THE LEGAL
Rights AND
Responsibilities
OF TEACHERS

D1219384

To our wonderful wives,
the two Debbies,
With all of our love, always and forever

and

In memory of
Carol Shiffer

THE LEGAL
Rights AND
Responsibilities
OF TEACHERS

ISSUES OF EMPLOYMENT
AND INSTRUCTION

ALLAN G. OSBORNE, JR.
CHARLES J. RUSSO

CORWIN
A SAGE Company

CORWIN
A SAGE Company

FOR INFORMATION:

Corwin
A SAGE Company
2455 Teller Road
Thousand Oaks, California 91320
(800) 233-9936
Fax: (800) 417-2466
www.corwin.com

SAGE Ltd.
1 Oliver's Yard
55 City Road
London EC1Y 1SP
United Kingdom

SAGE India Pvt. Ltd.
B 1/I 1 Mohan Cooperative Industrial Area
Mathura Road, New Delhi 110 044
India

SAGE Asia-Pacific Pte. Ltd.
33 Pekin Street #02-01
Far East Square
Singapore 048763

Acquisitions Editor: Arnis Burvikovs
Associate Editor: Desirée A. Bartlett
Editorial Assistant: Kimberly Greenberg
Production Editor: Cassandra Margaret Seibel
Copy Editor: Cate Huisman
Typesetter: C&M Digitals (P) Ltd.
Proofreader: Charlotte J. Waisner
Indexer: Jean Casalegno
Cover Designer: Scott Van Atta
Permissions Editor: Karen Ehrmann

Copyright © 2011 by Corwin

Printed in the United States of America

Library of Congress Cataloging-in-Publication Data

Osborne, Allan G.

The legal rights and responsibilities of teachers : issues of employment and instruction / Allan G. Osborne, Jr., and Charles J. Russo.

p. cm.
Includes bibliographical references and index.

ISBN 978-1-4129-7546-9 (pbk.)

1. Teachers—Legal status, laws, etc.—United States. I. Russo, Charles J. II. Title.

KF4175.O83 2011 344.73'078—dc22 2010051776

This book is printed on acid-free paper.

11 12 13 14 15 10 9 8 7 6 5 4 3 2 1

Contents

Preface   ix

Acknowledgments   xv

About the Authors   xix

1. Introduction: The Historical and Legal
   Foundations of Public Education   1

   Introduction   1
   A Brief History of Public Education in America   2
   Legal Fundamentals of Education   5
   Summary and Recommendations   16
   Frequently Asked Questions   17
   What's Next   18
   Endnotes   19

2. School Governance and the Teacher   23

   Introduction   23
   The Role of the Federal Government   24
   State Education Agencies   25
   Local School Boards   28
   School Finance and Use of Property   32
   Summary and Recommendations   36
   Frequently Asked Questions   37
   What's Next   38
   Endnotes   38

3. Basic Constitutional Rights and Freedoms   41

   Introduction   41
   First Amendment Rights   42
   Privacy   54
   Due Process   59
   Summary and Recommendations   62
   Frequently Asked Questions   63
   What's Next   65
   Endnotes   65

4. Employment Terms and Conditions   **71**
   Introduction   71
   Teacher Certification or Licensure   72
   Privacy Rights of Teachers   81
   Salaries and Terms of Employment   93
   Leaves of Absence   96
   Teacher Evaluations   100
   Resignations   102
   Summary and Recommendations   104
   Frequently Asked Questions   106
   What's Next   108
   Endnotes   108

5. Collective Bargaining   **115**
   Introduction   115
   Historical Background   116
   Bargaining Units and Their Composition   118
   Union Rights   121
   Dispute Resolution   124
   Summary and Recommendations   127
   Frequently Asked Questions   132
   What's Next   133
   Endnotes   133

6. Prohibitions Against Employment Discrimination   **137**
   Introduction   137
   Race, Color, Ethnicity, or National Origin   140
   Gender   144
   Religion   149
   Disability   152
   Age   158
   Genetic Information   161
   Retaliation   162
   Affirmative Action   162
   Summary and Recommendations   164
   Frequently Asked Questions   166
   What's Next   167
   Endnotes   167

7. Teacher Discipline, Dismissal, and Due Process   **173**
   Introduction   173
   Tenure Rights   174
   Progressive Discipline and Dismissal of Teachers   178
   Reduction in Force   196
   Summary and Recommendations   201

Frequently Asked Questions   203
What's Next   204
Endnotes   205

8. Curricular and Instructional Issues   **217**
Introduction   217
Control of the Curriculum and Academic Freedom   218
Student Records   232
Copyright Law   239
Using Technology in the Classroom   240
Special Education and Programs for
   English Language Learners   242
Summary and Recommendations   251
Frequently Asked Questions   254
What's Next   255
Endnotes   255

9. Tort Liability   **265**
Introduction   265
Definitions and Types of Torts   266
Educational Malpractice   289
Civil Rights Violations   290
Summary and Recommendations   292
Frequently Asked Questions   293
Endnotes   295

Resource A: Court Systems and the Authority of Courts   **299**
Functions and Duties of the Courts   299
Organization of the Federal Court System   299
State Courts   301
Court Jurisdictions   301

Resource B: Legal Resources and References   **303**
Laws and Regulations   303
Court Decisions   303
Understanding Legal Citations   304

**Resource C: Basic Legal Research: Maintaining Currency
in an Evolving Legal Environment**   **305**
Keeping Abreast of Legal Developments   305
Useful Education Law Websites   306

Glossary of Terms, Acronyms, and Abbreviations   **309**

Index   **315**

Preface

WHY WE WROTE THIS BOOK

As we note in the introduction to the first chapter, well over 3 million teachers currently work in American public schools. Yet, teachers in most states are not required to take a course or courses in education law in order to obtain certification or licensure. As a result, the majority of teacher preparation programs in our colleges and schools of education do not require courses in education law, and many do not even offer it as an elective. Generally, teachers do not even take such a course in their graduate programs, unless they have enrolled in programs leading them to prepare for roles as school administrators.

Over the past six decades the role of teachers has become intimately intertwined with legal issues. Since the Supreme Court's landmark school desegregation decision in *Brown v. Board of Education* (*Brown*) in 1954, teachers in public schools have had to become more concerned with their legal rights as employees. In fact, *Brown* also stands out as the birth of the extensive field that is known today as education (or school) law. At the same time, just as educators, whether teachers, administrators, or other staff members, are aware of their rights, they are also cognizant of their professional duties in schools. Although the responsibility for implementing all of the myriad laws and regulations that affect education largely rests on administrators, insofar as teachers and other staff share in the duty of safeguarding the rights of the students in their care, they must have knowledge of how the law impacts their professional roles. In particular, teachers need to know their rights and responsibilities, both regarding their employment and as these rights and responsibilities apply to the instructional process.

In our experiences as former K–12 educators who now teach graduate courses and conduct professional development seminars on an array of topics in education law, we have found that there is a dearth of information about education law targeted specifically for teachers. We have thus written this book to help fill the knowledge gap in education law by providing a concise, practical guide specifically targeting the areas of the law that are of most concern to teachers. In addition to addressing the concerns expressed by teachers in our courses and professional development seminars, prior to undertaking this project we conducted an informal survey with a representative group of teachers to see which topics are foremost in their minds.

Turning to the employment context, the book presents information about teacher certification, employment, tenure, evaluation, and dismissal, along with issues related to collective bargaining. The book also reviews the constitutional rights of teachers, including freedom of speech and religion. In addition, the book provides information on how teachers can avoid liability when dealing with discrimination and harassment based on race, ethnic origin, gender, sexual orientation, age, religion, or disability, regardless of whether it is at the hands of supervisors, peers, or students.

In the instructional domain, the book explores the rights and responsibilities teachers have in the instructional process. This includes topics such as what may be taught, academic freedom, methodology, grading policies, student records, and copyright law. The book also provides information about tort liability and teachers' responsibilities regarding the safety and well-being of their students as well as their own protections from defamation.

Prior to writing this book we circulated a proposed table of contents to many teachers and colleagues in higher education who had taught in K–12 schools asking for their input. Many of the topics that we included directly respond to the concerns expressed by those teachers and colleagues. The book also provides useful, practical suggestions for dealing with specific situations, and there are answers to frequently asked questions at the end of each chapter. These are questions that our graduate students, who are practicing teachers, asked in our graduate school law courses, seminars, and professional development presentations. Moreover, the third through ninth chapters include summaries of leading judicial opinions to give readers a sense of how the law is applied to actual situations.

For ease of reading, we use endnotes to cite our sources and references throughout the book, as is common in legal writing, rather than in-text citations. However, we recognize that most readers are not familiar with standard legal citations. Thus, we have used a modified version of the law review style outlined in *The Bluebook: A Uniform System of Citation*. We deviate from this style in many instances by borrowing elements of American Psychological Association style to make our endnotes more reader friendly.

We would like to point out that this book is intended to be one of a two-book set. The second book will address student rights. Although each book will stand alone in its own right, the volumes could be used together to form a comprehensive treatment of education law.

WHO SHOULD READ THIS BOOK

As indicated above, this book is targeted specifically for teachers. Even so, it can be useful to administrators, particularly those at the building level, who need a refresher on school law as it applies to teachers' rights and responsibilities. Although the book is designed to be read by in-service teachers, particularly those just entering the field, it could be useful for students currently in programs leading to teacher licensure. The book could also be used as a text in an introductory course on school law or in professional development seminars.

As is the case with all of our books, this one is not intended to replace the advice and counsel of competent attorneys. Rather, the book is designed to make school personnel more aware of how various laws provide them with rights, protections, and responsibilities. We hope that educators who understand these laws will be in a better position to meet their myriad legal requirements and make legally correct decisions. Accordingly, we caution readers to consult competent legal counsel when difficult situations arise. In this respect, although the book presents information about teachers' rights and responsibilities, it does not provide information about legal procedures.

HOW THE BOOK IS ORGANIZED

The first chapter, which serves as an introduction, begins with a brief look at the history of public education in America. The bulk of the chapter deals with the legal foundations of education, including a review of relevant constitutional provisions and major laws. This introductory chapter is important insofar as it provides a brief synopsis of the constitutional provisions and the statutes that are discussed throughout the book.

Chapter 2 continues the discussion of the legal foundations of education by providing an overview of school governance. Specifically, this chapter provides additional information about the expanding role of the federal government along with laws regulating state and local educational agencies as well as a section on school finance and the use of school property. All of this is covered from the perspective of how school governance affects teachers.

The third chapter provides a brief overview of the constitutional rights and freedoms of all citizens. In doing so it lays the foundation for many of the issues that are discussed in more detail in subsequent chapters. The chapter includes discussions of the basic freedoms: speech, association, religion, and privacy, in addition to due process. It places particular emphasis on how these rights and freedoms interact with teachers' responsibilities and the limitations placed on them as public employees. The purpose of the chapter is to provide an introduction to the constitutional principles underlying many of the issues presented throughout the book.

Chapter 4 outlines the legal issues involved in employment terms and conditions. The chapter begins with a discussion of the requirements for teacher certification and the reasons for which such certification can be revoked. It continues with information about the privacy rights of teachers and issues regarding employment terms such as salaries, leaves of absence, evaluations, and resignations.

Chapter 5 discusses collective bargaining. The chapter begins with an overview of the history of teacher associations, their role in the process, and how bargaining units are formed. It next outlines the topics of bargaining before reviewing dispute resolution processes that are used in teacher labor relations disagreements. The chapter concludes with practical suggestions for unions and school boards to use before, during, and after bargaining.

The sixth chapter focuses on discussions of discrimination. This chapter outlines federal statutes and constitutional provisions that provide teachers with protections against workplace discrimination. It begins with information on those areas specifically enumerated in Title VII of the Civil Rights Act of 1964, continuing with an overview on more recent statutes protecting teachers from other forms of discrimination.

Chapter 7 deals with the important issues of teacher discipline and dismissal, emphasizing the due process rights of teachers. Opening with information on tenure and the privileges it entails before continuing with topics related to progressive discipline and the steps school boards must follow to dismiss teachers for cause, the chapter concludes with a discussion on dismissals that occur due to reductions in force.

Chapter 8, which deals exclusively with curricular and instructional topics, starts by providing information on the authority of school boards to establish and control curricular topics, including those that must be taught, that may not be taught, and that are discretionary. The chapter also speaks to issues such as graduation requirements, testing, grading policies, and student records. It rounds out by reviewing other curriculum-related topics such as special instructional programs, copyright law, and technology in classrooms.

The final chapter covers the different types of torts and the standard of care that teachers must exercise in order to avoid civil liability. Chapter 9 begins with the definition of a tort and descriptions of the various types of torts. Next, the chapter reviews the intentional torts of assault, battery, false imprisonment, and defamation. It continues with discussions of negligence, the standard of care expected of educators, the elements of negligence, how to avoid negligence, and defenses to negligence. The chapter also covers educational malpractice and civil rights torts.

Appendices to this book, which are designed to familiarize readers with the technical aspects of law, should be particularly beneficial for readers with little background in educational law. As a result, readers with little background in school law may wish to review the first two of these resources before reading the book itself. Other readers may find it helpful to consult these references when questions arise. Resource A provides a brief, but fairly comprehensive, overview of the court systems and how they operate. This resource affords readers a better understanding of the various levels of courts and the significance that should be placed on decisions from each court. Resource B explains where legal documents, such as copies of statutes and court opinions, can be found; it also provides an explanation of legal citations that should be helpful to readers unfamiliar with the structure and format of the legal citations contained in the endnotes of each of the book's chapters. Since the law is constantly evolving, it is difficult for practitioners to maintain their currency in the field. Resource C thus provides references and suggestions for readers who wish to keep up with new developments in education law via a list of websites providing further information.

Acknowledgments

W e could not have written this book without the encouragement, support, advice, and assistance of many colleagues, former colleagues, friends, and family members. It is impossible to acknowledge all who have influenced us in some way and so contributed to this book, but we would at the very least like to extend our gratitude to those who have had the greatest impact in our professional and personal lives. This group includes all who have contributed to our knowledge and understanding of the subject matter of this book, most notably our many friends and colleagues who are members of the Education Law Association. These professionals have not only consistently shared their knowledge with us but also, more important, provided constructive criticism and constantly challenged our thinking. We also include in this group our graduate students, who, as educational practitioners, have kept us abreast of the problems they face daily in their schools. Sincere appreciation is extended to Jim Hennessy, Joe O'Neill, Peggy O'Neill, and Denise Ready for reading and reacting to the original proposal for this book and reviewing chapters while they were being written. Their comments provided us with much insight into the legal concerns of teachers and helped us to make this book much more user friendly. Many topics were included in this book due to their suggestions.

We are also most fortunate to work with professional educators who understand the importance of our work and provide us with the support and resources to continue our research. The contributions of many colleagues from the Quincy Public Schools and University of Dayton can never be adequately acknowledged.

I (Allan Osborne) especially thank the entire administrative team of the Quincy Public Schools for all of their encouragement and support during my years in that school system. In that respect I want to extend a special thank you to my good friend and former colleague, Dennis Carini, for his unending support and encouragement, along with his unlimited patience when I bounced ideas off him. I am now happily retired, but for 24 years I served as a special education teacher, assistant principal, and principal of the Snug Harbor Community School. I would like to extend a very sincere and warm thank you to the faculty, parents, and students of that school for many years of rewards and inspiration.

Heartfelt gratitude is also extended to Dr. Timothy Ernst, Melissa Hopp-Woolwine, and the wonderful staff of Charles River Oncology, and to Dr. Edwin Alyea and the medical team at the Dana Farber Cancer Institute, for their exceptional care and treatment during my recent illness. Their care, along with the hope and encouragement they provided, allowed me to continue work on this book.

In all of our recent books I have acknowledged my good friend Carol Shiffer for the inspiration she has given me. In spite of living with a terminal illness for over 20 years, Carol always maintained a positive outlook and zest for life. She became even more of an inspiration when I, myself, was diagnosed with cancer. Sadly, Carol passed away as this book was being written. She will always be my hero and I dedicate this book to her with love.

In the School of Education and Allied Professions at the University of Dayton, I (Charlie Russo) would like to express my thanks to Rev. Joseph D. Massucci, Chair of the Department of Educational Leadership; Dr. Kevin. R. Kelly, Dean; Dr. Dan Raisch, Associate Dean; Dean Lisa Kloppenberg of the University of Dayton School of Law; and Dr. Thomas J. Lasley, Jr., my former Dean, for their ongoing support and friendship. I also extend a special note of thanks to my assistant Ms. Elizabeth Pearn for her valuable assistance in helping to process the manuscript and proofreading its final version as well as to Mrs. Ann Raney of the Curriculum Materials Center for the many times that she has helped me to find information for this book and many other projects. I would also like to thank the late David B. Evans who, even when I was an undergraduate at St. John's University in New York City, taught me a great deal about the skills necessary to succeed in an academic career. In addition, I would like to thank my doctoral mentor, Dr. Zarif Bacilious, again at St. John's in New York City, for helping me to complete my formal education as I prepared for my entry into the Academy.

We would both like to thank our acquisitions editor at Corwin, Arnis Burvikovs, associate editor Desirée Bartlett, production editor Cassandra Seibel, and editorial assistant Kim Greenberg for their support as we conceptualized, wrote, and revised this book. It is a pleasure working with such outstanding professionals and their colleagues at Corwin. They certainly helped to make our jobs easier. We also wish to thank the reviewers who provided helpful comments on an earlier draft of this book. Many of their suggestions have been incorporated into the final product.

Special thanks are extended to our skilled copyeditor Cate Huisman, who has worked with us on several of our books. Cate not only caught many of our errors, but helped us to clarify portions of the original text to make it much more understandable and readable. Most important, however, Cate showed great patience as we continued to make changes throughout the copyediting process.

On a more personal note, we both extend our appreciation to our late parents, Allan G. and Ruth L. Osborne, and James J. and Helen J. Russo. We can never adequately express our gratitude to our parents for the profound influences that they have had on our lives.

I (Charlie Russo) also extend a special note of thanks and appreciation to my two wonderful children, Emily Rebecca and David Peter, and to David's wife Li Hong. The bright and inquisitive children that my wife Debbie and I had the pleasure of raising have grown to be wonderful young adults who provide us both with a constant source of inspiration and love.

Our wonderful wives, affectionately known as the two Debbies, have been the major influence in our lives and professional careers. Our best friends, they encourage us to write, show great patience as we ramble on endlessly about litigation in education, and understand when we must spend countless hours working on a manuscript. We would not be able to do all that we do if it were not for their constant love and support. Thus, as we do with all of our work, we dedicate this book to them with all of our love.

A. G. O.
C. J. R.

About the Authors

Allan G. Osborne, Jr., EdD, is the former principal of the Snug Harbor Community School in Quincy, Massachusetts. Retired after 34 years as a special education teacher and school administrator, he currently spends his time writing and teaching graduate courses in school law and special education law. He received his doctorate in educational leadership from Boston College. Allan Osborne has authored or coauthored numerous articles, monographs, textbooks, and textbook chapters on special education law, along with textbooks on other aspects of special education. A past president of the Education Law Association (ELA) and recipient of the McGhehey Award for lifetime achievement in educational law, he has been a frequent presenter at ELA conferences and writes the "Students with Disabilities" chapter of the *Yearbook of Education Law,* which is published by ELA. Allan Osborne is on the Editorial Advisory Committee of *West's Education Law Reporter* and is coeditor of the "Education Law Into Practice" section of that journal. He also serves as an editorial consultant for many other publications in education law, administration, and special education.

Charles J. Russo, JD, EdD, is the Joseph Panzer Chair in Education in the School of Education and Allied Professions and Adjunct Professor in the School of Law at the University of Dayton, Ohio. The 1998–1999 president of the Education Law Association and 2002 recipient of its McGhehey (Lifetime Achievement) Award, he is the author of more than 200 articles in peer-reviewed journals and the author, coauthor, editor, or coeditor of 39 books. He has been the editor of the *Yearbook of Education Law* for the Education Law Association since 1995 and has written or coauthored more than 750 publications; he is also the editor of two academic journals and serves as a member of more than a dozen editorial boards. He has spoken and taught extensively on issues in education law in the United States and in 29 other nations on all six inhabited continents. In recognition of his work in education law in other countries, he received an honorary PhD from Potchefstroom University, now the Potchefstroom Campus of North-West University, in Potchefstroom, South Africa, in May of 2004.

Other Corwin Books by Osborne and Russo

Special Education and the Law: A Guide for Practitioners, Second Edition

Essential Concepts and School-Based Cases in Special Education Law

Section 504 and the ADA

Discipline in Special Education

Introduction: The Historical and Legal Foundations of Public Education

KEY CONCEPTS IN THIS CHAPTER

❖ The Roots of Public Education in America

❖ Constitutional Provisions Applicable to Education

❖ Important Statutes Governing Education

❖ Case or Common Law

INTRODUCTION

Public education in America has grown significantly from its early beginnings in colonial times. What was once considered to be primarily the responsibility of the family is now a major function of governments at all levels. Currently, there are approximately 98,793 public schools[1] serving students in grades kindergarten through 12 in the 13,862 school districts in the United States.[2] These districts and schools serve approximately 49,300,000 students[3] who are taught by 3,180,000 million teachers.[4] Public education in this country has become a major source of expenditure at the federal, state, and local levels with over $520 billion being spent annually[5] at an average of $10,889 per student.[6] Further, although they are beyond the scope of this book, nonpublic schools and home schooling families educate in excess of another 6 million students.[7]

Initially, the responsibility for public education was borne almost exclusively by local communities. However, during the past two centuries, state and federal governments have increasingly become involved in the running and financing of public schools.

This chapter begins with a brief overview of the history of public education from its meager beginnings as a purely local function in colonial times to the present day in which the federal government is involved in education more than ever. Next, the chapter provides a primer on the legal foundations of public education. This section includes a synopsis of the major constitutional and statutory provisions governing public education. Throughout this book the authors reference decisions by federal and state courts. Readers lacking the background knowledge of court systems should consult "Resource A: Court Systems and the Authority of Courts," at the back of the book, which provides an overview of the organization of federal and state court systems. Readers who are unfamiliar with legal materials also may wish to consult "Resource B: Legal Resources and References," which provides information on reading and understanding legal citations.

A BRIEF HISTORY OF PUBLIC EDUCATION IN AMERICA

When settlers first arrived on the shores of what is now the United States, the task of educating children was the responsibility of the family and was done largely at home. During these times parents taught their children the rudiments of reading, writing, and arithmetic. Much of what children were taught was based on what they needed to know in an agrarian society. Thus, boys were also expected to acquire basic vocational skills and girls learned how to run a household. As the nation developed and expanded, formal schools became more common but were largely private institutions that educated children whose parents could afford to pay tuition. Even so, the first publicly supported secondary school, Boston Latin, was founded in 1635.

In 1647, Puritans in Massachusetts enacted what became known as the "Ye old deluder Satan" law requiring towns of 50 households to provide instruction in reading and writing to their children, and towns of 100 households or more to establish grammar schools to prepare children for the universities. One main purpose of the law, and thus its name, was to combat the attempts of Satan to keep people ignorant of the scriptures. Even though this law provided for the establishment of schools, attendance was not compulsory, but rather was at parental discretion. Students generally attended school for only a few weeks during the winter; they studied in poorly equipped schoolhouses and were taught by untrained teachers.[8]

The idea of publicly financed schools did not take hold until the mid-19th century, when social reformers in Massachusetts, Connecticut, and New York succeeded in passing legislation that required school attendance and provided for tax-supported schools. Massachusetts passed the first compulsory school law in 1853, and New York followed suit one year later. Early schools, particularly in rural areas, were supported partially by property taxes and partially by tuition paid by parents. More options existed in the cities, where many schools were operated by churches.

> The idea of publicly financed schools did not take hold until the mid-19th century, when social reformers in Massachusetts, Connecticut, and New York succeeded in passing legislation that required school attendance and provided for tax-supported schools.

Education remained principally a local and state function until the mid-20th century, when Congress passed the National Defense Education Act of 1958 (NDEA),[9] largely in response to the Soviet Union's launch of Sputnik, and the Elementary and Secondary Education Act of 1965 (ESEA),[10] now reauthorized as the No Child Left Behind Act (NCLB).[11] These two landmark pieces of legislation sought to improve instruction in commonly neglected subjects such as science, mathematics, and foreign languages and to expand educational opportunities to students from poor families. The NDEA marked the first time the federal government directly intervened in public school policy and curricula, when Congress earmarked funds to support more intense instruction in science and mathematics. The ESEA, on the other hand, provided funds for school districts that had large numbers of children living in poverty. The legislation also funded Head Start, a program designed to help prepare low-income toddlers for school. Although these were not the first pieces of educational legislation passed by Congress, the NDEA and ESEA did mark the beginning of the federal government's increased involvement in public education. During this period many school officials began to see public education as the key to individual success and the nation's prosperity.

Unfortunately, since public schools in many areas of the country were still segregated by race midway through the 20th century, educational opportunities were not fully available to all children during this time. That began to change in the second half of the 20th century when public schools became instrumental in assuring equal opportunity to all citizens. Initially, change came about through court orders, but further change was instituted through federal legislation. In 1954, in its landmark school desegregation ruling, *Brown v. Board of Education* (*Brown*), the Supreme Court characterized education as "perhaps the

> Unfortunately, since public schools in many areas of the country were still segregated by race midway through the 20th century, educational opportunities were not fully available to all children during this time. That began to change in the second half of the 20th century, when public schools became instrumental in assuring equal opportunity to all citizens.

most important function of state and local governments."[12] Chief Justice Warren, writing for the unanimous Court, pointed out that education was necessary for citizens to exercise their most basic civic responsibilities:

> In these days, it is doubtful that any child may reasonably be expected to succeed in life if he is denied the opportunity of an education. Such an opportunity, where the State has undertaken to provide it, is a right that must be made available to all on equal terms.[13]

Two decades later, in *Lau v. Nichols*,[14] the Supreme Court insisted that the failure to provide remedial English language instruction to non-English-speaking students violated Section 601 of Title VI of the Civil Rights Act of 1964.[15] The Court held that denying such students the chance to receive remedial instruction denied them meaningful opportunities to participate in public education. The Court emphasized that recipients of federal funds were bound by Title VI of the Civil Rights Act of 1964, and a Department of Health, Education, and Welfare regulation required public school systems, as recipients of federal assistance, to take affirmative steps to rectify language deficiencies.

Federal involvement in public education reached a new height one year later in 1975 when Congress passed the Education for All Handicapped Children Act,[16] currently known as the Individuals with Disabilities Education Act (IDEA).[17] This landmark legislation mandated that all states provide a free, appropriate public education in the least restrictive environment for all students with disabilities between the ages of 3 and 21. The IDEA required school officials to develop individualized education programs for all students with disabilities who required special education and related services. The IDEA also provided parents with unprecedented rights and created an elaborate system for the resolution of disputes that might develop over the provision of special education services. The IDEA not only opened the doors of our public schools to children who had previously been excluded but also provided a guarantee that the education they received would be meaningful.

The 1983 publication of an extensive report on the condition of the country's public schools, *A Nation at Risk: The Imperative for Educational Reform*, generated much interest and controversy.[18] This report suggested that students from other developed countries outperformed U.S. students on international measures. In response, most states implemented educational reform laws that mandated more frequent testing of students in core academic subjects and that increased state-mandated curriculum requirements. This led to the passage of the No Child Left

Behind Act (NCLB)[19] almost two decades later. The key purposes of the NCLB are to improve the academic achievement of students, assure that students are taught by highly qualified personnel, make school systems accountable for student achievement, require school systems to use effective, research-based teaching methods, and afford parents choices in educational programs.[20] The NCLB provides for accountability through annual testing and the use of proven instructional methods.[21] It represents the federal government's most extensive involvement in public education to date. Even so, the NCLB affords states flexibility in terms of setting standards, choosing tests, and spending federal dollars, but the states must show results.

LEGAL FUNDAMENTALS OF EDUCATION

There are four sources of law in the United States: constitutions, statutes, regulations, and judicial opinions. These sources exist at both the federal and state levels. A constitution is the fundamental law of a nation or state, while a statute is an act of a legislative body—a law enacted by Congress or another legislative body.[22] Statutes must be consistent with their controlling constitutions. Inasmuch as most statutes are general mandates, they are typically supplemented by implementing regulations or guidelines written by officials in the agencies that are charged with their implementation and enforcement. Regulations are thus more specific than the statutes they are designed to implement, because they interpret legislative intent as to how laws should work in practice. Constitutions, statutes, and regulations are all subject to judicial interpretation. The many court decisions applying constitutions, statutes, and regulations to specific situations compose a body of law known as *case law* or *common law*. Judicial opinions rely heavily on the concept of *binding precedent*, or the theory that a ruling of the highest court in a jurisdiction is binding on all lower courts in that jurisdiction. Cases from other jurisdictions that are of no binding effect are referred to as *persuasive precedent*, meaning that courts are free to consult the judgments of other courts but are not bound to follow their holdings.

Constitutions

In addition to the U.S. Constitution, each state has its own constitution. State constitutions must be compatible with the provisions of the federal Constitution and typically deal with many of the same topics. State constitutions do, however, address many functions not covered by their

> Education is considered to be a function of the states insofar as education is not mentioned in the federal Constitution. The Tenth Amendment reserves to the states all powers not delegated to the federal government, as long as those powers are not prohibited by the Constitution.

federal counterpart. Thus, education is considered to be a function of the states insofar as education is not mentioned in the federal Constitution. The Tenth Amendment reserves to the states all powers not delegated to the federal government, as long as those powers are not prohibited by the Constitution. In fact, the Supreme Court went so far as to declare that

Education, of course, is not among the rights afforded explicit protection under our Federal Constitution. Nor do we find any basis for saying it is implicitly so protected.[23]

Even so, many aspects of the federal Constitution have a direct impact on the daily operations of our public schools.

Federal Constitution

The sections of the Constitution that are generally implicated in litigation involving the public schools are those protecting individual rights. As much of the school-related litigation over the past several decades has shown, teachers and students do not surrender their individual rights when they enter school buildings. In addition to the body of the Constitution, its first ten amendments, adopted as the Bill of Rights in 1791, play a major role in the daily lives of teachers, students, and their school systems. The following provides a thumbnail sketch of key clauses and amendments, most of which are discussed in more detail later in this book.

General Welfare and Spending Clause.[24] Although education is largely a state function, over the years the federal government has had its hand in educational matters. In recent years Congress has enacted a great deal of far-reaching legislation that has imposed conditions and standards on the public schools. The federal government derives its authority to pass such legislation from Article I, Section 8, which gives Congress the power to collect taxes, pay debts, and provide for the common defense and general welfare of the country.

Contracts Clause.[25] Article I, Section 10 of the Constitution, known as the Contracts Clause, prohibits states from passing laws impairing the obligation of contracts. The Contracts Clause essentially prevents state legislatures from passing laws that change the provisions of teachers' contracts or collective bargaining agreements regarding tenure, salaries, or even retirement benefits. Yet, this does not prohibit state legislatures from changing laws if they do not implicate contracts. For example, states are generally free to alter teacher licensure or certification requirements.

First Amendment.[26] The First Amendment provides basic freedoms and has been the subject of much litigation in education, involving both teachers' and students' rights. Although the wording of the First Amendment indicates that it applies to Congress, it has been extended to the states by way of the Fourteenth Amendment. According to the First Amendment,

> Congress shall make no law respecting an establishment of religion, or prohibiting the free exercise thereof; or abridging the freedom of speech, or of the press; or the right of the people peaceably to assemble, and to petition the Government for redress of grievances.

The religion clauses of the First Amendment have significant implications for teachers regarding their rights to practice their religion. For example, cases have come before the courts on topics as varied as teachers being able to take time off from work for religious observances, their rights to wear religious garb when working in public schools, and bans on proselytizing in class.

A long line of case law has clearly established that teachers do not lose their constitutional rights as citizens simply because they are public employees. To this end, the Supreme Court clearly stated that neither students nor teachers "shed their constitutional rights to freedom of speech or expression at the schoolhouse gate."[27] Still, there has been much litigation over teachers' rights to speak out or write letters to the editors of local newspapers regarding matters of public concern. However, some restrictions can be placed on teachers' free speech rights, particularly if the speech can result in disrupting the educational environment. The final clause of the First Amendment, which grants the right to assemble and petition the government, has many implications for teachers' associations or unions.

Fourth Amendment.[28] The Fourth Amendment, which prohibits unreasonable searches and seizures, has been the subject of much litigation involving student discipline. Moreover, it offers privacy protections to teachers. Specifically, the Fourth Amendment states,

The right of the people to be secure in their persons, houses, papers, and effects, against unreasonable searches and seizures, shall not be violated, and no Warrants shall issue, but upon probable cause, supported by Oath or affirmation, and particularly describing the place to be searched, and the persons or things to be seized.

Although most of the litigation under the Fourth Amendment in a school setting has involved students, it has implications for teachers as well, particularly regarding their expectations of privacy in such areas as drug testing.

Fifth Amendment.[29] The Fifth Amendment is best known for protections against self-incrimination and double jeopardy for those accused of crimes. Even so, there is much more to the Fifth Amendment, which reads in part,

No person . . . shall be compelled in any criminal case to be a witness against himself, nor be deprived of life, liberty, or property, without due process of law; nor shall private property be taken for public use, without just compensation.

The second clause of the Fifth Amendment provides due process protections for parties to federal actions. It is important to note that it does not apply to state actions; however, as shown below, the Fourteenth Amendment includes a Due Process Clause applicable to the states. In the school context, the last clause, which prohibits the taking of private property for public use without fair compensation, is significant. In this respect the Fifth Amendment may come into play when private property needs to be acquired for educational purposes, such as with the taking of land by eminent domain for building a new school.

Ninth Amendment.[30] The Ninth Amendment simply states that "the enumeration in the Constitution, of certain rights, shall not be construed to deny or disparage others retained by the people." While this amendment has been interpreted to prevent the expansion of the powers of the federal government, it also frequently has been interpreted to imply personal privacy rights.

Tenth Amendment.[31] When the founding fathers wrote the Constitution, there were many compromises between those who wanted a strong federal government and those who advocated states' rights. The Tenth Amendment was included in the Bill of Rights to preserve the powers and governmental functions of the states. Specifically, the Tenth Amendment provides that the "powers not delegated to the United States by the Constitution, nor prohibited by it to the States, are reserved to the States respectively, or to the people." Insofar as education is a function not addressed in the federal Constitution, it is left to the states by the terms of the Tenth Amendment.

As will be shown later in this chapter and throughout this book, this does not mean that the federal government lacks any authority to become involved in the process of education. In fact, in recent years a significant amount of federal legislation has had a profound impact on the daily operation of public schools. Further, under the General Welfare and Spending Clause of the federal Constitution, Congress may pass legislation and attach conditions to the states' acceptance of funds under that legislation as long as it makes its intent known in clear and unambiguous terms.

Eleventh Amendment.[32] The concept of sovereign immunity as established in common law did not find its way into the original articles of the Constitution. This oversight was rectified with the enactment of the Eleventh Amendment, which affirms that

> the Judicial power of the United States shall not be construed to extend to any suit in law or equity, commenced or prosecuted against one of the United States by citizens of another State, or by Citizens or Subjects of any Foreign State.

The Eleventh Amendment's grant of sovereign immunity has been interpreted as granting states and state officials immunity from suit by their own citizens. However, Congress can abrogate a state's immunity to suit as long as it does so explicitly in clear and unambiguous language. States also may waive their Eleventh Amendment immunity. In this respect, states may be considered to have waived their immunity under an act of Congress by accepting federal funds provided under the legislation.

Fourteenth Amendment.[33] The Fourteenth Amendment includes a Due Process Clause similar to that in the Fifth Amendment except that it applies to the states. Equally important to education is the amendment's Equal Protection Clause. The amendment reads, in part,

> No State shall make or enforce any law which shall abridge the privileges or immunities of citizens of the United States; nor shall any State deprive any person of life, liberty, or property, without due process of law; nor deny to any person within its jurisdiction the equal protections of the laws.

It is important to understand that there are two types of due process: substantive and procedural. Substantive due process refers to the notion that a law must have a function within the rightful power of the government and be judiciously related to the achievement of that goal. Procedural due process, on the other hand, refers to the process of informing charged individuals about what they are accused of and giving them the opportunity to defend themselves before an impartial decision maker.

The right to due process has many implications for teachers, especially within the employment context. For example, when facing discharge, tenured teachers have the right to be notified of the reasons for their contemplated dismissal and to be given the opportunity to respond, generally during an impartial hearing. Teachers who are not tenured ordinarily lack this protection, since they have yet to achieve the substantive due process rights that would afford them full procedural due process.

The last part of the Fourteenth Amendment, the Equal Protection Clause, conveys the principle that people in similar circumstances should be treated similarly. Thus, any differences in how individuals are treated must be based on legitimate criteria that are not prohibited by law. The Equal Protection Clause has been prominent in much of the discrimination litigation in education, such as *Brown*. As will be shown below, federal statutes have corrected disparities in how individuals are treated. Prime examples are the statutes that have been passed to afford greater opportunities to individuals with disabilities in terms of both educational and employment opportunities.

State Constitutions

All states have constitutions of their own that grant rights and privileges similar to those found in the federal Constitution. Nevertheless, state constitutions usually address many areas not covered by the national document, such as education. Under what is known as the Supremacy Clause of the federal Constitution, conflicts between federal and state constitutional provisions (or federal and state laws for that matter) are resolved in favor of the federal mandate. The purpose of most state constitutions is to define the powers of the state legislatures. In that respect, state constitutions often spell out what a state legislature must do, may do, and may not do.

Most state constitutions have sections that require the state legislature to provide for the establishment, maintenance, and support of a system of public schools. The Ohio Constitution is typical in this respect:

Most state constitutions have sections that require the state legislature to provide for the establishment, maintenance, and support of a system of public schools.

The general assembly shall make provisions, by taxation, or otherwise, as with the income arising from the school trust fund, will secure a thorough and efficient system of common schools throughout the State; but, no religion or other sect or sects, shall ever have any exclusive right to, or control any part of the school funds of this state.[34]

The term "thorough and efficient" appears in many state constitutions to describe the types of systems to be established. Further, as with Ohio, many states include clauses to make sure that public or common schools are free from religious influence. This provides an example of an acceptable difference that can occur between the federal Constitution and its state counterparts. While some forms of aid to students attending sectarian schools are allowed under the Establishment Clause of the First Amendment, state constitutions may place further restrictions on such aid.

Statutes and Regulations

A statute is an act of a legislative body, such as a law enacted by Congress or a state legislature.[35] All statutes, either federal or state, must be consistent with the constitutions within their jurisdictions. Inasmuch as statutes only provide general mandates without specifying how those mandates are to be implemented in actuality, most are accompanied by regulations or guidelines issued by the agencies responsible for their execution and enforcement. Regulations are thus more specific than the statutes they are designed to implement, because they interpret legislative intent as to how the laws should work in practice.

As noted, under the Tenth Amendment, education is reserved to the states. Nevertheless, Congress has the power to enact laws under the General Welfare and Spending Clause of Article I, Section 8 of the Constitution by offering funds for purposes that it believes will serve the public good. Over the years Congress has enacted a series of statutes, such as the NCLB, that have provided funds to states and school districts to put certain mandates into practice. By accepting the funds under these statutes, states and school districts become bound by the terms of the statutes. For example, states receiving federal financial assistance under the NCLB must take steps to improve academic achievement by instituting reforms such as using teaching methods that are research based and that have been proven effective.

Over the years Congress has enacted a series of statutes, such as the No Child Left Behind Act, that have provided funds to states and school districts to put certain mandates into practice.

Regulations promulgated by the U.S. Department of Education, in addition to those from other federal and state administrative agencies, afford executive officers the means to implement statutes by carrying out their full effect. In other words, while statutes set broad legislative parameters, regulations allow administrative agencies to provide details to satisfy the requirements of the law. For example, statutes may set the number of days that children must attend school to satisfy state compulsory attendance laws, while regulations fill in such details as how long class days should be and what subjects students must study. Regulations carry the full force of the law and are presumptively valid unless or until courts strike them down as conflicting with the underlying legislation.

> Regulations carry the full force of the law and are presumptively valid unless or until courts strike them down as conflicting with the underlying legislation.

Civil Rights Statutes

Congress has enacted many statutes to protect the civil rights of individuals. These laws prohibit discrimination in areas including employment on the basis of characteristics such as race, color, national origin, ethnicity, gender, age, and disability. Some of these statutes, such as the Civil Rights Act of 1964, specifically target recipients of federal funds.

Title IV of the Civil Rights Act of 1964.[36] Title IV of the Civil Rights Act of 1964 requires public school boards to desegregate their districts while prohibiting officials from making student assignments based on a student's race, color, religion, or national origin. Congress enacted Title IV both to provide an enforcement mechanism for *Brown* and to authorize the withdrawal of federal funds from programs that practiced discrimination.

Title VI of the Civil Rights Act of 1964.[37] Title VI of the Civil Rights Act prohibits recipients of federal funds, including public school systems, from discriminating against individuals on the basis of race, color, or national origin. If recipients of federal funds violate Title VI, they are subject to litigation by the U.S. Department of Justice, as often occurred during the era of desegregation, or the threat of the future loss of those funds or other actions by the U.S. Department of Justice.

Title VII of the Civil Rights Act of 1964.[38] Title VII of the Civil Rights Act of 1964 is designed to provide equal employment opportunity by prohibiting workplace harassment and discrimination. Title VII covers private employers as well as government agencies and educational institutions that have 15 or more employees. Title VII prohibits discrimination on the basis of race, color, national origin, religion, and sex and has been extended to prohibit discrimination on the basis of pregnancy. Even so, employers may treat individuals differently on account of their traits if a trait constitutes a bona fide occupational qualification. Therefore, officials in religious schools may require employees to belong to the faiths that operate their schools.

Title IX of the Education Amendments of 1972.[39] Title IX prohibits discrimination on the basis of sex in any program or activity receiving federal financial assistance. Congress enacted Title IX to eliminate sex discrimination in schools and other educational institutions. Initially best known for providing parity in sports and athletic programs, Title IX also protects students from sexual harassment at the hands of teachers and their peers. Title IX prohibits discrimination due to sex in a wide range of services and activities, such as admission to programs, athletics, and financial assistance. Like other civil rights statutes, Title IX applies to recipients of federal funds, and its enforcement mechanism authorizes the withdrawal of funding from institutions when violations are found. At the same time, the Supreme Court has interpreted Title IX as authorizing private causes of action for monetary damages by students when they can prove that they were victims of intentional discrimination.[40] Interestingly, while Title IX protects students from discrimination based on sex, aggrieved teachers generally must seek redress under Title VII.

Section 504 of the Rehabilitation Act of 1973.[41] Section 504 prohibits recipients of federal funds from discriminating against individuals with disabilities in their programs or activities. Section 504 was the first civil rights legislation specifically guaranteeing the rights of individuals with disabilities. Section 504's antidiscrimination provisions against individuals with disabilities in programs receiving federal funds are similar to those in Titles VI and VII of the Civil Rights Act of 1964.[42]

Americans with Disabilities Act.[43] The Americans with Disabilities Act (ADA), passed in 1990, extends the reach of Section 504 by prohibiting discrimination against individuals with disabilities in the private sector as well as the public sector. The ADA's impact on schools is most significant in the areas of reasonable accommodations for employees and academic program accommodations for students.[44]

Age Discrimination in Employment Act.[45] The Age Discrimination in Employment Act (ADEA), enacted in 1967, prohibits discrimination against individuals 40 years of age and older. The ADEA's antidiscrimination provisions are substantively similar to those found in Title VII of the Civil Rights Act of 1964. The ADEA applies to employers with 20 or more employees and protects older workers in areas such as hiring, compensation, benefits, transfers, promotions, demotions, and dismissal. As with Title VII, age may be a factor when it is a bona fide occupational qualification. By way of illustration, for reasons of public safety, school boards[46] may institute policies that place restrictions on older bus drivers.

Individuals with Disabilities Education Act

The Individuals with Disabilities Education Act (IDEA)[47] (formerly the Education for All Handicapped Children Act[48]) was first enacted in 1975. The IDEA mandates a free, appropriate public education (FAPE) in the least restrictive environment (LRE) for all students with disabilities between the ages of 3 and 21 based on the contents of their individualized education programs (IEPs). School officials must develop IEPs in conferences with students' parents for any children who require special education and related services. The IDEA specifies how IEPs are to be developed and the elements they must contain. Additionally, the IDEA includes elaborate due process safeguards to protect the rights of students and ensure that its provisions are enforced. As part of the IDEA's funding formula, which allows all school districts to qualify for funds, boards receiving funds are subject to rigid auditing and management requirements.[49]

No Child Left Behind Act

One of the more controversial federal education laws enacted in recent memory is the No Child Left Behind Act (NCLB)[50] that was passed in 2002 as an extension of the Elementary and Secondary Education Act of 1965.[51] The key elements in the NCLB are to improve the academic achievement of students who are economically disadvantaged; assist in preparing, training, and recruiting highly qualified teachers; provide improved language instruction for children of limited English proficiency; make school systems accountable for student achievement, particularly by imposing standards for annual yearly progress for students and districts; require school systems to rely on teaching methods that are research based and that have been proven effective; and afford parents better choices while creating innovative educational programs, especially where local school systems are unresponsive to parents' needs.[52]

State Statutes

Most of the laws directing the day-to-day operation of public schools are state statutes. While state legislatures are subject to the limitations of federal law and of state constitutions, they are relatively free to establish and change their own systems of education. The law is well settled that state and local school boards, administrators, and teachers have the authority to adopt and enforce reasonable rules and regulations to ensure the smooth operation and management of schools. Even so, rules and regulations are subject to the same constitutional limitations as statutes passed by legislative bodies. Accordingly, if it is unconstitutional for Congress or state legislatures to enact laws violating the free speech rights of children, it is also impermissible for school administrators to do so by creating rules that apply only in their school buildings. Thus, while school officials have the authority to institute their own rules, their rules may not violate students' constitutional rights. It is also significant to note that legislation or rule-making on any level, whether federal or state, cannot conflict with a higher authority.

> The law is well settled that state and local boards of education, administrators, and teachers have the authority to adopt and enforce reasonable rules and regulations to ensure the smooth operation and management of schools.

Case or Common Law

Another source of law that significantly influences the daily operation of public schools is case law, also known as judge-made or common law. Common law refers to judicial interpretations of legal questions. Judges "interpret the law" by examining issues that may have been overlooked in the legislative or regulatory process or that may not have been anticipated when statutes were enacted. The Supreme Court, in the landmark case of *Marbury v. Madison*,[53] asserted its authority to review the actions of other branches of government. Although there is an infrequent tension between the three branches of government, the legislative and executive branches generally defer to judicial interpretations of their actions. Of course, whether judges are interpreting or making laws is subject to a great deal of controversy and often comes down to an individual's judicial perspective.[54]

A major tenet of common law is the concept of precedent, or the proposition that a majority ruling of the highest court in a given jurisdiction is binding on all lower courts within its jurisdiction. Accordingly, a ruling of the Supreme Court is binding throughout the nation, while a decision of a state's high court is binding only in a given state. Persuasive precedent, a ruling from another jurisdiction, is actually not precedent at all. Put another way, when courts in one state seek to resolve novel legal issues, the judges typically review precedent from other jurisdictions to determine whether those jurisdictions have addressed the same legal question, so that the judges might rely on that opinion for guidance. However, since courts are not bound to follow precedent from different jurisdictions, these cases remain persuasive in nature.

A substantial body of case law has developed from the application of both federal and state laws in the public schools. As indicated above, executive or administrative agencies develop sets of regulations to provide guidance on implementing statutes passed by legislative bodies. Even though these regulations provide significant guidance on how the law is to be put into operation, all possible scenarios cannot be fully anticipated. Thus, conflicts arise over how specific aspects of the statute are to be applied. Insofar as the resulting case law provides even more guidance because of the concept of precedent, the analysis and study of judicial opinions can provide valuable insight into how laws are to be applied to everyday situations.

> A substantial body of case law has developed from the application of both federal and state laws in the public schools.

SUMMARY AND RECOMMENDATIONS

Public education in America has evolved during the past four centuries as the country has moved from being a largely agrarian society to the industrial-technological economy of today. During this time education moved from being primarily the responsibility of the family to a major function of local and state governments. Although education is primarily a state responsibility, during the last century the federal government has increasingly become involved in public education.

Over the course of this history, Congress, state legislatures, and administrative agencies have enacted almost countless laws and regulations addressing education. These enactments impact the daily lives of teachers by regulating their employment status while spelling out their instructional duties. As time goes on, education is becoming more regulated, as the federal government continues to assume a greater role in the daily operations of schools, and states pass educational reform measures. Increasingly, teachers are finding that the laws affecting their jobs are becoming more complex. Add to this the thousands of judicial opinions that are handed down each year on education-related issues, and it is easy to see why teachers must develop an awareness of their legal rights and responsibilities in the area known as school or education law.[55] In this respect, we offer the following recommendations:

- Teachers should become familiar with federal and state education laws, particularly those relating to their employment and instructional responsibilities. In this respect, a major federal law, the No Child Left Behind Act, was scheduled to undergo reauthorization as this book was being written. Teachers should pay close attention to any changes that may be enacted, particularly those pertaining to professional qualifications, overall standards, and student testing requirements.
- Since the law is constantly evolving, teachers should develop a means to remain up to date on the issues presented in this book. To do so, teachers should supplement this book by attending workshops on school law offered by their professional organizations, teachers' associations, or local schools of education and by regularly visiting websites providing information on education law.
- Although courses in school law are not required by most graduate programs in education, except those leading to licensure as an administrator, teachers seeking graduate degrees should consider taking such a course as an elective to help themselves become better informed.
- If in doubt, ask. Since school administrators are generally fairly well versed in school law, as are teachers' association officials, teachers should seek information before acting on matters with legal consequences.
- Teachers should seek competent legal counsel in situations that may lead to litigation. Most teachers' associations provide a degree of legal protection to their members as a benefit.

FREQUENTLY ASKED QUESTIONS

Q. If education is not mentioned in the U.S. Constitution, why is it necessary to become familiar with constitutional provisions?

A. As the Supreme Court stated in *Tinker v. Des Moines Independent Community School District*,[56] neither students nor teachers lose their constitutional rights when they enter schools. Teachers, therefore, need to be aware of their own constitutional rights as well as those of their students. Knowledge of their own rights should help to prevent those rights from being unfairly violated. Knowledge of students' constitutional rights can help to prevent teachers from violating their students' rights and, we hope, avoid legal action as a result.

Q. Are there limitations on teachers when they seek to exercise their constitutional rights in schools?

A. Just as someone may not yell "fire" in a crowded theater when no fire is present and later claim it was a protected act of free speech, school boards may limit the free speech rights of teachers and students under certain circumstances. Thus, restrictions may be placed on the rights of both students and teachers due to the unique nature of our educational systems. These restrictions and limitations are discussed in later chapters of this book.

Q. Is it necessary to understand the court systems in order to understand school law fully?

A. No, but it helps. For example, in order to understand fully how a new court case can affect a school, an individual teacher, or a group of teachers, it is important to understand its full reach. The significance of a given case very much depends on the jurisdiction and level of the court. Lacking a full understanding of the court systems, it is difficult to analyze how a case impacts a school or teacher. Resource A at the end of this book provides additional guidance on the levels and jurisdictions of courts and how their decisions affect education.

Q. If education law is continuing to evolve, how is it possible for a teacher to keep up with changes?

A. Professional organizations and teachers' associations are generally a good source of information about new developments in school law. Teachers should read the monthly publications and literature put out by these groups. For example, the newsletters of many organizations contain regular columns on legal issues. If your organization or association does not regularly provide information on legal issues, as a member you should encourage it to do so. In addition, many websites provide useful information and updates on developments in education law. Resource C at the end of this book provides guidance on additional sources of information that can be used to remain current.

WHAT'S NEXT

The second chapter continues the discussion of the legal foundations of education by covering the topic of school governance and how it affects teachers. Specifically, this chapter provides additional information about the expanding role of the federal government along with laws regulating state and local educational agencies. The chapter also includes a section on school finance and the use of school property.

ENDNOTES

1. National Center for Educational Statistics. (2008). *Digest of Educational Statistics,* Chapter 2, Table 87. Number of public school districts and public and private elementary and secondary schools: Selected years, 1869–70 through 2006–07. Retrieved from http://nces.ed.gov/programs/digest/d08/tables/dt08_087.asp

2. National Center for Educational Statistics. (2008). *Digest of Educational Statistics,* Chapter 2, Table 94. Public elementary and secondary schools, by type of school: Selected years, 1967–68 through 2006–07. Retrieved from http://nces.ed.gov/programs/digest/d08/tables/dt08_094.asp

3. National Center for Educational Statistics. (2008). *Digest of Educational Statistics,* Chapter 1, Table 2. Enrollment in educational institutions, by level and control of institution, fall 1980 through fall 2008. Retrieved from http://nces.ed.gov/programs/digest/d08/tables/dt08_002.asp

4. National Center for Educational Statistics. (2008). *Digest of Educational Statistics,* Chapter 2, Table 65. Public elementary and secondary teachers, by level and state or jurisdiction: Selected years, fall 2000 through fall 2006. Retrieved from http://nces.ed.gov/programs/digest/d08/tables/dt08_065.asp

5. National Center for Educational Statistics. (2008). *Digest of Educational Statistics,* Chapter 2, Table 171. Revenues for public elementary and secondary schools, by source of funds: Selected years, 1919–20 through 2005–06. Retrieved from http://nces.ed.gov/programs/digest/d08/tables/dt08_171.asp

6. National Center for Educational Statistics. (2008). *Digest of Educational Statistics,* Chapter 2, Table 181. Total and current expenditures per pupil in public elementary and secondary schools: Selected years, 1919–20 through 2005–06. Retrieved from http://nces.ed.gov/programs/digest/d08/tables/dt08_181.asp

7. National Center for Educational Statistics. (2008). *Digest of Educational Statistics,* Chapter 2, Table 58. Private elementary and secondary enrollment, teachers, and schools, by orientation of school and selected school characteristics: Fall 2005. Retrieved from http://nces.ed.gov/programs/digest/d08/tables/dt08_058.asp

8. Commager, H. S. (Ed.). (1965). *Documents of American History, Vol. I: to 1898* (7th ed.). New York: Appleton-Century-Crofts.

9. National Defense Education Act of 1958, P.L. 85-864.

10. Elementary and Secondary Education Act of 1965, P.L. 89-10, 20 U.S.C. § 6301 *et seq.* (1965).

11. No Child Left Behind Act, 20 U.S.C. §§ 6301 *et seq.* (2006).

12. 347 U.S. 483 at 493 (1954).

13. *Id.*

14. 414 U.S. 563 (1974).

15. Civil Rights Act of 1964, Title VI, 42 U.S.C. §§ 2000d *et seq.* (2006).

16. Education for All Handicapped Children Act, 20 U.S.C. § 1400 *et seq.* (1975).

17. Individuals with Disabilities Education Act, 20 U.S.C. § 1400–1491 (2006).

18. National Commission on Excellence in Education. (1983). *A Nation at Risk: The Imperative for Educational Reform.* Washington, DC: Author.

19. No Child Left Behind Act, 20 U.S.C. §§ 6301 *et seq.* (2006).

20. Wenkart, R. D. (2003). The No Child Left Behind Act and Congress' power to regulate under the Spending Clause. *Education Law Reporter, 174,* 589–597. Raisch, C. D., & Russo, C. J. (2006). The No Child Left Behind Act: Federal over-reaching or necessary educational reform? *Education Law Journal, 7*(4), 255–265.

21. U.S. Department of Education. (2009). *Great expectations: Holding ourselves and our schools accountable for results.* Washington, DC: Author.

22. Garner, B. A. (2004). *Black's Law Dictionary* (8th ed.). St. Paul, MN: West.

23. San Antonio Independent School District v. Rodriguez, 411 U.S. 1 at 35 (1973).

24. U.S. Constitution, Article I, § 8.

25. U.S. Constitution, Article I, § 10

26. U.S. Constitution, Amendment I.

27. Tinker v. Des Moines Independent Community School District, 393 U.S. 503 at 506 (1969).

28. U.S. Constitution, Amendment IV.

29. U.S. Constitution, Amendment V.

30. U.S. Constitution, Amendment IX.

31. U.S. Constitution, Amendment X.

32. U.S. Constitution, Amendment XI.

33. U.S. Constitution, Amendment XIV.

34. Constitution of the State of Ohio, Article VI.

35. Garner, B. A. (2004). *Black's Law Dictionary* (8th ed.). St. Paul, MN: West.

36. Civil Rights Act of 1964, Title IV, 42 U.S.C. § 2000c *et seq.* (2006).

37. Civil Rights Act of 1964, Title VI, 42 U.S.C. §§ 2000d *et seq.* (2006).

38. Civil Rights Act of 1964, Title VII, 42 U.S.C. § 2000e *et seq.* (2006).

39. Education Amendments of 1972, Title IX, 20 U.S.C. § 1681(a) (2006).

40. Franklin v. Gwinnett County Public Schools, 503 U.S. 60 (1992).

41. Rehabilitation Act, Section 504, 29 U.S.C. § 794 (2006).

42. Russo, C. J. & Osborne, A. G. (2009). *Section 504 and the ADA.* Thousand Oaks, CA: Corwin.

43. Americans with Disabilities Act, 42 U.S.C. § 12101 *et seq.* (2006).

44. Russo, C. J. & Osborne, A. G. (2009). *Section 504 and the ADA.* Thousand Oaks, CA: Corwin.

45. Age Discrimination in Employment Act, 29 U.S.C. § 621 *et seq.* (2006).

46. School boards are also known by other names, such as school committees, boards of education, boards of directors, or boards of trustees. For the sake of simplicity, the term *school boards* will be used throughout this book to signify the governing body of local education agencies or school districts.

47. Individuals with Disabilities Education Act, 20 U.S.C. § 1400–1491 (2006).

48. Education for All Handicapped Children Act, 20 U.S.C. § 1400 *et seq.* (1975).

49. Osborne, A. G. & Russo, C. J. (2007). *Special education and the law: A guide for practitioners.* Thousand Oaks, CA: Corwin.

50. No Child Left Behind Act, 20 U.S.C. §§ 6301 *et seq.* (2006). As this is being written, Congress is working on legislation to reauthorize the NCLB.

51. Elementary and Secondary Education Act of 1965, P.L. 89-10, 20 U.S.C. § 6301 *et seq.* (1965).

52. Raisch, C. D., & Russo, C. J. (2006). The No Child Left Behind Act: Federal over-reaching or necessary educational reform? *Education Law Journal, 7,* 255–265.

53. 5 U.S. 137 (1803).

54. Russo, C. J. (2009). Judges as umpires or rule makers? The role of the judiciary in educational decision making in the United States. *Education Law Journal, 10*(1), 33–47.

55. *See* Russo, C. J. (2010). School law: An essential component in your tool-box. *School Business Affairs, 75*(9), 36–38.

56. 393 U.S. 503 (1969).

School Governance 2 and the Teacher

INTRODUCTION

Public educational systems in the United States are governed by school boards subject to federal and state laws. Local school boards are fairly free to establish policy and set the rules and regulations for the operation of their respective districts as long as these rules do not conflict with federal and state laws or constitutional provisions. School boards are charged with the responsibility for ensuring that a school system is staffed by competent and properly licensed administrators, teachers, and other staff. Further, local boards have the authority to establish the annual budget for their districts by prioritizing needs and efficiently spending revenue available from local, state, and federal sources.

As indicated in the first chapter, education is primarily a function of states rather than the federal government. To this end, all states have laws and regulations governing the operation of their schools that prescribe specified subjects that must be included in their curricula and that establish criteria for the proper licensing or certification of professional educators.

State laws also may establish minimum academic standards and graduation requirements for students. Again, as indicated in the first chapter, the federal government has taken on an increased role in the governance of school systems during the past several decades. Thus, school systems are now subject to the mandates of federal education and civil rights statutes such as the No Child Left Behind Act (NCLB),[1] the Individuals with Disabilities Education Act (IDEA),[2] and the Americans with Disabilities Act.[3] Further, local school boards are responsible for ensuring that federal and state laws are properly implemented within their school systems.

This chapter begins with a discussion of the roles of the federal and state governments in the operation of public school systems with an emphasis on how federal and state mandates affect teachers and classroom instruction. The chapter next reviews the authority and responsibilities of local school boards. Finally, the chapter presents information on the important area of school financing and the use of public school property.

THE ROLE OF THE FEDERAL GOVERNMENT

As noted in the first chapter, education is primarily a function of the states. Nevertheless, over the past five decades the federal government has taken on a greater role in the day-to-day operation of the schools through legislation designed to foster specific programs and improve the general condition of our schools. Further, much of the federal legislation pertaining to the general citizenry—notably that addressing civil rights and privacy—applies equally to students and school employees. Congress annually allocates billions of dollars in education funds. State and local school boards, by accessing those funds, agree to the conditions and requirements of federal laws. Consequently, the federal government has a strong role in education today.

> Congress annually allocates billions of dollars in education funds. State and local school boards, by accessing those funds, agree to the conditions and requirements of federal laws.

In 1979 President Carter created the U.S. Department of Education (ED) as a separate federal agency by the Department of Education Organization Act,[4] largely to fulfill one of his campaign promises. Prior to 1979 the federal education agency had been part of the Department of Health, Education, and Welfare. ED is administered by the secretary of education, who is a member of the president's cabinet. Among the subdivisions in the ED most significant to the daily operation of public schools are these:

- Office for Civil Rights
- Office of Elementary and Secondary Education

- Office of English Language Acquisition, Language Enhancement, and Academic Achievement for Limited English Proficient Students
- Office of Innovation and Improvement
- Office of Safe and Drug Free Schools
- Office of Special Education and Rehabilitation Services

The primary purposes of ED are to administer federal education funds, promulgate regulations to accompany federal education statutes, and enforce civil rights and privacy laws in the context of educational institutions. Its mission is "to promote student achievement and preparation for global competitiveness by fostering educational excellence and ensuring equal access."[5] In addition to administering federal education funds, the agency collects data and disseminates research information, focuses attention on critical educational issues, and enforces federal laws and regulations particularly in regard to discrimination, equal educational access, and civil rights. More specifically, the act establishing the ED requires it to

> In addition to administering federal education funds, ED collects data and disseminates research information, focuses attention on critical educational issues, and enforces federal laws and regulations particularly in regard to discrimination, equal educational access, and civil rights.

- strengthen the federal commitment to assuring access to equal educational opportunity for every individual;
- supplement and complement the efforts of states, local school systems and other instrumentalities of the states, the private sector, public and private nonprofit educational research institutions, community-based organizations, parents, and students to improve the quality of education;
- encourage the increased involvement of the public, parents, and students in federal education programs;
- promote improvements in the quality and usefulness of education through federally supported research, evaluation, and sharing of information;
- improve the coordination of federal education programs;
- improve the management of federal education activities; and
- increase the accountability of federal education programs to the president, the Congress, and the public.[6]

STATE EDUCATION AGENCIES

All states, other than Minnesota and Wisconsin, have state-level boards of education with general authority over public schools.[7] Further, all states have agencies or departments of education, generically known as state education agencies (SEAs), which coordinate and oversee the operation of local school boards. SEAs operate by delegation of powers under the authority of state legislatures and are charged with the administrative responsibility of developing educational policy and implementing state laws. Most SEAs are headed by a chief school officer, variously known by titles such as the state commissioner of education or state superintendent of schools, who is appointed by and works under the direct control of a state board of education. The method of selecting individuals to serve on the state boards of education is established by state law and consequently varies from state to state; most commonly, members are either appointed by governors or elected.

> SEAs operate by delegation of powers under the authority of state legislatures and are charged with the administrative responsibility of developing educational policy and implementing state laws.

As with the federal ED, SEAs are subdivided into a number of departments, each with specific functions. For example, most SEAs have divisions supervising special education. A state's special education division would be responsible for distributing federal and state funds and making sure that each local board properly implements federal and state laws governing the education of students with disabilities. In this respect, special education divisions investigate complaints of noncompliance and periodically conduct program reviews and financial audits of districts. Depending on the state, other subdivisions might be responsible for some or all of the following:

- Elementary education
- Secondary education; career, technical, and vocational programs
- Charter schools
- Curriculum implementation
- Teacher certification or licensure
- Distribution of grants
- Programs for non-English speakers
- Accountability
- Testing and assessment
- Technology

Authority

Inasmuch as SEAs are created and operated under the auspices of state legislatures, their authority varies from state to state. Generally speaking, state laws grant SEAs general supervision and control over school systems within their respective states.[8] Beyond that, individual SEAs may have specific executive powers as granted by their legislatures.

One of the major functions of an SEA is rule-making. Typically, as with Congress and the ED, state legislatures enact education laws but leave it to the SEAs to establish rules and regulations for their implementation. For example, legislatures may enact laws requiring individuals to possess valid certificates or licenses to teach within their states. The laws may even provide general minimum requirements for certification, such as possession of a bachelor's degree in education. Even so, it is usually left to SEAs to establish the specific criteria for obtaining teaching licenses. Thus, SEAs may set requirements regarding course content or knowledge that applicants for certification must demonstrate before they can seek employment.

Once they have granted certification to teachers and other educational professionals, SEAs also may have the authority to rescind it for just cause. Further, SEAs may have the authority to grant approval for college programs designed to prepare students for careers in education.

Within the limits established by federal and state law, SEAs have control over the operation of public schools. Nevertheless the powers of SEAs are subject to judicial review. By way of illustration, if SEA officials revoke a teacher's certification for just cause, the individual may seek judicial review. Ordinarily, as long as the decisions made by SEA officials are consistent with the law, are within their authority, and are not arbitrary or capricious, the courts uphold those actions.

> Within the limits established by federal and state law, SEAs have direct control over the operation of public schools. Nevertheless, the powers of SEAs are subject to judicial review.

Other Duties and Powers

SEAs often have quasi-judicial powers allowing them to settle disputes via administrative due process hearings. The best example of this is in special education. The IDEA, the federal special education statute, mandates that states must establish systems of due process hearings through which parents can bring complaints regarding matters related to the provision of special education services to their children.[9] Under this mechanism, states must establish either a one- or two-tiered dispute resolution system. In a one-tiered system, a single administrative due process hearing is held at the state level. In a two-tiered system, a hearing is held at the local level, but an aggrieved party may bring an appeal to the state level. In both systems parties may appeal final hearing decisions to either state or federal courts. The role of hearing officers or hearing tribunals is to gather the important facts in disputes and render decisions consistent with federal and state laws and regulations. Unless overturned on appeal, orders of hearing officers or tribunals have the full force of law. In addition, state law may allow SEAs to settle disputes over other educational issues such as the allocation of funds or teacher dismissal.

In many states, SEAs are also charged with the responsibility for accrediting school districts to ensure that they meet minimum standards. Accreditation is important to make sure that students receive an adequate education and that taxpayer dollars are being spent wisely and efficiently. Typically, the accreditation process involves extensive reviews of district curricula and the overall quality of instruction. Further, accountability reviews may include financial audits along with reviews of student achievement. A number of remedies exist for school systems that are found to be lacking; these range from placing them on remedial plans to withholding of state funds to a complete state takeover of the school district.

LOCAL SCHOOL BOARDS

With the exception of Hawaii,[10] where the entire state is a single district, states are organized into school systems that may be coterminous with county or municipal boundaries. In some states, districts are organized along county lines, while in others they coincide with city or town borders. In yet other jurisdictions, districts may be formed as completely separate entities that cross geographic boundaries. Further, small geographic locales may join together to form regional districts. At the same time, some states form intermediate districts or collaborative units for specific purposes such as providing vocational or special education. School districts are governed by school boards, or school committees as they are known in New England. Most local school boards are elected, while boards in some large cities are appointed by executive authorities such as mayors or city councils.

> School districts are governed by school boards, or school committees as they are known in New England. Most local school boards are elected while boards in some large cities are appointed by executive authorities such as mayors or city councils.

Authority

Since education is a state function, school boards are "creatures of the state" operating at the local level. Thus, school board members are deemed to be state officials as opposed to local officials. State legislatures authorize local schools boards to administer their systems. So authorized, school boards typically develop and administer annual budgets, hire personnel, establish curricular and course offerings, and set overall policy. Even so, school boards do not, or should not, run school systems on a day-to-day basis, since they vest this responsibility in the professional educational administrators that they employ. Districts are commonly administered by chief school officers, usually with the title of superintendent of schools, and management teams consisting of lower-level administrators with specific responsibilities.

> State legislatures authorize local schools boards to administer their systems. So authorized, school boards typically develop and administer annual budgets, hire personnel, establish curricular and course offerings, and set overall policy.

The duties of school boards and district administrators may be either discretionary or ministerial. Discretionary duties are those that require judgment by the decision makers. On the other hand, ministerial duties are those mandatory functions that statutes or regulations direct boards to complete and do not require the exercise of judgment; duties here include hiring a superintendent, levying taxes, and choosing whether to purchase property to erect new school buildings. Discretionary duties are, as the name suggests, those functions that boards are not obligated to carry out, such as creating extracurricular activities or academic electives. In reality the line between discretionary and ministerial duties is not always distinct and is often blurred.

School boards have two types of authority or power: express and implied. *Express powers* are those that are specifically granted by legislation. *Implied powers* are those that are assumed to be reasonably necessary for school boards to carry out their duties effectively, although they are not specifically delineated in statute. An example of an express power is hiring and entering into employment contracts for superintendents of schools. Implied powers include hiring contractors to complete repairs on school buildings. Implied powers are grounded in language included in most state statutes that allow boards to take such actions as are reasonable and necessary for the proper functioning of their schools.

To the extent that school boards are established and governed by state law, the authority vested in them varies from one jurisdiction to the next. For example, in most jurisdictions school boards have the authority to hire the instructional staff. However, in some jurisdic-

> To the extent that school boards are established and governed by state law, the authority vested in them will vary from one jurisdiction to the next.

tions, such as Massachusetts, the superintendent of schools appoints principals, who have the authority to hire the teachers within their respective schools.[11]

School Board Members

Regardless of whether school board members are elected or appointed, state legislatures generally establish minimum qualifications for individuals to serve. It should go without saying that one such qualification is that individuals must be residents in the districts in which they wish to serve. Minimum age requirements also may be set, but where none exist it may be assumed that candidates must be of voting age.[12] Some officials may serve *ex officio* or as a legislated function of their position. For example, in some cities the mayor may automatically be a member of the school board by local ordinance.

By the same token, state legislatures may place restrictions on who may serve as school board members. Typically, to avoid conflict of interest, school employees are forbidden to serve on school boards in the districts where they work. Still, for the most part, teachers and other employees may serve on boards in their districts of residence. In addition, antinepotism statutes may place restrictions on close relatives of school employees sitting on school boards or, at the very least, if employees' relatives do serve, may prevent them from voting on issues that directly affect their related employees. Further, conflict of interest laws usually prevent board members from doing business with their own school districts. For instance, a board member who owns a business would not be allowed to supply the district with goods or services.

> To avoid conflict of interest, school employees are forbidden to serve on school boards in the districts where they work. Still, for the most part, teachers and other employees may serve on boards in their districts of residence.

Legislatures also establish the criteria and means by which school board members may be removed from office. Generally, whether elected or appointed, school board members have no guarantee that their terms of office will be renewed upon expiration. Most state statutes provide for the removal of board members for cause, such as misconduct or dereliction of duty. Typically, the removal of board members may be by recall elections (in the case of elected officials) or by the appointive authorities (in the case of appointed officials).

Meetings and Procedures

In almost all states, school boards operate under open meeting or sunshine laws. These laws provide a significant degree of transparency by requiring boards to take nearly all actions in meetings open to the public rather than in private. The purpose of these laws is to prevent boards from taking action in secret or excluding a member from a meeting. Under most sunshine statutes, notice of meetings must be posted a designated number of days prior to the meetings so that all board members are aware of the meetings and, in some states, to

> In almost all states, school boards operate under open meeting or sunshine laws. These laws provide a significant degree of transparency by requiring boards to take nearly all actions in meetings open to the public rather than in private.

allow the citizenry to attend. At a minimum, meeting notices must include the date, time, and place of the meeting. State statutes also may require notice of agenda items or a summary of the business to be conducted. When meetings convene on a regular basis and the schedule is established and made public in advance, further notice may not be required. Deviations to the set schedule, such as canceling or rescheduling meetings or calling special meetings, require notice. In some jurisdictions, boards set aside a portion of the agenda to allow citizens to speak on matters of public concern. Meetings are also often broadcast on the local access channels of cable television.

There are exceptions to the requirement to hold meetings in the open. Most sunshine statutes allow for certain types of business to be held in closed or executive sessions. Boards can enter into executive sessions to discuss sensitive matters such as employee dismissals or collective bargaining agreements. Requiring such discussions in open sessions would compromise school boards' abilities to negotiate effectively. Although boards may discuss these sensitive matters in executive sessions, they must vote in open sessions. Another exception might be hearings to take disciplinary action against school employees, although state laws typically allow those who are subjects of the proceedings to request that they be open to the public. Even so, many statutes require that the actions taken in closed or executive sessions be released as soon as the need for privacy no longer exists. By way of illustration, the minutes of negotiation strategy sessions may have to be released once employees' contracts are signed.

Some state statutes prescribe certain rules of procedure for school board meetings so that business proceeds in an orderly fashion. Absent specific statutory rules of procedure, boards are generally free to adopt their own rules. These rules may determine how many members present constitute a quorum or spell out how many votes are necessary to take certain actions. Most

> Absent specific statutory rules of procedure, school boards are generally free to adopt their own rules.

motions may be passed by a simple majority of those present and voting. Yet, some important actions, such as the appointment of a superintendent or the approval of the annual budget, may require a majority of all board members even if not all are present and voting. Other actions even may require a vote greater than a simple majority, such as a two-thirds majority. Other rules spell out how motions can be made, seconded, and amended. Rules of procedure also may dictate how discussions take place and how discussions can be cut off so that votes may be taken. The rules followed by most boards are generally based on *Robert's Rules of Order*,[13] although strict adherence to that protocol is normally not required.

As indicated above, statutes or rules of procedure normally determine how votes are taken and how many votes are needed for motions to be passed. There are situations, though, where board members may fail to vote. In these instances a nonvote is by and large considered to be a vote for the majority. For example, if a five-member board takes a vote with two members in favor, one opposed, and two not voting, the motion is considered to have passed four to one. Although a board member's failure to vote may be considered an abdication of duty, exceptions exist. Thus, as indicated above, in some states antinepotism or conflict of interest laws may require members to abstain or recuse themselves in matters in which they have personal interests. Most votes may be taken by a simple hand count, but important votes often require a roll call tally.

State laws or regulations commonly require that the business of school boards be recorded and kept in the form of meeting minutes. The form and content of minutes may be set by either statute or rules of procedure and normally do not require a verbatim record of all discussion. At a minimum, minutes must record votes or actions taken but should also include a summary of the discussion that proceeded any vote. It is important for meeting minutes to be accurate. For this reason, as soon as it is practical, generally at the next meeting, minutes are approved and entered into the record by formal vote. At this time minutes may be corrected or amended if necessary. Once approved, the minutes of a board meeting become the official record of the board's proceedings and must be made available to the public unless they are minutes of closed or executive sessions. Minutes of those meetings must be made public when the need for privacy has passed.

SCHOOL FINANCE AND USE OF PROPERTY

The tasks involved in overseeing and managing school systems' finances and property are among the primary responsibilities of school boards. It can be argued that nothing is more important than safeguarding the taxpayers' investments. Although the tasks of managing the budget, spending school district funds, and caring for property on a day-to-day basis are almost always delegated to the professional staff, school boards are ultimately responsible for seeing that the school systems' resources are managed wisely and in accordance with all laws. In other words, although school administrators may handle the everyday functions of placing orders and paying bills, school boards are the final authority on how funds are spent and how district property is used, and ultimately boards are legally responsible for the fiscal management of the school system. Thus, all expenditures must be approved by school boards, which can then be held accountable for any misspent funds.

Financial Responsibilities

Public education in the United States is financed through a combination of federal, state, and local funds. Federal monies most often come to local school districts in the form of grants. For the most part, there are two types of grants: entitlement and competitive. School districts receive entitlement grants as long as they meet certain criteria. For example, districts with

> Public education in the United States is financed through a combination of federal, state, and local funds.

qualifying numbers of students from low-income families receive funds to help provide additional remedial instruction to those students through the Title I program of the NCLB. While receipt of these funds is contingent on districts completing the proper paperwork and application forms, it is fairly automatic, and districts do not compete against each other for funds. Competitive grants, on the other hand, typically require school personnel to complete detailed applications that describe how the monies will be used and what outcomes the districts hope to achieve. As the name suggests, school boards compete against each other for grants that are awarded to those making the best proposals through the application process. Federal grants are provided for specific purposes. An example of a competitive federal grant is the Reading First program of the NCLB, which provides funds to improve literacy instruction.

State funds also may be distributed to local school districts in the form of grants for targeted purposes. Even so, most state monies are provided directly to school boards to assist in financing their schools. The allocation of funds is based on often-complicated funding formulas that take into account factors such as the number of students in districts, the wealth of local communities, and the efforts of local taxpayers.

In most states the major portion of school district funding comes from the local level, generally in the form of taxes on real property. School boards do not have the power to tax, but that authority is delegated to them either through constitutional provisions or by the state legislature. In locales where districts are coterminous with county or municipal borders, school taxes may be levied as part of overall taxes that

> In most states the major portion of school district funding comes from the local level, generally in the form of taxes on real property.

finance county or municipal governments. In other areas, school taxes may be levied as separate entities. School boards also may borrow money from time to time for large capital outlays such as building a new school, but generally they may not borrow to pay for normal yearly expenses. Inasmuch as each state has its own unique school financing mechanism, a complete discussion of taxation and procurement of school funds is beyond the scope of this book.

Regardless of the source of school funds, school boards are charged with managing those funds wisely. In order to plan effectively, school boards begin by developing an itemized budget that projects how funds will be spent. Most budgets have two major categories: salaries and expenses. These categories are further broken down to provide explanations of the purposes for which funds are allocated. For example, the salary portion of the budget is further broken down to itemize how much will be spent to pay for administrators, teachers, teacher aides, custodians, cafeteria workers, and all other personnel. Once budgets are approved, boards generally are free to transfer funds approved for one purpose to another as needs change. For example, if the heating system in one school unexpectedly broke down, to pay for repairs a school board could divert funds intended for another less urgent purpose at another school, such as painting classrooms. A board may not exceed its total budget.

> Regardless of the source of school funds, school boards are charged with managing those funds wisely. In order to plan effectively, school boards begin by developing an itemized budget that projects how funds will be spent.

By far the largest part of school districts' budgets is set aside for salaries. It is not at all unusual for salaries to compose up to 80% or more of the total district budget. Not surprisingly, teacher salaries make up the largest portion of the salary budget. School boards in most states are vested with the authority to negotiate salaries and benefits with both professional and nonprofessional staff either on an individual or collective-bargaining basis. Once contracts have been negotiated, boards must establish the needs of the school system for proper staffing and set the budget accordingly. Since school boards in most jurisdictions do not enjoy fiscal autonomy, there are limits on how much they can spend, regardless of what they might consider to be necessary to educate their students properly. The task of school boards, then, is to determine proper staffing levels within the limits of their budget allocations. In difficult economic times this often means prioritizing needs and making difficult choices, inasmuch as most budgets do not allow for funding everything a board may feel is reasonable or even necessary.

Another source of potential funding for school systems is competitive grants from private corporations; such grants are available for specific purposes. For example, many high-tech companies offer grants to encourage and improve the use of technology in the schools. Even though these monies come from private sources, school personnel in charge of these grants must account for how the funds are spent and must administer the grant programs consistent with state law and standard accounting requirements.

Use of School Property

For purposes of this section, school property includes not only school buildings and the land on which they sit but also supplies and equipment. School boards are legally responsible for the management and control of the use of school property. Since almost all school property is either purchased or constructed with tax dollars, it is considered to be public property. School boards are thus responsible for protecting the property and making sure that it is used for its intended purposes. Even so, insofar as school property is public property, boards may permit other reasonable uses of school property such as allowing their facilities to be used for meetings and functions of community groups. Boards also may rent out school property and use the funds obtained for other school purposes. For example, boards can rent school gymnasia to local youth basketball leagues and use the funds to help maintain the athletic facilities.

In granting the use of school facilities to outside groups, boards must be cognizant of constitutional principles. In other words, if a board regularly opens its buildings for meetings of local political organizations, it may not deny use to a group simply because it disagrees with that group's point of view or political philosophy. On the other hand, boards may set policies to deny use of their facilities when there are compelling interests in doing so. For example, access could be denied to a group that advocated the violent overthrow of the government.

School employees do not have any inherent right to use school property for uses not related to their employment without permission. To this end, teacher associations may be allowed to use school buildings for after-school meetings as long as proper permission is obtained prior to the meetings, but they do not have the right to use facilities without authorization.

School boards' authority to manage school property properly does not give them free reign to dispose of property. The disposal of public property, including school property, is generally governed by state statute. Naturally, school boards from time to time will have the need and desire to dispose of surplus or no longer needed property, and most states have procedures or policies for doing so. Generally speaking, as long as the sale or lease of the property is in the school district's best interests and does not conflict with state statutes, courts do not interfere.[14]

School Fees

In an era of tight budgets school boards often look to other forms of revenue. One such form is charging fees for activities and services offered by the school district. School boards generally cannot charge parents for tuition or expenses directly related to the education of their children, such as the use of textbooks, since this would be contrary to the concept of providing free schools. Even so, in some states boards charge participation fees for nonessential, albeit important, activities. Thus, it is not uncommon for boards to assess fees for participation in extracurricular programs or even for school transportation where it is not mandated by law. Since participation in such activities is optional, courts have upheld the use of fees. In establishing fee schedules, most boards make provisions to waive fees for students who may not be able to afford the cost and even cap the amount of fees that may be charged to a student or family in one academic year.

SUMMARY AND RECOMMENDATIONS

Although the basic level of school governance, particularly as it applies to teachers, emanates from local school boards, the state and federal governments play a large role in the operation of schools. As has been often stated in these first two chapters, education is primarily a function of the states. In this respect most of the legal requirements under which school systems operate are derived from state law. Even so, particularly in the past few decades, the federal government has become much more involved in setting school policy and influencing how students are educated through the passage of laws such as the NCLB and the IDEA.

The rights and responsibilities of teachers are established through a combination of federal and state laws along with local school board policies. Further, the programs and curricular offerings of all school systems are paid for through a combination of federal, state, and local funds. In view of the increased legal requirements that have been placed on school districts during the last half century, teachers need to be aware of the following:

- The federal government has the authority to provide funding for education under the General Welfare and Spending Clause of the Constitution. Since the federal government can attach requirements to the receipt of federal funds, these monies can be lost if school systems do not follow federal mandates.
- All states have established agencies charged with coordinating and overseeing the operation of their public schools. SEAs, acting with powers delegated by their state legislatures, may establish policies and procedures affecting daily school operations.
- Except for Hawaii, all states have delegated the management of public schools to local school boards. In discharging their duties, boards are responsible for setting local policy, seeing that qualified professional staff is retained, and setting the annual operating budget.

- Teachers may not serve on the school boards of the districts in which they are employed. However, most states allow them to serve on school boards in other jurisdictions.
- Most of the business of school boards must be conducted in the open. Exceptions to this rule exist, however, in certain circumstances, such as to protect the privacy rights of teachers or to develop negotiating strategies for collective bargaining.
- Funding for school systems comes from a variety of federal, state, and local sources. While most of these funds are for the general operation of the schools, others are specifically targeted for a set purpose.
- Grants from private corporations are often a good source of funds for specific purposes such as improving the use of technology in the schools. Although the origin of these funds is private, school personnel are accountable for their use.
- School boards may charge fees for participation in elective activities such as sports and other extracurricular programs.

FREQUENTLY ASKED QUESTIONS

Q. If education is a function of the states, why is the federal government involved?

A. As indicated in Chapter 1, the General Welfare and Spending Clause in Article I of the Constitution gives the federal government the authority to pass legislation for the general welfare of the country. It goes without saying that strong educational systems are in the best interests of the nation as a whole. For this reason, the federal government has increasingly become involved in education by providing funds to achieve specific national goals such as the education of students with disabilities or the improvement of the overall literacy of the population. As we move toward a more global economy we may expect to see even greater federal involvement in education in the future.

Q. What is the role of state education agencies?

A. The major role of state education agencies, or SEAs, is to oversee the operation of the public schools within states. The authority of SEAs is derived from the state legislatures, and in essence they act on behalf of state legislatures. Depending on the state, SEAs coordinate educational activities within the state, serve as watchdogs to make sure that the applicable laws are carried out, provide technical assistance to local school boards, and distribute state funds. Further, SEAs make local school boards accountable for the funds they receive and for educational outcomes.

Q. What do school boards derive their authority from?

A. Like SEAs, local school boards derive their authority from state legislatures and in essence act on behalf of the legislatures at the local level. School board powers may be either express, meaning that they are specifically granted by statute, or implied, meaning that they are assumed as necessary to carry out boards' express functions. School board duties may be either discretionary, which require judgment, or ministerial, which are mandatory.

Q. Where do the funds required to operate schools come from?

A. School funds come from a variety of sources. Most funds are raised at the local level, generally through taxes on real property. Other funds come from the state and federal governments. Most federal and many state funds come in the form of grants. Entitlement grants are given to school districts on the basis of established criteria and are fairly automatic as long as the districts meet the eligibility requirements. Competitive grants are given for very specific purposes, and, as the name suggests, districts must compete for these funds by submitting detailed proposals for how the monies will be used. Districts submitting the best proposals are usually the ones that obtain these grants.

WHAT'S NEXT

The third chapter covers the constitutional rights and freedoms of teachers. Specifically, the chapter deals with free speech and association, freedom of religion, privacy rights, and aspects of due process.

ENDNOTES

1. No Child Left Behind Act, 20 U.S.C. §§ 6301–7941 (2006).
2. Individuals with Disabilities Education Act, 20 U.S.C. § 1400–1491 (2006).
3. Americans with Disabilities Act, 42 U.S.C. § 12101 *et seq.*
4. Department of Education Organization Act, P.L. 96-88 (1979).
5. U.S. Department of Education. (n.d.). *About ED overview.* Retrieved from http://www.ed.gov/about/landing.jhtml
6. U.S. Department of Education. (n.d). *Mission.* Retrieved from http://www.ed.gov/about/overview/mission/mission.html
7. National Association of State Boards of Education. http://www.nasbe.org/index.php/web-links/2-state-boards

8. Russo, C. J. (2009). *Reutter's the law of public education* (7th ed.). New York: Foundation Press.

9. 20 U.S.C. § 1415.

10. Hawaii Department of Education. (n.d.). *About us.* Retrieved from http://doe.k12.hi.us/about/index.htm

11. 71 Massachusetts General Laws § 59B (2009).

12. Vittoria v. West Orange Board of Education, 300 A.2d 356 (N.J. App. Div. 1973).

13. Robert, H. N., Evans, W. J., Honemann, D. H., & Balch, T. J. (2000). *Robert's rules of order: Newly revised* (10th ed.). New York: Da Capo Press.

14. Russo, C. J. (2009). *Reutter's the law of public education* (7th ed.). New York: Foundation Press.

Basic Constitutional Rights and Freedoms

3

KEY CONCEPTS IN THIS CHAPTER

- ❖ Free Speech Rights
- ❖ Rights of Association
- ❖ Freedom of Religion
- ❖ Privacy Rights
- ❖ Due Process

INTRODUCTION

The U.S. Constitution outlines the basic rights of all Americans. Teachers enjoy their constitutional rights even when they are within the walls of public school buildings.[1] Even so, school officials may curtail the constitutional rights of teachers when there is a legitimate governmental interest in doing so. Although school boards cannot insist that teachers surrender their basic rights as a prerequisite for employment, since teachers are in sensitive positions, some limitations may be placed on their full exercise of those rights, particularly in the classrooms where, for example, they may not endorse political candidates or profess their religious beliefs.

This chapter is not intended to be a comprehensive review of teachers' rights. Rather, this chapter provides a brief introduction to and overview of the constitutional principles underlying the legal controversies in the issues presented in much greater detail in later chapters. Specifically, the chapter deals with the rights of free speech and association, freedom of religion, privacy, and aspects of due process. Insofar as each of these topics is discussed in greater detail later in the book, the intent of this chapter is to establish the constitutional foundation, with a few examples taken from case law, for many of the rights and freedoms to which teachers are entitled. A second purpose of the chapter is to provide a brief introduction to some of the more contentious issues that have been litigated. Because many of the basic rights of teachers were established through court decisions from other areas of public employment, some of the cases discussed in this chapter do not involve teachers; they are cited because the legal principles that they enunciated are applicable to educators.

FIRST AMENDMENT RIGHTS

According to the First Amendment, enacted in 1791 as part of the Bill of Rights, the first ten amendments to the federal Constitution,

> Congress shall make no law respecting an establishment of religion, or prohibiting the free exercise thereof; or abridging the freedom of speech, or of the press; or the right of the people peaceably to assemble, and to petition the Government for a redress of grievances.

Since the Supreme Court has extended the First Amendment to the states via case law, the same limits that apply to the federal government also apply to the states and to local school boards as arms of their states.

Freedom of Speech

It almost goes without saying that teachers continue to enjoy the First Amendment right of free speech and that they do not forfeit the basic right of all citizens to speak out on matters of public concern. This is true even when teachers may voice criticisms of school board policies or speak out on school matters, as long as they are issues of public concern.[2] Even so, teachers cannot air private grievances under the guise of free speech.[3] Also, just as the freedom of speech does not give individuals the right to yell "fire" in a crowded theater, officials may curtail speech that disrupts the educational environment. By the same token, teachers do not have the same freedom of speech in the classroom as they might enjoy at public meetings or in their homes.

Matters of Public Concern

Issues around the free speech rights of teachers began to emerge in light of a series of cases starting with the Supreme Court's 1968 landmark decision in *Pickering v. Board of Education of Township High School District 205 (Pickering).*[4] In *Pickering* the Court ruled that the rights of teachers to speak on matters of public concern could not be abridged, unless there was a compelling state interest to curtail those free speech rights. The controversy began when a school board discharged a teacher who had written a

> In 1968 the Supreme Court… acknowledged that the rights of teachers to speak on matters of public concern could not be abridged, unless there was a compelling state interest to curtail those free speech rights.

letter to a newspaper criticizing the board's allocation of school funds and its methods of informing the public regarding its need for additional taxes. The board claimed that it dismissed the teacher due to the detrimental effect the publication of the letter had on the operation and administration of the schools. Although not all of the statements in the teacher's letter were true, those that were not were determined to result from poor research as opposed to being intentionally made knowingly false statements. The teacher challenged his dismissal on First Amendment grounds.

In *Pickering* the Supreme Court held that the school board could not dismiss the teacher because of his exercise of his First Amendment right to speak on matters of public concern absent a showing that his false statements were made knowingly or with a reckless disregard for the truth. However, the Court noted that the teacher's rights needed to be balanced against the school board's interests in maintaining efficient schools. In so doing, the Court indicated that if the teacher's expression dealt with a matter of public concern and did not interfere with the operation of the schools, he could not be discharged inasmuch as he enjoyed the same First Amendment protection as any member of the general public. In its opinion the Court created a two-part shifting burden of proof: First, the Court explained that teachers must produce evidence that they spoke as private citizens on a subject matter that was a matter of public concern; second, the Court decided that school boards assume the burden of producing evidence that the speech, albeit on a matter of public concern, interfered with the teacher's duties or the efficient operation of the school district.

The Supreme Court further emphasized the proposition that teachers do not give up their free speech rights in its 1972 judgment in *Perry v. Sinderman.*[5] In a dispute admittedly set in higher education, the litigation arose after officials chose not to renew the contract of an experienced

CASE SUMMARY 3.1: FREE SPEECH RIGHTS

*Pickering v. Board of Education of Township
High School District 205*

391 U.S. 563 (1968)

Factual Summary: A teacher wrote a letter to the editor of a local newspaper critical of how the school board had allocated funds between educational and athletic programs. In essence the letter attacked the school board's handling of bond issue proposals. Although most of the statements in the teacher's letter were true, some were false. Even so, the false statements appeared to be based on faulty research rather than on a malicious intent to mislead. After a hearing, the teacher was dismissed for actions that were detrimental to the efficient operation and administration of the school system. The teacher challenged his dismissal, claiming that his letter was protected speech under the First Amendment. State courts in Illinois rejected that argument, reasoning that his acceptance of a teaching position required him to refrain from making statements about the operation of the public schools.

Issue: Do public school teachers relinquish the right to speak out on matters of public concern regarding the operation of the school districts in which they are employed?

Decision: No, the Supreme Court reversed and remanded the case to the state courts with instructions, thus deciding in favor of the teacher.

Summary of Court's Rationale: In the absence of statements that are knowingly or recklessly made, teachers may not be dismissed for exercising their right to speak out on issues of public concern. Even though teachers' First Amendment rights must be balanced against their school boards' interests in maintaining efficient schools, when teachers' statements concern matters of public interest and do not interfere with the administration of the schools, the teachers may not be discharged. The First Amendment affords teachers the same protection as other citizens, and they cannot be required to relinquish those rights as a condition of employment. Since the question of how school funds are allocated is a matter of public concern, the Supreme Court decided that teachers should be free to speak out on such matters without fear of retaliation.

Texas state college instructor. Prior to his nonrenewal, which occurred after he had completed ten years of employment, the instructor publicly criticized the Board of Regents' policies. The instructor then challenged the nonrenewal of his contract, claiming that officials violated his First Amendment free expression rights and his Fourteenth Amendment rights to procedural due process. Even though the college did not have a formal tenure system, the instructor claimed that in essence he had tenure insofar as the college's faculty guide indicated that teachers who had a minimum of seven years of employment were considered to have permanent status.

The Supreme Court ruled that the instructor's public criticism of a matter of public concern was protected by the Constitution and could not form the basis for the nonrenewal of his contract regardless of his tenure status. The Court reasoned that under the First Amendment, the board could not deny the instructor a benefit because of his exercise of a protected right. Although not germane to this section, the Court added that the teacher's expectation of tenure created a property interest in employment that could not be withheld without due process of law, a topic that is discussed later in this chapter and book.

In *Mt. Healthy City Board of Education v. Doyle (Mt. Healthy)*,[6] the Supreme Court reviewed the impact of including a constitutionally protected right as a factor in not renewing the contract of a nontenured teacher with a record of being difficult in school. The teacher filed suit, claiming that the board violated his rights after he called a radio talk show and criticized an internal school policy on a faculty dress code. The Court reversed an earlier order from the Sixth Circuit that the teacher was entitled to reinstatement with back pay, since part of the reason for his contract nonrenewal was his exercise of a protected activity. In reversing, the high Court emphasized that the Sixth Circuit's decision would have placed the teacher in more favorable circumstances than if he had not exercised his free speech rights. The Court pointed out that in cases, where teachers claim that officials nonrenewed their contracts in response to their having exercised a protected right, boards must be given the chance to show that they would not have retained the employees regardless of whether the employees exercised a protected right. On remand, the board reported that it would not have renewed the teacher's contract even if he had not placed the call to the radio talk show.[7]

The above opinions show that teachers, as citizens, may speak out on issues of public concern, but it soon became clear that this protection does not extend to matters of personal concern. In another landmark decision, *Connick v. Myers* (*Connick*),[8] the Supreme Court posited that the First Amendment does not protect employees who speak out on subjects concerning their personal interests. This case began when an assistant district attorney was dismissed after she had distributed a questionnaire to her coworkers soliciting their views of office policies and procedures, employee morale, confidence in supervisors, and pressure to work on political campaigns; her employer considered this to be an act of insubordination. The Court was convinced that the First Amendment did not provide protections against adverse employment actions for employees whose expression was related to personal interests. Further, the Court observed that even when an employee speaks out on a matter of public concern, the First Amendment does not provide protection when the government's interest in efficiency outweighs the value of the statement to the public.

> Free speech rights do not extend to matters of personal concern . . . the First Amendment does not protect employees who have spoken out on subjects concerning their personal interests.

In *Connick* the Supreme Court addressed the shifting burden of proof it created in *Pickering* by stating that "the state's burden in justifying a particular discharge varies depending upon the nature of the employee's expression."[9] Since the employee's questionnaire touched on matters of public concern in only a limited way, the Court was of the view that the questionnaire could only be characterized as an employee grievance that the employer reasonably believed disrupted the office, undermined his authority, and destroyed close working relationships. Recognizing that government offices could not function if every employment decision became a constitutional issue, the Court acknowledged that government officials should have wide latitude in managing their offices, without intrusive oversight by the courts.[10]

The Supreme Court refined the guidance it created in *Pickering* and *Connick* in its 2006 opinion in *Garcetti v. Ceballos*,[11] another case that is outside of education but applicable because it applies to public employment. This dispute involved an assistant district attorney who alleged that he suffered an adverse employment action as a result of a memorandum he had prepared on a case his office was prosecuting. The high Court ruled that statements that are made as part of an employee's official duties are not protected by the First Amendment inasmuch as the employee is not speaking as a private citizen. The Court noted that public employers need a degree of control over their employees' words and actions to maintain the efficient delivery of public services. Accordingly, the Court pointed out that employers must determine whether employee expression was on a matter of public concern, and if the person engaging in that expression was doing so as a citizen or as part of his or her official responsibilities.[12]

In sum, teachers may not be dismissed for speaking out on matters of public concern, as long as they do so in a nondisruptive manner, but the exercise of free speech will not protect teachers when school boards have other legitimate reasons for their discharge. Thus, dismissed teachers must show that the exercise of their constitutional rights was a substantial or motivating factor in their discharge.[13] As long as school boards can show that their primary reasons for dismissing teachers are legitimate, the fact that the teachers may have spoken out publicly will not provide the teachers with any recourse.

Expression in the Classroom

The free expression rights of teachers are limited in classrooms. Inasmuch as school boards have the authority to control curricula and teachers at the elementary and secondary level do not enjoy extensive academic freedom, teachers' speech within the classroom can be regulated. The Supreme Court, while acknowledging that teachers retain their First Amendment free speech rights in school, added that classroom speech may be limited to promote educational goals.[14] In this respect, teachers particularly need to guard against expressing political and religious views in the classroom.

> Inasmuch as school boards have the authority to control the curriculum and teachers at the elementary and secondary level do not enjoy extensive academic freedom, teachers' speech within the classroom can be regulated.

Courts have long recognized that school boards may restrict teachers' speech for pedagogical reasons. The Tenth Circuit emphasized that since classrooms are not public forums, teacher speech during class could be treated as school sponsored for First Amendment purposes.[15] To this end, the court upheld a school board's disciplinary actions against a teacher who had an in-class discussion of rumors of students' sexual activity. The court was convinced that the school board had legitimate pedagogical interests in limiting classroom speech and that their actions were reasonably related to those interests. Similarly, in a dispute involving a nontenured biology teacher whose contract was not renewed after she had a discussion in class about the abortion of fetuses with Down syndrome, the First Circuit recognized that classroom speech may be limited to promote educational goals.[16] The court noted that boards may regulate teachers' classroom speech as long as their actions are reasonably related to legitimate pedagogical concerns and the teachers are provided notice that the conduct was prohibited. Further, in affirming the trial court's decision in favor of the board, the court acknowledged that a teacher's classroom speech is part of the curriculum.

The Seventh Circuit emphasized that the fact that students in a classroom are a captive audience restricts the right of teachers to express or advocate viewpoints that depart from the official curriculum.[17] The court further wrote that the Constitution does not entitle teachers to present personal views to students against the instructions of the school board. In another case the Fourth Circuit indicated that classroom speech is curricular if it imparts particular knowledge by conveying a message or information to students.[18] The court specified that this includes information on social or moral values. In the same way, teachers are not free to speak about their own religious values or to proselytize students in the classroom.[19] Similarly, the Seventh Circuit affirmed that a teacher did not have a constitutional right to introduce his own views on the creation of the world in the classroom and could be required to limit discussion to the prescribed curriculum.[20]

A case from the Ninth Circuit demonstrates that teachers may be restricted from presenting viewpoints in class that are contrary to those advocated by their school boards.[21] A high school teacher filed suit after he was ordered to remove materials he posted on a school bulletin board that presented a viewpoint different from that of materials that had been posted by school officials regarding the school's gay and lesbian awareness month. The court determined that the materials posted by school officials were not individual speech; they were, instead, attributable to the district and board pursuant to board policy. The court reasoned that since the board was not subject to viewpoint neutrality, the teacher did not have the right to contribute to the speech contained on the bulletin board. Further, since the bulletin board was not a free speech zone, the court ruled that the school board could exclude materials that harmed, rather than helped, its goals without violating the First Amendment. The Fourth Circuit, noting that public school officials may limit classroom speech to promote educational goals, stated that they do not need to tolerate speech that is inconsistent with their basic educational mission, even though they could not censor similar speech outside of the school.[22]

Teachers must exercise caution in making comments critical of their school systems, since these are not necessarily protected by the First Amendment. In one such case, the federal trial court in Connecticut held that a teacher's speech, in the form of an e-mail to an assistant principal, was not protected, because it did not address a matter of public concern.[23] In the e-mail the teacher complained about missing textbooks and threatened to give her students a study hall until the books came in and send a letter home to parents explaining the situation.

Freedom of Association

The Constitution does not explicitly state that Americans have the right to association such as by forming labor unions, a topic that is discussed at length in Chapter 5. Even so, this right can be inferred from the final clause of the First Amendment, which grants the right to assemble peaceably and petition the government for redress of grievances. In fact, in *Healy v. James*[24] the Supreme Court found that the rights of individuals to associate to further their own personal beliefs are implicit in the freedoms of speech, assembly, and petition. Although it was not always the case, it is now well recognized that teachers may maintain membership in organizations and may be involved in political and labor union activities. Further, the rights to marry, raise a family, enter into personal relationships with others, and form friendships may be implied from the First Amendment's basic freedoms. Even so, school boards may impose prohibitions on activities that have the effect of disrupting the educational environment or that interfere with teaching responsibilities.

An important aspect of teachers' associational rights is that these rights can protect them from adverse employment actions because of their political activities. While political activity inside school walls may be restricted, it has long been recognized that public employees such as teachers have the right to engage in political activities outside of school as long as their doing so does not interfere with the fulfillment of their job responsibilities. In making such determinations, courts typically weigh the employees' rights to engage in protected activities against the employers' interest in efficient service.

> An important aspect of teachers' associational rights is that these rights can protect them from adverse employment actions because of their political activities.

When it can be shown that the exercise of constitutional rights interferes with the discharge of employees' duties, the courts are inclined to rule that employees' rights must yield to the government's interest in maintaining effectiveness and efficiency. Teachers, for the most part, are not considered to be in policy-making positions so that their political activities do not necessarily affect their day-to-day job performance. For example, the Sixth Circuit affirmed a jury verdict that a teacher's political differences with the superintendent resulted in the teacher's not being reappointed to a position he had previously held.[25] The appellate panel instructed the lower court to enter an order of reinstatement as an appropriate remedy for the constitutional violation, overriding concerns that the superintendent could no longer work with the teacher because of the differences.

On the other hand, high-level school administrators, such as superintendents, who work much more closely with school boards, may face adverse employment actions if they engage in political activities, such as opposing candidates who were eventually elected. In one such situation, the Fifth Circuit upheld the dismissal of a superintendent who supported unsuccessful candidates for the school board, since this created a strained relationship between the board and the superintendent.[26] Further, high-level administrators may be removed due to their political associations if they occupy policy-oriented and politically sensitive positions.[27] Midlevel administrators may have greater protections. By way of illustration, the Sixth Circuit agreed that party affiliation was not an appropriate consideration for filling a position as gifted and talented teacher/coordinator, since the job involved neither significant discretionary authority nor considerable advising on policy making.[28]

Public employment has often been connected to patronage practices, whereby jobs are given to individuals who supported successful candidates. Although teaching positions have not been as subject to patronage systems as other forms of public employment, they have not been entirely immune either. The Supreme Court, in *Elrod v. Burns,*[29] stated that patronage actions severely restrict individuals' political beliefs and association and that the government may not force public employees to relinquish their rights to political association. The Court explained that conditioning public employment on employees' support of the party in power can survive constitutional scrutiny only if it furthers some vital government interest, and the benefit gained must outweigh the loss of constitutionally protected rights. Later, in *Branti v. Finkel,*[30] the Court added that unless the government can show an overriding interest in requiring that individuals' private beliefs conform to those of the hiring authority, such beliefs cannot be the sole basis for depriving the individuals of continued public employment. Thus, most low-level employees are protected from adverse actions on the basis of political affiliations.[31]

As is discussed in Chapter 5, the First Amendment provides teachers with the freedom to join unions and engage in union activities. Moreover, boards may not discipline teachers or subject them to adverse employment actions as a consequence for union activities. Courts have consistently struck down state statutes prohibiting government employees from joining unions or labor organizations.[32] The Seventh Circuit recognized that the First Amendment grants public school teachers the right to form and join unions as part of their right of free association.[33]

Courts have invalidated adverse employment actions for individuals protected by this right, such as when school boards dismissed teachers for participating in union activities. In one such case the Sixth Circuit

---

CASE SUMMARY 3.2: UNION ACTIVITIES
Hickman v. Valley Local School District Board of Education

619 F.2d 606 (6th Cir. 1980)

Factual Summary: A teacher whose contract was not renewed by the school board at the end of her probationary period, and was thus denied tenure, filed suit, alleging that the nonrenewal was in retaliation for her union activities. The facts revealed that although the teacher had received excellent ratings in her first probationary year, her ratings declined in subsequent years. A comment on one evaluation advised her to reduce her activities outside of the classroom. A federal trial court in Ohio ruled in favor of the school board, finding that the board would have dismissed her even in the absence of her union activities. The teacher appealed.

Issue: Was the teacher's contract impermissibly nonrenewed in retaliation for her engagement in protected activities?

Decision: Yes, the Sixth Circuit reversed and remanded the trial court's decision, thus ruling in favor of the teacher.

Summary of Court's Rationale: The Sixth Circuit disagreed with the trial court's finding that the teacher would have been dismissed even in the absence of her union activities. The appeals court was convinced that the decline in the teacher's evaluation ratings and a personality conflict with her principal could be traced to her union activities, particularly in light of many comments on her evaluations that were critical of her union activities. Thus, the court held that the board's decision not to renew her contract was made for constitutionally impermissible reasons.

---

determined that a teacher's discharge was unjustified, since an alleged personality conflict with her principal and declining evaluations could be traceable to her union activities.[34] By the same token, teachers may not be subjected to adverse employment actions for exercising their rights under collective bargaining agreements.[35]

It has long been recognized that the First Amendment establishes individuals' freedoms to marry, raise families, enter into personal relationships, and form friendships with other persons. As is shown in the next chapter, while school boards may not restrict those rights, since public employment is a privilege rather than a right, employment may be denied to those who exercise associational rights in this regard. For example, courts have upheld antinepotism laws that prohibit close relatives of school board members from working in the school system or married couples from working in the same building.[36] In essence, the courts generally agree that these laws do not prevent people from exercising their right to marry, but rather, merely restrict their access to public employment based on legitimate governmental concerns in the smooth operation of school systems.

Freedom of Religion

Freedom of religion is one of the First Amendment's basic liberties. The country was founded, in part, on the proposition that Americans have the right to the religious beliefs of their choosing and may exercise their beliefs as they see fit without government interference as long as their actions do not violate the law. Accordingly, the government is not allowed to favor one religion over another, or even religion over nonreligion,[37] and may not interfere with individuals' exercise of their religion. Insofar as public employment may not be conditioned on religious beliefs, courts have agreed that teachers may not be denied public school positions because they have elected to send their children to private sectarian schools.[38] It is well established that parents have the fundamental right to direct the education of their children, and this right may not be abridged as a condition of employment in public schools.

Nonetheless, as Chapter 6 demonstrates, teachers may not use their positions to proselytize or indoctrinate others or insist on the right to exercise their religious beliefs when it interferes with their job responsibilities. In one recent example, the Seventh Circuit agreed that a school board was justified in not renewing the contract of a guidance counselor who prayed with students, advocated abstinence, and disapproved of contraception.[39] The court explained that the First Amendment did not give teachers a license to engage in uncontrolled expression that varied with the established curricular content. In essence, as in other areas, teachers' exercise of religious freedom may be limited if it encroaches on the rights of students or interferes with the efficient performance of the schools.

CASE SUMMARY 3.3: FREE EXERCISE RIGHTS

Grossman v. South Shore Public School District

507 F.3d 1097 (7th Cir. 2007)

Factual Summary: A school board decided to not renew the contract of a probationary guidance counselor. During her probationary period the counselor had removed from her office literature designed to instruct students on the use of condoms and replaced it with literature advocating abstinence. Also, on more than one occasion the counselor prayed with students in her office. With the exception of matters relating to her religion, the guidance counselor's performance during her probationary period had been exemplary. The counselor appealed the nonrenewal of her contract, claiming that it was based on hostility toward her religious beliefs in violation of the First Amendment's Free Exercise Clause. A federal trial court in Wisconsin ruled in favor of the school board, and the counselor appealed.

Issue: Did the decision to nonrenew the counselor's contract violate her free expression rights under the First Amendment?

Decision: No, the Seventh Circuit affirmed the trial court's decision in favor of the school board.

Summary of Court's Rationale: School system employees do not have the right to make the promotion of religion a part of their job description. In promoting their own religious values, teachers precipitate possible First Amendment Establishment Clause violations, even when the religious composition of their communities makes legal challenges unlikely. Further, the school board was within its right to control policy, and the First Amendment does not give the counselor the right to uncontrolled expression at variance with established curricular content.

As in other areas when conflicts arise, the duty of teachers to carry out essential job functions takes precedence over their rights to the free exercise of religion. Again, to the extent that public employment is a privilege and not a right, courts have agreed that school boards may restrict freedom of religion when there is an overriding government interest. The rationale is that the teachers' free exercise of their religion is not being abridged, as they are free to seek employment elsewhere if carrying out their job responsibilities interferes with their religious beliefs or obligations. This means that teachers may be required to provide instruction on aspects of curricula that may be contrary to their own personal religious beliefs. In such a case, the Seventh Circuit ruled that a public school teacher was not free to disregard the prescribed curriculum regarding patriotic matters because it conflicted with his religious beliefs.[40] Similarly, the Ninth Circuit was convinced that requiring a teacher to teach evolution did not violate his right to free exercise of religion.[41]

At the same time, teachers may not introduce their own religious values or beliefs into their classes when it conflicts with the proscribed curriculum.[42] Teachers also may be prohibited from wearing religious garments in the classroom. Courts have maintained that such prohibitions further the legitimate objective of maintaining neutrality in the public schools.[43] Such prohibitions do not inhibit religious beliefs, but rather, apply only to the wearing of religious garb by teachers while in the performance of their duties.[44]

Another area of possible conflict arises when teachers are required to take time off for religious observances. For the most part courts have agreed that it is not unreasonable to allow teachers to take a limited number of days off each year for this purpose.[45] Depending on state law and the terms of negotiated agreements, these days may be taken off either with or without pay. On the other hand, school boards are not required to grant excessive leaves of absence, since doing so could result in a disruption of the educational process, place an undue hardship on other teachers, or result in excessive expenditures. Again, the courts agree that if job responsibilities interfere with the exercise of teachers' religious beliefs, they are free to seek employment elsewhere.

PRIVACY

The Constitution does not explicitly spell out privacy rights. Even so, privacy rights can be inferred from several constitutional provisions. For example, the rights to marry, raise families, enter into personal relationships with others, and form friendships are basic, although they are not clearly enumerated in the Constitution. Privacy rights may be inferred from the Fourth Amendment's protections against unreasonable searches and seizures and the Fourteenth Amendment's equal protection rights and prohibitions against government actions that impair personal liberties without due process of law. Further, the Ninth Amendment has been interpreted as implying that individuals have personal privacy rights.

The Supreme Court has not addressed a case dealing with searches of public school employees, but it has examined privacy issues in three applicable cases outside of education. The first decision, in *O'Connor v. Ortega*[46] in 1987, concerned a search by public hospital officials of a doctor's locked office, ostensibly for the purpose of conducting an inventory and looking for evidence that the doctor allegedly sexually harassed two females. The Court upheld the search, relying heavily on the reasonableness standard established in *New Jersey v. T.L.O.*,[47] a case involving an assistant principal's search of a student's purse. The Court ruled that hospital officials could enter a locked office at any time for business-related purposes, such as conducting inventories, looking for files or records, or investigating alleged acts of wrongdoing. Although it didn't address the question, the Court indicated that searches of the personal property of employees, such as briefcases or purses, would require reasonable suspicion.

Two years later, the Supreme Court reviewed two other cases involving public employees. In *Skinner v. Railway Labor Executives' Association*,[48] the Court allowed drug and alcohol testing of railroad employees after serious accidents occurred, even without showings of individualized suspicion. In *National Treasury Employees Union v. Von Raab*,[49] the Court upheld the practice of the U.S. Customs Service of drug testing employees who applied for promotions or transfers to drug interdiction positions that required them to carry firearms. In both decisions, the Court reasoned that testing was justified based on the government's showing of compelling interests.

Workplace Privacy

All Americans, including teachers, are protected by the Fourth Amendment's prohibition against unreasonable searches. Insofar as the Constitution prohibits only unreasonable searches, searches that have a rational basis are not unconstitutional. The fact that there is a limited expectation of privacy in educators' workplaces restricts their rights, particularly when school officials can present valid reasons for searches. In this respect a clear distinction exists between searches by police officers, which under most circumstances require probable cause and a warrant, and those conducted by school officials, which require that school officials meet the lesser standard of reasonable suspicion but do not require a warrant. For example, a police officer's classroom search for contraband as part of a criminal

> The fact that there is a limited expectation of privacy in educators' workplaces restricts their rights, particularly when school officials can present valid reasons for searches.

investigation would require a warrant, while a similar search by a school principal with the intent of using the evidence only for purposes of dismissal would not require a warrant. Another distinction can be made between searches of teachers' personal items, such as cell phones, and those belonging to the school but provided for teachers' use, such as laptop computers.

Courts have routinely upheld warrantless searches of teachers' classrooms, file cabinets, and school-owned computers by school administrators, especially when they have been necessary to conduct legitimate business of the school or to protect students. Since classrooms and their contents are accessible to a wide range of individuals, including students and other school employees, courts generally agree that there is no expectation of privacy in classrooms or their contents.[50] For example, in a situation involving school custodians but having implications for teachers, an appellate court in Ohio upheld the installation of video surveillance equipment in a break room.[51] Since the room was open to other employees, the court thought that the custodians, who were disciplined for spending unauthorized time there, did not have any expectation of privacy in this room. Generally, though, teachers do have an expectation of privacy when it comes to their own personal belongings, such as purses or briefcases. In this regard, as a case from the Second Circuit revealed, expectations of privacy may be reduced under specified circumstances, such as when individuals have been given the opportunity to remove personal items from classrooms but have failed to do so.[52]

Many questions have arisen regarding the degree of privacy to which teachers are entitled with respect to the contents of their personnel files, an issue that is typically addressed in state statutes, local board policies, and even collective bargaining agreements. On the one hand, teachers should be able to expect that many items in their personnel files are confidential. Even so, under some states' right-to-know laws, specified aspects of personnel records may be subject to public inspection. As is discussed in the next chapter, the type of information that may be accessible to the public varies from state to state. For the most part, information that is of a highly personal nature, such as health records, is confidential, whereas data regarding teachers' qualifications for their positions is more often open for inspection. As Chapter 4 discusses in greater detail, courts are divided when it comes to records that fall in between, such as teachers' performance evaluations.

Another area where teachers' privacy rights may be diminished due to the sensitive nature of their positions arises when they may be required to submit to drug and alcohol testing, a topic that has been controversial. Courts have reached mixed results in this sensitive area, often depending

CASE SUMMARY 3.4: PRIVACY RIGHTS OF EMPLOYEES

Brannen v. Kings Local School District Board of Education

761 N.E.2d 84 (Ohio Ct. App. 2001)

Factual Summary: A supervisor of custodians, suspecting that some custodians were not working during portions of their shifts, installed a hidden video camera in a break room. After reviewing videotapes the supervisor determined that four custodians had been taking unauthorized breaks. Instead of being terminated, the custodians were suspended and their pay was docked by the superintendent of schools in accord with a settlement negotiated with union representatives. Even so, the custodians filed suit, alleging that the surveillance amounted to an unlawful search in violation of the Fourth and Fourteenth Amendments. A state trial court in Ohio granted a judgment in favor of the school board, and the custodians appealed.

Issue: Did the installation of the hidden surveillance cameras in the break room amount to an unlawful search and seizure?

Decision: No, the appellate court affirmed the trial court's earlier decision in favor of the school board.

Summary of Court's Rationale: The appeals court first determined that Constitutional rights are implicated only when the conduct of a supervisor infringes on a reasonable expectation of privacy in the workplace. To the extent that break rooms were open to other employees who had unfettered access to the room, the court found that the custodians did not have a reasonable expectation of privacy there. Thus, the court rejected the custodians' claim that the school board violated their constitutional rights. Further, noting that a court must balance the employee's legitimate expectation of privacy against a government employer's need for supervision and efficiency, the court determined that the surveillance of the break room was reasonable and justified in light of the supervisor's suspicions of misconduct.

on the individual factual circumstances of each case, such as whether there was a reasonable suspicion of substance abuse either for an individual teacher or among a group of teachers. This issue is discussed in greater detail in the next chapter.

Personal Privacy

Consistent with long-held positions, and as is stressed throughout this book, teachers are role models for their students. In order to fulfill their responsibilities in this regard, teachers sometimes may be required to give up a degree of their personal privacy. Although the private lives of most citizens are their own business, teachers generally are held to a higher standard of personal behavior than are employees in other fields. The freedom teachers are given in the conduct of their private lives and lifestyle choices is directly related to their effectiveness in the classroom. In other words, teachers may be limited in their lifestyle choices when those choices compromise their abilities to effectively carry out their professional duties.

> Teachers are role models for their students ... to fulfill their responsibilities in this regard, teachers sometimes may be required to give up a degree of their personal privacy.

As overall social and community standards have evolved, teachers now enjoy much greater freedom in their personal lives and lifestyle choices than they once did. For example, while teachers in the past could be dismissed for cohabiting or maintaining homosexual relationships, such is not the case today. In spite of having greater freedoms in their personal relationships and private behavior, teachers still may be constrained when it comes to activities such as having sexual relationships with students or using controlled substances. In one recent case an appellate court in Texas upheld a section of the state's penal code prohibiting primary and secondary school employees from engaging in sexual conduct with students in the schools where they work.[53] The court ruled that the statute did not implicate any rights protected by the Constitution and was rationally related to the legitimate state interest in protecting minors from sexual abuse and exploitation. Further, as is discussed in Chapter 7, behavior that compromises teachers' abilities to be positive role models, such as criminal activity, may be cause for dismissal.

The Fourth Amendment right of teachers, and other school employees, to be free from unreasonable searches and seizures has been subject to a fair amount of contentious litigation with mixed results, particularly with regard to drug and alcohol testing. It must be stressed, however, that since a "teacher's employment in the public schools is a privilege, not a right,"[54] absent contrary language in state constitutions, statutes, or collective bargaining agreements, school boards have some authority to define their employees' privacy expectations with regard to drug testing. This issue is discussed in greater detail in the next chapter.

DUE PROCESS

The rights to due process of law are grounded in both the Fifth and Fourteenth Amendments. The Fifth Amendment, which applies to the federal government, clearly states that no person shall "be deprived of life, liberty, or property, without due process of law. . . ."[55] The Fourteenth Amendment, which was ratified following the Civil War, includes a similar phrase but specifically applies due process to the states. There are essentially two aspects of due process, substantive and procedural, that work together. At the same time, it is important to understand that teachers' interest in continued employment is created by state tenure statutes or contracts, not by the Constitution.

Substantive Due Process

Substantive due process refers to the concept that a law must have a function within the rightful power of the government and be rationally related to the achievement of that goal. In an early decision, the Supreme Court recognized that the Fourteenth Amendment protected teachers' rights to practice their profession.[56] It is now well settled that tenured teachers have an important property interest in their employment inasmuch as they have an expectation of continued employment.

> Substantive due process refers to the concept that a law must have a function within the rightful power of the government and be judiciously related to the achievement of that goal.

Therefore, the employment of teachers cannot be terminated without justification. In this respect procedural due process protects teachers from the unjust deprivation of their employment. The Constitution simply guarantees that the right cannot be taken away without due process. Therefore, as the Supreme Court has made clear, individuals have a property interest in continued employment only when they have a legitimate claim or entitlement to it.[57] Conversely, when the right to continued employment has not been created, as is the case with non-tenured teachers, due process is ordinarily not required when school boards choose not to extend their contracts.

Teachers also have liberty and property interests in their good names and reputations. This means that actions by school boards that could damage teachers' reputations or compromise their abilities to obtain jobs in the future could implicate due process. In this respect, performance-related criticisms or disciplinary actions against teachers for failure to properly carry out their duties do not create any stigmatization.[58] On the other hand, allegations of improper conduct[59] or that impute individuals' character,[60] and that can carry over into their personal lives, may implicate due process,[61] particularly when those allegations are made public.[62] When stigmatizing charges are made public, affected employees are entitled to name-clearing hearings to defend themselves against the possibility of their character being falsely maligned.

Procedural Due Process

In an educational context, procedural due process refers to the measures that school boards must take to inform individuals who are faced with the loss of their jobs with notice of what they are accused of doing and affording them the opportunity to defend themselves before fair and impartial third-party decision makers. Procedural due process has many implications for administrators, teachers, parents, and students. For instance, tenured teachers facing discharge have the rights to notification of the reasons for the contemplated board actions and the opportunity to respond, generally through impartial hearings. Students have similar due process rights, including the rights to notice and a hearing when facing serious disciplinary sanctions such as expulsions. Further, statutes such as the Individuals with Disabilities Education Act[63] provide parents of students with disabilities with significant due process rights regarding the identification, evaluation, and provision of services to their children.[64]

It is beyond dispute that tenured teachers are entitled to impartial hearings before they can be discharged. Although probationary teachers usually are not entitled to hearings,[65] they may be entitled to due process when school boards intend to dismiss them prior to the expiration of their contracts. In other words, school boards are not required to provide probationary teachers with a hearing when they simply do not renew their contracts for another year but must provide a hearing to terminate the contracts at any time during the contractual period. In addition, probationary teachers may be entitled to due process when they can adequately

CASE SUMMARY 3.5: PRETERMINATION DUE PROCESS

Cleveland Board of Education v. Loudermill

470 U.S. 532 (1985)

Factual Summary: School boards dismissed a security guard for dishonesty on his job application and a bus mechanic for failing an eye test. The boards dismissed the employees without giving them prior notice or hearings, although they were afforded posttermination notice and hearings consistent with state law. The employees were classified as civil servants who, under state law, could be dismissed only for cause. The employees filed suit, claiming that their dismissals violated the Due Process Clause. A federal trial court in Ohio dismissed their claims, deciding that the posttermination notices and hearings provided the employees with adequate due process. The Sixth Circuit, on the other hand, determined that the employees had been deprived of due process and that their interest in retaining employment outweighed the administrative burden in providing pretermination hearings.

Issue: Did the employees' dismissal, without prior notice and a hearing, violate their due process rights?

Decision: Yes, the Supreme Court affirmed that the board's actions violated the due process rights of the employees.

Summary of Court's Rationale: The Court determined that under state law the employees possessed property rights in continued employment. The Court, noting that dismissals of public employees for cause often involves factual disputes, posited that such employees are entitled to notice of the charges against them, an explanation of the evidence, and an opportunity to present their side of the case before being dismissed.

allege that boards are discharging them for exercising constitutionally protected rights.

Due process, as it applies to teacher dismissals, normally involves notice of the reasons for the contemplated school board actions and impartial hearings in which teachers may defend themselves against the charges.[66] Notice that the teachers receive must include a summary of the charges and the evidence against them, be specific enough to provide them with the opportunity to refute the charges and prepare defenses, and allow a reasonable amount of time before hearings are scheduled. Hearings, although less formal than judicial proceedings, must afford teachers the opportunity to be represented by counsel, present evidence, challenge evidence presented against them, call witnesses, and question witnesses. As is discussed in greater detail in Chapter 7, hearings must be fair and impartial, but this does not mean that they may not be conducted by school boards.

SUMMARY AND RECOMMENDATIONS

The Constitution provides Americans with basic rights and freedoms. As Americans, teachers may exercise those rights and enjoy those freedoms. Be that as it may, the government may abridge individuals' rights and freedoms when it can demonstrate an overriding interest in their curtailment. School boards usually can satisfy this requirement when they can justify restrictions for the sake of efficient school operations. A good example is in the area of political speech: While teachers may speak out on political issues outside of school, they may not use their positions of authority to indoctrinate captive students in classrooms.

The practical applications of teachers' basic rights and freedoms, as they relate to employment terms and instructional responsibilities, are discussed in greater detail in the remaining chapters. Even so, the following general principles are provided by way of background information:

- Teachers, as private individuals, may speak or otherwise issue expressions on matters of public concern. Teachers also may join political parties, support candidates for office, and even run for public office in their private lives. However, while teachers may serve on school boards in their home districts, they may not be members of school boards in the systems where they work due to potential conflicts of interest.
- Teachers may not exercise their free speech rights in a manner that disrupts the educational environment or otherwise interferes with efficient school operations.
- Academic freedom, to the limited extent it exists in elementary and secondary education, does not afford teachers the right to express personal viewpoints in classrooms when doing so is contrary to school board policy or curricular objectives.

- The First Amendment's implied freedom of association gives teachers the right to form and join labor organizations and participate in union activities without fear of retaliation.
- Courts consistently uphold antinepotism policies, since public employment is not a right.
- Employment may not be conditioned on membership in particular religious bodies or adherence to specific religious beliefs.
- All parents, including teachers, have the right to direct the upbringing of their children. Thus, teachers may not be denied employment in the public schools because they choose to send their children to religiously affiliated nonpublic schools.
- The First Amendment's religion clauses do not give teachers the right to refuse to teach portions of the curriculum that may be inconsistent with their own religious beliefs.
- Teachers have diminished expectations of privacy in classrooms and other public areas of school buildings.
- Teachers do have reasonable expectations of privacy regarding their personal possessions even when those items are kept or used in the workplace.
- Teachers, like all Americans, have the freedom to make certain lifestyle choices. Even so, the private behavior of teachers may be regulated when it has the effect of compromising their teaching effectiveness, especially to the extent that they are expected to be positive role models for their students.
- Employees, such as tenured teachers, who have a legitimate expectation of continued employment have a substantive due process property right in their positions and thus are entitled to procedural due process before their contracts may be terminated.

FREQUENTLY ASKED QUESTIONS

Q. Since issues regarding tax levies for schools are matters of public concern, may teachers speak out on these issues even if their opinions differ from the school board's official position?

A. Yes, as taxpayers teachers may speak out on such issues in their capacity as private citizens. This means that teachers may write letters to the editors of local newspapers or speak at public forums to express their thoughts on referenda before the voters. However, since this right does not extend to classrooms, teachers may not use their official positions to indoctrinate students or influence parents.

Q. May teachers be dismissed, demoted, or denied promotions for having actively campaigned for individuals who unsuccessfully sought election to the school board?

A. No, teachers are not considered to be in policy-making positions and do not regularly advise their school boards on matters of policy. To the extent that there is a degree of distance between teachers and boards, courts consistently agree that teachers may not be subjected to adverse employment decisions on the basis of their support for candidates or other political activities.

Q. For religious reasons I do not agree with several aspects of the science curriculum. I consider the requirement that I teach these concepts to be a violation of my religious freedom, as it forces me to present information that I believe to be false. How can I be required to teach this subject matter when it offends my religious principles?

A. The First Amendment grants all Americans the right to adopt whatever religious beliefs they choose. Nonetheless, the Constitution does not give anyone the right to public employment. In accepting a teaching contract you agree to certain conditions, including the requirement to teach the prescribed curriculum. Such a requirement does not infringe on your religious liberties, because it does not prevent you from believing as you wish. If you are unable to teach the required subject matter, and thus fulfill your job responsibilities, you may seek employment elsewhere. Nothing in the requirement infringes on your First Amendment rights.

Q. How can school administrators establish standards for teachers' behavior outside of the school building?

A. Teachers must fulfill many roles and responsibilities. Courts have long recognized that part of teachers' roles is to set an example for their students. When teachers fail to fulfill that essential responsibility, school administrators may take disciplinary action, just as they may when teachers fail to teach the prescribed curriculum or fail to maintain control over their students. In essence, individuals who are unable to be positive role models are unfit to be teachers, because they cannot fulfill all job requirements. A good illustration is that part of the mission of all schools is to teach students to be law-abiding citizens. Since teachers who break the law set a bad example for their students by failing to advance that aspect of the schools' missions, they are not qualified to continue in their positions.

Q. After I completed two years as a probationary teacher, my contract was not renewed. During my probationary period my evaluations indicated some deficiencies but were generally favorable. I was never told that my performance did not meet standards or that I was in danger of being released. Am I not entitled to a hearing, since I expected to be reemployed?

A. No. Although you may have thought that you would be rehired, as a nontenured teacher you had no legal right, claim, or entitlement to continued employment. In order to be entitled to procedural due process prior to discharge, teachers must have more than abstract expectations of reemployment. It has long been recognized that probationary teachers do not have any such entitlement, regardless of what they may have expected.

WHAT'S NEXT

The next chapter continues the discussion of teachers' rights, particularly as they apply to employment, outlining the legal issues involved in teacher employment terms and conditions. The chapter begins with information regarding the requirements for teacher certification and the reasons for which it may be revoked. It continues with a discussion of the privacy rights of teachers and issues regarding employment terms such as salaries, leaves, evaluations, and resignations.

ENDNOTES

1. As noted in Chapter 1, the U.S. Supreme Court in Tinker v. Des Moines Independent Community School District, 393 U.S. 503, 506 (1969) ruled that neither students nor teachers "shed their constitutional rights to freedom of speech or expression at the schoolhouse gate." Still, teachers do not lose other constitutional rights by accepting public employment.

2. A *matter of public concern* has been defined as one that is of interest to the community for social, political, or other reasons. Dill v. City of Edmond, 155 F.3d 1193 (10th Cir. 1998).

3. *See, e.g.*, Fox v. Traverse City Area Public Schools Board of Education, 605 F.3d 345 (6th Cir. 2010) (holding that a teacher did not speak as a citizen when she made complaints to school administrators about the size of her teaching load); Stroman v. Colleton County School District, 981 F.2d 152 (4th Cir. 1993) (finding that complaints about conditions of employment or expressions about other issues of personal concern do not constitute matters of public concern protected by the First Amendment).

4. 391 U.S. 563 (1968).

5. 408 U.S. 593 (1972).

6. 429 U.S. 274 (1977).

7. Doyle v. Mt. Healthy City School District Board of Education, 670 F.2d 59 (6th Cir. 1982).

8. 461 U.S. 138 (1983).

9. *Id.* at 150.

10. The Supreme Court also addressed teacher free speech in two relatively minor cases. In Givhan v. Western Line Consolidated School District, 439 U.S. 410 (1979), the Justices, although refusing to reinstate a teacher who was described as loud and hostile in being critical of her school board, interpreted *Pickering* as requiring courts to consider on-the-job working relationships when reviewing petitioners' First Amendment rights. In Waters v. Churchill, 511 U.S. 661 (1994), a dispute involving a nurse in a public hospital, the Court essentially reiterated the principle that the First Amendment does not protect employees who criticize internal operating policies, since these policies are not matters of public concern.

11. 547 U.S. 410 (2006).

12. Mawdsley, R. D., & Osborne, A. G. (2007). The Supreme Court provides new direction for employee free speech in Garcetti v. Ceballos. *Education Law Reporter, 214,* 457–465.

13. Mt. Healthy City School District v. Doyle, 429 U.S. 274 (1977).

14. Tinker v. Des Moines Independent Community School District, 393 U.S. 503 (1969).

15. Miles v. Denver Public Schools, 944 F.2d 773 (10th Cir. 1991).

16. Ward v. Hickey, 996 F.2d 448 (1st Cir. 1993).

17. Mayer v. Monroe County Community School District, 474 F.3d 477 (7th Cir. 2007).

18. Lee v. York County School Division, 484 F.3d 687 (4th Cir. 2007).

19. *See, e.g.,* Williams v. Vidmar, 367 F. Supp. 2d 1265 (N.D. Cal. 2005); Helland v. South Bend Community School Corp., 93 F.3d 327 (7th Cir. 1996); Peloza v. Capistrano Unified School District, 37 F.3d 517 (9th Cir. 1994).

20. Webster v. New Lenox School District No. 122, 917 F.2d 1004 (7th Cir. 1990).

21. Downs v. Los Angeles Unified School District, 228 F.3d 1003 (9th Cir. 2000).

22. Lee v. York County School Division, 484 F.3d 687 (4th Cir. 2007).

23. Carone v. Mascolo, 573 F. Supp. 2d 575 (D. Conn. 2008).

24. 408 U.S. 169 (1972).

25. Banks v. Burkich, 788 F.2d 1161 (6th Cir. 1986).

26. Kinsey v. Salado Independent School District, 950 F.2d 988 (5th Cir. 1992). *But see* Kercado-Melendez v. Aponte-Roque, 829 F.2d 255 (1st Cir. 1987) (affirming a reinstatement order and back pay award for a school superintendent who was discharged because of her affiliation with a political party that was no longer the majority party in power).

27. *See, e.g.,* Steigmann v. Democratic Party of Illinois, 406 F. Supp. 2d 975 (N.D. Ill. 2005).

28. Hager v. Pike County Board of Education, 286 F.3d 366 (6th Cir. 2001). *See also* Chadwell v. Lee County School Board, 535 F. Supp. 2d 586 (W.D. Va. 2008) (ruling that an administrator's demotion was in retaliation for her support of an unsuccessful candidate in a prior election).

29. 727 U.S. 347 (1976).

30. 445 U.S. 507 (1980).

31. Rutan v. Republican Party of Illinois, 497 U.S. 62 (1990) (ruling that conditioning employment decisions on political belief and association violates the First Amendment in the absence of a vital government interest).

32. *See, e.g.,* Atkins v. City of Charlotte, 296 F. Supp. 1068 (W.D.N.C. 1969) (voiding a state statute prohibiting public employees from joining a labor organization, as it abridges their freedom of association).

33. McLaughlin v. Tilendis, 398 F.2d 287 (7th Cir. 1968).

34. Hickman v. Valley Local School District Board of Education, 619 F.2d 606 (6th Cir. 1980). *See also* Springdale Education Association v. Springdale School District, 133 F.3d 649 (8th Cir. 1998 (pointing out that school officials may not terminate or otherwise act against employees who join unions).

35. *See, e.g.,* Stellmaker v. DePetrillo, 710 F. Supp. 891 (D. Conn. 1989) (forbidding a school board from transferring a teacher in retaliation for filing a grievance).

36. *See, e.g.,* Montgomery v. Carr, 101 F.3d 1117 (6th Cir. 1996) (affirming school board policy requiring one member of a married couple to transfer to another building following their marriage).

37. *See, e.g.,* Torcasco v. Watkins, 367 U.S. 488 1961) (explaining that it is unconstitutional to impose requirements that aid adherents of all religions as opposed to nonbelievers).

38. *See, e.g.,* Barrow v. Greenville Independent School District, 332 F.3d 844 (5th Cir. 2003) (affirming that school officials violated a teacher's constitutional right to direct the education of her children by denying her consideration for an administrative position because her children attended a sectarian school); Barrett v. Steubenville City Schools, 388 F.3d 967 (6th Cir. 2005) (reasoning that a school board could not condition employment on where a teacher's child attended school and violated the teacher's right to direct the education of his child by terminating his employment when he enrolled his son in a sectarian school).

39. Grossman v. South Shore Public School District, 507 F.3d 1097 (7th Cir. 2007).

40. Palmer v. Board of Education of Chicago, 603 F.2d 1271 (7th Cir. 1979).

41. Peloza v. Capistrano Unified School District, 37 F.3d 517 (9th Cir. 1994).

42. *See, e.g.,* LeVake v. Independent School District, 625 N.W.2d 502 (Minn. Ct. App. 2001) (ruling that a teacher was not allowed to teach a biology class in a manner that circumvented the prescribed curriculum).

43. *See, e.g.,* Cooper v. Eugene School District, 723 P.2d 298 (Or. 1986) (finding that the state legislature had a legitimate objective of maintaining neutrality in the public schools in enacting a statute prohibiting wearing of religious garb in school).

44. Commonwealth v. Herr, 78 A. 68 (Pa. 1910) (finding that legislation prohibiting the wearing of religious garb applied to teachers only while in the performance of their duties and did not inhibit their beliefs).

45. *See, e.g.,* Ansonia Board of Education v. Philbrook, 479 U.S. 60 (1986) (ruling that a school board must provide a reasonable accommodation for an employee's religious beliefs if it does not cause an undue hardship).

46. 480 U.S. 709 (1987).

47. 469 U.S. 325 (1985). The reasonableness test established by the Court requires that the search of a student at its inception is based on the reasonable suspicion that it will turn up evidence that the student has either violated the law or school rules. Further, the scope of the search must reasonably be related to the student's age and sex and to the nature of the alleged infraction.

48. 489 U.S. 602 (1989).

49. 489 U.S. 656 (1989).

50. *See, e.g.*, Shaul v. Cherry Valley–Springfield Central School District, 363 F.3d 177 (2d Cir. 2004) (ruling that a teacher had no expectation of privacy in his classroom or its contents).

51. Brannen v. Kings Local School District Board of Education, 761 N.E.2d 84 (Ohio Ct. App. 2001).

52. Shaul v. Cherry Valley–Springfield Central School District, 363 F.3d 177 (2d Cir. 2004) (indicating that a teacher had no expectation of privacy where he had been asked to turn in his keys and had been given the opportunity to remove personal items from the classroom).

53. Ex Parte Morales, 212 S.W.3d 483 (Tex. Ct. App. 2006), *citing* Texas Penal Code Annotated § 21.12 (West Supp. 2005).

54. Board of Education of City of Los Angeles v. Wilkinson, 270 P.2d 82, 85 (Cal. Ct. App. 1954).

55. U.S. Constitution, Amendment V.

56. Meyer v. Nebraska, 262 U.S. 390 (1923). *See also* Board of Regents v. Roth, 408 U.S. 564 (1972) (noting that the Fourteenth Amendment requires due process when state action impairs a person's life, liberty, or property interest).

57. Board of Regents v. Roth, 408 U.S. 564 (1972).

58. *See, e.g.*, Brammer-Hoelter v. Twin Peaks Charter Academy, 81 F. Supp. 2d 1090 (D. Colo. 2000) (finding that statements relating to neglect of duties and insubordination that are not stigmatizing do not warrant a name-clearing hearing); Gray v. Union County Intermediate Education District, 520 F.3d 803 (9th Cir. 1975) (affirming that charges of insubordination, incompetence, hostility toward authority, and difficulty getting along with others do not create a stigma that interferes with an individual's ability to obtain other employment); Shrick v. Thomas, 486 F.2d 691 (7th Cir. 1973) (affirming that charges regarding performance of work duties do not create a stigma even when they make a teacher less attractive to other employers).

59. *See, e.g.*, Winegar v. Des Moines Independent Community School District, 20 F.2d 895 (8th Cir. 1994) (ruling that allegations of unjustified child abuse were sufficiently stigmatizing to implicate constitutionally protected liberty interests).

60. *See, e.g.*, Bomhoff v. White, 526 F. Supp. 488 (D. Ariz. 1981) (finding that published statement that a teacher was not rehired because she had an apparent emotional disability involved a liberty interest); Wellner v. Minnesota State Junior College Board, 487 F.2d 153 (8th Cir. 1973) (affirming that a nontenured teacher who was allegedly dismissed for racism, with the charges being placed in his file, was entitled to a hearing).

61. *See, e.g.*, Burke v. Chicago School Reform Board of Trustees, 169 F. Supp. 2d 843 (N.D. Ill. 2001) (finding that publicly disclosed allegations of criminal behavior diminished a teacher's reputation making it unlikely that she would find future employment in education).

62. *See, e.g.,* Gibson v. Caruthersville School District, 336 F.3d 768 (8th Cir. 2003) (ruling that a probationary teacher who was dismissed for volatile, erratic, and potentially abusive behavior toward students was entitled to a name-clearing hearing); *see also* Chisolm v. Michigan AFSCME Council 25, 218 F. Supp. 2d 855 (E.D. Mich. 2002) (pointing out that a discharged custodian did not have a property or liberty interest where the school board had not published or disclosed any stigmatizing information that prevented him from obtaining other employment); Lancaster v. Independent School District, 149 F.3d 1228 (10th Cir. 1998) (affirming that a school board's failure to disclose its reasons for suspending a teacher did not rise to the level of a public stigma).

63. 20 U.S.C. §§ 1400–1482 (2006).

64. 20 U.S.C. § 1415.

65. *See, e.g.,* Goodman v. Hasbrouck Heights School District, 275 F. App'x 106 (3d Cir. 2008) (affirming that a nontenured teacher did not have a property interest entitling him to due process prior to his termination); Halfhill v. Northeast School Corporation, 472 F.3d 496 (7th Cir. 2006) (affirming that nontenured teachers do not have property rights regarding the nonrenewal of their contracts).

66. In Cleveland Board of Education v. Loudermill, 470 U.S. 532 (1985), the U.S. Supreme Court held that public employees who can be discharged only for cause are entitled to oral or written notice of the charges brought against them, an explanation of the employer's evidence, and an opportunity to present their side of the story.

Employment Terms and Conditions

4

INTRODUCTION

As the previous chapter demonstrated, teachers do not forfeit their constitutional rights when they are employed by public school systems. Even so, the fact that teachers are expected to be role models for their students places some restrictions on the exercise of their rights. Further, teachers have responsibilities and rights that are created by state law, such as a duty to obtain proper certification and a right not to have their certificates revoked except for cause as defined in the law. State laws also spell out many other conditions of employment for teachers. At the same time federal laws impact the employment rights and responsibilities of teachers.

71

Federal laws, such as the No Child Left Behind Act (NCLB),[1] which requires that students be taught by highly qualified teachers in core subjects, have an unquestionable impact on state laws and the conditions of employment in public schools. Insofar as federal and state laws regulate employment terms and working conditions for professional staff, they are of utmost importance and have generated a fair amount of litigation. Even so, for the most part courts do not interfere with the judgments of state and local officials unless the officials' actions are clearly unconstitutional, contrary to statutes, or arbitrary.

This chapter outlines legal issues involved in teacher employment terms and conditions. The chapter begins with a discussion of the requirements for teacher certification and the reasons for which it can be revoked. The chapter next discusses the privacy rights of teachers and issues regarding employment terms such as salaries, leaves, evaluations, and resignations. This chapter does not include information on the procedures that must be followed for teacher dismissals, since this topic is covered in Chapter 7. Inasmuch as the employment of teachers is largely governed by state law and the laws of the 50 states vary, it is beyond the scope of this chapter to provide comprehensive information about the laws of each individual state. Thus, the purpose of this chapter is to outline the legal issues that are common to most states with examples, taken from case law, of where and how individual state laws may vary.

TEACHER CERTIFICATION OR LICENSURE

In the context of obtaining teaching credentials, the terms *certification* and *licensure* are synonymous. Some states use the former term, while others use the latter. In either event, professional certification or licensure refers to the process of state education agencies issuing a form of confirmation that individuals have met specified criteria and are qualified and competent to teach in that state. The NCLB requires school boards to employ only highly qualified teachers to teach the core subjects in both elementary and secondary schools. One aspect of the NCLB's definition of highly qualified requires teachers to be certificated by the state in which they teach.[2] Proper certification in most states is a prerequisite to obtaining teaching positions, although some states do grant waivers or issue temporary certificates.[3]

Certification or licensure is obtained by application to an individual teacher's state education agency (SEA). While state certification requirements vary, the NCLB now mandates that teacher certification candidates have earned a bachelor's degree at a minimum, and some states require a master's degree for full certification. State standards for certification are fairly specific and require prospective teachers to pass specified courses or complete a program of study approved for the certification of teachers. The NCLB also requires new teachers to pass rigorous state tests on subject matter knowledge and teaching skills. Additional state requirements such as being a citizen or being of good moral character are not unusual. It is important to understand that although obtaining proper certification is a prerequisite for employment, it is not a contract to teach and does not guarantee a teaching position.

> While state certification requirements vary, the NCLB now requires a bachelor's degree at a minimum. . . . The NCLB also requires new teachers to pass a rigorous state test on subject matter knowledge and teaching skills.

Requirements

Certification or licensure requirements for teachers are established by state legislatures, which delegate the task of issuing certificates to their SEAs. As noted, the NCLB requires, at a minimum, that teachers have bachelor's degrees and pass state-administered tests. Many states have established additional standards such as requiring a minimum number of credits in specific pedagogical and subject matter courses. For example, certification as a high school chemistry teacher may require a specified number of credits in courses related to the art of teaching as well as chemistry and the sciences. Generally, courts uphold the decisions of SEAs denying licenses to applicants who do not meet current standards.[4] In this respect it is important to note that as a rule candidates must meet the requirements that exist when they submit their applications, not the criteria that existed when they began their programs of study.

Insofar as state legislatures establish teacher certification standards, they may alter the requirements for licensure as the need arises. Academic and practical prerequisites for certification may be increased, or additional requirements may be added at any time. For example, the highest court in Massachusetts refused to strike down a new regulation requiring mathematics teachers in schools with low-performing programs to demonstrate subject-matter competence by taking assessment tests before they could have their licenses renewed.[5]

> Following the passage of the NCLB, many states passed their own education reform statutes establishing more rigorous standards for teacher certification to bring the states' standards in line with the federal law.

Following the passage of the NCLB, many states passed their own education reform statutes establishing more rigorous standards for teacher certification to bring the states' standards in line with the federal law.

Certification may be granted after transcript reviews, whereby applicants submit documentation that they have met the statutory requirements, or when applicants provide proof that they completed approved courses of study leading to certification. In the latter process, SEAs typically approve college or university programs and issue certificates once campus officials verify that applicants successfully completed their programs. Even so, it is important to note that the states, not the institutions of higher learning, are the licensing agencies.

Basic Standards

As indicated earlier, most states require teacher candidates to complete prescribed programs of studies leading to receipt of bachelors' degrees for certification. Depending on the level or area of certification, programs of study normally include specific courses in pedagogy or teaching methods along with classes in content or cognate areas. Programs also include a practical component, such as student teaching. For the most part, SEAs have the discretion to waive or accept alternatives to the stated requirements in specified circumstances. Thus, SEAs may establish alternative paths to certification or issue temporary licenses to candidates who have not met all requirements. By the same token, courts uphold the judgments of SEAs when they refuse to accept alternatives. In such a case, an appellate court in Pennsylvania agreed with an SEA's decision that work experience was insufficient to meet its practicum requirement.[6]

Some states establish a tiered system of certification, whereby teachers may start out with initial or provisional certificates but must earn standard certification within specified numbers of years by completing additional requirements. Teaching certificates may be permanent or may be issued for a set number of years with continuing education requirements for renewal. As an example of a tiered system with periodic renewal, Massachusetts issues initial licenses to candidates who earned bachelors' degrees, completed approved teacher preparation programs, and passed the commonwealth's licensure test.[7] Initial licenses are good for five years but may be extended once for another five years, after which time teachers must qualify for professional licenses in order to maintain their employment. Candidates for professional licenses must have earned masters' degrees. Teachers in Massachusetts must renew their professional licenses every five years by completing a specified number of continuing education credits.

Generally speaking, teaching certificates are issued for specific areas, such as identified grade levels and/or subject matter. At the elementary level, certificates may be issued for a range of grades such as preschool to Grade 2 or Grades 3 to 5. At the high school level, certificates are normally issued for certain subjects such as English or mathematics. Except in emergency situations, teachers should not be assigned to teach outside of their areas of certification. In other words, a teacher with a preschool to Grade 2 license should not be assigned to teach Grade 5, while a teacher with a secondary history certificate should not be assigned to teach physics.

A teaching certificate by itself does not allow an individual to obtain employment for another position within a school system. In other words, in most jurisdictions individuals must obtain additional or alternate certifications if they wish to pursue employment as school administrators or support personnel. Often, support personnel must meet qualifications established by professional organizations in addition to or in place of those established by the SEA, since professionals such as physical therapists may work in schools, hospitals, or clinical settings. Those employed by school boards might need to be licensed as physical therapists by the appropriate state medical board and certified by their SEAs.

Citizenship

State certification statues may require applicants to be citizens of the United States. In 1979, when two applicants unsuccessfully challenged a New York law that prohibited aliens from being certificated to teach, the U.S. Supreme Court held that such a requirement did not violate the federal constitution.[8] The Court explained that the state satisfied its burden of demonstrating that there was a rational relationship between the requirement and a legitimate governmental interest. The Court found that since teaching is an important governmental function, the legislature's determination that citizens are better qualified than noncitizens to promote the aims of public education and civic virtues was reasonable.

Loyalty Oaths

Applicants for teacher certification may be required to take loyalty oaths as long as the oaths themselves are not unconstitutional. On more than one occasion the Supreme Court has upheld statutes requiring public employees to swear to uphold the federal and state constitutions.[9] Similarly, the courts have upheld requiring applicants to affirm that they will not advocate the forceful overthrow of the government. For the most part, oaths addressing future rather than past conduct are allowed. On the other hand, membership in subversive organizations by itself cannot be grounds for denying teaching certificates absent evidence that applicants were actively involved in working toward the illegal goals of the organization.[10]

Good Moral Character

Many state statutes require applicants for teacher certification to be of good moral character. While it is easy to understand why teachers, who are in positions where they may influence young students, should be of good moral character, the term itself is difficult to define. Changing times also can modify the perception of what constitutes good moral character. To this end, over the past century sexual mores have evolved so that human behavior that once was considered to be evidence of a lack of morality now may be generally accepted by society.

CASE SUMMARY 4.1: DENIAL OF TEACHING CERTIFICATE FOR CRIMINAL CONDUCT

Arrocha v. Board of Education of the City of New York

690 N.Y.S.2d 503 (N.Y. 1999)

Factual Summary: An applicant for a teaching certificate disclosed that he had been convicted of selling cocaine but submitted evidence that he was rehabilitated. Nevertheless, the licensing board denied his application on the grounds that he posed a risk to the safety and welfare of students and school employees. The teacher filed suit challenging that decision, arguing that it was arbitrary and capricious and in violation of a section of the state's correction laws that prohibited discrimination against exoffenders. A state trial court ruled in his favor, ordering the licensing board to issue the applicant a certificate. In a split decision, the state appeals court affirmed, and the licensing board appealed.

Issue: Was the licensing board justified in denying the applicant a teaching certificate due to his prior criminal activity?

Decision: Yes, the state's highest court reversed the appellate court's decision, thus ruling that the licensing board was justified in denying the applicant's request for a teaching certificate.

Summary of Court's Rationale: In reviewing the trial court's record, the state's high court was convinced that the licensing board considered all necessary factors and balanced positive factors against negative factors in making its decision. Specifically, the court reasoned that in denying the certificate, the licensing board was concerned that the applicant's prior conviction might impact his ability to serve as a role model inasmuch as teachers must serve as role models to their students and are held to a high ethical standard. The court concluded that the licensing board was entirely justified in considering the nature and seriousness of the applicant's crime in denying his application for certification.

Courts have upheld the denial of certification to applicants who engaged in criminal activity. Since teachers are expected to be good role models, conviction of crimes, which can constitute evidence that candidates lack good moral character, is often sufficient cause for denying teaching certificates.[11] In New York, for instance, the state's highest court upheld the SEA's denial of a teaching certificate to an applicant who had been convicted of selling cocaine.[12]

Examinations

As stated above, the NCLB requires new teachers to pass state-administered tests to earn the designation of "highly qualified" under the act. Accordingly, states now routinely require new applicants to pass tests demonstrating skills in areas such as communication, pedagogy, and subject matter knowledge. While the content of these tests is by and large left to the states to determine, the administration of the tests must not be discriminatory. Under Section 504 of the Rehabilitation Act,[13] applicants with disabilities must be given reasonable accommodations in test-taking situations. This does not mean that the content of test items must be modified. Rather, this means that the circumstances under which tests are administered might need to be altered to accommodate test takers' disabilities. Thus, an applicant who is sight-impaired must be allowed to take a large-print or Braille version of a test, but the actual questions should be the same as those given to other applicants. Even so, failure to pass a state-administered test is grounds for denying a teaching certificate.[14]

Revocation

Teaching certificates may be revoked for cause. Most states specify reasons for revocation of licenses and outline the steps officials must take to rescind individuals' certifications. Insofar as the revocation of teaching certificates affects individuals' abilities to gain or retain employment, it is a serious matter subject to procedural due process requirements and court review. Not surprisingly, many states have included provisions for hearings and appeals in their revocation procedures. Moreover, it must be kept in mind that revocation of a license and termination from a professional position are separate matters even though the reasons for each may be similar. Although revocation of teaching certificates would automatically disqualify teachers from continued employment, termination from positions, even for cause, does not routinely result in the revocation of licenses. By the same token, teaching certificates may be revoked only by SEAs, the agencies granting licenses. In addition to outright revocation, teaching certificates may become invalid because they no longer meet the state's requirements or have simply expired.

> The most frequent reasons for the revocation of teaching certificates are unprofessional conduct or conduct unbecoming a teacher, sexual misconduct, immorality, incompetence, and neglect of duty.

The most frequent reasons for the revocation of teaching certificates are unprofessional conduct or conduct unbecoming a teacher, sexual misconduct, immorality, incompetence, and neglect of duty. As long as proper procedures are followed and school officials' actions are not arbitrary or capricious, courts almost always uphold SEA decisions to revoke teaching certificates.[15]

Criminal Activity

The teaching certificates of individuals who are convicted of criminal charges may be revoked in most states even when the crimes are unrelated to the teachers' professional duties. In this respect, many states differentiate between convictions for felonies, which are more serious criminal infractions, and conviction for less serious offenses known as misdemeanors. Engaging in criminal conduct can also be evidence of not having good moral character. For example, an appellate court in Pennsylvania agreed that a teacher who pled guilty to mail fraud could have his license revoked, since this crime fell within the rubric of moral turpitude.[16] In two cases from Ohio, appellate courts upheld the revocations of licenses of teachers who were convicted of the theft of drugs and money[17] and receiving stolen property, respectively.[18]

Sexual Misconduct

Sexual misconduct, especially when it involves students or minors, is certainly grounds for the revocation of teachers' licenses, as courts uniformly agree that such misbehavior demonstrates unfitness to teach. In an egregious case, an appellate court in Connecticut upheld the SEA's revocation of a teacher's license in light of evidence indicating that the teacher engaged in sexual behavior with students over a long period of time.[19] As reflected in a case from New York, even a single incident may be cause for revocation. Here an appellate court affirmed the SEA's revocation of the license of a teacher who engaged in sexual relations with a student and had given her alcohol.[20] Similarly, in Oregon, an appellate court upheld the revocation of a teacher's certificate after he engaged in improper sexual contact with female students.[21] As cases from New York[22] and New Hampshire[23] demonstrate, teaching certificates can be revoked even when inappropriate sexual behavior does not involve a teacher's students but does involve minors.

Unprofessional Conduct

A great variety of actions, ranging from cheating to acts that put students at risk of harm, can be deemed to amount to unprofessional conduct or conduct unbecoming a teacher. In many situations the conduct serves as grounds for rescinding teaching certificates, particularly where courts agree that the actions are irremediable or where an investigation results in findings that individuals are unfit to teach. In many cases, teachers engaged in behavior that, while inappropriate, was not criminal. In this respect it must be kept in mind that teachers may be held to a higher standard than individuals in other professions, not only because they are expected to act as role models for their students but also because "employment in the public schools is a privilege, not a right."[24]

Courts generally uphold the revocation of the certificates of teachers who engage in unprofessional behavior, particularly if the teachers' actions are deemed to have impaired their abilities to function effectively or work in a professional environment. Further, courts are particularly reticent to overturn adverse measures against teachers whose misconduct has subjected students or minors to physical or emotional harm. In the first of five illustrative cases, an appellate court in Illinois agreed with the SEA's suspension of a teacher's license after he gave students the option of trading detention for electric shocks from a small engine.[25] An appellate court in Florida upheld the license revocation of a teacher who e-mailed files containing profanity and sexual material to some of her students.[26] Similarly, an appellate court in Missouri refused to disturb the revocation of the certificate of a teacher who engaged in sexually explicit conversations with students, noting that the revocation was necessary to protect children.[27] In Florida, an appellate court affirmed the revocation of the certificate of a teacher who had exhibited inappropriate behavior toward students, parents, and coworkers.[28] In yet another example, an Arizona court upheld the SEA's revocation of the certification of a teacher who displayed threatening and aggressive behavior toward children.[29] As the above cases make clear, teachers who engage in behaviors that either subject students to harm or impede their own abilities to teach effectively are often subject to license revocations.

Four cases from Georgia demonstrate that unethical behavior can be cause for decertification. In the first case, an appellate court affirmed the suspension of the license of a teacher who altered answers on a student's test, in violation of the professional ethics code.[30] The court later supported the suspension of a teacher's certificate in light of evidence that he coached students on a standardized test.[31] Further, a teacher who also served as a coach had his license revoked due to his involvement in a scheme to change the grades of ineligible athletes so they could play football.[32] In yet another case involving a code of ethics, the court sustained the suspension of the license of a teacher who was unable to control his anger in altercations with a cafeteria manager and a student.[33] In keeping with the proposition that teachers may be held to a higher standard of conduct than others, an appellate court in Pennsylvania upheld the revocation of the license of a teacher who submitted false information with her job application.[34]

Adoption of New Standards

The fact that teaching certificates were originally issued as permanent or for life does not necessarily prohibit states from revising their licensure statutes and requiring teachers who were certificated under the old laws to meet the new standards. As stated above, many states have revised their standards for teacher certification, particularly in light of the NCLB. In some circumstances, licenses that were originally issued as permanent certificates were annulled in favor of certificates that expired and needed to be renewed. For the most part, courts have supported these initiatives.

In an early case North Carolina's high court upheld a new regulation requiring teachers to earn six college credits within five years in order to renew their licenses.[35] Similarly, the Supreme Court of Texas approved a new condition requiring teachers with permanent certification to pass a basic skills test to retain their certificates.[36] Also, the Supreme Court of Connecticut affirmed the SEA's power to replace permanent certificates with ones that were subject to renewal every five years.[37]

When new standards are issued and currently employed teachers are expected to meet them, basic principles of due process require that current teachers be given notice of the new requirements and a reasonable amount of time to meet the updated standards. Since there is no set amount of time for what would be considered to be reasonable for meeting new requirements, courts need to rule on challenges to the time allocated on case-by-case bases.

Procedural Issues

Insofar as the revocation of teaching certificates implicates a property right, individuals must ordinarily be afforded hearings before their licenses may be rescinded. Hearings grant teachers opportunities to refute the charges or challenge whether the allegations, if proven, constitute sufficient cause to warrant the revocation of their certificates. In a case on point, an appellate court in Pennsylvania struck down the commonwealth's revocation procedures, because they did not provide for at least minimal due process.[38]

PRIVACY RIGHTS OF TEACHERS

The Constitution does not explicitly enumerate privacy rights, but courts have interpreted its provisions to imply the existence of such rights. In accepting public employment, teachers do not automatically lose their constitutional rights.[39] Even so, since teachers are role models for their students and can be held to higher standards, school boards and SEAs may place limitations on the exercise of their rights.[40] As Chapter 3 demonstrated, the general rule is that the private lives of teachers are their private lives unless or until their lives impact their abilities to perform their jobs or would substantially interfere with the educational process.[41] Since there is no right to public employment, then, teachers have the choice between seeking employment in public schools with the accompanying limitations or looking for work elsewhere. As discussed below, the right to marry does not necessarily trump state antinepotism laws if teachers choose to marry members of school boards.

> In accepting public employment, teachers do not automatically lose their constitutional rights. Even so, since teachers are role models for students and can be held to higher standards, school boards and SEAs may place limitations on the exercise of their rights.

The status of teachers as role models is apparent in the area of privacy rights. Individuals' privacy rights allow them to make certain lifestyle choices. Teachers, in some situations, may find that their choices bring them into conflict with their responsibilities as public employees and role models. While standards have changed dramatically from the days when female teachers in many places were prohibited from marrying, teachers generally are expected to conform to the behavioral and social norms of their communities. In some cases, the failure of teachers to comply with these standards may cause others to lose respect for them in such a way that it impairs their effectiveness and may subject them to dismissal.

An important privacy issue is emerging as a direct result of technology. The widespread use of the Internet has raised many issues that before now were not even considered. Thus, since the privacy rights of teachers in the electronic age are evolving along with advances in technology, many questions have arisen regarding teacher and student use of e-mail and the Internet. Of particular concern is what students may post about teachers on their own sites. A corollary issue involves what teachers may or may not post on social networking sites.

Private Lives

The rights to marry, raise a family, enter into personal relationships with others, and form friendships, although not explicitly stated in the

Constitution, are basic. Rights of association, as they are known, may be implied from the First Amendment's elucidation of basic freedoms. Further, the Fourteenth Amendment's guarantees of personal liberty imply additional rights in this regard. Although it was once commonplace to prohibit teachers, particularly females, from marrying, at present there is no question that teachers may marry, raise families, and retain their jobs. More recent disputes involve living arrangements and lifestyles that may not meet with the approval of school officials or the community at large. Such issues entail both heterosexual and homosexual relationships outside of marriage, extramarital affairs, and relationships with students or former students. Much of the controversy stems from disagreement over what constitutes immorality, particularly as it pertains to the conduct expected of teachers as role models. The dismissal of teachers for immorality or unprofessional conduct is discussed in greater detail in Chapter 7.

In an older case, the Supreme Court of Pennsylvania provided a fluid definition of immorality that has withstood the test of time and is often quoted by other courts. The court explained that immorality is behavior that offends the morals of the community and sets a bad example to the children whose ideals a teacher is supposed to foster and elevate.[42] Community values have evolved in recent decades so that behavior that was once considered to be immoral or deviant is no longer deemed to be so. Further, since standards vary from one community to the next, with behavior that is accepted in one locale frowned on in another, judicial opinions may vary from one jurisdiction to the next.

Although one would expect that teachers' private lives are their own business, it must be kept in mind that teachers generally are held to a higher standard than employees in other fields due to their status as role models. Thus, the latitude teachers are accorded in their private lives often hinges on the impact their behavior has on their effectiveness as educators. By way of illustration, in an early case, the Eighth Circuit refused to overturn the dismissal of a female teacher in South Dakota who openly lived with a male without benefit of marriage.[43] The court was persuaded that the school board was justified in its action, because the negative reaction the living arrangement spawned within the community could have had a harmful effect on the teacher's students. While it is unlikely that this case would be decided the same way today, it demonstrates the proposition that violating community standards may put teachers in jeopardy of losing their jobs. In a more relevant

> Although one would expect that teachers' private lives are their own business, it must be kept in mind that teachers generally are held to a higher standard than employees in other fields due to their status as role models.

example, an appellate court in Pennsylvania upheld the dismissal of a teacher who was convicted following multiple offenses of driving under the influence and with a suspended license.[44] After hearing testimony that the teacher's behavior offended community standards, the court concluded that her conduct made her a bad role model.[45]

Community standards have evolved considerably since 1975 such that teachers who enter into nonmarital living arrangements are unlikely to be dismissed today, as is evidenced by the lack of cases in the interim. Also, in light of the widespread recognition of the rights of individuals who are homosexual, and with some states sanctioning gay marriages, today most school boards do not attempt to dismiss teachers solely because of their sexual orientation.[46] Even having a child out of wedlock no longer carries the disapproval it once did. Interestingly, in the same year the Eighth Circuit upheld the dismissal of a female teacher for cohabitating with a male, the Fifth Circuit struck down a school board rule in Mississippi, which is now part of the Eleventh Circuit, that prohibited unwed parents from working in the system.[47] The court was not convinced that the birth of a child out of wedlock, by itself, was evidence of immoral conduct. The contrast between these two cases shows how community standards can affect the final outcome of a court case.

Today, it is even unlikely that a board could successfully discharge a teacher who has engaged in an adulterous affair absent evidence that the behavior had a negative impact on the teacher's effectiveness.[48] For the most part, courts now require substantial evidence that teachers' conduct or lifestyle choices have a negative effect on their duties or abilities to carry out their professional responsibilities before dismissals will be supported.

As would be expected, courts consistently upheld the dismissal of teachers who engaged in sexual relations with students. Any sexual contact with a minor could result in a criminal conviction that would clearly be grounds for termination.[49] Further, courts almost always support the dismissal of teachers who enter into consensual relationships with students even if the students are over the age of consent. In such a case, an appellate court in Oklahoma affirmed the dismissal of a female teacher who had a romantic relationship with a 17-year-old male student.[50] Courts are also inclined to support the firings of teachers who engage in relationships with former students, especially those who have only recently graduated. In fact, the Sixth Circuit upheld the denial of tenure to a teacher in Michigan who had a romantic relationship with a former student.[51] Also, as a second case from Michigan illustrates, teachers can be liable for inappropriate sexual activity with students even when the charges stem from incidents that occurred many years in the past.[52]

Off-campus conduct, such as using illegal drugs, also constitutes a basis for teachers' dismissal. As in other areas, teacher arrests and convictions on drug charges may result in the revocation of licenses and can be grounds for dismissal. Nonetheless, teachers can be dismissed for using drugs even absent criminal convictions. Generally speaking, the standard of proof in dismissal hearings is less than is required for criminal convictions, such that teachers can be fired if school boards can show that their misconduct renders the teachers ineffective. In one such case an appellate court in Connecticut affirmed the dismissal of a tenured teacher who was charged with possession of cocaine and drug paraphernalia but was never convicted of the crime, because he completed rehabilitation.[53] The court agreed that the teacher's conduct undermined his ability to work with other faculty, set a poor example for students, and reflected personal values that were inconsistent with his role as a teacher. In another case, West Virginia's high court upheld the discharge of a teacher who had been arrested but acquitted of selling marijuana to an undercover police officer.[54] Since the teacher admitted during his trial to smoking marijuana, the school board subsequently received petitions opposing his continued employment. The court agreed that the notoriety surrounding the teacher was sufficient cause for his dismissal.

As Chapter 2 discussed, many states have antinepotism statutes that prohibit the employment of close relatives of school board members. Moreover, in some jurisdictions, policies forbid employees from reporting to related school administrators or even prohibit spouses from working together in the same building. Generally speaking, courts have upheld antinepotism statutes even in the face of challenges that they violate employees' associational rights. A case from the Sixth Circuit is illustrative: Two teachers in Ohio challenged a school board policy requiring one of them to transfer to another building following their marriage. Recognizing that the right to marry is fundamental, the court nevertheless ruled in favor of the policy, reasoning that it was rationally related to legitimate goals and did not place a substantial burden on the teachers' right to marry.[55] In essence, the court was of the opinion that the policy did not prevent the couple from marrying, but rather, only stopped them from working together after their marriage. Since there is no right to public employment, most antinepotism statutes or policies are likely to withstand challenges, as long as there are legitimate reasons for their implementation.

Personnel Records and Personal Information

School systems, as public entities, operate in an environment where their business is open to public scrutiny. Under the rubric of the public's right to know, school officials are required to release information about many aspects of district operations. At the same time, this openness may conflict with the rights of teachers, who have a right to expect a degree of confidentiality regarding their personal information. By way of example, while parents may have the right to know the qualifications of their children's teachers, they are not entitled to information about why teachers may have taken medical leaves.

> Under the rubric of the public's right to know, school officials are required to release information about many aspects of district operations. At the same time, this openness may conflict with the rights of teachers, who expect a degree of confidentiality regarding their personal information.

One of the more contentious questions concerns items in teachers' personnel files. Whether such information must be made available to the public depends largely on individual state freedom of information or right-to-know laws. In balancing the need for disclosure against confidentiality, the Supreme Court in Connecticut noted that performance evaluation materials were exempt from disclosure.[56] Conversely, an appellate court in Michigan observed that information such as teacher evaluations, disciplinary and attendance records, and other similar items were not protected from disclosure.[57] Similarly, the Supreme Court of Connecticut maintained that records about the number of days of sick leave taken by a school employee were a matter of public concern subject to disclosure.[58]

Teachers facing disciplinary actions or dismissal have some right to privacy.[59] This right to privacy is particularly important, since charges leveled against teachers may be unfounded, and their mere existence could damage the teachers' reputations even if they are later completely exonerated. In one such case, the Supreme Court of Minnesota ruled that the release of a teacher's personnel information was contrary to state law, even when the teacher was subject to disciplinary action.[60] The court indicated that all that could be disclosed until the final disposition of the disciplinary action was the existence and status of complaints lodged against the teacher. As a case from Connecticut demonstrates, disciplinary action may be disclosed once proceedings have been finalized.[61]

Courts generally agree that information on employment applications is confidential. As evidenced by an order of an appellate court in Pennsylvania, a newspaper did not have a right to obtain copies of teacher employment applications.[62] The court ascertained that even though the applications might be public records, they contained confidential information about the candidates that was protected from disclosure. In dealing with a similar request, an appellate court in Indiana decided that the state's public disclosure laws applied only to current or former employees, not prospective employees.[63]

Two cases from Ohio demonstrate how complicated public records laws can be. In the first, the state's high court ruled that materials submitted by applicants that were reviewed by school board members in executive session and then returned to the candidates after their interviews were not public records insofar as the materials were not retained.[64] On the other hand, under the theory that questions must be settled in favor of disclosure, an appellate court asserted that newspapers could obtain information about candidates for superintendent, including their resumes, under the state's public records statute.[65]

As noted earlier in this section, parents may not necessarily have the right to know teachers' reasons for medical leaves. Conversely, teachers' privacy rights do not prevent school boards from requiring health information, particularly when it implicates fitness to teach. In one case the Second Circuit affirmed that a school board in New York was justified in requesting the health records of a teacher who was returning from a medical leave so that its physician could evaluate her fitness to resume her duties.[66]

Search and Seizure and Drug/Alcohol Testing

Teachers, like all Americans, enjoy the Fourth Amendment protection against unreasonable searches. Even so, subject to provisions in their collective bargaining agreements, teachers have an expectation of privacy on school premises.[67] A distinction can be made between searches by police officers, which usually require probable cause and warrants, and those conducted by school officials, which require the lesser standard of reasonable suspicion but not a warrant. A further distinction can be made between searches of teachers' personal items and those that belong to the school but are provided for teachers' use. For example, school officials do not have the right to search teachers' purses or briefcases without warrants, but they have greater latitude when conducting searches of teachers' desks, file cabinets, or computer hard drives, since these are owned by the school boards.

> Teachers, like all citizens, enjoy the Fourth Amendment protection against unreasonable searches. Even so, subject to provisions in their collective bargaining agreements, teachers have diminished expectations of privacy on school premises.

The Second Circuit explained that teachers lack an expectation of privacy in their classrooms, because the classrooms are accessible to others such as students, teachers, administrators, and custodians.[68] In such a case, a trial court in the District of Columbia dismissed a challenge to a warrantless entry into common areas of a school building and a subsequent search and seizure by police officers.[69] The court reasoned that since the school's front door was unlocked, there was no expectation of privacy.

Drug and alcohol testing of employees is a timely topic that has led to mixed judicial results. For the most part, the courts acknowledge that school boards have the authority to order employees to undergo drug and alcohol testing when there is evidence, based on reasonable suspicion, of abuse. The Sixth Circuit upheld a school board policy from Tennessee that required preemployment testing of employees whose job performance or behavior may have been affected by the use of illegal drugs.[70] The court ruled that the policy was constitutional, because its detailed provisions for testing required reasonable cause and individualized suspicion.[71] Similarly, the Eleventh Circuit affirmed the dismissal of a teacher who refused to take a drug test after a sniff dog detected the presence of marijuana in her car.[72] The court was of the view that since the board acted under a policy calling for a drug free workplace, it had the authority to act. Nevertheless, suspicions of drug or alcohol use must be well founded. In this regard, a federal trial court in Missouri decided that the fact that a teacher had difficulty getting along with her peers was not a sufficient basis for subjecting her to drug tests.[73]

Due to the nature of their positions, where they are entrusted with the care and safety of children, school employees, including teachers, may be subject to suspicionless drug tests.[74] As noted, the Sixth Circuit upheld suspicionless preemployment testing and suspicion-based individualized testing for teachers and other school employees who already worked in child safety sensitive positions.[75] The court recognized that the school board had a strong interest in ensuring the safety and security of children entrusted to the care of educators while acknowledging that due to the nature of their jobs, teachers have a diminished privacy interest in not being tested. Citing the previous decision, a federal trial court in Kentucky dismissed teacher challenges to a board's random drug-testing policy, particularly in light of the fact that there was evidence of a drug problem among the staff.[76] Similarly, the Fifth Circuit upheld a random drug-testing policy for school bus drivers, emphasizing that the testing was minimally intrusive and that the board had an interest in protecting its students.[77]

Courts have been reluctant to permit drug-testing programs that target classes of employees absent reasonable suspicion or compelling governmental interests. The Fifth Circuit struck down policies requiring employees who were injured on the job to undergo drug testing.[78] The court pointed out that the disputed policies were unconstitutional, because they allowed for the testing absent individualized suspicion of drug use. Similarly, New York's highest court struck down a school board policy that required all probationary teachers to submit to urine tests to detect potential drug use.[79] The court reasoned that the requirement to submit to urine tests constituted an impermissible search absent reasonable suspicion or evidence of a drug problem.[80] In sum, the court concluded that searches conducted by the government without reasonable suspicion are permitted only "when the privacy interests implicated are minimal, the government's interest is substantial, and safeguards are provided to insure that the individual's reasonable expectation of privacy is not subjected to unregulated discretion."[81] A federal trial court in Georgia struck down a state law requiring applicants for state employment, including teaching positions, to submit to urine tests.[82] In ruling that the law was unconstitutional, the court noted that the state failed to identify a governmental interest that was sufficiently compelling to justify testing all applicants. According to the court, a generalized governmental interest in maintaining a drug-free workplace was insufficient.

As should be apparent from the above discussion, the issue of drug and alcohol testing of teachers is far from settled. What is allowed varies by jurisdiction and special circumstances that may exist. Drug and alcohol testing is almost always allowed when school officials have a reasonable suspicion that individual employees are using illegal drugs or are under the influence of alcohol. Further, courts allow suspicionless testing of groups when there is a special need for testing, such as when there is evidence of a drug problem among a particular group of employees or in situations where employees are in safety sensitive positions.

Use of E-Mail and Social Networking Sites

The widespread use of technology in today's schools has ushered in a host of new legal issues that were not even contemplated just a few years ago.[83] How teachers access and use the Internet is dictated more by school board policy than law. Therefore, it is critical for teachers to be familiar with and understand their districts' Internet use policies. In fact, most districts today require teachers and students to read and sign their acceptable use policies. These policies may vary significantly from one district to the next, but most address the types of sites or content that can be accessed, instructional use of the Internet, personal use of district-provided computers, and copyright issues. Further, Internet use policies

> How teachers access and use the Internet is dictated more by school board policy than law. Therefore, it is critical for teachers to be familiar with and understand their districts' Internet use policies.

usually spell out the parameters for using a district's e-mail system with most limiting its use to job-related correspondence.

As an initial matter, it is important to understand that there is no expectation of privacy in the use of computers and other technology devices that are supplied by school boards. As a result, school officials have the authority to search the hard drives and computer files of computers used by employees.[84] Again, this is usually spelled out in school systems' acceptable use policies.

E-mail provides teachers with a quick and convenient means of communicating with school administrators, colleagues, parents, and even students. Unfortunately, the ease of use of e-mail may lead to carelessness. Given the nature of electronic communications, teachers must exercise caution in the use of e-mail and should treat it as they would any other written communication. Due to the number of issues that can arise, particularly regarding confidentiality, it is important for teachers to be familiar with their districts' policies and expectations regarding e-mail. Teachers must be cognizant of the fact that e-mails sent through school districts' electronic systems are not always private. Also, deleting e-mail messages does not necessarily permanently erase them, as they may remain on school districts' servers indefinitely. Teachers need to be particularly cautious when it comes to e-mails that are sent to parents and students, as these may become part of the students' records. In fact, due to the lack of privacy that exists with e-mails, teachers should be very careful when discussing students with colleagues via e-mail. Inasmuch as there is little litigation to date on this topic, and the law is not clearly established, it is important for school boards to provide guidelines for teachers regarding the use of e-mail and even more important for teachers to follow those guidelines.

In recent years teachers and students have had the unprecedented ability to create websites, blogs, and profiles and to post messages on social networking sites. Even when this is done off campus utilizing private computers, items posted on the Internet by both students and teachers can have carryover effects into the classroom and can result in disciplinary action. In this regard two issues of great concern to teachers have arisen. The first involves postings by students about teachers, and the second relates to postings by teachers themselves.

Teachers are naturally concerned when students post negative items about them on the Internet for all to see. Litigation has arisen when school administrators have attempted to discipline students for derogatory, defamatory, and threatening items they have posted about teachers on social networking sites. Challenges to disciplinary actions taken against students have alleged unconstitutional censorship on the part of school officials and questioned the rights of administrators to discipline students for off-campus activities.

CASE SUMMARY 4.2: STUDENT HARASSMENT OF TEACHERS ON SOCIAL NETWORKING SITES

J.S. v. Bethlehem Area School District

807 A.2d 847 (Pa. 2002)

Factual Summary: A middle school student created a website on his home computer that included derogatory, profane, offensive, and threatening comments about one of his teachers and the school's principal. Among the most egregious statements on the website were suggestions that the principal was having sex with another school employee, a list of reasons why the teacher should die, and a solicitation for funds to hire a hit man. After seeing the website herself, the teacher experienced such stress and anxiety that she was unable to finish the school year and took a medical leave the following year. Following a full investigation and a hearing, the school board expelled the student. The student and his parents filed suit in a state court to appeal that decision. The state court supported the school board's action, and the parents appealed to the state's supreme court, arguing that the expulsion violated the student's constitutionally guaranteed right of free speech.

Issue: Did the student's expulsion violate his First Amendment right to free speech?

Decision: No, the court affirmed the lower court's decision, ruling that school officials did not violate the student's First Amendment free speech rights in expelling him.

Summary of Court's Rationale: The court ascertained that although the student's website did not contain true threats, he could be expelled because his Internet postings caused an actual and substantial disruption to the school. The court observed that the website created disorder and adversely impacted the delivery of instruction. Specifically, the court noted that the teacher's absence, and the consequent need to use substitutes, disrupted the delivery of instruction. Further, the court acknowledged that the website posting had a negative impact on the school's atmosphere and the morale of students and staff. Thus, the court ruled that school officials did not violate the student's First Amendment free speech rights by expelling him, because his rights did not extend to speech that disrupted instruction.

In one of the first cases on point, the Supreme Court of Pennsylvania supported the expulsion of a student who posted negative comments about teachers, suggested that the principal had engaged in sex with another administrator, and even solicited funds to hire a hit man.[85] The court recognized that the student's comments were sophomoric and did not constitute a real threat, but nonetheless upheld the school board's decision, because the postings resulted in actual disruption of the school. One of the teachers targeted by the student was so distraught by the postings that she took a medical leave of absence. In another case, the Second Circuit affirmed the long-term suspension of a middle school student who created a drawing and text on the Internet suggesting that a named teacher should be shot and killed.[86] Although a criminal investigation and a psychological evaluation indicated that the student did not pose a real threat, school officials suspended him after a hearing officer concluded that his actions created a disruption to the school environment. The court affirmed that the student's postings constituted a threat that crossed the boundary of acceptable free speech and therefore was not protected.

In another Second Circuit case, the court upheld a lower court's denial of a student's request for a preliminary injunction to void disciplinary action taken against him. The student had posted a vulgar message on her website in order to anger the superintendent, urging others to contact the superintendent to protest the canceling of a school activity.[87] The court concluded that the student failed to show a likelihood of success on the merits, because her conduct "created a foreseeable risk of substantial disruption to the work and discipline of the school."[88] In another Pennsylvania case, a student unsuccessfully challenged his suspension for creating a fake MySpace profile of his school's principal that contained the principal's picture and insinuated that he was a sex addict and pedophile. The Third Circuit acknowledged that the disruption caused by the student's actions was not substantial but nevertheless affirmed her suspension, since it was reasonably foreseeable that the disruption could continue.[89]

School authorities have been unsuccessful in disciplining students for Internet postings when they have been unable to show that the offensive material caused a disruption to the educational process. In a case from Missouri, a federal trial court ruled in favor of a student who posted vulgar and insulting comments critical of the school, its administration, and its teachers.[90] The court could find no evidence of disruption and commented that disliking or being upset by the content of the posting was insufficient grounds for limiting student speech. A principal in Florida suspended a student for violating school rules regarding cyberbullying and harassment of a staff member after she created a group on Facebook encouraging her peers to express dislike of a named teacher. The federal trial court ruled that the posting fell within the umbrella of protected speech, noting that it expressed an opinion about a teacher, did not cause a disruption, and was not lewd, vulgar, or threatening.[91]

A decision by a federal trial court in Pennsylvania shows the importance of presenting strong evidence of a substantial disruption. Initially, the court agreed that educators were justified in disciplining a student who created an unflattering profile of the school's principal on a social networking site. In denying the student's request for an order to prevent the disciplinary action, the court was satisfied that school authorities had presented sufficient evidence that the posting created a material and substantial disruption of the school. Specifically, students accessed the website so frequently on school computers that officials had to shut down the network and install additional firewall protections. Following a trial with a more fully developed record, the court changed its view, determining that the disruption of the school was not substantial and did not warrant curtailment of the student's free speech rights. The Third Circuit affirmed, agreeing that the suspension violated the student's free speech rights, since his posting did not result in a foreseeable or substantial disruption of the school.[92]

Social networking sites are used by teachers as well as students. At this writing there are only two published opinions involving disciplinary action taken against teachers because of content they published on such sites. In the first, a federal trial court allowed the nonrenewal of the contract of a nontenured teacher from Connecticut for inappropriate postings on MySpace.[93] Similarly, a federal trial court in Pennsylvania rejected the claims of a student-teacher who was dismissed from her program due to making inappropriate postings on her MySpace page.[94] Further, news reports indicate that teachers have been disciplined and have even faced termination for posting inappropriate content, such as derogatory comments about students or items about themselves that might conflict with their role model status.[95] Therefore, prospective and current teachers need to be aware that school districts routinely review applicants' social networking sites before offering positions.[96]

The limited amount of case law in this area aside, teachers must be careful with what they post on the Internet, because it can lead to the nonrenewal or termination of their contracts for inappropriate or unprofessional conduct. In this respect any content that substantially disrupts the educational environment could be grounds for disciplinary action. Inappropriate comments about students or fellow employees, even if the individuals are not named, could conceivably interfere with teachers' relationships with students, parents, and colleagues in a way that consequently impairs the teachers' effectiveness. Comments that are critical of schools' or districts' administration or school boards' policies fall into a grey area. On the one hand, comments on issues of public concern fall within the sphere of protected free speech. Conversely, speech that is related to individuals' job responsibilities is not protected. Further, postings that either depict or describe teachers' participation in activities that would otherwise result in discipline can result in adverse employment consequences. Thus, teachers need to be vigilant when posting anything on the Internet, particularly content that is or can be made public, keeping in mind that they should not post anything on the Internet that they would not want to be in the news the next day.

SALARIES AND TERMS OF EMPLOYMENT

Salary schedules in most districts are negotiated between teacher associations or unions and their school boards. Where individual teachers are placed on salary schedules is usually spelled out in their contracts and typically based on a grid including years of experience and academic degrees or credits earned. As straightforward as this may sound, disputes do arise, particularly over issues such as credit for prior work experience. Absent statutes or contractual provisions to the contrary, courts generally defer to the discretion of school officials on salary matters as long as their actions were fair and reasonable. By the same token, courts are reluctant to interfere with school board decisions about the assignment and reassignment of teachers as long as such actions are consistent with state laws and contractual provisions.

Salary Schedules

New teachers are usually placed on the lowest step of salary schedules, with consideration given for advanced degrees or academic credits. Teachers then proceed through the steps on their schedules as they gain additional years of experience and academic credits. Teachers who are new to districts may come with relevant prior experience such as teaching in nonpublic schools or related work in other fields. Unless specifically obligated to do so by state law or contractual agreements, school boards are neither required to grant credit to new teachers for prior experience nor are they prohibited from doing so. Yet, salary schedules cannot be applied arbitrarily. Thus, if board officials grant credit to one teacher for experience in a nonpublic school, then they must do so for another, unless there is a rational basis for a differential application of the schedule.

School boards also may grant credit for relevant experience in a field related to a teacher's assignment. For example, it is not uncommon to give credit to vocational and career teachers with years of experience working in the trades in which they teach. Further, some states and school systems routinely grant credit for military service even though it may not be related to teaching assignments.[97]

Although merit pay is not in widespread use, the issue of merit pay has generated a great deal of discussion.[98] Courts support administrators' decisions regarding salary increases due to merit, unless it can be shown that such pay was awarded arbitrarily. At the same time officials may deny teachers advancement on salary schedules for good cause, such as inefficiency,[99] unsatisfactory performance,[100] or failure to earn required professional development credits. In an early case, a federal trial court in Illinois held that since a teacher lacked a legitimate expectancy of a merit salary increase, she had no rights to a written explanation of why it was denied.[101]

> Although merit pay is not in widespread use, the issue of merit pay has generated a great deal of discussion.

In 1963 Congress passed the Equal Pay Act (EPA)[102] to abolish wage disparities based on sex. Enacted to establish salary equality for women, the EPA prohibits employers from paying members of one sex more than members of the other for the same work on jobs that require equal skills, effort, and responsibility and that are performed under similar working conditions. To this end, school boards cannot establish different salary schedules for males and females.

Assignments

Insofar as school employees do not have a right to work in specific buildings, boards have almost complete discretion to assign and transfer teachers as needed, as long as assignments are made within the teachers' areas and levels of certification. Even teachers' attainment of tenure does not prohibit boards from reassigning them. Courts generally do not interfere with boards' assignments of teachers unless the actions of school officials violate collective bargaining agreements or were made in retaliation for teachers' participation in protected activities.[103] In one case, the federal trial court in Connecticut refused to overturn a school board's reassignment of a seventh grade language arts teacher to teach mathematics and writing,

> Insofar as school employees do not have a right to work in specific buildings, boards have almost complete discretion to assign and transfer teachers as needed, as long as assignments are made within the teachers' areas and levels of certification.

subjects for which she was certificated but had not taught for some time, since she was qualified for the assignment.[104]

Assigning additional duties without extra compensation or without relieving educators of other duties is usually impermissible, since it may contravene contracts.[105] Moreover, reassignments resulting in substantially less compensation may not be permissible unless officials follow nonrenewal procedures, because such actions could be construed as the nonrenewal of contracts.[106] Conversely, officials may reassign teachers from one school to another if the teachers' duties and status remain the same or are similar.[107] A teacher's refusal to accept such a reassignment could result in the termination of the teacher's contract.[108]

Additional Compensation

Teachers need to be aware of state laws or school district policies that may affect additional compensation. It is common for school boards to compensate teachers for extra duties such as coaching, teaching summer school, or supervising other extracurricular programs. Salary differentials could also be given for hard-to-fill positions, those requiring additional certification(s), or those including added responsibilities. Most often, supplementary compensation is spelled out in teachers' negotiated collective bargaining agreements. Again, courts generally support such arrangements as long as they are not contrary to state law. Supplementary contracts usually do not come with any expectation, right, or guarantee that they will be renewed or continued in the future.

Teachers may provide tutoring to students on their own as a means of supplementing their incomes. As with any type of additional employment teachers might have, private tutoring is not problematic, unless it interferes with their abilities to carry out their normal school responsibilities. Put another way, conflict of interest policies may prohibit teachers from tutoring their own students for a fee, even if they do this off campus during nonschool hours.

Conflict of interest or ethics statutes could prohibit teachers from accepting gifts from parents. Although most conflict of interest laws have been enacted to discourage public officials from taking bribes, many add that public employees may not accept gifts that are given to them because of their official positions. By way of example, Massachusetts recently

> Conflict of interest or ethics statutes could prohibit teachers from accepting gifts from parents.

amended its conflict of interest law to prohibit the solicitation or acceptance of gifts of substantial value, interpreted as anything over $50, by public employees.[109]

LEAVES OF ABSENCE

Allowable leaves of absence are by and large described in detail in teachers' collective bargaining agreements. As a rule, these agreements permit teachers to take specified numbers of days off per year for illness, to conduct personal business that cannot be taken care of during nonschool time, for religious observances, and to attend professional development workshops. In addition, many boards grant both paid and unpaid sabbatical leaves. Moreover, since many teachers serve in the armed forces and may require leaves for military duty, federal law requires boards to reinstate them when they return from active duty.

Contracts typically allow teachers to carry over or accumulate unused sick days into future years, up to a set maximum, while other types of leaves typically cannot be rolled over. Further, some contracts allow teachers to "buy back" unused sick leave on retirement, giving them the option of collecting a sum of money at retirement, based on the number of days of accrued leave, in return for not having used all of their allotted sick leave. While leaves of absence are subject to collective bargaining, all contractual provisions must be consistent with state and federal laws.

Personal and Family Medical Leave

In 1993 Congress enacted the Family and Medical Leave Act (FMLA)[110] to permit eligible employees to take unpaid leaves of absence of up to 12 weeks due to serious health conditions or to care for ill immediate family members or new children.[111] The FMLA, which is administered by the Department of Labor, defines eligible employees as those who work for businesses with 50 or more employees or public agencies, including schools. Employees must have worked for the businesses or agencies for at least 12 months and a total of 1,250 hours to be eligible.

The FMLA provides that employees taking leaves of absence must be restored to the same or substantially similar positions when they return to work and must have all benefits restored as well. Further, employers may not retaliate against employees for exercising their statutory rights. In addition to state laws that may offer more extensive coverage than the FMLA by expanding the definition of family, collective bargaining contracts may provide even greater benefits.

Under the FMLA teachers may use a combination of accumulated paid time and unpaid leave if doing so is permitted by school policies or their collective bargaining agreements. Individuals may request leaves either due to their own serious health conditions that render them unable to work or those of immediate family members who require care. Leaves may also be requested for the birth, adoption, or assumption of foster care of children. School boards may require documentation that requested leaves are necessary.

The FMLA includes specific provisions applicable to teachers to minimize disruptions to the educational process. In particular, these provisions affect how leaves may be taken at or near the end of school terms.

> Most collective bargaining agreements provide for specified numbers of days per year of sick leave. Even so, abuse of contractual leave may subject teachers to discipline and even dismissal.

Most collective bargaining agreements provide for specified numbers of days per year of sick leave. Even so, abuse of contractual leave may subject teachers to discipline and even dismissal. For example, an appellate court in Pennsylvania upheld the discharge of two teachers who used sick leave to go on a ski trip.[112] Further, teachers can be dismissed for excessive absences.[113]

CASE SUMMARY 4.3: DISCHARGE FOR UNAUTHORIZED USE OF SICK LEAVE

Riverview School District v. Riverview Education Association

639 A.2d 974 (Pa. Commw. Ct. 1994)

Factual Summary: Two teachers submitted requests to take four days of personal leave to go on a ski trip and filed grievances after their superintendent denied the requested leave. Although the superintendent's decision was upheld by the school board, the teachers took the time off and later presented certificates stating that their absence was due to personal illness. After the superintendent and school board took steps to dismiss the teachers, the matter proceeded to arbitration. An arbitrator sustained the teachers' grievances and ordered the school board to reinstate them. The school board appealed. A state trial court disagreed with the arbitrator's decision but did not feel that it had the authority to overturn the award.

Issue: May the school board dismiss the teachers for unauthorized use of sick time?

Decision: Yes, the appellate court reversed the trial court's decision, vacated the arbitrator's award, and reinstated the dismissals.

Summary of Court's Rationale: The court was convinced that the arbitrator's factual findings regarding the teachers' actions supported the school board's determination. The court viewed the evidence, as established by the arbitrator, as showing that the teachers violated the school board's sick leave policy. Once the arbitrator found that the teachers violated the policy, the court maintained that the question of appropriate discipline was a matter reserved to the school board.

Courts generally uphold requirements for teachers to submit confirmation of their illnesses when they have taken sick leave.[114] Again, collective bargaining agreements normally spell out the circumstances of when documentation of illness may be requested. Further, school officials may require documentation that teachers are fit to return to work after extended leaves due to illness.[115]

Maternity and Child Rearing

In addition to state law and collective bargaining agreements, the FMLA also covers maternity and child-rearing leaves. In one case, the Eleventh Circuit affirmed that a teacher in Alabama who requested a maternity leave within her first 12 months of employment was not covered by the FMLA, because her requested leave would have begun several days before she was eligible for FMLA coverage.[116]

Whether teachers may use paid sick leave for at least part of their maternity leaves depends on state law and contractual provisions. Sick leave normally may be used when teachers are incapacitated due to their conditions. Thus, in most situations teachers may use sick leave for a period of time prior to the birth of a child if they are unable to work.

Religious Obligations

A fair amount of litigation involving leaves has concerned absences for religious observances. Title VII of the Civil Rights Act of 1964,[117] as amended, prohibits employers from discriminating against employees because of race, color, sex, religion, or national origin. The Supreme Court has interpreted Title VII as requiring school boards to make reasonable efforts to accommodate teachers' religious obligations.[118] Even so, accommodations do not need to be the ones requested by the teachers. In this case, the school board allowed the teacher to use only three days of paid leave to meet his religious obligations, which required a total of six days of absence. The Court noted that requiring the teacher to take the remaining three days without pay was an acceptable option. When the case was returned to the lower court, it was satisfied that the board did not discriminate against the teacher.[119] In an earlier noneducation case, the Supreme Court interpreted Title VII as not requiring employers to suffer undue hardships to accommodate employees.[120]

> The Supreme Court has interpreted Title VII as requiring school boards to make reasonable efforts to accommodate teachers' religious obligations.... Even so, those accommodations do not need to be the ones requested by the teachers.

CASE SUMMARY 4.4: LEAVE FOR RELIGIOUS OBSERVANCE

Ansonia Board of Education v. Philbrook

479 U.S. 60 (1986)

Factual Summary: A high school teacher filed suit challenging his school board's religious observances leave policy. According to the tenets of his religion, the teacher was required to miss six days of work each school year for observance of holy days. The board's leave policy, as defined in a collective bargaining agreement, allowed teachers three days of paid leave for religious holidays. Since the policy did not allow teachers to use other types of leave such as personal or sick days for religious observances, he was forced to take three days without pay. When the board rejected the teacher's request either to be allowed to use personal leave for holy days or to pay for his own substitute on the additional days, he filed suit under Title VII's prohibition against discrimination on the basis of religion. A federal trial court ruled in the school board's favor, but the Second Circuit reversed and remanded on behalf of the teacher.

Issue: Did the school board make a proper accommodation to the teacher's need to take additional days off for religious observances?

Decision: Yes, the U.S. Supreme Court held that unpaid leave was a reasonable accommodation.

Summary of Court's Rationale: As an initial matter the Court held that the school board was not required to provide the teacher's preferred accommodation as long as the board offered a reasonable accommodation. The Court added that once the board demonstrated that its accommodations were reasonable, it was not required to prove that granting the employee's requested accommodation would present an undue hardship. The Court next declared that allowing the teacher to take unpaid days was reasonable, because Title VII did not require employers to accommodate religious observances at all costs. Further, the Court noted that unpaid leave required only that the teacher lose compensation; it did not affect his employment status.

School calendars typically accommodate Christian holidays but do not necessarily make allowances for the holidays of other religions. In a case where a teacher needed more than the days allowed by contract for religious observances, the federal trial court in Colorado commented that it would violate Title VII to punish teachers by placing them in a position where they must ignore their religious obligations to retain employment.[121] Still, the court was convinced that allowing employees to use unpaid leave was a reasonable accommodation. In essence, school boards must make reasonable efforts to accommodate teachers' needs for leaves of absence for religious purposes but are not obligated to grant extensive leaves if doing so causes an administrative hardship.

Military Duty

Teachers also may require leaves of absence to serve in the armed forces. The Uniformed Services Employment and Reemployment Rights Act of 1994[122] guarantees that those who serve in the armed forces, including the Reserves and National Guard, are not disadvantaged in their civilian jobs because of their service. Therefore, teachers who take leaves of absence for military duty must be promptly reinstated on their return and should be given the same, or substantially similar, positions to the ones they held before deployment. Further, teachers may not be discriminated against in their employment due to past, present, or future military service.

TEACHER EVALUATIONS

School boards have both the right and duty to evaluate teachers' job performance. If not specifically dictated by statute, the frequency and form of evaluations commonly are subjects for collective bargaining. Even so, administrators have the right to evaluate teachers more frequently than called for by statute. More frequent evaluations are common when administrators have concerns about individual teachers and may be considering the termination of their contracts. Evaluations take two forms: formative and summative. Formative evaluations are conducted for the purpose of teacher improvement, while the main reason for summative evaluations is making personnel decisions regarding rehiring, dismissal, tenure, promotion, and/or merit pay. A comprehensive evaluation system can protect teachers from subjective or arbitrary personnel decisions. Since critical decisions are based on the results of teacher evaluations, they have been the subject of a fair amount of litigation.

Most states have laws requiring teacher evaluations. Even so, teacher evaluation laws vary widely in what they require. Requirements range

> Most states have laws requiring teacher evaluations. Even so, teacher evaluation laws vary widely in what they require. Requirements range from a simple mandate for school districts to establish an evaluation mechanism to very specific criteria regarding the content of those evaluations.

from simple mandates for school boards to establish evaluation mechanisms to specific criteria regarding the content of evaluations. It is well settled that boards have the right to evaluate teachers even in the absence of statutes directing them to do so. Of course any evaluation system must be fair.

Essential elements of evaluation systems include notifying teachers of the criteria and procedures to be used in assessing them; using valid, reliable criteria directly related to teacher competence and effectiveness; and providing teachers written copies of final evaluations. At the same time, evaluation systems should afford teachers a full opportunity to correct their deficiencies.[123] More often than not, courts uphold the dismissal of teachers who have received notice of their shortcomings but have not improved their performances after a reasonable time.[124] At the same time, a distinction must be made between the nonrenewal of the contracts of teachers lacking tenure and the termination of contracts of tenured teachers. The contracts of teachers who are not tenured can simply be allowed to expire or not be renewed for any lawful reason, while dismissals of teachers with tenure are subject to much greater procedural due process. This will be discussed in greater detail in Chapter 7.

Courts do overturn adverse personnel decisions if school boards fail to comply with mandated evaluation protocols. For example, courts may order the reinstatement of dismissed teachers if the teachers were not evaluated as called for by state statutes or contractual agreements under the theory that teachers cannot improve if their deficiencies are not brought to their attention.[125] On the other hand, courts generally uphold personnel decisions when they are based on evaluations that substantially comply with established practices. For the most part, courts do not substitute their judgment for that of competent school administrators. Rather, courts limit their review to procedural issues.

Evaluation systems often involve targeted observations of teachers in the classroom, and, in a change that is controversial, considerations of the academic progress of students. It is fairly well settled that test scores may be used as part of a comprehensive teacher evaluation system.[126] In light of provisions in the No Child Left Behind Act requiring all students to achieve proficiency in reading and mathematics by 2014, and allowing the dismissal of educators in schools that fail to reach this goal, it will be interesting to observe how the subsequent dismissal of teachers plays out.[127]

One issue that has emerged is whether teachers may be videotaped as part of the evaluation process. Unless such a practice is prohibited by statute or contractual agreement, administrators have the right to use videotapes as an evaluation tool. An appellate court in Texas ruled that the use of videotapes in a teacher's evaluation did not violate her privacy rights, since her teaching in a public classroom did not fall within a zone of privacy.[128]

RESIGNATIONS

As is the case with employees in other occupations, most teachers do not serve for life. While retirement is probably the most common reason for teachers' separation from service, many resign their positions to accept employment in other school districts, move on to promotional positions, enter other professions, raise families, and/or relocate. Some, unfortunately, must resign because of incapacity or illness.

Retirements

Although it was not always the case, all states have provisions for teacher retirements. Many states have set up retirement systems exclusively for educators, while others incorporate teachers into retirement systems established for state or municipal employees. While retirement systems vary from state to state, most require teachers to contribute portions of their salaries to funds from which they later draw annuities or pensions. For the most part, pensions may be based on teachers' ages at retirement, years of service, and average salaries over a specified number of years, or on the total amount of contributions over all years of employment.

> While retirement systems vary from state to state, most require teachers to contribute portions of their salaries to funds from which they later draw annuities or pensions.

Some plans allow teachers who have worked in other jurisdictions to transfer their former retirement credits into their new plans. Often this is done by cashing out of the former retirement systems and purchasing an equivalent number of years in the new system. Further, some jurisdictions permit teachers with previous employment in nonpublic schools, the military, public agencies, or nonprofit organizations to buy into their systems. Provisions also exist in some plans for teachers who left and reenter the profession to buy back into the retirement system if their contributions from their first term of service had been refunded. Typically, systems that have buy in or buy back policies require teachers to elect this option within a specified period of time. By and large, courts support decisions of retirement boards about teachers' rights to receive credit for other employment as long as those decisions comport with statutes and the boards' regulations and are not arbitrary.[129]

Now that retirement plans are well established, the litigation in this area has subsided somewhat; still, questions arise concerning the benefits to be paid upon retirement, especially when changes occur in how benefits are calculated. A common issue of litigation is whether extra compensation teachers received should be included in pension calculations. Some systems specifically allow retirement benefits to include credit for compensation for extra duties, such as coaching, while others calculate benefits on base pay alone. How courts rule on benefit changes varies depending on whether claimants were retired at the time the changes were instituted. In one case, the First Circuit approved changes implemented in Maine as they applied to teachers who had not yet begun receiving pensions, including those who were already vested.[130]

When pensions are based on an average salary over a set number of years, retirement boards are frequently suspicious of unusually large salary increases or bonuses that may be granted to potential retirees during that time period. Courts have approved retirement boards' decisions to exclude disproportionate raises in their calculations of former employees' pensions.[131] By the same token, severance pay may be excluded from pension calculations.[132]

School boards often offer early retirement incentives. Typical packages may afford teachers extra raises in salaries or bonuses for a specified numbers of years with the agreement that they will retire on agreed upon dates. For obvious reasons, teachers who fail to retire on those dates may be required to repay the early retirement incentives. On the other hand, teachers who retire before agreed upon dates usually do not pose problems.[133]

Other Resignations

As indicated earlier, teachers resign their positions for a variety of reasons. In order to avoid disruptions to the educational process, contracts commonly specify that except in emergency situations, teachers may resign only at the end of contract periods or school terms. Most agreements also require a specified amount of notice before teachers may terminate their contracts. The failure of teachers to sign contracts on or before specified dates for continuing employment can amount to resignations.[134] As would be expected, a teacher's resignation terminates all claims to tenure.[135]

Teacher resignations may, in most cases, be rescinded up to the point where they have been accepted by superintendents or school boards. In one case where a teacher's resignation had not been accepted formally but his replacement had been hired, an appellate court in Ohio ruled that hiring of the new teacher implied the acceptance of the former teacher's resignation.[136] Similarly, an appellate court in Alabama would not allow a school employee to rescind a resignation that had been accepted by the superintendent but had not yet been acted on by the board.[137]

SUMMARY AND RECOMMENDATIONS

Along with employment rights, teachers have many responsibilities. Thus, the rights of teachers must constantly be balanced against the responsibilities they willingly accept when offered public employment. Even in view of the fact that teachers do not lose their rights as citizens in accepting public employment, it must always be kept in mind that they can be subjected to a higher standard of personal behavior, because they are expected to be role models for their students.

Teachers must be certificated to be employed in public school systems except in rare circumstances when individuals are granted waivers. States establish certification requirements, which generally involve completion of a program of studies leading to bachelors' degrees. Additional requirements such as citizenship and having good moral character are common. Since states set certification standards, states may also amend their standards such that individuals may be required to meet the new standards. Further, teacher certification may be revoked for cause.

Teachers have the right to expect a degree of privacy in how they conduct their personal lives. Even so, individuals may be dismissed if school boards can show that teachers' private behavior has a negative impact on their professional standing and effectiveness. Not surprisingly, teachers may be discharged and have their certificates revoked for involvement in criminal activities. Teachers have a much lesser expectation of privacy when it comes to classrooms and equipment supplied by the school board. Moreover, due to privacy concerns, mandatory drug testing requirements have met with mixed results in the courts.

Salary schedules in most school systems are established through negotiations between boards and teacher unions. Courts usually do not interfere with board actions regarding the placement of teachers on salary schedules, unless the boards' decisions were arbitrary. Further, collective bargaining agreements normally include provisions for teachers to take leaves of absence for illness, conducting personal business, and other legitimate reasons.

In light of maintaining the balance between teachers' rights and professional responsibilities, the following principles have emerged:

- To become certificated or licensed as teachers, individuals must complete prescribed courses of study that meet the standards enumerated by their SEAs. Additional requirements may exist, such as citizenship, swearing loyalty, and having good moral character.
- Teacher certificates may be revoked for cause, such as conviction of felonies, sexual misconduct, and conduct unbecoming teachers.

Naturally, revocation of their certificates renders teachers ineligible for public school employment. Teachers may be dismissed for the same reasons even if their certificates have not been revoked.

- States are free to adopt new teacher licensure standards. Current teachers may be required to meet those new standards even if their existing certificates were issued for life.

- In recent years there have been few attempts to discharge teachers for alternative living arrangements, sexual orientation, or being an unwed parent. Even so, teachers may be dismissed if their lifestyles or choices interfere with their classroom effectiveness.

- Involvement in inappropriate sexual activities with students is cause for discharge and revocation of teacher certificates. Intimate relationships with former students may also be cause for dismissal.

- Teachers may be dismissed for illegal use of drugs even if they do not face criminal charges.

- Courts largely uphold antinepotism laws or policies that prohibit relatives of board members from working in public school systems or that forbid close relatives from working in the same building.

- Information that is contained in teachers' personnel files is generally confidential. However, other information, such as data about teacher credentials, may be considered part of the public record. Although it is rare, in some jurisdictions teachers' evaluations may be made public.

- Teachers lack a reasonable expectation of privacy in classrooms or with regard to items provided by their school boards, such as desks, file cabinets, and computers. Therefore, teachers may be more readily subjected to workplace searches than searches of their private belongings.

- Teachers may be required to submit to drug tests if school authorities have well-founded suspicions that they are using illegal substances. Schools may institute suspicionless drug testing programs only when they have compelling governmental interests.

- Teachers have limited protection against postings that students make about them on social networking websites. While many student postings that are critical of teachers fall into the realm of protected free speech, those that are threatening or cause substantial disruptions in schools are unprotected.

- Teachers need to be careful when posting information or items about themselves on the Internet. Although the law in this area is still emerging, it is likely that courts would support disciplinary action against teachers if their postings cause a substantial disruption to school environments or fall into the category of unprofessional conduct.

- While salary schedules must be applied fairly, school boards have great latitude in how they establish and administer pay scales.
- Insofar as courts recognize that school boards need flexibility, judges are reluctant to interfere with the assignment, reassignment, or transfer of teachers.
- Eligible teachers may take up to 12 weeks of unpaid leave due to their own serious illness or that of family members, or to care for new children. School boards may require appropriate documentation that such leave is needed.
- School boards may not deny teachers leave for religious reasons, unless granting leave would create undue hardships. Even so, leave days need not be paid.
- School boards have the right to evaluate teachers and make personnel decisions based on those evaluations. Still, an overriding theme of teacher evaluation systems is that they must be fair.
- Evaluation criteria should be clearly communicated to teachers in advance of any assessments of their performances.
- Teachers' resignations may normally be rescinded up until the point at which they are accepted.

FREQUENTLY ASKED QUESTIONS

Q. May applicants who refuse to take loyalty oaths be denied teacher certification?

A. Yes, the U.S. Supreme Court has ruled that loyalty oaths for government employees that are general but not overly broad are not unconstitutional. Since employees may be required to take these oaths, prospective employees may be held to the same standard. Thus, typical loyalty oaths—where applicants swear to uphold federal and state constitutions and not engage in activities such as the violent or forceful overthrow of the government—are allowed.

Q. May teachers' certification be revoked for off-campus misconduct or actions?

A. Since the revocation of teacher certification is controlled by state law, the causes for revocation vary from one state to the next. By and large, courts support the revocation of teacher certificates if there is a sufficient nexus between the conduct and an individual's fitness or ability to teach. While it may be easier to demonstrate a nexus when incidents took place on campuses, off-campus misconduct also may subject students to disciplinary sanctions. Conviction of felonies or substantiated charges of sexual misconduct or immorality almost always result in the revocation of teaching credentials. Whether misdemeanors or conduct that is considered to be inappropriate warrants the revocation of teachers' licenses depends on the nature of the offenses and how they impact the individual's future ability to complete profession duties.

Q. May teachers be dismissed for having alternative lifestyles?

A. Teachers may not be dismissed solely because their lifestyle choices or sexual orientation do not agree with the expectations of school administrators or school board members. However, teachers may be dismissed if their lifestyle choices interfere with their teaching. The extent to which unconventional behavior or alternative lifestyles impact teachers' effectiveness may depend on what is considered to be acceptable in given communities.

Q. May individual teachers be required to submit to drug tests as a condition of continued employment?

A. Individual teachers may be subjected to drug testing only when school officials have reasonable suspicion that teachers have been using illegal drugs or when drug testing is permitted under their collective bargaining agreements. Reasonable suspicion exists if teachers are found to be in possession of illegal substances or if they are observed frequently exhibiting signs of drug abuse. Erratic behavior, by itself, is usually insufficient cause to require teachers to submit to drug tests.

Q. Are teachers whose religion observes the Sabbath on a day when school is typically in session entitled to leave on that day of the week every week?

A. Under most circumstances the answer is no. Title VII requires school boards to make reasonable accommodations for teachers' religious beliefs. Granting teachers one day of leave each week, even if it is unpaid, would not be reasonable due to the disruption it would cause to school operations. The exception would be if the teacher could be given an assignment that required attendance only four days per week.

Q. If the law in the area of teachers' postings on social networking sites is still emerging, what guidelines can be provided?

A. Although the law in this area is developing, parallels can be drawn from other aspects of education law. First, as with students' postings, teachers' postings that are disruptive to the educational environment, such as negative comments about students or colleagues, could subject teachers to discipline. Second, postings that could compromise teachers' classroom effectiveness also can be cause for discipline. For example, pictures that show teachers engaging in activities that would be considered conduct unbecoming a teacher could be problematic. In light of the unsettled nature of this topic in the law, it is best to err on the side of caution.

WHAT'S NEXT

The next chapter continues the discussion of issues related to conditions of employment. Specifically, Chapter 5 addresses the legal status of collective bargaining and teacher contracts. Topics include the right to bargain, subjects for collective bargaining, and dispute resolution.

ENDNOTES

1. No Child Left Behind Act, 20 U.S.C. §§ 6301–7941 (2006).
2. NCLB, 20 U.S.C. § 7801(23).
3. *See, e.g.,* Guthrie v. Independent School District, 958 P.2d 802 (Okla. Ct. App. 1997) (holding that a teacher's contract was void because she failed to obtain proper certification in a timely manner).
4. *See, e.g.,* Bhatt v. New York State Education Department, 843 N.Y.S.2d 737 (N.Y. App. Div. 2007) (finding that the denial of a teaching certificate was not irrational, arbitrary, or capricious).
5. Massachusetts Federation of Teachers v. Board of Education, 767 N.E.2d 549 (Mass. 2002).
6. Miller v. Commonwealth of Pennsylvania, 752 A.2d 451 Pa. Commw. Ct. 2000).
7. 71 Massachusetts General Laws § 38G (2009).
8. Ambach v. Norwick, 441 U.S. 68 (1979).
9. Cole v. Richardson, 405 U.S. 676 (1972); Connell v. Higginbotham, 403 U.S. 207 (1971).
10. *See, e.g.,* Keyishian v. Board of Regents, 385 U.S. 589 (1967); Whitehill v. Elkins, 389 U.S. 54 (1967).
11. *See, e.g.,* Newchurch v. Louisiana State Board of Elementary and Secondary Education, 713 So. 2d 1269 (La. Ct. App. 1998); Burstein v. Board of Examiners, 589 N.Y.S.2d 554 (N.Y. App. Div. 1992).
12. Arrocha v. Board of Education of the City of New York, 690 N.Y.S.2d 503 (N.Y. 1999).
13. Rehabilitation Act, Section 504, 29 U.S.C. § 794 (2006).
14. *See, e.g.,* Dauer v. Department of Education, 874 A.2d 159 (Pa. Commw. Ct. 2005); Feldman v. Board of Education of the City School District of New York, 686 N.Y.S.2d 842 (N.Y. App. Div. 1999).
15. Russo, C. J. (2009). *Reutter's the law of public education* (7th ed.). New York: Foundation Press.
16. Startzel v. Commonwealth of Pennsylvania, 562 A.2d 1005 (Pa. Commw. Ct. 1989).
17. Crumpler v. State Board of Education, 594 N.E.2d 1071 (Ohio Ct. App. 1991).
18. Steltzer v. State Board of Education, 595 N.E.2d 489 (Ohio Ct. App. 1991).
19. Joyell v. Commissioner of Education, 696 A.2d 1039 (Conn. Ct. App. 1997).
20. Grohl v. Sobol, 604 N.Y.S.2d 279 (N.Y. App. Div. 1993).
21. Reguero v. Teacher Standards and Practices Commission, 789 P.2d 11 (Or. App. Ct. 1990).

22. Welcher v. Sobol, 642 N.Y.S.2d 370 (N.Y. App. Div. 1996).

23. *In re* Appeal of Morrill, 765 A.2d 699 (N.H. 2001).

24. Board of Education of City of Los Angeles v. Wilkinson, 270 P.2d 82 at 85 (Cal. Ct. App. 1954).

25. Rush v. Board of Education of Crete-Monee Community Unit School District, 227 N.E.2d 649 (Ill. App. Ct. 2000).

26. Wax v. Horne, 844 So. 2d 797 (Fla. Dist. Ct. App. 2003).

27. Howard v. Missouri State Board of Education, 913 S.W.2d 887 (Mo. Ct. App. 1995).

28. Knight v. Winn, 910 So. 2d 310 (Fla. Dist. Ct. App. 2005).

29. Winters v. Arizona Board of Education, 83 P.3d 1114 (Ariz. Ct. App. 2004).

30. Professional Standards Commission v. Denham, 556 S.E.2d 920 (Ga. Ct. App. 2001).

31. Professional Standards Commission v. Smith, 571 S.E.2d 443 (Ga. Ct. App. 2002).

32. Brewer v. Schact, 509 S.E.2d 378 (Ga. Ct. App. 1998).

33. Professional Standards Commission v. Valentine, 603 S.E.2d 792 (Ga. Ct. App. 2004).

34. Nanko v. Department of Education, 663 A.2d 312 (Pa. Commw. Ct. 1995).

35. Guthrie v. Taylor, 185 S.E.2d 193 (N.C. 1971).

36. State of Texas v. Project Principle, 724 S.W.2d 387 (Tex. 1987).

37. Connecticut Education Association v. Tirozzi, 554 A.2d 1065 (Conn. 1989).

38. Slater v. Pennsylvania Department of Education, 725 A.2d 1248 (Pa. Commw. Ct. 1999).

39. Tinker v. Des Moines Independent Community School District, 393 U.S. 503 (1969).

40. *See, e.g.,* Ambach v. Norwick, 441 U.S. 68 (1979).

41. DeMitchell, T. (1994). Private lives: Community control vs. professional autonomy. *Education Law Reporter, 78,* 187–197.

42. Horosko v. Mount Pleasant Township School District, 6 A.2d 866 (Pa. 1939).

43. Sullivan v. Meade City Independent School District, 530 F.2d 799 (8th Cir. 1975).

44. Zelno v. Lincoln Intermediate Unit, 786 A.2d 1022 (Pa. Commw. Ct. 2001).

45. Courts in a number of cases have sanctioned the dismissal of teachers after determining that their private actions made them poor role models for students. *See, e.g.,* Green v. New York City Department of Education, 793 N.Y.S.2d 405 (N.Y. App. Div. 2005) (upholding the termination of a teacher who was convicted of grand larceny); Walthart v. Board of Directors of Edgewood-Colesburg Community School District, 694 N.W.2d 740 (Iowa 2005) (upholding a school board's decision to discharge a teacher who allowed students to drink on her property); Kinniry v. Abington School District, 673 A.2d 429 (Pa. Commw. Ct. 1996) (upholding dismissal of a teacher who was convicted for trafficking in counterfeit goods or services); Satterfield v. Board of Education of the Grand

Rapids Public Schools, 556 N.W.2d 888 (Mich. Ct. App. 1996); (upholding the discharge of a teacher who pled guilty to a charge of embezzling funds); Board of Directors of the Lawton-Bronson Community School District v. Davies, 489 N.W.2d 19 (Iowa 1992) (upholding the dismissal of a teacher who was arrested for shoplifting).

46. *But see* Glover v. Williamsburg Local School District, 20 F. Supp. 2d 1160 (S.D. Ohio 1998) (finding that a motivating factor in a teacher's non-renewal was his sexual orientation).

47. Andrews v. Drew Municipal Separate School District, 507 F.2d 611 (5th Cir. 1975).

48. *See, e.g.,* Bertolini v. Whitehall City School District Board of Education, 744 N.E.2d 1245 (Ohio Ct. App. 2000) (finding that an assistant superintendent's adulterous affair was not grounds for termination).

49. *See, e.g.,* Baltrip v. Norris, 23 S.W.3d 336 (Ten. Ct. App. 2000) (upholding the termination of a teacher who had been charged with sexual battery but pled guilty to assault, a misdemeanor).

50. Andrews v. Independent School District, 12 P.3d 491 (Okla. Civ. App. 2000). *See also* Dixon v. Clem, 492 F.3d 665 (6th Cir. 2007) (upholding the firing of a teacher who took topless photographs of a female student, presumably with her consent); Welch v. Board of Education of Chandler Unified School District No. 80, 667 P.2d 746 (Ariz. Ct. App. 1983) (upholding the dismissal of a teacher who failed to cooperate with an investigation into his relationship with a student that culminated in marriage).

51. Flaskamp v. Dearborn Public Schools, 385 F.3d 935 (6th Cir. 2004).

52. Parker v. Board of Education of the Byron Center Public Schools, 582 N. W.2d 859 (Mich. Ct. App. 1998).

53. Gedney v. Board of Education of the Town of Groton, 703 A.2d 804 (Conn. Ct. App. 1997).

54. Woo v. Putnam County Board of Education, 504 S.E.2d 644 (W.Va. 1998). *See also* Bergerson v. Salem-Keizer School District, 144 P.2d 918 (Or. 2006) (upholding the dismissal of a teacher who pled no contest to criminal mischief charges and parents objected to her returning to teaching).

55. Montgomery v. Carr, 101 F.3d 1117 (6th Cir. 1996).

56. Board of Education of the Town of Somers v. Freedom of Information Commission, 556 A.2d 592 (Conn. 1989).

57. Herald v. Ann Arbor Public Schools, 568 N.W.2d 411 (Mich. Ct. App. 1997).

58. Perkins v. Freedom of Information Commission, 635 A.2d 783 (Conn. 1993).

59. *See, e.g.,* Bellevue John Does v. Bellevue School District, 120 P.3d 616 (Wash. Ct. App. 2005) (ruling that the names of teachers who were falsely accused of sexual misconduct could not be released to a newspaper).

60. Navarre v. South Washington County Schools, 652 N.W.2d 9 (Minn. 2002).

61. Wiese v. Freedom of Information Commission, 847 A.2d 1004 (Conn. Ct. App. 2004).

62. Cypress Media v. Hazelton Area School District, 708 A.2d 866 (Pa. Commw. Ct. 1998).

63. South Bend Tribune v. South Bend Community School Corporation, 740 N.E.2d 937 (Ind. Ct. App. 2000).

64. State *ex rel.* Cincinnati Enquirer v. Cincinnati Board of Education, 788 N.E.2d 629 (Ohio 2003).

65. State *ex rel.* Dayton Newspapers v. Dayton Board of Education, 747 N.E.2d 255 (Ohio Ct. App. 2000).

66. Strong v. Board of Education of Uniondale Free School District, 902 F.2d 208 (2d Cir. 1990).

67. Russo, C. J., & Mawdsley, R. D. (2008). *Searches, seizures and drug testing procedures: Balancing rights and school safety* (2nd ed.). Sarasota, FL: LRP.

68. Shaul v. Cherry Valley–Springfield Central School District, 363 F.3d 177 (2d Cir. 2004).

69. Gatlin v. United States, 833 A.2d 995 (D.C. Ct. App. 2003).

70. Knox County Education Association v. Knox County Board of Education, 158 F.3d 361 (6th Cir. 1998).

71. For a discussion of Knox County Education Association v. Knox County Board of Education *see* Russo, C. J., & Mawdsley, R. D. (1999). Drug testing of teachers: Student safety v. teacher rights or an overreaching school board? *Education Law Reporter, 134,* 661–674.

72. Hearn v. Board of Public Education, 191 F.3d 1329 (11th Cir. 1999), *rehearing and suggestion for rehearing en banc denied,* 204 F.3d 1124 (11th Cir. 1999), *cert. denied,* 529 U.S. 1109 (2000).

73. Warren v. Board of Education of St. Louis, 200 F. Supp. 2d 1053 (E.D. Mo. 2001).

74. A variety of courts have upheld suspicionless drug testing of school employees other than teachers. *See, e.g.,* Jones v. McKenzie, 878 F.2d 1476 (D.C. Cir. 1989) (school bus attendants); English v. Talladega County Board of Education, 938 F. Supp. 775 (N.D. Ala. 1996) (a mechanic's helper); Cornette v. Commonwealth, 899 S.W.2d 502 (Ky. Ct. App. 1995) (public school bus drivers); Aubrey v. School Board of Lafayette Parish, 148 F.3d 559 (5th Cir. 1998) (custodians and other safety-sensitive school personnel).

75. Knox County Education Association v. Knox County Board of Education, 158 F.3d 361 (6th Cir. 1998).

76. Crager v. Board of Education of Knott County, 313 F. Supp. 2d 690 (E.D. Ky. 2004).

77. Aubrey v. School Board of Lafayette, 148 F.3d 559 (5th Cir. 1998).

78. United Teachers of New Orleans v. Orleans Parish School Board, 142 F.3d 853 (5th Cir. 1998).

79. Patchogue-Medford Congress of Teachers v. Board of Education of the Patchogue-Medford Union Free School District, 517 N.Y.S.2d 456 (N.Y. 1987).

80. For a discussion of Patchogue-Medford Congress of Teachers v. Board of Education of the Patchogue-Medford Union Free School District, *see* Russo, C. J. (1987). Drug testing of teachers: Patchogue-Medford Congress of Teachers revisited. *Education Law Reporter, 40,* 607–614.

81. Patchogue-Medford Congress of Teachers v. Board of Education of the Patchogue-Medford Union Free School District, 517 N.Y.S.2d 456 at 462 (N.Y. 1987).

82. Georgia Association of Educators v. Harris, 749 F. Supp. 2d 1110 (N.D. Ga. 1990).

83. McCarthy, M. (2010). Cyberspeech controversies in the Third Circuit. *Education Law Reporter, 258,* 1–14.

84. *See, e.g.,* Biby v. Board of Regents of the University of Nebraska, 419 F.3d 845 (8th Cir. 2005); United States v. Angevine, 281 F.3d 1130 (10th Cir. 2002).

85. J.S. v. Bethlehem Area School District, 807 A.2d 847 (Pa. 2002).

86. Wisniewski v. Board of Education of the Weedsport Central School District, 494 F.3d 34 (2d Cir. 2007).

87. Doninger v. Niehoff, 527 F.3d 41 (2d Cir. 2008). It must be noted that this case has not been settled on the merits and is still active. In Doninger v. Niehoff, 594 F. Supp. 2d 211 (D. Conn. 2009), the trial court denied a motion for summary judgment, finding that a fact issue existed as to whether school administrators punished the student for her speech or for her blog entry's potential disruption. At this writing that decision is on appeal to the Second Circuit.

88. Doninger v. Niehoff, 527 F.3d 41, 53 (2d Cir. 2008).

89. J.S. *ex rel.* Snyder v. Blue Mountain School District, 593 F.3d 286 (3d Cir. 2010).

90. Beussink v. Woodland R-IV School District, 30 F. Supp. 2d 1175 (E.D. Mo. 1998).

91. Evans v. Bayer, 2010 WL 521119 (S.D. Fla. 2010).

92. Layshock v. Hermitage School District, 412 F. Supp. 2d 502 (W.D. Pa. 2006), 496 F. Supp. 2d 587 (W.D. Pa. 2007), *affirmed* 593 F.3d 249 (3d Cir. 2010).

93. Spanierman v. Hughes, 576 F. Supp. 2d 292 (D. Conn. 2008).

94. Snyder v. Millersville University, 2008 WL 5093140 (E.D. Pa. 2008).

95. *District disciplines teachers for Facebook entries.* (2009, January 1). *Quinlan School Law Bulletin, 36*(1), 8.

96. For a discussion of Snyder v. Millersville University, *see* Russo, C. J. (2009). Social networking sites and the free speech rights of school employees. *School Business Affairs, 75*(4), 38–41.

97. *See, e.g.,* North Plainfield Education Association v. Board of Education of North Plainfield, 476 A.2d 1245 (N.J. 1984) (an annual increment in a teacher's salary for time spent in military service accrues regardless of the teacher's performance).

98. Ellis, T. I. (1984). Merit pay for teachers. *ERIC Clearinghouse on Educational Management: ERIC Digest, Number Ten.* ERIC Identifier: ED259453.

99. *See, e.g.,* North Plainfield Education Association v. Board of Education of North Plainfield, 476 A.2d 1245 (N.J. 1984) (an award of an annual salary increment was not a statutory right but was subject to denial for inefficiency).

100. *See, e.g.,* Probst v. Board of Education of Haddonfield, 606 A.2d 345 (N.J. 1992) (a teacher whose salary increments were withheld for unsatisfactory performance was not entitled to restoration of previously denied increments).

101. Kanter v. Community Consolidated School District, 558 F. Supp. 890 (N.D. Ill. 1982)

102. Equal Pay Act of 1963, 29 U.S.C. § 206(d) (2006).

103. *See, e.g.,* Bernasconi v. Tempe Elementary School District, 548 F.2d 857 (9th Cir. 1977) (finding that a teacher's transfer was, in part, in retaliation for her exercise of protected First Amendment free speech rights).

104. Gordon v. Nicoletti, 84 F. Supp. 2d 304 (D. Conn. 2000).

105. *See, e.g., Ex Parte* Ezell, 545 So. 2d 52 (Ala. 1989) (finding that the addition of another teaching assignment was an impermissible amendment to a teacher's contract).

106. *See, e.g.,* Quarles v. McKenzie Public School District, 325 N.W.2d 662 (N.D. 1982).

107. Thomas v. Smith, 897 F.2d 154 (5th Cir. 1989) (ruling that nonrenewal procedures must be followed when an adjustment in duties results in a severe reduction in salary).

108. *See, e.g.,* Miller v. Houston Independent School District, 51 S.W.3d 676 (Tex. Ct. App. 2001) (upholding the dismissal of a teacher who failed to report to work following a transfer).

109. 268a Massachusetts General Laws Annotated, §§ 3-4, (2009), as amended by Chapter 20 of the Acts of 2009 (2009).

110. Family and Medical Leave Act, 29 U.S.C. § 2601 *et seq.* (2006).

111. Russo, C. J., & Massucci, J. D. (2000). Update on statutory protections for school employees: The Americans with Disabilities Act and Family and Medical Leave Act. *School Business Affairs, 66*(6), 48–53.

112. Riverview School District v. Riverview Education Association, 639 A.2d 974 (Pa. Commw. Ct. 1994).

113. *See, e.g.,* McKinnon v. Board of Education of North Bellmore Union Free School District, 709 N.Y.S.2d 104 (N.Y. App. Div. 2000) (upholding the termination of an employee for incompetence due to his excessive absenteeism).

114. *See, e.g.,* Crowston v. Jamestown Public School District, 335 N.W.2d 775 (N.D. 1983) (finding that teachers who had taken six weeks of sick leave following the birth of their babies were entitled to only three weeks of leave because the documentation submitted did not show that they were unable to work for the six weeks).

115. *See, e.g.,* Strong v. Board of Education of Uniondale Free School District, 902 F.2d 208 (2d Cir. 1990) (ruling a school board did not violate a teacher's rights by refusing to allow her to return from an extended medical absence until she provided medical records and submitted to a physical examination).

116. Walker v. Elmore County Board of Education, 379 F.3d 1249 (11th Cir. 2004).

117. Civil Rights Act of 1964, Title VII, 42 U.S.C. § 2000e *et seq.* (2006).

118. Ansonia Board of Education v. Philbrook, 479 U.S. 60 (1986).

119. Philbrook v. Ansonia Board of Education, 925 F.2d 47 (2d Cir. 1991), *cert. denied,* 501 U.S. 1218 (1991).

120. Trans World Airlines v. Hardison, 432 U.S. 63 (1977).

121. Pinsker v. Joint District No. 28J, 554 F. Supp. 1049 (D. Colo. 1983).

122. Uniformed Services Employment and Reemployment Rights Act of 1994, 38 U.S.C. §§ 4301–4335 (2006).

123. *See, e.g.,* Independent School District v. Orange, 841 P.2d 1177 Okla. Ct. App. 1992) (affirming the reinstatement of a teacher who had not been given proper notice of her deficiencies).

124. *See, e.g.,* Keesee v. Meadow Heights R-11 School District, 865 S.W.2d 818 (Mo. Ct. App. 1993) (finding that evidence supported a school board's determination that a teacher failed to improve her competency and efficiency to a sufficient degree during the curative period after she received a warning letter).

125. *See, e.g.,* Chicago Board of Education v. Smith, 664 N.E.2d 113 (Ill. Ct. App. 1996) (voiding a teacher's dismissal due to the principal's failure to follow proper dismissal procedures); Snyder v. Mendon-Union Local School District, 661 N.E.2d 717 (Ohio 1996) (reversing teacher dismissals when the school board failed to follow state statute regarding teacher evaluations).

126. *See, e.g.,* St. Louis Teachers Union v. St. Louis Board of Education, 652 F. Supp. 425 (E.D. Mo. 1987); Whaley v. Anoka-Hennepin Independent School District, 325 N.W.2d 128 (Minn. 1982); Scheelhaase v. Woodbury Central Community School District, 488 F.2d 237 (8th Cir. 1973).

127. Raisch, C. D., & Russo, C. J. (2006). The No Child Left Behind Act: Federal over-reaching or necessary educational reform? *Education Law Journal, 7,* 255–265.

128. Roberts v. Houston Independent School District, 788 S.W.2d 107 (Tex. Ct. App. 1990).

129. *See, e.g.,* Dube v. Contributory Retirement Appeal Board, 733 N.E.2d 1089 (Mass. Ct. App. 2000); Cain v. Public School Employees' Retirement Board, 651 A.2d 660 (Pa. Commw. Ct. 1994), *appeal denied* 659 A.2d 560 (Pa. 1995).

130. Parker v. Wakelin, 123 F.3d 1 (1st Cir. 1997).

131. *See, e.g.,* Holbert v. New York State Teachers' Retirement System, 840 N.Y.S.2d 655 (N.Y. App. Div. 2007); Cooper v. New York State Teachers' Retirement Board, 795 N.Y.S.2d 802 (N.Y. App. Div. 2005).

132. *See, e.g.,* Laurito v. Public School Employees' Retirement Board, 606 A.2d 609 (Pa. Commw. Ct. 1992).

133. *See, e.g.,* Upper St. Clair Education Association v. Upper St. Clair School District, 576 A.2d 1176 (Pa. Commw. Ct. 1990).

134. *See, e.g.,* Petrini v. United States, 19 Cl. Ct. 41 (1989) (upholding the nonrenewal of a contract of a teacher who had not timely accepted an offer to renew).

135. *See, e.g.,* Kilgore v. Jasper City Board of Education, 624 So. 2d 603 (Ala. Civ. App. 1993); Gould v. Board of Education of Sewanhaka Central High School District, 584 N.Y.S.2d 910 (N.Y. App. Div. 1992).

136. Mullen v. Fayettesville-Perry Local School District, 557 N.E.2d 1235 (Ohio Ct. App. 1988).

137. Mitchell v. Jackson County Board of Education, 582 So. 2d 1128 (Ala. Civ. App. 1991).

Collective Bargaining

5

INTRODUCTION

The previous chapter on teacher employment reviewed the actual terms and conditions impacting the employment rights of teachers. This chapter takes the process one step further, focusing on the rights of teachers to engage in collective bargaining that shapes the terms and conditions of their employment. Insofar as the practice of collective bargaining is governed by laws of individual states where it is permitted, it is beyond the scope of this chapter to provide a comprehensive analysis of the laws of all jurisdictions. Thus, this chapter provides an overview of key legal issues that are common to most states with examples taken from case law to illustrate where and how individual courts vary with regard to the implementation of collective bargaining agreements between teacher unions and school boards.

This chapter outlines the process of collective bargaining in education. It begins with a brief review of the history and development of labor relations in American public schools before examining the actual process of bargaining. The chapter then discusses bargaining units and their composition, the topics of bargaining, union rights, and dispute resolution, including strikes and work stoppages. The chapter rounds out by offering practical recommendations for parties involved in bargaining.

Collective bargaining, in public education, is a process whereby teacher unions, acting as sole negotiating agents of their members, meet with their school boards to negotiate the terms and conditions of their members' employment, such as salary and benefits. Collective bargaining agreements typically cover three-year periods but may exist for any length of time allowed by state law.

HISTORICAL BACKGROUND

Unions of public school teachers that engage in collective bargaining on behalf of their members are part of a professional labor movement in education that traces its origins to the mid-19th century. In 1857, the National Education Association (NEA), which describes itself as a professional organization rather than a union and is one of two bodies representing teachers, was created in Philadelphia. An organization that was initially created for male school administrators, the NEA admitted its first female member in 1866 and has grown to about 3.2 million members today.[1]

The other major teacher organization, the American Federation of Teachers (AFT), was created in Chicago in April 1916 and within a month received a charter from the private sector American Federation of Labor.[2] Today, the AFT has about 1.5 million members.[3] Although they maintain their separate identities, and stopped short of a hoped-for merger in 2001,[4] the AFT and NEA agreed to form the "NEAFT Partnership" calling for collaboration in areas of mutual interest.[5] These joint efforts have met with mixed success.

The differences between the public and private sectors aside, teacher collective bargaining is modeled largely after the process that has been used in private sector industrial labor relations since the 1930s. Following a stormy history, in an effort to instill labor peace, in 1935 Congress enacted the National Labor Relations Act (NLRA),[6] also known as the Wagner Act. Congress subsequently modified federal labor law in the Taft-Hartley Act of 1947[7] and the Landrum-Griffin Act of 1950.[8] Via mechanisms that are developed on a state-by-state basis, and that vary widely, school

> The differences between the public and private sectors aside, teacher collective bargaining is modeled largely after the process that has been used in private sector industrial labor relations since the 1930s.

boards and the unions of their teachers and other staff engage in collective bargaining over the terms and conditions of employment.

In apparently the first reported case on the question of teacher unions, *Norwalk Teachers' Association v. Board of Education of the City of Norwalk*,[9] Connecticut's highest court recognized the right of public school teachers to organize and bargain collectively with their school boards. The court added that teachers lack the right to strike or engage in concerted activities when they are unable to reach agreements with their boards over issues relating to their employment.

CASE SUMMARY 5.1: RIGHT OF UNION TO ORGANIZE

Norwalk Teachers' Association v. Board of Education of the City of Norwalk

83 A.2d 482 (Conn. 1951)

Factual Summary: Negotiations between the teachers' association and the school board ended in a dispute over salaries. After 230 teachers rejected the individual contracts that the board offered and refused to return to work, subsequent negotiations produced an agreement with teachers returning to work. Even so, questions remained regarding the interpretation of several aspects of the agreement, the rights and duties of each party, and the construction of state statutes. The parties agreed to join this action seeking the advice of the court via a declaratory judgment to resolve those issues.

Issue: Is the teachers' association permitted by state law to organize itself as a labor union for the purpose of collective bargaining?

Decision: Yes, the court ruled that the association could organize itself as a labor union.

Summary of Court's Rationale: Absent a statute or regulation prohibiting such organizations, the court saw no good reason why public employees could not organize and form labor unions. The court explained that if the school board wished to negotiate with the association over matters such as salaries, benefits, and working conditions, nothing in state law forbade it from doing so. However, the court specified that the association's organization for the purposes of demanding recognition and collective bargaining had to be kept within legal bounds. In this respect the court made it clear that the association could not engage in actions such as strikes, work stoppages, or a collective refusal to conduct teaching duties. The court added that arbitration and mediation were acceptable means of settling specific labor disputes.

The move toward teacher unions took a major step forward in 1958 when the Mayor of New York City, Robert F. Wagner, issued Executive Order 49, allowing public employees to engage in union activities.[10] A year later, in 1959, Wisconsin "passed one of [the] nation's first collective bargaining laws for public employees."[11] Three years later, 1962, became a watershed year for public employees starting with President Kennedy's Executive Order 10998, which allowed federal workers to unionize and was subsequently reinforced by President Nixon's Executive Order 11491.[12]

A one day work stoppage of public school teachers in New York City led by the United Federation of Teachers in April of 1962[13] initiated a change in labor relations that has led to large-scale teacher unionization. As of 2010, 35 states have enacted statutes permitting collective bargaining in education.[14] Moreover, data reveal that four out of five public school teachers are represented by unions or some form of professional organization.[15]

In acknowledging that not all states have enacted collective bargaining statutes, it is worth noting that the Supreme Court explained that the "first amendment does not require the government to recognize or bargain with an association of employees, but it does protect the right of an individual 'to associate with others, and to petition his government for redress of grievances'"[16] even in so-called "right to work states" where bargaining is generally not practiced.[17] Moreover, at least three state legislatures—those in North Carolina,[18] Texas,[19] and Virginia[20]—specifically prohibit collective bargaining between governmental units, including school boards and employees. Against this background, the remainder of the chapter examines the legal parameters of teacher collective bargaining.

BARGAINING UNITS AND THEIR COMPOSITION

It almost goes without saying that before teachers' unions can begin their primary responsibility of engaging the school boards of their members in negotiations, educators in local units need to select bargaining representatives to represent their interests. Depending on state law, once unions are formed, they are ordinarily recognized as the exclusive bargaining agents of their members to negotiate written agreements over the terms and conditions of their employment with their school boards.[21]

> It almost goes without saying that before teacher unions can begin their primary responsibility of engaging the school boards of their members in negotiations, educators in local units need to select bargaining representatives to represent their interests.

Once local boards and state labor relations bodies recognize exclusive bargaining representatives, these representatives alone have the duty to act on behalf of all employees in good faith[22] during negotiations. Union representatives have this duty even to individuals who are not members and who must pay so-called *agency* or *representation fees*, a topic that is discussed later in this chapter.

In order to avoid conflicts of interest, state laws usually require various school employees to organize around specific, and different, "communities of interest" such that teachers, typically referred to as professional staff, are in one unit, while other employees such as office workers and maintenance personnel, usually referred to as classified staff, are in another. For example, the Supreme Court of Minnesota affirmed that part-time early childhood family education teachers were not members of the same community of interest as the board's other teachers, because they did not provide academic instruction that was part of the school's curriculum.[23] Although exceptions exist in some large urban school systems such as in New York City, administrators who work in personnel offices and may have access to potentially sensitive employee information, and others specified by state law, are ordinarily not permitted to join or form unions.[24]

Topics of Bargaining

Insofar as the process of collective bargaining is defined by state laws that vary in specificity and that have led to a significant amount of judicial interpretation, not all jurisdictions or courts agree on which terms and conditions of employment are subject to mandatory, permissive, and prohibited subjects of bargaining.[25] One of the more controversial topics of bargaining is teacher evaluations, as some states treat it as excluded from bargaining as a prohibited topic[26] while others treat it as a mandatory[27] or a permissive[28] topic of negotiations. While conceding the difficulty in attempting to categorize the topics neatly into the three sometimes overlapping categories, the following sections review major topics under each, highlighting judicial exceptions in various jurisdictions.

Mandatory Topics of Bargaining

Mandatory topics of bargaining are those going to the heart of terms and conditions of employment such as salaries, leave, and mileage reimbursement for teachers,[29] along with fringe benefits.[30] Among the other items that courts have found to be subjects of mandatory bargaining due to their impact on terms and conditions of employment are whether teachers should be paid for specified holidays even if they were out on sick leave,[31] whether a board could subcontract out for services ordinarily performed by teachers or staff,[32]

> Mandatory topics of bargaining are those going to the heart of terms and conditions of employment such as salaries, leave, and mileage reimbursement for teachers, along with fringe benefits.

benefits that a teacher would receive under an early retirement program,[33] placement on a pay scale,[34] a proposed dress code policy for teachers,[35] whether a board could pay moving expenses for a new teacher,[36] a school board's wish to increase the number of class periods that teachers taught,[37] and job security provisions.[38]

Permissive Topics of Bargaining

Permissive topics of bargaining are those that are not prohibited by law as managerial prerogatives but that impact basic terms and conditions of employment. In considering whether topics are subject to mandatory or permissive bargaining, some courts, rather than simply proclaiming matters subject to mandatory bargaining, have suggested guidelines beyond such basic restatements as conditions of employment, managerial prerogatives, and basic policy issues. The courts caution that such judgments must be made on case-by-case bases.

> Permissive topics of bargaining are those that are not prohibited by law as managerial prerogatives but that impact basic terms and conditions of employment.

Among the permissive topics that courts have recognized are so-called zipper clauses, which allow parties to renegotiate items in midcontract,[39] whether a board would have its students and teachers participate in academic summer school program,[40] whether a school board could adopt a year-around school calendar,[41] a board's harassment-violence policy,[42] teacher preparation periods,[43] and teacher assignments and transfers.[44]

Prohibited Topics of Bargaining

> States generally prohibit bargaining on topics of educational policy or managerial prerogatives.

States generally prohibit bargaining on topics of educational policy or managerial prerogatives.[45] As stated by Pennsylvania statute, this means that boards are not

required to bargain over matters of inherent managerial policy, which shall include but shall not be limited to such areas of discretion or policy as the functions and programs of the public employer, standards of services, its overall budget, utilization of technology, the organizational structure and selection and direction of personnel.[46]

Courts have found that such issues as requiring teachers to take written assessment tests prior to the renewal of their licenses;[47] hiring teachers,[48] principals[49] and department heads;[50] granting tenure;[51] abolishing jobs;[52] and nonrenewing teacher contracts[53] are prohibited.

UNION RIGHTS

Unions of public school teachers seeking to represent their members, unlike those in the private sector, which is governed by the NLRA, are forbidden from establishing "union" or "closed" shops requiring all employees to join unions within set periods of time after being hired.[54] Since state laws do not mandate that teachers join unions, but most do allow them to do so, unions operate with one of two kinds of "shops." In *agency* or *fair share* shops, teachers are not required to join unions but are expected to pay a "fair share" of the expenses that unions expend on their behalf; these fees often come close to equaling the cost of becoming a union member. On the other hand, in *open* shops, employees are neither obligated to join unions nor to pay fair share fees.

Insofar as fair share fee arrangements are common, two key issues have arisen over the payment of union dues. In order to keep labor peace, the laws in most states permitting teacher collective bargaining allow school boards to collect union fees on behalf of labor organizations by asking employees to "check off" their consent in the box on an appropriate form.[55] By checking off the box, union members signify that they are permitting their school board to deduct portions of their salary and pay it directly to their union. Whether boards can permit such "checking off" is typically a permissive subject of bargaining.[56]

The second issue associated with unions, which concerns whether nonmembers must pay fees, has been much more contentious. As noted, the NLRA permits agency shop arrangements, whereby nonmembers must pay unions for the services that the unions render in negotiating terms and conditions of employment for all employees.[57]

Consistent with Supreme Court precedent,[58] albeit from the private sector, and following the lead of the NLRA, 19 jurisdictions have adopted laws allowing teacher unions to collect agency fees in order to receive additional financial support.[59] Even so, in light of significant disagreements over how unions may spend these funds, the Court has seen fit to address the constitutionality of fair share fees in five different disputes that have been litigated in educational contexts since 1977. These cases also raised important related First Amendment free speech claims about the extent to which teachers who are not members of unions may be required to provide financial support for causes they do not support or activities with which they do not agree.

> In its first case addressing fair share fees in a K–12 context, . . . the Supreme Court upheld the constitutionality of an agency shop agreement.

In its first case addressing fair share fees in a K–12 context, *Abood v. Detroit Board of Education*,[60] the Supreme Court upheld the constitutionality of an agency shop agreement. In so doing, the Court explained that while unions may collect fees for their legitimate expenses, they may not charge nonmembers for expenses supporting ideological causes that are unrelated to bargaining.

The Supreme Court's judgment in *Chicago Teachers Union v. Hudson*[61] reiterated that unions may not use agency fees to pay for activities that are irrelevant to bargaining and that, in this case, the procedures that the union had used to calculate the amount of fees had been inadequate. At the heart of its analysis, the Court rejected what was essentially a rebate plan for nonmember teachers, where the union returned funds to nonmembers that it had not spent on bargaining. The court invalidated this plan as deficient, because union officials had neither offered adequate information justifying the amount of agency fees they charged nor provided reasonably prompt answers about how they spent fees they collected.

Lehnert v. Ferris Faculty Association,[62] a dispute from higher education, is important for the K–12 context, because in it the Supreme Court clarified which expenses unions may charge to dissenters in their ranks and to nonmembers. The Court pointed out that the dissenters and non-union members could be charged a pro rata share of costs for activities of state and national union affiliates even if these activities did not directly benefit their bargaining units. More important, the Court specified that unions may not charge objecting employees for expenses of legislative lobbying and other political activities, for litigation, or for public relations activities that are unrelated to local bargaining units.

The Supreme Court placed greater restrictions on the ability of unions to spend the fair share fees of nonmembers in *Davenport v. Washington Education Association*.[63] The Court unanimously decided that state law could require a teachers' union to obtain affirmative written approval from nonmembers before spending their agency fees for election-related purposes. The Court ruled that teachers who did not belong to the union should have been able to enjoy the benefits of membership without having to support all of its related political activities.

Most recently, in *Ysursa v. Pocatello Education Association*,[64] the Supreme Court placed further limits on the ability of teachers' unions to spend the fair share fees of nonmembers. The Court upheld a ban on public employee

CASE SUMMARY 5.2: VALIDITY OF AGENCY SHOP PROVISIONS

Abood v. Detroit Board of Education

431 U.S. 209 (1977)

Factual Summary: Teachers who opposed collective bargaining for public employees filed suit challenging a Michigan statute authorizing a union and a public employer to agree on an agency shop arrangement whereby the employees represented by the union would pay union dues or face dismissal. The teachers also contested the allocation of a portion of the union dues to support a variety of activities that were economic, political, professional, or religious but were not directly related to collective bargaining. After an intermediate state appellate court upheld the constitutionality of the agency shop clause in the teachers' contract but reversed and remanded on other grounds, and the Supreme Court of Michigan refused to intervene, the teachers sought further review by the U.S. Supreme Court.

Issue: May teachers who do not belong to the union but benefit from collective bargaining be charged an agency fee?

Decision: Yes, the Supreme Court vacated the state court's decision and remanded the case back to the court for additional consideration of the extent to which nonmembers could be required to pay to support ideological positions with which they did not agree.

Summary of Court's Rationale: The Supreme Court ruled that the agency shop clause of the teachers' collective bargaining agreement was valid and did not violate the First Amendment as long as the charges were used to finance collective bargaining, contract administration, and grievance adjustments. However, the Court observed that the Constitution forbids requiring teachers to pay for union expenditures for ideological causes that are irrelevant to the union's organizational duties as a collective bargaining representative. The Court added that when teachers object to how their money is being spent, they must notify union officials of their objections in general terms so that they do not have to reveal their positions on specific issues. Thus, the Court held that the First Amendment prohibited the union and school board from requiring teachers to contribute to the support of ideological causes they might oppose as a condition of holding jobs as public school teachers.

payroll deductions for political activities at the local level, because it was satisfied that the law advanced the state's interest in separating the operation of government from partisan politics.

DISPUTE RESOLUTION

As can readily be expected, labor relations between school boards and the unions of their employees do not always run smoothly, particularly when there are constraints on financial resources. Consequently, collective bargaining contracts ordinarily specify the types of dispute resolution processes that unions and school boards are to use in the event that disagreements arise.

> Collective bargaining contracts ordinarily specify the types of dispute resolution processes that unions and school boards are to use in the event that disagreements arise.

Depending on state law and local contracts, disagreements between unions and boards begin with what may be multiple levels of grievances that operate pursuant to local procedures before heading to the more significant step of arbitration and ultimately potential litigation over the rights of individuals or unions as a whole.

Arbitration and Mediation

As part of the dispute resolution process, teacher unions and their boards ordinarily include provisions in their collective bargaining agreements voluntarily agreeing to submit their disputes to arbitration. In arbitration, the parties agree to abide by the authority of an independent third party decision maker that they have chosen to resolve their disagreements in quasi-judicial or administrative settings in which the rules of evidence and court procedures are relaxed. Insofar as arbitration is an alternative to judicial review, as long as arbitrators draw their judgments from the essence of the underlying collective bargaining contracts, the courts tend to leave original adjudications in place, especially if dissatisfied employees failed to exhaust administrative remedies under their negotiated agreements.[65]

It is important to distinguish arbitration from mediation, fact-finding, or other forms of conflict resolution that do not result in orders that are legally binding. There are two different types of arbitration. *Interest arbitration* concerns the terms of an agreement, while *rights* or *grievance arbitration* focuses on a provision's application to an existing agreement. Grievance arbitration, which is more widely used in public schools, considers whether a term in a bargaining contract is subject to the authority of a third party arbitrator or whether it is exempt from arbitration as a managerial prerogative.

After some initial reluctance to permit grievance arbitration, the majority of courts have agreed that it is permissible as long as the parties voluntarily agreed to participate in the process and boards have the statutory power to do so. In other words, courts examine whether boards that consent to arbitration to resolve labor disputes have impermissibly delegated their authority to third parties. In other words, courts ask whether it was allowable for the parties to have gone to arbitration in the first place.

> After some initial reluctance to permit grievance arbitration, the majority of courts have agreed that it is permissible as long as the parties voluntarily agreed to participate in the process and boards have the statutory power to do so.

The use of grievance arbitration has led to a fair amount of litigation in which courts typically have avoided the merits of claims, instead focusing on whether contractual language in the parties' original agreement expressed an intent to submit disagreements to arbitrators. If courts are content that arbitration was permissible, they generally do not disturb the results of the arbitration, as long as the arbitrators have rationally drawn their results from the essence of underlying language in collective bargaining agreements[66] and, as discussed below, as long as the proposed remedies violate neither the law nor the managerial authority of school boards, such as to terminate the employment of staff members for cause. Still, courts have reached varied results on what topics may properly be subject to arbitration.

Topics that courts have agreed were subject to arbitration included the following:

- Upholding an order that a 10-day suspension was a more appropriate punishment than dismissal for a teacher who used questionable force against a student[67]
- Entitling new teachers to credit on their pay scale for time they worked as substitutes[68]
- Interpreting the meaning of teacher overloads and planning time[69]
- Reviewing whether a school board improperly directed teachers to add duties as bus aides to their job responsibilities[70]
- Agreeing that long-term substitute teachers who were part of a bargaining unit were entitled to pay and benefits identified in a bargaining agreement[71]
- Reinstating a teacher who had been suspended without just cause and paying his legal fees[72]
- Allowing sick leave to be used to attend a medical appointment with a family member[73]
- Failing to advance teachers on a pay scale[74]
- Awarding back pay to a teacher who had been improperly compensated[75]

On the other hand, topics that courts agreed were not subject to arbitration included these:

- Reviewing whether a teacher used excessive force against a sixth grader[76]
- Determining qualifications for a substitute teacher[77]
- Distinguishing between the duties of computer technicians and their assistants[78]
- Suspending a teacher for one year for engaging in an improper relationship with a 16-year-old student[79]
- Awarding salary and health insurance buyouts to a probationary teacher whose contract was not renewed[80]
- Considering whether an employee had medical clearance to return to work after suffering from a psychological condition after having been robbed at gunpoint[81]
- Deciding whether a teacher who lost her professional certification could have been reinstated[82]
- Reinstating a classroom assistant who was found unconscious in a restroom suffering from a drug overdose[83]

When unions engage in their primary responsibility of negotiating agreements but are unable to reach agreements with their school boards at the expiration of their contracts, the parties may declare an impasse and, depending on state law, move on to mediation and/or fact-finding.[84] Since these disagreements can often lead to strikes or work slowdowns, the next section of the chapter examines what happens under these circumstances.

Work Stoppages and Strikes

Throughout the history of the American labor movement, strikes have been a tool that labor has used commonly in attempting to achieve its goals in resolving disagreements with management. At the same time, though, legislatures and courts have been much less willing to permit strikes by teachers and other public employees because of the essential duties that they perform. Further, to the extent that teachers appropriately wish to be considered professionals, an argument can be made that professionals do not engage in strikes and other concerted labor stoppages.[85] Fortunately, since strikes by teachers, whether legal or illegal, are uncommon, some of the litigation in

> Throughout the history of the American labor movement, strikes have been a tool that labor has used commonly in attempting to achieve its goals in resolving disagreements with management. At the same time, though, legislatures and courts have been much less willing to permit strikes by teachers and other public employees because of the essential duties that they perform.

this section, particularly with regard to sanctions, is a bit dated, because these are such well-settled issues of law.

As noted earlier, Connecticut's highest court, although conceding that educators had the right to bargain collectively, reasoned that teacher strikes were illegal.[86] Along with common law barriers against teacher strikes, courts continued to uphold long-standing statutory prohibitions against strikes.[87] A limited number of jurisdictions grant teachers a qualified right to strike,[88] meaning, for example, that they may typically do so only after negotiations have broken down and the parties have declared an impasse in bargaining.[89]

When teachers threaten either to strike or to engage in illegal work stoppages, school boards,[90] but not private citizens,[91] can seek injunctions to prevent them from doing so. With respect to actions short of actually striking, courts have ruled that teachers may not engage in mass absences,[92] large-scale resignations,[93] or picketing. However, courts have been reluctant to prevent teachers from engaging in so-called informational picketing while work continues, unless the teachers' actions have been likely to be disruptive to school environments.[94]

Courts have the authority to punish union leaders, unions, and teachers who participate in strikes. For instance, an appellate court in New York found a union leader who led a strike in contempt of court,[95] while the highest courts in Delaware[96] and Massachusetts[97] fined officials and their unions. Also, the Second Circuit affirmed an order of the New York State Labor Relations Board denying a union the dues check-off privilege in the interest of ensuring labor peace in light of its having participated in an illegal strike.[98] Courts have punished teachers who took part in illegal strikes by allowing their employment to be terminated,[99] withholding salary for days missed during strikes,[100] and imposing fines on striking teachers as means of essentially reimbursing their boards for the expenses incurred, such as paying substitutes, in response to their missing work while on strike.[101]

SUMMARY AND RECOMMENDATIONS

Collective bargaining agreements are legally binding contacts to the extent that they are written agreements between parties specifying the duties and obligations of school boards and the unions of their teachers, such as terms and conditions of employment, while also stipulating how the parties are to resolve any resulting labor disputes. At the same time, since state statutes set forth minimal expectations in bargaining, the parties are free to negotiate greater rights, such as in dispute resolution processes or the nonrenewal of teacher contacts, to the extent that these modifications grant individuals greater, rather than less, protection than would be afforded by law.

At the same time, collective bargaining agreements differ from most contracts, because even though they ordinarily are not permitted to exceed three years in length,[102] they are essentially ongoing legal relationships that do not terminate completely on expiration. Put another way, since educators, particularly at the building level, whether they serve as union representatives or administrators, must monitor contracts on an almost daily basis to ensure compliance on both sides, they are well aware of how labor agreements are "living documents." Further, by paying regular attention to ensure that collective bargaining contracts are interpreted and applied consistently, educators on both sides can help to avoid having to rely on their dispute resolution provisions. Keeping the need to ensure smooth labor relations in school systems in order to focus on educating children in mind, the following recommendations—offering suggestions to be followed before, during, and after bargaining—should assist teachers, their unions, and boards to negotiate the bargaining process more smoothly.[103]

Before Bargaining

- As both sides prepare for renewing or reopening bargaining agreements under so-called zipper agreements that allow parties to open their contracts up at times other than when their terms have expired, leadership should select teams that are representative of various constituencies. In other words, both sides at the table should include teachers from different types of schools (elementary, middle, secondary), while the team from the school board also should include representatives from the central office and building level.
- It is important to keep in mind that both superintendents and school board members are eligible to become members of their bargaining teams. Even so, it is unwise to include either superintendents or board members on teams, because insofar as they ultimately are responsible for implementing and approving contracts, it is best that they not participate in the bargaining. That way, if there has been acrimony at the bargaining table, it should not carry over into their jobs.
- Depending on the circumstances, boards might wish to consider using outside negotiators, because, by avoiding direct involvement in what can be a contentious process, superintendents, in particular, can keep open minds in communications with their board members and various constituencies, including the unions.

- If a superintendent participates in the bargaining process with one union (such as that of teachers) but does not do so for all unions, another union (such as administrative assistants) may be offended, regardless of whether there may have been different circumstances. This leaves the door open to labor strife that could easily have been avoided.

- Especially in smaller districts where labor relations have proceeded smoothly, superintendents and/or board members may wish to become involved in negotiations, especially if this has been done in the past. However, if it appears that negotiations are going to be difficult, it is all the wiser to rely on an outside negotiator, so that the superintendent and other educational leaders can, if things become difficult, "blame the outsider," who is unlikely to be present once negotiations are over and the parties are implementing the bargaining agreement.

- In a closely related point, unions and school boards should think about how many members will actually participate in bargaining sessions. To this end, it is important to keep in mind that having more than five or six members at the bargaining table can become unwieldy when discussions heat up. Thus, it is better to have fewer, rather than more, individuals engaged in the actual bargaining process, and all members of a team should be under the direction of one designated negotiator. This position can rotate depending on the issue under consideration.

- Both sides should encourage team members to express their viewpoints in planning sessions and, if interest-based bargaining is used, in actual negotiations. If, as noted above, the parties engage in traditional bargaining, each side should identify a spokesperson who will do most of the talking during negotiating sessions.

- Both sides should agree to develop ground rules for bargaining sessions. Prior to the first meeting, the parties should agree on important considerations, such as whether to engage in traditional (and typically more adversarial) or interest-based (also referred to as collaborative) bargaining. The teams should also decide where to meet, whether in the board office, a school, or a neutral location, and designate a meeting time and date.

- In what initially seems like a small matter, it may be very important to members of the employee unions to determine in advance whether meetings will take place during school hours or after-school hours. It appears to be in the best interest of school boards to be open on this latter point and to do all that they can to ensure that negotiations get off to a smooth start.

- Prior to engaging in bargaining there are two additional items that unions and boards need to address. First, both sides should provide training sessions for members of their bargaining team in order to prepare for negotiations. Second, teams should develop planned strategies. In other worlds, along with making note of which items are mandatory, permissive, and prohibited topics of bargaining, each side should identify and prioritize what they believe they need to gain in order to reach an agreement on their terms.

- More specifically, unions and boards should prioritize items they are willing to compromise on to reach an agreement while identifying topics that they are willing to "give away" as bargaining chips in order to procure more significant items. It is important, during the initial session, to share items for consideration and to make sure that each item is clearly understood by both parties.

- In a final prebargaining step that overlaps with the negotiation process, even though meetings typically take place at the central offices of school boards, education officials should treat both sides equally. This means, for instance, that the sides should take turns selecting meeting times, so the sessions do not always convene at times that are inconvenient for one side. This is particularly important when teachers are involved, so that they will not have to miss classes.

- Both sides need to be sure to share and agree on accurate data such as financial information and the number of employees, since these will occupy vital roles in the final agreement. In this regard, it is essential that board officials ensure that both bargaining teams have equal access to technology including telephones, faxes, and computers that are invaluable during the negotiations process.

- It is essential that board officials ensure that both bargaining teams have equal access to separate rooms to caucus during breaks.

During Bargaining

- Once bargaining is under way, union and school board negotiators must be mindful of applicable legal constraints, keeping in mind that legal requirements vary from one state to the next. An issue that both sides need to be cognizant of concerns the dates by which nonrenewal and tenure decisions must be made, since these frequently relate to questions that arise in bargaining and implementing contracts.

- Both sides should come to and leave the bargaining table with a collaborative, winning attitude. Each party should develop a positive, agreement-based momentum by trying to start out with easier items that can be resolved with little or no conflict. Adopting a positive approach can avoid adversarial stances and can help to build a basis of trust between the parties that can lead to a quick and successful round of negotiations. Along these lines, it would be wise for the spokespersons to meet before and after each session to ensure understanding of all issues and to provide each other with an overview of where negotiations are headed.

- Parties should formalize verbal agreements in writing as soon as possible, meaning before the end of bargaining sessions, and have formal confirmations that the agreements meet the expectations of both sides.

- Once bargaining teams have agreed on contract language, they should reduce it to writing and finalize preliminary acceptance of those terms subject to final approval by voting members of unions and school boards accordingly.

- Unions and boards should have their attorneys present at bargaining sessions to ensure that they have the precise language that all have accepted in negotiating preliminary contractual agreements. Adopting such an approach can help to eliminate confusion at the bargaining table and later when the agreement is shared with the remainder of the school community. Further, the chairpersons of both teams should meet after each session to confirm the content of the items that the parties have resolved.

After Bargaining

Once the bargaining process is complete and contracts are signed, two important points need to be considered:

- First, both union and school board officials must act in good faith in implementing their agreements, particularly with regard to the dispute resolution process, because it can generate a great deal of conflict that can be avoided with some careful planning and follow-through.

- Second, since collective bargaining is an ongoing legal relationship or process that is revisited every three years, leaders on both sides of the table should keep a running list of items that may have to be reviewed the next time that contracts are up for renegotiation. Keeping a list of items that need to be addressed can help to reduce the stress of preparing for sessions while also helping to ensure a smoother process. This benefits all participants and culminates in good labor relations in public school systems.

FREQUENTLY ASKED QUESTIONS

Q. I work in a small school district with a union, but all I do with the union is pay my dues; I do not have the time or desire to become involved in negotiations. Why should I read about collective bargaining?

A. There are two reasons why you should want to read this chapter. First, since what occurs in bargaining impacts your job as a teacher, the chapter will help to keep you better informed as to what takes places when your contract is being renegotiated. Second, since you are in a small district, some day you may be asked to step up and become involved in bargaining. If this happens, the chapter is designed to provide you with a good overview of the process, making it possible for you to be up-to-date and informed when you participate in sessions and other union activities.

Q. I do not want to join the union in my school. What are my options?

A. As a public school teacher, you may not be obligated to join the union in your district. However, depending on state law, you may have to pay a fair agency fee that compensates the union for its efforts on your behalf in negotiating the terms and conditions of your employment, such as salary raises and medical benefits. Depending on local circumstances, fair share fees can cost almost the same amount as union dues.

Q. A few years ago, there was talk of a strike in our district that never materialized. What might have happened if the teachers went out on strike?

A. The answer depends on where you live. In some states, teachers have a limited right to engage in strikes but can do so only after their union has declared an impasse signaling a breakdown in bargaining with their school boards. Then, before a strike may occur, a specified number of days, identified in state statute, may first have to pass. If the union had followed all of the statutory procedures and you had gone out on strike, you would not have had to worry about the loss of your job, but, again, depending on the law in your state, you may have had your pay docked for the days you missed work. In other states, where teacher strikes are against the law, you could have lost your pay, been fined, and/or been fired from your job.

WHAT'S NEXT

The next chapter outlines the various federal statutes and constitutional provisions that provide teachers with protections against discrimination in the workplace. Specifically, it includes discussions of those areas expressly enumerated in Title VII of the Civil Rights Act of 1964 along with information on more recent statutes protecting teachers from other forms of discrimination.

ENDNOTES

1. National Education Association. (2010). *Our history.* Retrieved from www.nea.org/home/1704.htm

2. American Federation of Teachers. (2010). *American Federation of Teachers, AFL-CIO.* Retrieved from www.aft.org/about

3. *Id.*

4. Archer, J. (2001). NEA board approves AFT 'partnership' pact. *Education Week, 20*(23), 3.

5. Archer, J. (2001). Unions cement partnership to work on range of projects. *Education Week, 20*(43), 9.

6. 29 U.S.C. §§151–169 (2006).

7. 29 USC §§ 141 *et seq.* (2006).

8. 29 USC §§ 401 *et seq.* (2006).

9. 83 A.2d 482 (Conn. 1951).

10. Tyler, G. (1976). Why they organize. In A. M. Cresswell & M. J. Murphy (Eds.), *Education and collective bargaining: Readings in policy and research*, pp. 12–21. Berkeley, CA: McCutchan.

11. Wisconsin Labor History Society. (2010). *Primer.* Retrieved from http://wisconsinlaborhistory.org/?page_id=34

12. Cresswell, A. M., & Murphy, M. J., with Kerchner, C. T. (1980). *Teachers, unions, and collective bargaining in public education.* Berkeley, CA: McCutchan.

13. Kerchner, C. T., & Mirchell, D. E. (1988). *The changing idea of a teachers' union.* London: Falmer Press.

14. Education Commission of the States. (2010). *State notes.* Retrieved from http://mb2.ecs.org/reports/Report.aspx?id=173

15. Moe, T. M. (2006). Political control and the power of the agent. *Journal of Law, Economics and Organization, 22*(1), 1–29.

16. Smith v. Arkansas State Highway Employees, Local 1315, 441 U.S. 463, 464 (1979).

17. Russo, C. J. (2002). Right-to-work and fair share agreements: A delicate balance. *School Business Affairs, 68*(4), 12–15.

18. North Carolina General Statutes Annotated §§ 95–98 (2010).

19. Texas Government Code Annotated § 617.002 (2010).

20. Virginia Code Annotated § 40.1–57.2 (2010).

21. Appeal of Londonderry School District, 707 A.2d 137 (N.H. 1998).

22. Fratus v. Marion Community Schools Board of Trustees, 749 N.E.2d 40 (Ind. 2001).

23. Education Minnesota-Chisholm v. Independent School District No. 695, 662 N.W.2d 139 (Minn. 2003).

24. Niles Township High School District 219, Cook County v. Illinois, 900 N.E.2d 336 (Ill. App. Ct. 2008). *See also* 71 Massachusetts General Laws § 41, which states that "School principals . . . shall not be represented in collective bargaining. . . ."

25. Colonial School Board v. Colonial Affiliate, NCCEA/DSEA/NEA, 449 A.2d 243 (Del. Super. Ct. 1982).

26. Bethlehem Township Board of Education v. Bethlehem Township Education Association, 449 A.2d 1254 (N.J. 1982).

27. Board of Education, Unified School District No. 314, Brewster, Thomas County v. Kansas Department of Human Resources By and Through Dick, 856 P.2d 1343 (Kan. Ct. App. 1993), *review denied* (Kan. 1993).

28. In re White Mountain Regional School District, 908 A.2d 790 (N.H. 2006).

29. Fort Stewart Schools v. Federal Labor Relations Authority, 495 U.S. 641 (1990).

30. Crete Education Association v. Saline County School District No. 76-0002, 654 N.W.2d 166 (Neb. 2002).

31. Cadott Education Association v. Wisconsin Employment Relations Commission, 540 N.W.2d 21 (Wis. Ct. App. 1995).

32. Matter of Watkins Glen Central School District/Watkins Glen Faculty Association, 628 N.Y.S.2d 824 (N.Y. App. Div. 1995).

33. Ringgold School District v. Ringgold Education Association, 694 A.2d 1163 (Pa. Commw. Ct. 1997).

34. Waterloo Community Education Association v. Public Employment Relations Board, 650 N.W.2d 627 (Iowa 2000).

35. Polk County Board of Education v. Polk County Education Association, 139 S.W.3d 304 (Tenn. Ct. App. 2004).

36. Ekalaka Unified Board of Trustees v. Ekalaka Teachers' Association, 149 P.3d 902 (Mont. 2006).

37. Kent County Education Association/Cedar Springs Education Association v. Cedar Springs Public Schools, 403 N.W.2d 494 (Mich. Ct. App. 1987).

38. Peninsula School District No. 401 v. Public School Employees of Peninsula, 924 P.2d 13 (Wash. 1996).

39. Mt. Vernon Education Association, IEA–NEA v. Illinois Education Labor Relations Board, 663 N.E.2d 1067 (Ill. App. Ct. 1996).

40. Webster Central School District v. Public Employment Relations Board of State of N.Y., 555 N.Y.S.2d 245 (N.Y. 1990).

41. Racine Education Association v. Wisconsin Employment Relations Commission, 571 N.W.2d 887 (Wis. Ct. App. 1997).

42. Lipka v. Minnesota School Employees Association, Local 1980, 537 N.W.2d 624 (Minn. Ct. App. 1995), *affirmed,* 550 N.W.2d 618 (Minn. 1996).

43. Dodgeland Education Association v. Wisconsin Employment Relations Commission, 639 N.W.2d 733 (Wis. 2002).

44. Bonner School District No. 14 v. Bonner Education Association, 176 P.3d 262 (Mont. 2008).

45. Montgomery County Education Association, v. Board of Education of Montgomery County, 534 A.2d 980 (Md. 1987).

46. 43 Pennsylvania Statutes § 1101.72 (2010).

47. Massachusetts Federation of Teachers, AFT, AFL-CIO v. Board of Education, 767 N.E.2d 549 (Mass. 2002).

48. Board of Directors of Maine School Administrative District No. 36 v. Maine School Administrative District No. 36 Teachers Association, 428 A.2d 419 (Me. 1981).

49. Berkshire Hills Regional School District Committee v. Berkshire Hills Education Association, 377 N.E.2d 940 (Mass. 1978).

50. Maine School Administrative District No. 61 Board of Directors. v. Lake Region Teachers Association, 567 A.2d 77 (Me. 1989).

51. Cohoes City School District v. Cohoes Teachers Association, 390 N.Y.S.2d 53 (N.Y. 1976).

52. School Committee of Braintree v. Raymond, 343 N.E.2d 145 (Mass. 1976).

53. Sunnyvale Unified School District v. Jacobs, 89 Cal. Rptr. 3d 546 (Cal. Ct. App. 2009).

54. *See, e.g.,* Ohio Revised Code § 4117.09(C) (2010).

55. *See, e.g.,* 43 Pennsylvania Statutes § 1101.75 (2010).

56. *See, e.g.,* 43 Pennsylvania Statutes § 1101.75 (2010).

57. 29 U.S.C. § 158(a)(3).

58. Machinists v. Street, 367 U.S. 740 (1961).

59. National Institute for Labor Relations Research. (2010). *Compulsory unionism in the United States.* Retrieved from http://www.nilrr.org/node/13

60. 431 U.S. 209 (1977).

61. 475 U.S. 292 (1986).

62. 500 U.S. 507 (1991).

63. 551 S. Ct. 177 (2007).

64. 129 S. Ct. 1093 (2009).

65. Davis v. Chester Upland School District, 786 A.2d 186 (Pa. 2001).

66. Juniata Mifflin Counties Area Vocational-Technical School v. Corbin, 691 A.2d 924 (Pa. 1997).

67. Union River Valley Teachers Association v. Lamoine School Commission, 748 A.2d 990 (Me. 2000).

68. Chambersburg Area School District v. Chambersburg Area Education Association, 811 A.2d 78 (Pa. Commw. Ct. 2002).

69. MTI v. Madison Metropolitan School District, 678 N.W.2d 311 (Wis. Ct. App. 2004).

70. Crow v. Wayne County Board of Education, 599 S.E.2d 822 (W. Va. 2004).

71. Somerset Area School District v. Somerset Education Association, 899 A.2d 1170 (Pa. Commw Ct. 2006).

72. Marion Community School Corporation v. Marion Teachers Association, 873 N.E.2d 605 (Ind. Ct. App. 2007).

73. Allegheny Valley School District v. Allegheny Valley Education Association, 943 A.2d 1021 (Pa. Commw. Ct. 2008).

74. Northwest Area School District v. Northwest Education Association, 954 A.2d 111 (Pa. Commw. Ct. 2008).

75. Baldwin-Woodville Area School District v. West Central Education Association–Baldwin Woodville Unit, 766 N.W.2d 591 (Wis. 2009).

76. School District of Beverly v. Geller, 737 N.E.2d 873 (Mass. App. Ct. 2000).

77. United Federation of Teachers, Local 2 v. Board of Education of the City School District of the City of N.Y., 746 N.Y.S.2d 7 (N.Y. App. Div 2002).

78. District 318 Service Employees Association v. Independent School District No. 318, 649 N.W.2d 896 (Minn. Ct. App. 2002).

79. In re Binghamton City School District, 823 N.Y.S.2d 231 (N.Y. App. Div. 2006).

80. In re Liberty Central School District, 808 N.Y.S.2d 445 (N.Y. App. Div. 2006).

81. National Association of Government Employees Local R1-200 v. City of Bridgeport, 912 A.2d 539 (Conn. Ct. App. 2007).

82. New York State Office of Children & Family Services v. Lanterman, 879 N.Y.S.2d 247 (N.Y. App. Div. 2009).

83. Westmoreland Intermediate Unit # 7 v. Westmoreland Intermediate Unit # 7 Classroom Assistants Education Support Personnel Association, 977 A.2d 1205 (Pa. Commw. Ct. 2009).

84. *See, e.g.,* Ohio Revised Code § 4117.14(C) (2010).

85. Geisert, G., & Lieberman, M. (1994). *Teacher union bargaining: Practice and policy.* Chicago: Precept Press.

86. Norwalk Teachers' Association v. Board of Education, 83 A.2d 482 (Conn. 1951).

87. Commonwealth Employment Relations Board v. Boston Teachers Union, 908 N.E.2d (Mass. App. Ct. 2009).

88. Martin v. Montezuma-Cortez School District RE-1, 841 P.3d 237 (Colo. 1992).

89. *See, e.g.,* Ohio Revised Code § 4117.01(I) (2010).

90. *See, e.g.,* Ohio Revised Code §§ 4117.15, 16 (2010), and Central Lakes Education Association v. Independent School District No. 743, Sauk Centre, 411 N.W.2d 875 (Minn. Ct. App. 1987).

91. Wilson v. Pulaski Association of Classroom Teachers, 954 S.W.2d 221 (Ark. 1997).

92. Pruzan v. Board of Education of the City of N.Y., 217 N.Y.S.2d 86 (N.Y. 1961).

93. Board of Education of the City of N.Y. v. Shanker, 286 N.Y.S.2d 453 (N.Y. App. Div. 1967).

94. Board of Education of Danville Community Consol. School District No. 118 v. Danville Education Association, 376 N.E.2d 430 (Ill. App. Ct. 1978).

95. Board of Education of the City of N.Y. v. Shanker, 286 N.Y.S.2d 453 (N.Y. App. Div. 1967).

96. Wilmington Federation of Teachers v. Howell, 374 A.2d 832 (Del. 1977).

97. Labor Relations Commission v. Fall River Education Association, 416 N.E.2d 1340 (Mass. 1981).

98. Buffalo Teachers Federation v. Helsby, 676 F.2d 28 (2d Cir. 1982).

99. Hortonville Joint School District No. 1 v. Hortonville Education Association, 426 U.S. 482 (1976).

100. Board of Education of Marshallton-McKean School District v. Sinclair, 373 A.2d 572 (Del. 1977).

101. Passaic Township Board of Education v. Passaic Township Education Association, 536 A.2d 1276 (N.J. Super. Ct. App. Div. 1987).

102. *See, e.g.,* Ohio Revised Code § 4117.09(R) (2010).

103. Raisch, C. D., & Russo, C. J. (2005). How to succeed at collective bargaining. *School Business Affairs, 71*(11), 8–10.

Prohibitions Against Employment Discrimination

6

INTRODUCTION

Discrimination can be defined as the unfair treatment or denial of normal privileges to individuals because of innate characteristics such as their race, sex, age, nationality, or religion. Discrimination occurs when people are treated unequally due to those characteristics. The Equal Protection Clause of the Fourteenth Amendment to the U.S. Constitution[1] along with a variety of important federal and state statutes protect employees and applicants for public employment from discrimination based on factors such as race, color, ethnicity, national origin, religion, gender, age, and disability.

Prohibitions against discrimination extend to any aspect of employment, including hiring, training, firing, layoffs, wages, fringe benefits, job assignments, promotions, and any other condition of employment. Various sections of the Civil Rights Act of 1964,[2] particularly Title VII, provide many of these protections.

The Civil Rights Act of 1964 was initially proposed by President John F. Kennedy but was signed into law by President Lyndon B. Johnson following Kennedy's assassination. The most sweeping civil rights statute enacted since the Reconstruction period following the Civil War, the Civil Rights Act of 1964 prohibited discrimination in public places while mandating the integration of public facilities, including schools. While this statute addressed discrimination based on race, color, national origin, religion, and sex, later legislation makes it illegal to discriminate on the basis of other factors such as age, disability, and genetics.

Title VII of the Civil Rights Act of 1964,[3] arguably the most far-reaching statute prohibiting employment discrimination and the model for other federal and state antidiscrimination statutes, declares, in part, that it is illegal for an employer

(1) to fail or refuse to hire or to discharge any individual, or otherwise to discriminate against any individual, with respect to his compensation, terms, conditions, or privileges of employment, because of such individual's race, color, religion, sex, or national origin; or

(2) to limit, segregate, or classify his employees or applicants for employment in any way which would deprive or tend to deprive any individual of employment opportunities or otherwise adversely affect his status as an employee, because of such individual's race, color, religion, sex, or national origin.[4]

Based on Supreme Court guidance, lower courts examine discrimination claims on two theories: *disparate treatment* and *disparate impact*. Litigants alleging disparate treatment need to show that they were treated unequally, with the intent to discriminate, due to their membership in a protected class. On the other hand, to prove disparate impact, claimants need to demonstrate that what appear to be neutral criteria, in fact, have a discriminatory result. Thus, employers are required to remove artificial, arbitrary, or unnecessary barriers that result in discrimination on the basis of an impermissible classification.[5]

An example of a disparate treatment claim would be a case where a female teacher files suit after a less qualified male is granted a promotional position. A case from the Fourth Circuit provides a good example of disparate impact. An unsuccessful minority applicant for a teaching position in Virginia challenged the school board's practice of advertising vacant positions by word of mouth and hiring relatives of current employees. Ruling in favor of the applicant, the court found that even though the board's failure to consider her for a job opening was a mistake rather than intentional discrimination, since most of its then-current employees were white, the board's reliance on nepotism had a disparate impact on minorities, in violation of Title VII. Consequently, the court ordered the board to discontinue the use of its discriminatory hiring practices.[6]

Most civil rights laws also forbid employers from retaliating against individuals who exercise their rights under the statutes by filing formal complaints or who may have participated in employment discrimination investigations or legal proceedings. Further, the statutes prohibit discrimination by association. For example, employers may not discriminate against individuals because they are married to or associate with persons of a certain race, national origin, or religion. In addition to prohibiting discrimination, civil rights statutes forbid harassment on the basis of innate characteristics. Harassment may include such acts as making offensive or derogatory remarks. It is illegal when it is so frequent or severe that it creates a hostile or offensive work environment or when it results in an adverse employment decision.

The Equal Employment Opportunity Commission (EEOC) is responsible for enforcing antidiscrimination statutes as they apply to employment situations. The EEOC is authorized to investigate charges of discrimination, make findings, and attempt to reach a resolution where it finds evidence of discrimination. As part of its enforcement authority, the EEOC may file suits in federal courts to protect the rights of individuals and the interests of the public. After investigating complaints, the EEOC may issue notices giving complainants the right to file private actions in federal courts.

This chapter outlines the various federal statutes and constitutional provisions that provide teachers with protections against discrimination in the workplace. It begins with discussions of those areas specifically enumerated in Title VII of the Civil Rights Act of 1964 and continues with information on more recent statutes protecting teachers from other forms of discrimination. While many state statutes provide additional protections or extend the protections afforded by federal statutes, a discussion of these laws is beyond the scope of this chapter and book, since it is designed to provide a broad overview of federal antidiscrimination law.

RACE, COLOR, ETHNICITY, OR NATIONAL ORIGIN

Titles VI and VII of the Civil Rights Act of 1964 prohibit discrimination in the workplace on the bases of individuals' race, color, ethnicity, or national origin.

> Titles VI and VII of the Civil Rights Act of 1964 prohibit discrimination and harassment in the workplace on the bases of individuals' race, color, ethnicity, or national origin.

Title VI[7] forbids recipients of federal funds, including public schools, from discriminating against individuals on the basis of race, color, or national origin. Recipients of federal funds that are found to have violated Title VI are subject to loss of future funding or other actions by the Department of Justice. Title VII,[8] on the other hand, covers private employers that have 15 or more employees as well as government agencies and educational facilities. Further, the Equal Protection Clause of the Fourteenth Amendment, which mandates that similarly situated people must be treated similarly, has played a prominent part in many cases alleging discriminatory treatment.

Race discrimination involves treating individuals unfavorably because they belong to a certain race or due to personal characteristics associated with race, such as hair texture, skin color, or facial features. Color discrimination involves treating people unfavorably because of their skin color or complexion. In like manner, national origin discrimination involves treating persons unfavorably due to the fact that they are from particular countries or parts of the world, because of their ethnicity or accents, or since they appear to be of certain ethnic backgrounds.

Creating Racial Balance Among Faculty

When school systems were desegregating, many boards tried to establish a racial balance among their faculty. In doing so, school boards often adopted one of two approaches, either matching the racial composition of their faculties to that of their student populations or employing faculties that reflected the racial composition of the labor market. In this respect in 1977, in *Hazelwood School District v. United States*,[9] the Supreme Court expressed the opinion that the teachers in a school system should be representative of the labor market. In the aftermath of *Hazelwood*, statistics assessing the racial composition of the labor market played a prominent part in judicial determinations as to whether school boards made progress in terms of nondiscriminatory hiring practices.[10] In one case, the Fifth Circuit decided that a school board was not using discriminatory employment practices where statistics showed that the

> Courts agreed that students do not have a constitutional right to attend schools with particular staff racial compositions.

percentage of black teachers increased even though the percentage of the qualified black applicants in the labor market decreased during the same time period.[11] Other courts agreed that students do not have a constitutional right to attend schools with particular staff racial compositions.[12]

Discrimination Claims

As an initial matter, employees bringing discrimination claims must show that they are members of a protected class. When teachers or applicants for positions sufficiently allege that actions against them were taken for discriminatory reasons, the burden is then placed on school boards to show that their decisions were made for legitimate nondiscriminatory reasons. If school boards are able to offer seemingly justifiable reasons for their adverse actions, the burden then shifts back to the plaintiffs to try to show that the stated reasons were not true or were pretexts for discriminatory treatment. For instance, dismissed teachers must be able to prove that the reasons provided for the termination of their employment, such as incompetence or neglect of duty, were simply pretexts for discriminatory intent. In one such case, a Hispanic teacher failed to show that a school board's explanation for not renewing her contract—that students could not understand her because she spoke rapidly and with an accent—was a pretense for national origin discrimination.[13] Similarly, a black applicant for a promotional position was unable to show that the school board's reason for not giving him the position—that he did not perform as well in an interview as the successful candidate—was a pretext for discrimination.[14] When teachers are able to show that boards demonstrated a discriminatory animus, boards still may be able to prevail in court if they can show that they acted for legitimate, nondiscriminatory reasons.

Courts are reluctant to substitute their judgments for those of school officials when it comes to evaluating either the qualifications of candidates for positions or which qualifications are most important with respect to final hiring decisions. Accordingly, courts have upheld school board actions regarding various candidates' education, experience, performance in interviews, and recommendations.[15] By the same token, courts are hesitant to overturn dismissals when boards can show that they acted for legitimate reasons such as incompetence, poor evaluations, lack of classroom discipline, misconduct, failure to meet legitimate job expectations, or insubordination, unless plaintiffs can prove that the stated reasons were false or a pretext for discrimination.[16]

> Courts are reluctant to substitute their judgment for those of school officials when it comes to evaluating either the qualifications of candidates for positions or which qualifications are most important with respect to final hiring decisions.

CASE SUMMARY 6.1: NONDISCRIMINATORY REASONS FOR ADVERSE ACTION

Pittman v. Cuyahoga Valley Career Center

451 F. Supp. 2d 905 (N.D. Ohio 2006)

Factual Summary: A principal verbally reprimanded an African American with a nonrenewable full-time substitute teaching contract and formally put him on notice for having released students early. The notice concerned expectations for dismissal of students and coverage of assigned areas. The teacher was later placed on suspension for two separate instances of insubordination. Due to the timing of the suspension, the teacher did not meet a minimum requirement of working 60 days as called for in his contract. Following the suspension, when the teacher was reverted to "on call" status but was not called back as a substitute teacher, he filed suit, claiming, among other things, racial discrimination. The school board responded by stating that the teacher's suspension resulted from insubordination and failure to follow rules and regulations.

Issue: Was the teacher's suspension the result of unlawful racial discrimination?

Decision: No, a federal trial court granted the school board's motion for summary judgment, essentially dismissing the teacher's claim.

Summary of Court's Rationale: Since the parties agreed that the teacher was a member of a protected class, was qualified to be a substitute teacher, and suffered an adverse employment action, the only question that remained was whether he was treated differently than other similarly situated nonminority employees. Looking at the evidence in a light most favorable, the applicable standard when dealing with a motion for summary judgment, the court concluded that the teacher failed to demonstrate that he was treated differently. Further, the court concluded that the school board articulated legitimate, nondiscriminatory reasons for the teacher's suspension and that the teacher failed to offer any evidence that those reasons were a pretext for intentional discrimination.

Teachers can allege that they were subject to pretexts for discrimination if they can demonstrate that others who are not in the protected class received more favorable treatment under similar circumstances. In a dispute involving national origin discrimination, a federal trial court in New York entered a judgment in favor of an unsuccessful candidate who established that school board members acted pretextually, since some of them had not read her resume or listened to her tape-recorded interview and that she was not asked the same questions as the successful applicant.[17] More recently, the Third Circuit upheld the dismissal of a superintendent from Pennsylvania who claimed that he was subject to discrimination based on his national origin.[18] The court affirmed that the board did not discriminate against the superintendent when it terminated his employment after a lengthy investigation that demonstrated that his many misdeeds had a negative financial impact on the district.

Employment Tests

Tests that are used for hiring or promotional purposes must be related to the competencies required of a teacher and must not be unreasonable or arbitrary. Further, the tests must be reliable and valid for the purposes for which they are used. In an early case, during the heyday of desegregation litigation, the Fifth Circuit upheld an order of a federal trial court in Mississippi striking down a school board's requirement that applicants and teachers attain a minimum score on the Graduate Record Exam as a condition of employment; the Fifth Circuit determined that the test was not job related.[19] Subsequently, the Fifth Circuit affirmed another ruling of the court from Mississippi invalidating a school board's use of the National Teachers Examination for similar purposes, inasmuch as the board had neither addressed the examination's validity and reliability for selecting teachers nor established its relationship to teaching skills.[20] In both cases the court ascertained that use of the tests had a discriminatory result.

> Tests that are used for hiring or promotional purposes must be related to the competencies required of a teacher and must not be unreasonable or arbitrary. Further, the tests must be reliable and valid for the purposes for which they are used.

Conversely, a federal trial court in South Carolina upheld the use of the National Teachers Examination for purposes of certification and placement on a salary scale.[21] The court was convinced that the test had a rational relationship to the employment objectives and was valid in light of the fact that the test developer had conducted validity studies for this purpose. Even though use of the test resulted in the disqualification of a disproportionate number of black candidates, the court did not find that its use violated the Equal Protection Clause. A comparison of the South Carolina decision, which the Supreme Court affirmed, and the earlier Mississippi verdict involving the same examination, demonstrates the importance of validating any tests that are used for employment-related purposes.

GENDER

Title VII also prohibits discrimination based on a person's sex or gender, but the statute was extended by the Pregnancy Discrimination Act (PDA)[22] to forbid discrimination on the basis of pregnancy, childbirth, or a medical condition caused by pregnancy or childbirth. The PDA is now incorporated into Title VII.

> Title VII also prohibits discrimination based on a person's sex or gender, but the statute was extended by the Pregnancy Discrimination Act to forbid discrimination on the basis of pregnancy, childbirth, or a medical condition caused by pregnancy or childbirth.

Title VII does allow employers to treat men and women differently if gender is a bona fide occupational qualification. The Equal Pay Act of 1963[23] makes it illegal to pay different wages to males and females who perform essentially equal work in the same workplace. This statute has little impact on teachers, because they are generally paid according to a gender-neutral scale based on years of experience and graduate credits. Title IX of the Educational Amendments of 1972[24] further prohibits discrimination on the basis of sex in any educational program or activity at an institution receiving federal financial assistance. This latter act, however, is predominantly used in claims involving students rather than employees. By and large employees alleging discrimination based on gender rely on Title VII.

Harassment on the basis of individuals' sex is strictly prohibited by these laws. Harassment includes not only sexual harassment or unwelcome sexual advances, requests for sexual favors, and other verbal or physical harassment of a sexual nature but also may include offensive remarks about gender. For example, making offensive comments about women in general would be a form of harassment. Both the victim and the offender can be either a woman or a man, and the victim and offender can be the same sex.[25]

Discrimination Claims

Claims of gender discrimination are similar to those of racial or national origin discrimination in that employees raising such allegations must show that they were treated differently because of their sex. As with all discrimination claims, teachers making such allegations initially bear the burden of showing that they were subjected to discriminatory treatment. The burden then shifts to school boards to demonstrate that their actions were, in fact, taken for legitimate gender-neutral reasons. When boards can successfully make this case, the burden then shifts back to the employees to disprove the boards' contentions.

CASE SUMMARY 6.2: INTENTIONAL SEX DISCRIMINATION

Willis v. Watson Chapel School District

899 F.2d 745 (8th Cir. 1990)

Factual Summary: A teacher who taught business education for over 25 years unsuccessfully applied for administrative positions on eight occasions. On each of those occasions the successful applicant was a male. When the teacher filed suit alleging sex discrimination, the trial court found that the school board refused to hire her because she was a woman. The court noted that in four instances the superintendent preferred males over females even though the males' credentials and experience were similar or inferior to those of the females. The court further observed that on another occasion the superintendent stated that he was leery of a female in the position but later acknowledged that the female applicant was better qualified than the successful male candidate. The school board was ordered to appoint the plaintiff to the next available position.

Issue: Did the school board engage in impermissible sex discrimination by not hiring the female teacher for an administrative position?

Decision: Yes, the Eighth Circuit affirmed that the board discriminated against the female applicant.

Summary of Court's Rationale: The appeals court agreed that the record amply supported the trial court's decision that the reasons the board gave for not promoting the plaintiff were pretextual in at least four instances. The panel thus affirmed that the trial court's finding of intentional sex discrimination was not clearly erroneous.

Plaintiffs are successful in discrimination suits when they can show overt discriminatory animus. The Eighth Circuit was convinced that a female teacher who had been passed over for promotion numerous times was the victim of discrimination where all of the positions she applied for were given to males.[26] The superintendent's statement that he was leery of appointing a female to a junior high school principal position along

> Plaintiffs are successful in discrimination suits when they can show overt discriminatory animus.

with evidence that the female teacher was, in some instances, better qualified than the successful males proved fatal to the school board's case. Similarly, an appellate court in Massachusetts interpreted comments by school committee (as boards are referred to there) members that they did not want a woman as superintendent and that they needed a strong man to be evidence of sex discrimination.[27] West Virginia's highest court ruled that an unsuccessful female candidate for an administrative position, who had more seniority than the successful male applicant, sufficiently alleged discrimination by presenting statistical evidence of gender disparity between teachers and administrators.[28] A teacher from New Jersey also used statistics to convince an appellate court of possible discrimination when she showed that a disproportionate number of female teachers over the age of 45 had been denied tenure as opposed to males in that age category.[29]

In contrast, school boards are successful when they can demonstrate legitimate reasons for their employment decisions. As a rule, courts do not second-guess the judgment of those making hiring decisions, unless it can be shown that their stated reasons were merely pretexts for discrimination. For example, a federal trial court in Missouri accepted a school board's explanation that a successful female candidate had more experience and performed better in an interview than a male applicant even though the male had a degree in the field and the female did not.[30] The Eleventh Circuit agreed that a female teacher who was unsuccessful in two bids for promotion to administrative positions that were given to males was not discriminated against.[31] The court accepted the school board's contentions that the teacher would not have been promoted even if she were a man where evidence indicated that her personality and lack of positive recommendations, not her gender, caused her to be passed over for the promotions.

> As a rule, courts do not second-guess the judgment of those making hiring decisions, unless it can be shown that their stated reasons were merely pretexts for discrimination.

Harassment and Hostile Work Environments

Many of the cases brought under Title VII allege either harassment or the creation of hostile work environments by employers or supervisors. Harassment allegations generally involve charges that employees were subjected to unwelcome sexual conduct. In order to establish claims of hostile work environments, employees must show that the actions of employers or supervisors resulted in intolerable working conditions.

In cases that arose in a noneducation context, the Supreme Court established the criteria for lower courts to consider in deciding employee claims of harassment and hostile work environment under Title VII. The Supreme Court noted that claims of harassment and hostile work environment were actionable under Title VII and outlined the elements that can form such claims.[32] The impetus for this suit concerned allegations brought by a former employee asserting that she was forced to go on sick leave and was eventually dismissed because of a supervisor's demands for sexual relations. The Court observed that the elements of a viable claim include the following:

> Harassment allegations generally involve charges that an employee was subjected to unwelcome sexual conduct. In order to establish claims of hostile work environments, employees must show that the actions of employers or supervisors resulted in intolerable working conditions.

- The claimant belongs to a protected class.
- The claimant was subjected to unwelcomed sexual conduct.
- The harassment was based on gender.
- The harassment affected a term, condition, or privilege of employment.
- The employer knew or should have known of the alleged harassment and failed to correct it.

In a later case, the Supreme Court elaborated that factors such as the frequency and severity of the conduct in question along with whether it was physically threatening or humiliating must be considered in establishing the existence of a hostile work environment.[33] Claims alleging misconduct by a member of the same sex also are actionable under Title VII[34] as are complaints that teachers were harassed by students.[35]

Even though most harassment and hostile work environment proceedings arise when employees allege that supervisors subjected them to unwelcomed sexual misconduct, employers can be liable if they knew or should have known of the wrongdoing and failed to take remedial action.[36] A case decided by a federal trial court in Florida illustrates the point that school boards must be aware of the misconduct for them to be deemed liable. A teacher leveled allegations that her principal created a hostile work environment by making sexual comments on several occasions. The court acknowledged that the teacher established a viable hostile work environment claim but held that the board was not liable for the principal's actions because it had a policy forbidding sexual harassment and was unaware of his behavior, since the teacher had not filed any previous complaints.[37] Further, an employee alleging that harassment created a hostile work environment as defined by Title VII must show that the offending activity was severe or pervasive.[38]

Sexual Orientation

Courts agree that the antidiscrimination laws also protect employees on the basis of their sexual orientation and transgendered status. In one

> Courts agree that the antidiscrimination laws also protect employees on the basis of their sexual orientation and transgendered status.

such case a federal trial court in Ohio determined that the true motivation for a school board's decision to not renew the contract of a gay teacher was his sexual orientation.[39] In another situation the Eighth Circuit ascertained that a school board did not create a hostile work environment when it allowed a transgendered teacher, who had transitioned from a male to a female, to use a women's restroom.[40] In the suit, filed by a female teacher who objected to the transgendered teacher's use of the restroom, the court determined that the objecting female teacher did not show that she suffered an adverse employment action by the board's decision, since she had single-stall unisex bathrooms available to her.

Pregnancy and Child Rearing

The Pregnancy Discrimination Act,[41] which is now incorporated in Title VII, bars discrimination on the basis of pregnancy. Under the PDA,

> The Pregnancy Discrimination Act, which is now incorporated in Title VII, bars discrimination on the basis of pregnancy. Under this statute leaves of absence for pregnancy must be treated in the same way as other leaves for illness or disability.

leaves of absence for pregnancy must be treated in the same way as other leaves for illness or disability. The PDA forbids school boards from taking adverse actions against pregnant teachers simply because of their conditions unless the boards can show that their actions are required due to business necessities. Thus, boards may not dismiss teachers simply because the teachers might need maternity leaves. Even the need for continuity of instruction is not sufficient cause to dismiss a pregnant teacher.

A decision from the Fourth Circuit invalidating a school board policy requiring teachers to report their pregnancies to school officials as soon as they knew they were pregnant is illustrative of the parameters of the PDA.[42] The teacher filed suit, alleging that her contract had not been renewed due to her pregnancy, pursuant to an unwritten school board policy of not renewing the contract of teachers who could not commit to a full year of service. The court determined that such a policy resulted in gender-related discrimination, in that it placed a burden on females that their male counterparts did not suffer. Further, as is evidenced by a case from the Second Circuit, boards may not take adverse action against teachers with young children in the mistaken belief that such teachers cannot adequately carry out their professional tasks due to their child care responsibilities.[43]

Title IX

Although the vast majority of suits filed under Title IX entail discrimination against students, the Supreme Court has declared that it also may apply to employees.[44] In this regard the Court upheld U.S. Department of Education regulations that prohibited federally funded education programs from discriminating on the basis of sex in employment.

> Although the vast majority of suits filed under Title IX entail discrimination against students, the Supreme Court has declared that it also may apply to employees.

More recently, in a dispute involving a coach, the Supreme Court indicated that, at least in some circumstances, Title IX creates a private right of action for school employees.[45] Here a dismissed girls' basketball coach filed suit, alleging that he was dismissed in retaliation for registering complaints that his team did not receive equal funding and equal access to equipment and facilities. Even though the coach may have been an indirect victim of discrimination, the Court concluded that he had the right to bring his claim forward under Title IX insofar as retaliation against a person who has complained of sex discrimination fell within the parameters of the statute's protections.[46] A year earlier, a federal trial court in New York maintained that Title IX may be used by employees as a vehicle to allege gender-based discrimination.[47]

RELIGION

Employees are protected against discrimination on the basis of their religion by Title VII of the Civil Rights Act[48] as well as the First Amendment to the U.S. Constitution.[49] Religious discrimination involves treating employees or applicants unfavorably due to their religious beliefs or practices. Title VII protects people who belong to traditional, organized religions, such as Christianity, Judaism, Buddhism, Hinduism, and Islam, as well as those who have sincerely held religious, ethical, or moral beliefs but are not necessarily members of an organized religion.

> Religious discrimination involves treating employees or applicants unfavorably due to their religious beliefs or practices.

Title VII requires employers to make reasonable accommodations for employees' religious beliefs or practices, unless doing so would cause the employers significant difficulty or expense. As a result, school boards may have to make reasonable adjustments to the work environment to allow employees to practice their religions. For example, as illustrated in Chapter 4, employees should be allowed to take a reasonable number of days off for religious observances. Another accommodation may involve the dress or grooming practices that employees adhere to for religious reasons. For instance, some employees may don particular head coverings or religious garb or customarily wear certain hairstyles or facial hair. Some employees may need to adhere to a religious prohibition against wearing certain garments. If it does not pose an undue hardship, school boards must grant requested dress or grooming accommodations.

Employees who allege that they were subject to adverse employment actions due to their religion must meet the same burden of proof requirements as plaintiffs claiming other forms of discrimination. Teachers filing religious discrimination claims need to substantiate that the adverse actions were taken because of their religious beliefs or practices and not for legitimate, nondiscriminatory reasons.

Accommodating Religious Needs

The Supreme Court has emphasized that Title VII requires school boards to make reasonable accommodations to meet the religious needs of teachers.[50] Even so, the Court recognized that the accommodations granted need not necessarily be the ones requested by the employees. An accommodation frequently requested by teachers is to take time off for religious observances. Many teacher contracts allow for a set number of days that employees may take each year for religious holidays or observances. School boards can accommodate teachers who need additional days off by allowing them to use contractual personal time or to take the days off without pay.[51] However, boards are not required to grant additional days off with pay or to allow teachers to take an excessive number of days off. Put another way, boards are not required to grant accommodations that would cause a substantial disruption to the educational process, place an undue hardship on other employees, or result in excessive costs.[52] Thus, it would not be unreasonable to expect boards to give teachers several days of leave per year for religious purposes. On the other hand, school boards are not obligated to grant leaves that could result in a disruption to the educational process.

It is not unusual for teachers to be required to work on weekends. For example, coaches need to be present if their teams have contests on

> The Supreme Court has emphasized that Title VII requires school boards to make reasonable accommodations to meet the religious needs of teachers.

CASE SUMMARY 6.3: RESTRICTIONS ON USE OF RELIGIOUS MATERIAL IN CLASS

Williams v. Vidmar

367 F. Supp. 2d 1265 (N.D. Cal. 2005)

Factual Summary: An elementary school principal sent a memo directing one of her teachers to stop using materials of a religious nature with his students. The memo further required the teacher to submit to the principal advance copies of all materials he would be sending home with students at least two days in advance. The memo was issued after the principal received a complaint from a parent but followed several discussions the principal had with the teacher regarding his use of religious materials. The teacher filed a lawsuit alleging that the restrictions on his use of supplemental materials with religious content violated his constitutional rights.

Issue: Do the restrictions placed on the teacher's use of supplemental materials violate his constitutional rights?

Decision: No, the court granted, in part, the school board's motion to dismiss the suit.

Summary of Court's Rationale: Although acknowledging that the teacher sufficiently alleged facts that, if proven, would show that he was treated differently than other teachers in his school, the court nonetheless rejected his claim that the school board violated his Free Speech and Establishment Clause rights. The court was convinced that the principal had a reasonable concern that the teacher was promoting a faith, and the principal did not violate the teacher's rights by ordering him to stop using religious-based materials. The court noted that a public school has an interest in avoiding Establishment Clause violations and that the principal's directives were designed to make sure that a violation did not occur. The court added that limiting the teacher's lesson plans neither burdened his religious practice nor indicated hostility to religion.

weekends. Also, teachers often are needed to supervise or chaperone school events on weekends. Courts have upheld the right of school boards to take adverse employment actions against teachers who refuse to work on weekend days for religious reasons where working on these days is an essential function of their positions and accommodating them would create undue hardships, such as by requiring other employees to cover their duties.[53]

Religious Expression and Curricular Objections

Litigation has arisen concerning employees' rights to express their religious views in classrooms or to refrain from teaching portions of the curriculum that may not agree with their religious beliefs. By and large, courts have upheld the actions of school boards in these disputes. For instance, courts have consistently sustained school board requirements for teachers to include evolution in their biology and science classes.[54] By the same token, teachers may not refuse to teach portions of the curriculum concerning patriotism even though it may conflict with their religious beliefs.[55] In like manner, courts have allowed school boards to bar teachers from speaking about religion or their own religious beliefs in their classrooms.[56] On the other hand, boards may not require teachers to participate in a flag salute if doing so conflicts with the teachers' religious beliefs, but boards may insist that teachers have their students recite the pledge.[57] In accepting employment, teachers are expected to carry out all of the essential functions of the position, and a refusal to do so, even on religious grounds, may result in termination.

Religious Garb

Another question that has arisen concerns teachers wearing religious garments or emblems or displaying religious symbols in their classrooms. Litigation on this topic is mixed. In two older cases, courts in Kentucky and North Dakota did not see a problem with public school teachers wearing religious dress or emblems.[58] Conversely, courts in Mississippi, New York, Oregon, and Pennsylvania endorsed regulations banning public school teachers from wearing religious clothing while performing their official duties.[59] For the most part, the courts have recognized the need for schools to be neutral when it comes to religion and that young, impressionable children might view the wearing of religious garments by teachers as a governmental endorsement of religion.

> For the most part the courts have recognized the need for schools to be neutral when it comes to religion and that young, impressionable children might view the wearing of religious garments by teachers as a governmental endorsement of religion.

DISABILITY

Section 504 of the Rehabilitation Act of 1973[60] prohibits recipients of federal funds from discriminating against otherwise qualified individuals with disabilities in any of their programs or activities. The first civil rights legislation that specifically guaranteed the rights of individuals with disabilities, Section 504 effectively prohibits discrimination by recipients of federal funds in the provision of services or employment. Its provisions are similar to those found in Titles VI and VII of the Civil Rights Act of 1964.

The Americans with Disabilities Act (ADA),[61] passed in 1990, extends Section 504's protections by prohibiting discrimination against individuals with disabilities in the private sector as well as the public sector. Title I of the ADA prohibits discrimination by private sector employers with 15 or more employees. Title II applies to public accommodations, such as schools, using language similar to that of Section 504. Congress enacted the ADA Amendments Act of 2008[62] to broaden the definition of individuals with disabilities in both statutes to include those who suffer from chronic illnesses such as epilepsy, diabetes, cancer, and multiple sclerosis.

The ADA forbids employers from inquiring about the type, nature, and severity of the impairments of job applicants, but employers may ask about applicants' abilities to perform job-related tasks.[63] Likewise, once school officials have offered positions to candidates, they may condition hiring on submission to medical examinations as long as all prospective employees must do so. On the other hand, the ADA prohibits school boards from requiring current employees to submit to medical examinations about the nature of their disabilities, unless boards can prove that examinations would provide essential information about employees' abilities to do their jobs.

As defined by both the ADA and Section 504, individuals with disabilities are those who have physical or mental impairments that substantially limit one or more of their major life activities, who have records of such impairments, or who are regarded as having such impairments. Thus, under this definition individuals who have impairments are not considered to be disabled if their conditions do not substantially limit one or more major life activities. Major life activities include caring for oneself, performing manual tasks, walking, seeing, hearing, speaking, breathing, learning, and working.

> As defined by both the ADA and Section 504, individuals with disabilities are those who have physical or mental impairments that substantially limit one or more of their major life activities, who have records of such impairments, or who are regarded as having such impairments.

In the employment context, both Section 504 and the ADA require employers to provide reasonable accommodations to otherwise qualified individuals with disabilities, unless doing so would cause significant difficulty or expense for the employers. A reasonable accommodation is any change in the workplace environment or in the ways tasks are usually accomplished to help individuals with disabilities perform the duties of a job or enjoy the benefits and privileges of employment.[64] Reasonable accommodation might include anything from providing a ramp for a wheelchair user to making adjustments to an employee's schedule.

Discrimination Claims

Litigants are unlikely to prevail in discrimination claims when their alleged disabilities are not covered by the ADA or Section 504. As stated above, impairments must substantially limit major life activities to qualify as disabilities under these statutes. In one case, a federal trial court in New York asserted that an instructor who had suffered a stroke was not discriminated against when his salary raises were less than those of other faculty members.[65] The court ascertained that the instructor was not disabled inasmuch as his stroke had not substantially limited a major life activity. Further, the court noted that the reasons for his lower salary raise were related to his overall performance. In another case, Maine's state court of last resort declared that the term "individual with disabilities" does not include a person with sexual behavior disorders.[66] Here an instructor, who had been fired for violating the school's sexual harassment policy, alleged that he was wrongfully dismissed, since he had a sexual addiction that was a mental disability under Section 504. On the other hand, the federal trial court in the District of Columbia wrote that degenerative arthritis that affected an art teacher's mobility and dexterity qualified as a disability under the ADA and Section 504.[67] Similarly the Seventh Circuit accepted medical evidence to determine that a teacher who suffered from fibromyalgia and seasonal affective disorder was disabled.[68]

In order to maintain discrimination claims under the ADA or Section 504, applicants or teachers must demonstrate that they were treated in different ways than their colleagues who were not disabled, or that they suffered adverse employment decisions because of their disabilities. For example, a part-time worker with a disability failed in his discrimination claim when he was laid off after he worked the maximum number of hours allowed for part-time workers. The court pointed out that the board did not violate the worker's rights, because nondisabled part-time employees were laid off for the same reason.[69]

> In order to maintain discrimination claims under the ADA or Section 504, applicants or teachers must demonstrate that they were treated in different ways than their colleagues who were not disabled, or that they suffered adverse employment decisions because of their disabilities.

Courts reject discrimination claims when school boards can show that adverse employment decisions were made for legitimate nondiscriminatory reasons. By way of illustration, the federal trial court in the District of Columbia thought that an employee with a disability was not discriminated against when the employer was able to show that the employee was not promoted because his work performance was not up to standards and it had not improved when he was provided with accommodations.[70]

Otherwise Qualified

The prohibition against discrimination in the ADA and Section 504 applies only to otherwise qualified individuals. The Supreme Court ruled that individuals with disabilities are otherwise qualified if they can perform all essential requirements of the positions in question in spite of their disabilities.[71] Thus, if persons cannot perform the essential functions of positions, even with reasonable accommodations, they are not otherwise qualified.

> The Supreme Court ruled that individuals with disabilities are otherwise qualified if they can perform all essential requirements of the positions in question in spite of their disabilities.

One essential requirement of most positions, especially those in school systems, is regular attendance. Employees who cannot be present at the workplace in a reliable and predictable fashion are not otherwise qualified.[72] The ADA and Section 504 do not protect excessive absenteeism, even when it is caused by disabilities.[73] In the same way, classroom teachers are expected to be able to be physically present in classrooms and interact with students. Teachers who, due to their disabilities, are unable to interact with students may not be entitled to assignments that do not involve sustained contact with students. It should go without saying that since classroom teaching is considered an essential function of teachers' jobs,[74] those who cannot perform in such a setting fail to meet all essential requirements of a teaching position. Even so, when nonclassroom positions exist, teachers with disabilities may be entitled to reassignment to one of those open positions.

Teachers must be properly certificated or licensed to hold their positions. For that reason a teacher from Virginia who alleged that she was learning disabled but had not passed the communications portion of the National Teachers Examination after numerous attempts was not successful in her discrimination claims.[75] The court reasoned that the skills measured by the communications test were basic for competent performance as a classroom teacher. Consequently, the court concluded that the teacher was not otherwise qualified in that she could not perform the essential functions of the position. In a similar situation in New York, the Second Circuit affirmed that the ADA and Section 504 did not require that an individual with disabilities be exempted from demonstrating the same level of competency on skills measured by a licensing examination as other applicants.[76] The court sanctioned the plaintiff's dismissal on the basis that she was not qualified because she was not licensed.

The ADA and Section 504 do not protect misconduct, even when it can be attributed to disabilities.[77] An appellate court in California affirmed the dismissal of an employee with alcoholism who repeatedly reported to work intoxicated and was unable to perform his duties.[78] The court maintained that the employee was fired because of his misconduct, not his alcoholism, and that Section 504 did not protect misconduct. Similarly, an appellate court in Connecticut upheld the dismissal of a teacher who was arrested and charged with possession of cocaine.[79] The court was satisfied that his criminal conduct undermined his ability to continue as a teacher.

Reasonable Accommodations

The ADA and Section 504 require employers to provide reasonable accommodations so that otherwise qualified employees with disabilities can work and compete with their nondisabled colleagues. The rationale for providing accommodations is to give employees with disabilities the opportunity to lead normal, productive lives. Accommodations may include alterations to physical environments, schedule adjustments, or minor changes in job responsibilities. School boards are not obligated to furnish accommodations when doing so places an undue burden on them. During litigation the burden is placed on school boards to show that accommodations were denied because they created an undue financial or administrative burden.[80]

The ADA and Section 504 do not mandate that school boards make accommodations that essentially change the nature of the employees' jobs. On the other hand, boards can be required to reassign employees with disabilities to other open positions. This occurs, for example, when employees are unable to perform the essential functions of their current jobs even with reasonable accommodations, and vacant positions are available for which the employees are qualified. Reassignments are not required when other positions are not available. School boards are not required to create new positions or accommodate teachers by eliminating essential aspects of their current positions. In one instance the Sixth Circuit held that a school board was not required to accommodate a teacher with a degenerative condition by creating a new position for her that would have a small class size and would not require her to discipline students.[81]

> The ADA and Section 504 do not mandate that school boards make accommodations that essentially change the nature of the employees' jobs.

CASE SUMMARY 6.4: EXCESSIVE ABSENTEEISM AND DISABILITY DISCRIMINATION

Ramirez v. New York City Board of Education

481 F. Supp. 2d 209 (E.D.N.Y. 2007)

Factual Summary: A teacher who had not passed all required tests for full certification was classified as a provisional preparatory teacher. The teacher had epilepsy and was also later diagnosed as having depression and high blood pressure. The school board terminated his employment after he received an unsatisfactory performance rating that was based on his excessive absenteeism. The teacher sued the school board, alleging disability discrimination under the ADA.

Issue: Did the school board discriminate against the teacher on the basis of his disabilities by discharging him for excessive absenteeism?

Decision: No, the court found that the school board's actions were not discriminatory and did not violate the teacher's rights under the ADA.

Summary of Court's Rationale: As an initial matter the court determined that the teacher was not disabled within the meaning of the ADA, because his impairments did not substantially limit him from the major life activity of work. Further, even if the teacher's impairments had constituted disabilities under the ADA, the court was convinced that his excessive absences prevented him from performing the essential functions of a teacher. For that reason the court held that since he was not otherwise qualified within the meaning of the ADA, the teacher's claim was without merit.

School boards are not required to let teachers with disabilities work only when their conditions allow, inasmuch as regular attendance is a necessary requirement of the job to maintain continuity of instruction. In a dispute involving undue absenteeism, a federal trial court in New York decreed that an employee who could not report to work on a consistent basis was not otherwise qualified.[82] Even so, the federal trial court in Maryland agreed that a board offered reasonable accommodations by hiring a long-term substitute to work alongside a teacher whose illness caused frequent absences.[83] Still, taking such action is not always necessary, since the cost of the full-time substitute could be deemed to be unreasonable.

AGE

Congress passed the Age Discrimination in Employment Act (ADEA)[84] in 1967, making it illegal for employers to discriminate against individuals 40 years of age and older. The ADEA's antidiscrimination provisions are substantively similar to those found in Title VII of the Civil Rights Act of 1964 pertaining to race, religion, gender, and national origin.

> The Age Discrimination in Employment Act's antidiscrimination provisions are substantively similar to those found in Title VII of the Civil Rights Act of 1964 that pertain to race, religion, gender, and national origin.

The ADEA applies to employers with 20 or more employees and protects older workers in areas such as hiring, compensation, benefits, transfers, promotions, demotions, and dismissal. The ADEA does not prevent employers from considering age as a factor when age is a bona fide occupational qualification, and it does not forbid the use of seniority in employment decisions. It is important to note that the ADEA forbids age discrimination only against people who are age 40 or older and does not protect workers under the age of 40. Further, the ADA does not prevent an employer from favoring an older worker over a younger one, even when both are over the age of 40.

Economic Factors

It is not unusual for school boards to hire inexperienced teachers over more experienced ones simply because of the lower cost. According to the Seventh Circuit, this practice does not necessarily violate the ADEA.[85] The court was convinced that the economic basis for hiring a less experienced, but younger, teacher was not discriminatory insofar as a teacher's salary is based on years of service, not age. Still, economic reasons cannot serve as a pretext for age discrimination.

> Economic factors may provide legitimate reasons for employment decisions, even when older workers are affected to a greater degree than younger workers.

As in other areas of antidiscrimination law, courts do not dismiss age discrimination claims where there are genuine issues of material fact that may indicate that actions were taken for impermissible reasons.[86] The bottom line is that economic factors may provide legitimate reasons for employment decisions, even when older workers are affected to a greater degree than younger workers.[87]

Assessing Qualifications

Younger workers also may be hired over older workers when their qualifications are better. A federal trial court in New York declared that a school board's reasons for hiring a younger applicant, with a master's degree and experience with the curriculum, were not a pretext for age discrimination.[88] Similarly, the Second Circuit accepted a school board's contention that it did not hire an older applicant because she interviewed poorly and was not familiar with new teaching methods.[89]

CASE SUMMARY 6.5: AGE DISCRIMINATION

Stone v. Board of Education of Saranac Central School District

153 F. App'x 44 (2d Cir. 2005)

Factual Summary: An unsuccessful candidate for a teaching position filed suit alleging age discrimination. In her suit she charged, among other things, that two younger, less-qualified teachers were hired and that the school board had a statistical track record of preferring younger applicants. The trial court ruled in favor of the school board, finding that it had legitimate, nondiscriminatory reasons for making its hiring decisions. The teacher appealed.

Issue: Was age discrimination a factor in the school board's hiring decisions?

Decision: No, the appeals court affirmed that the school board's actions were not discriminatory.

Summary of Court's Rationale: The court agreed with the trial court that the school board offered valid age-neutral reasons for its hiring decisions: The facts revealed that the unsuccessful applicant interviewed poorly and did not demonstrate sufficient familiarity with newer teaching methods. Once this was established, the court explained that the applicant was required to show that these proffered reasons were a pretext for age discrimination. In reviewing the trial record, the appeals court concluded that the applicant failed to present evidence to prove either that the school board's stated reasons were false or that age discrimination was a force behind its decisions. In its opinion, the court noted that it was aware that it should both respect the school board's discretion to choose among qualified candidates and not second-guess the board's judgments.

Qualifications do not necessarily accrue only by means of advanced degrees and experience. To this end, courts have accepted school boards' explanations that applicants performed better in interviews or came with better recommendations as being legitimate reasons for hiring a younger person.[90]

Early Retirement Incentives

Early retirement incentives have come under close court scrutiny. As the name implies, these plans are offered to induce employees to retire before they otherwise would have. School boards have a legitimate financial reason for offering such plans insofar as they typically hire teachers low on the pay scale to replace retiring teachers high on the salary schedule. Early retirement plans also may be offered as a way of minimizing layoffs during periods of budget cuts. The ADEA states that it is not unlawful for employers to observe the terms of voluntary early retirement incentive plans as long as the terms of the plans are consistent with the purpose of the statute. Given that the terms of early retirement incentives vary considerably, courts must make case-by-case findings of whether particular plans further the purposes of the ADEA.[91]

Early retirement incentives that exclude employees over specified ages or that tie benefits directly to participants' ages can be struck down. Many older workers may be ineligible for full retirement because they have not accumulated a sufficient number of years of service, while plans tied to age tend to exclude them from participation. In one such case, the Eighth Circuit decreed that a school board violated the ADEA when it instituted an early retirement program that excluded workers over the age of 65.[92] The court maintained that a plan that denied a benefit solely on the basis of an employee's age was not consistent with the ADEA's purpose. Similarly, the Second Circuit invalidated a plan that provided a three-year salary supplement to teachers who reached age 55 but excluded those who were over 55 at the time the plan was implemented.[93] The Seventh Circuit also found a plan that cut off benefits at age 62 without incentives for teachers beyond that age to retire before their target date amounted to age discrimination.[94] Plans providing lump sum payments that varied by the age of the participants also have been quashed when they were not based on any factors other than age.[95]

> Early retirement incentives that exclude employees over specified ages or that tie benefits directly to participants' ages can be struck down.

On the other hand, early retirement incentive plans that are tied to teachers' ages and years of service pass muster. A federal trial court in New York was of the view that a bona fide retirement plan that made distinctions based on age was not a subterfuge for discrimination and did not violate the ADEA.[96] The plan provided an incentive to teachers who reached the age of 55 and had 15 or more years of service. Insofar as early retirement plans are designed to encourage teachers to retire early, those with windows of time in which teachers may elect to participate—thus excluding employees who do not elect to retire during the specified time period—have been upheld. Moreover, another federal trial court in New York found that a plan that excluded employees beyond the eligibility window of 55 to 60 years of age with at least 20 years of employment was valid.[97] Similarly, the Second Circuit upheld a plan that gave all teachers the chance to receive a flat rate cash payment and an accumulated sick leave payment if they retired at the end of the first school year in which they became eligible for benefits in the state's retirement program.[98] The court was convinced that older teachers who elected to work beyond the year they first became eligible for retirement were not denied benefits of the plan due to their age but rather because they chose not to retire during the eligibility window. In the court's view the plan did not violate the ADEA.

GENETIC INFORMATION

The most recent addition to the federal arsenal of antidiscrimination laws is the Genetic Information Nondiscrimination Act of 2008 (GINA).[99] GINA prohibits discrimination in health coverage and employment based on genetic information. Genetic information includes facts about an individual's genetic tests or those of a family member or knowledge about any disease, disorder, or condition of a family member. Genetic tests are defined as any analysis of human DNA, RNA, chromosomes, proteins, or metabolites that detect genotypes, mutations, or chromosomal changes. Routine tests such as complete blood counts or cholesterol tests are excluded. Inasmuch as this law has only recently been implemented, there has been no litigation at this writing.

Title I of GINA makes it illegal for health insurers or health plan administrators to request or require genetic information on an individual or the individual's family members or to use genetic information to make decisions concerning coverage, rates, or preexisting conditions. These protections apply only to health insurance and do not extend to life, disability, or long-term care insurance. Various provisions of Title I were scheduled to take effect between May 2009 and May 2010.

Title II of GINA prohibits discrimination against employees or job applicants based on genetic information. Specifically, Title II forbids employers from using genetic information in making employment decisions and restricts employers from obtaining genetic information. As with other federal antidiscrimination laws, GINA applies to employers with 15 or more employees and provides protections in any aspect of employment, including hiring, firing, wages, fringe benefits, job assignments, promotions, layoffs, training, and conditions of employment. Also, consistent with other antidiscrimination laws, GINA makes it unlawful to harass individuals because of their genetic information or to retaliate against someone who files a charge of discrimination or participates in a discrimination investigation or legal proceeding. Title II became effective in November 2009.

RETALIATION

All of the antidiscrimination laws prohibit employers from retaliating against employees who have either filed discrimination claims or participated in discrimination investigations or legal proceedings. Retaliation can be difficult to prove, since litigants must show a direct causal relationship between an adverse employment action and their participation in a protected activity.

In examining retaliation claims, courts first consider whether school boards had legitimate reasons for taking adverse actions. Further, courts consider factors such as the proximity in time between when the employees engaged in the protected activity and when the adverse employment actions were taken as well as changes in the employees' situations following their participation in protected activities. For example, the Eighth Circuit decided that a school board had a legitimate reason for transferring an administrator who leveled age discrimination complaints and that the two-year lapse between the events was too great to establish a nexus for retaliation.[100] Similarly, the Third Circuit rejected a retaliation claim when the teacher failed to show a causal connection between her making complaints about racial discrimination and her discharge two years later.[101]

AFFIRMATIVE ACTION

It is not at all unusual to see statements on school districts' literature or websites indicating that the respective school boards are equal opportunity employers. In the aftermath of numerous suits in which courts found that school boards engaged in discriminatory hiring and employment practices, many boards were under direct orders to take steps to correct the situation. In attempting to remedy imbalances in their workforces directly caused by discriminatory practices, many school boards had to take proactive steps to recruit and promote members of protected classes.

Even school boards in districts where discrimination had not been proven developed voluntary affirmative action plans to ensure a balance in their employee populations. Still, many courts ruled that affirmative action plans should provide an equal opportunity, not a preference, to members of protected classes. Care must be taken to make sure that affirmative action plans do not result in illegal reverse discrimination.

Affirmative action plans are more likely to withstand court scrutiny where past discriminatory school board policies or practices created imbalanced teaching corps, or where statistical imbalances exist on factors specifically targeted by antidiscrimination laws, such as race or sex. Further, plans that do not overtly infringe on the rights of other employees and that are temporary have better chances of holding up in court. As is shown in the following paragraph, plans giving preferences to hiring or retention of staff in a protected class in the absence of evidence of past discrimination against members of that class are likely to be invalidated. In fact, the Third Circuit held that Title VII does not allow an employer with a racially balanced workforce to grant a nonremedial racial preference for the purpose of promoting diversity.[102]

> Affirmative action plans are more likely to withstand court scrutiny where past discriminatory school board policies or practices created imbalanced teaching corps, or where statistical imbalances exist on factors specifically targeted by antidiscrimination laws, such as race or sex.

At this point in time, most school districts have achieved the goal of creating diversity within their workforces. Even so, in an era when many school boards are forced to lay off staff due to budget cuts or declining enrollments, they are faced with the very real possibility that the layoffs will once again create an imbalance. This is true particularly where a reduction in force occurs on the basis of seniority. For example, in many school systems that were formerly racially segregated, the more senior members of a faculty may be white, and those most likely to be laid off may be recently hired minorities. Thus, many school boards have instituted reduction in force policies designed to preserve their diverse workforces. The Supreme Court struck down a plan that resulted in the retention of minority teachers with less seniority than nonminority teachers.[103] In a plurality, the Court reasoned that such a practice violated the Equal Protection Clause, inasmuch as it was based on racial or ethnic criteria and there was no evidence that the retained minority teachers had been the victims of individual discrimination. The following year a full panel of the Seventh Circuit agreed that a collective bargaining agreement violated the Equal Protection Clause because it included a provision that minority teachers would not be laid off in the event of a reduction in force.[104] A plurality of the court was convinced that the plan was not designed to remediate past discrimination but created a preference for one race. Accordingly, a reduction in force plan that gives retroactive seniority to individual teachers who were victims of past discrimination has a better chance of being upheld.

SUMMARY AND RECOMMENDATIONS

The Equal Protection Clause of the Fourteenth Amendment, as well as federal and state statutes, shield individuals from discrimination in employment. Most notably, Title VII prohibits discrimination on the bases of race, color, religion, sex, or national origin. Other federal statutes, predominantly based on Title VII, provide further protections from discrimination on the bases of pregnancy, age, and disability.

In order to succeed in discrimination claims, regardless of the bases on which such claims are premised, teachers first must show that they are members of a group protected by an antidiscrimination statute and that they have suffered adverse employment actions due to discrimination. Once teachers have met their initial burden, the burden shifts to school boards to establish evidence that the boards' actions were, in fact, taken for legitimate, nondiscriminatory reasons. Teachers are then given the opportunity to dispute the reasons and show that they are a pretext for discriminatory actions. Finally, the burden shifts back to the school boards to prove that the same action would have been taken in the absence of the discriminatory motive.

Early retirement incentive plans have been controversial. Most of these plans are designed to provide a financial motive for employees to retire earlier than they otherwise would have. The financial incentive is offered to somewhat offset the fact that early retirees will get a lower pension as a result of their early exit. Plans excluding employees over a specified age, without regard for other factors such as the retirees' years of service or eligibility for a full pension, have generally been struck down. On the other hand, plans providing a window for eligibility that does not exclude employees solely on the basis of their ages have been allowed. Thus, plans that exclude workers who have a combination of age and service that would give them their maximum pension are unlikely to be unlawful.

Over the past several decades many school boards have instituted affirmative action hiring plans to increase the diversity of their teaching corps. While care must be taken that such programs do not infringe on the rights of other employees or prospective employees, they will be upheld if their purpose is to provide equal opportunities in employment rather than create a preference for one class of applicants.

In light of the antidiscrimination laws implemented and legal opinions handed down during the past several decades, teachers need to be aware of the following principles that have emerged:

- Discrimination against members of protected classes is prohibited. Protected classes are those created due to race, color, sex, religion, national origin, ethnicity, age, or disability.
- In order to establish viable claims of discrimination, teachers must first show that they are members of a protected class and were subjected to adverse treatment on the basis of their membership in the class.
- Even when teachers can show that adverse action was taken, in part, for discriminatory reasons, school boards will be successful if they can show that the action was taken for nondiscriminatory reasons as well and would still have been taken in the absence of the discriminatory reasons.
- As a rule, courts do not substitute their judgments for those of competent decision makers, unless it can be shown that the decision-makers' actions were arbitrary or a pretext for discrimination. Thus, courts generally defer to school officials when it comes to assessing the qualifications of applicants for positions or promotions or to making decisions regarding termination.
- Age discrimination may be harder to prove than other discrimination claims. There are many factors other than age that may form legitimate bases for employment decisions even when those considerations have a greater negative impact on older workers.
- Retaliation against individuals who have filed discrimination claims or participated in investigations into alleged discrimination is strictly prohibited.
- Harassment of employees due to their membership in a protected class is unlawful.
- In order to maintain disability discrimination claims, teachers must show that their disabilities are covered under the ADA or Section 504, that adverse employment decisions were made because of the disabilities, and that they have the skills to perform the jobs.
- Employees are not otherwise qualified under the ADA and Section 504 if they cannot perform the essential functions of the positions even with reasonable accommodations.
- Antidiscrimination statutes require school boards to provide reasonable accommodations. Accommodations are not reasonable if providing them would create an undue financial or administrative burden.
- A new federal statute forbids discrimination on the basis of genetic information. Since this law has only recently been enacted and has yet to be tested in the courts, it is an area worth watching.

- Many school boards have enacted affirmative action plans to remedy past discrimination by creating equal employment opportunity practices. Even so, these practices may not create a situation of reverse discrimination.

FREQUENTLY ASKED QUESTIONS

Q. Do the civil rights laws protect incompetent teachers who belong to one of the groups targeted by the statutes?

A. No, teachers may be disciplined or dismissed for cause even if they belong to protected classes. When teachers allege that dismissals were implemented for discriminatory purposes, they must present evidence to back up those claims. As in all cases where dismissals are challenged, school boards must be able to substantiate that the actions were taken for legitimate reasons. In other words, boards must be able to show that the teachers were, in fact, dismissed for cause.

Q. Do voluntary affirmative action plans create a hiring preference for under-represented groups in the workforce?

A. No, voluntary affirmative action plans should be designed to create an equal employment opportunity for everyone. Those that have shown a preference for one group have been struck down by the courts as violating Title VII.

Q. If it is proven that an applicant for a teaching position was passed over for discriminatory reasons, what remedies are available to the applicant?

A. There are many possible remedies. Judicial remedies are based on the individual circumstances of the case. Remedies could include an order to give the applicant the next available similar position for which the applicant is qualified, an award of back pay, or a monetary award for actual damages. Punitive damages awards are not allowed. Courts are unlikely to require the school board to remove the successful applicant in favor of the unsuccessful one even when it was determined that the board engaged in discriminatory hiring practices.

Q. Does the Age Discrimination in Employment Act prohibit all mandatory retirement age policies?

A. No. While the ADEA prohibits mandatory retirement ages in most sectors, it grants exceptions when it can be shown that age is a bona fide occupational qualification. For example, if an employer can show a legitimate reason for instituting a mandatory retirement age policy, such as the need for workers to be in top physical condition for safety purposes, it will be allowed. The onus is on the employers to show that there is a reason for assuming that most persons over a given age are incapable of performing the functions of the job and that it would be impractical to make the determination on an individual basis.

WHAT'S NEXT

Chapter 7 covers the legal aspects of teacher discipline and dismissal. The chapter focuses on due process procedures that school boards must adhere to in the process of dismissing teachers for cause. The chapter also discusses tenure and reductions in force.

ENDNOTES

1. U.S. Constitution, Amendment XIV.
2. Civil Rights Act of 1964, 78 Stat. 241 (1964).
3. Civil Rights Act of 1964, Title VII, 42 U.S.C. § 2000e *et seq.* (2006).
4. 42 U.S.C. § 2000e-2(a).
5. Russo, C. J. (2009). *Reutter's the law of public education* (7th ed.). New York: Foundation Press.
6. Thomas v. Washington County School Board, 915 F.2d 922 (4th Cir. 1990).
7. Civil Rights Act of 1964, Title VI, 42 U.S.C. §§ 2000d *et seq.* (2006).
8. Civil Rights Act of 1964, Title VII, 42 U.S.C. § 2000e *et seq.* (2006).
9. 433 U.S. 299 (1977).
10. *See, e.g.,* Scoggins v. Board of Education of Nashville, Arkansas Public Schools, 853 F.2d 1472 (8th Cir. 1988).
11. Quarles v. Oxford Municipal Separate School District, 868 F.2d 750 (5th Cir. 1989).
12. *See, e.g.,* Oliver v. Kalamazoo Board of Education, 706 F.2d 757 (6th Cir. 1983); Fort Bend Independent School District v. City of Stafford, 651 F.2d 1133 (5th Cir. 1981).
13. Forsythe v. Board of Education of Unified School District No. 489, 956 F. Supp. 927 (D. Kan. 1997).
14. Morton v. City School District of New York, 742 F. Supp. 145 (S.D.N.Y. 1990).
15. *See, e.g.,* Weber v. Port Arthur School Board, 759 F. Supp. 341 (E.D. Tex. 1991) (finding that unsuccessful applicants for a promotional position failed to show that reasons stated for hiring the successful applicant were a pretext for discrimination).

16. *See, e.g.,* Pittman v. Cuyahoga Valley Career Center, 451 F. Supp. 2d 905 (N.D. Ohio 2006); Shanklin v. Fitzgerald, 397 F.3d 596 (8th Cir. 2005); Cherry v. Ritenour School District, 253 F. Supp. 2d 1085 (E.D. Mo. 2003); Villarreal v. Independent School District, 520 N.W.2d 735 (Minn. 1994); Mack v. Kent County Vocational and Technical School District, 757 F. Supp. 364 (D. Del. 1991).

17. Rosario-Olmedo v. Community School Board for District 17, 756 F. Supp. 95 (E.D.N.Y. 1991).

18. Hasson v. Glendale School District, 296 Fed. App'x 226 (3d Cir. 2008).

19. Armstead v. Starkville Municipal Separate School District, 325 F. Supp. 560 (D. Miss. 1971), *affirmed* 461 F.2d 276 (5th Cir. 1972).

20. Baker v. Columbus Municipal Separate School District, 329 F. Supp. 706 (N.D. Miss. 1971), *affirmed* 461 F.2d 1112 (5th Cir. 1972).

21. United States v. South Carolina, 445 F. Supp. 1094 (D.S.C. 1977), *affirmed sub nom.* National Education Association v. South Carolina, 434 U.S. 1026 (1978).

22. Pregnancy Discrimination Act, 42 U.S.C. 2000e(k) (2006).

23. Equal Pay Act of 1963, 29 U.S.C. § 206(d) (2006).

24. Education Amendments of 1972, Title IX, 20 U.S.C. § 1681(a) (2006).

25. *See, e.g.,* Madon v. Laconia School District, 952 F. Supp. 44 (D.N.H. 1996) (refusing to dismiss an action alleging same-sex sexual harassment).

26. Willis v. Watson Chapel School District, 899 F.2d 745 (8th Cir. 1990).

27. Northeast Metropolitan Regional Vocational School District v. Massachusetts Commission Against Discrimination, 575 N.E.2d 77 (Mass. Ct. App. 1991).

28. Perilli v. Board of Education of Monongalia County, 387 S.E.2d 315 (W.Va. 1989).

29. Greenberg v. Board of Education of Sewanhaka Central High School District, 3 F. Supp. 2d 280 (N.J. Super. Ct. 1998).

30. Collins v. School District of Kansas City, 727 F. Supp. 1318 (W.D. Mo. 1990).

31. McCarthney v. Griffin-Spalding County Board of Education, 791 F.2d 1549 (11th Cir. 1986).

32. Meritor Savings Bank v. Vinson, 477 U.S. 57 (1986).

33. Harris v. Forklift Systems, 510 U.S. 17 (1993).

34. *See, e.g.,* Oncale v. Sundowner Offshore Services, 523 U.S. 75 (1998) (ruling that sex discrimination consisting of same-sex harassment is actionable under Title VII).

35. *See, e.g.,* Plaza-Torres v. Rey, 376 F. Supp. 2d 171 (D.P.R. 2005) (finding that student-on-teacher sexual harassment was cognizable under Title VII).

36. *See, e.g.,* Burlington Industries v. Ellerth, 524 U.S. 742 (1998) (ruling that employers must show that they exercised reasonable care to prevent and promptly correct any sexually harassing behavior); Faragher v. City of Boca Raton, 524 U.S. 775 (1998) (affirming that an employer may raise an affirmative defense claiming that the employer sought to correct harassing conduct).

37. Mason v. School Board of Dade County, 36 F. Supp. 2d 1354 (S.D. Fla. 1999).

38. *See, e.g.*, Alagna v. Smithsville R-II School District, 324 F.3d 975 (8th Cir. 1998) (ruling that allegedly harassing actions by a colleague, although inappropriate, did not rise to the level of harm required for either hostile work environment or constructive discharge claims under Title VII).

39. Glover v. Williamsburg Local School District, 20 F. Supp. 2d 1160 (S.D. Ohio 1998).

40. Cruzan v. Special School District No. 1, 294 F.3d 981 (8th Cir. 2002).

41. Pregnancy Discrimination Act, 42 U.S.C. 2000e(k) (2006).

42. Mitchell v. Board of Trustees of Pickens County School District, 599 F.2d 582 (4th Cir. 1979).

43. Black v. Hastings on Hudson Union Free School District, 365 F.3d 107 (2d Cir. 2004).

44. North Haven Board of Education v. Bell, 456 U.S. 512 (1982).

45. Jackson v. Birmingham Board of Education, 544 U.S. 167 (2005).

46. Russo, C. J., & Thro, W. E. (2005). The meaning of sex: Jackson v. Birmingham School Board and its potential implications. *Education Law Reporter, 198*, 777–793.

47. A.B. *ex rel.* C.D. v. Rhineland Central School District, 224 F.R.D. 144 (S.D.N.Y. 2004).

48. Civil Rights Act of 1964, Title VII, 42 U.S.C. § 2000e *et seq.* (2006).

49. U.S. Constitution, Amendment I.

50. Ansonia Board of Education v. Philbrook, 479 U.S. 60 (1986).

51. *See, e.g.*, Maine-Endwell Teachers' Association v. Board of Education, 771 N.Y.S.2d 246 (N.Y. App. Div. 2004); Pinsker v. Joint School District, 554 F. Supp. 1049 (D. Colo. 1983); Wangsness v. Watertown School District, 541 F. Supp. 332 (D.S.D. 1982).

52. *See, e.g.*, Creusere v. Board of Education of Cincinnati, 88 F. App'x 813 (6th Cir. 2003); Bynum v. Fort Worth Independent School District, 41 F. Supp. 2d 641 (N.D. Tex. 1999); Favero v. Huntsville Independent School District, 939 F. Supp. 1281 (S.D. Tex. 1996), *affirmed mem.* 110 F.3d 793 (5th Cir. 1997).

53. *See, e.g.*, Bynum v. Fort Worth Independent School District, 41 F. Supp. 2d 641 (N.D. Tex. 1999) (finding that an employer accommodated an employee's need to not work on parts of every weekend as much as it could without causing an undue hardship).

54. *See, e.g.*, LeVake v. Independent School District, 625 N.W.2d 502 (Minn. Ct. App. 2001) (noting that a teacher's right to free speech did not allow the teacher to teach a biology class in a manner that circumvented the prescribed curriculum); Peloza v. Capistrano Unified School District, 37 F.3d 517 (9th Cir. 1994) (affirming that requiring a teacher to teach evolution did not violate his free exercise of religion rights).

55. *See, e.g.*, Palmer v. Board of Education of Chicago, 603 F.2d 1271 (7th Cir. 1979) (observing that a public school teacher was not free to disregard the prescribed curriculum regarding patriotic matters because it conflicted with his religious beliefs).

56. *See, e.g.*, Williams v. Vidmar, 367 F. Supp. 2d 1265 (N.D. Cal. 2005); Helland v. South Bend Community School Corp., 93 F.3d 327 (7th Cir. 1996); Peloza v. Capistrano Unified School District, 37 F.3d 517 (9th Cir. 1994).

57. *See, e.g.,* Russo v. Central School District No. 1, 469 F.2d 623 (2d Cir. 1972); Santiago v. Temple University, 739 F. Supp. 974 (E.D. Pa. 1990).

58. Rawlings v. Butler, 290 S.W.2d 801 (Ky. 1956); Gerhardt v. Heid, 267 N.W. 127 (N.D. 1936).

59. McGlothin v. Jackson Municipal Separate School District, 829 F. Supp. 853 (S.D. Miss. 1992); United States v. Board of Education of the School District of Pennsylvania, 911 F.2d 882 (3d Cir. 1990); Cooper v. Eugene School District, 723 P.2d 298 (Or. 1986); Commonwealth v. Herr, 78 A. 68 (Pa. 1910); O'Connor v. Hendrick, 77 N.E. 612 (N.Y. 1906).

60. Rehabilitation Act, Section 504, 29 U.S.C. § 794 (2006).

61. Americans with Disabilities Act, 42 U.S.C. § 12101 *et seq.*

62. ADA Amendments Act of 2008, 122 Stat. 3553 (2008).

63. *See, e.g.,* Adeyemi v. District of Columbia, 525 F.3d 1222 (D.C. Cir. 2008) (affirming that it was permissible for an interviewer to ask a hearing impaired applicant how he communicated in a work environment where no one knew sign language).

64. Russo, C. J., & Osborne, A. G. (2009). *Section 504 and the ADA.* Thousand Oaks, CA: Corwin.

65. Redlich v. Albany Law School, 899 F. Supp. 100 (N.D.N.Y. 1995).

66. Winston v. Maine Technical College System, 631 A.2d 70 (Me. 1993).

67. Gordon v. District of Columbia, 480 F. Supp. 2d 112 (D.D.C. 2007).

68. Ekstrand v. School District of Somerset, 583 F.3d 972 (11th Cir. 2009).

69. Spells v. Cuyahoga Community College, 889 F. Supp. 1023 (N.D. Ohio 1994).

70. Adrain v. Alexander, 792 F. Supp. 124 (D.D.C. 1992).

71. School Board of Nassau County v. Arline, 480 U.S. 273 (1987); Southeastern Community College v. Davis, 442 U.S. 397 (1979).

72. *See, e.g.,* Santiago v. Temple University, 739 F. Supp. 974 (E.D. Pa. 1990) (finding that an employee's excessive absenteeism could not be accommodated).

73. *See, e.g.,* Carr v. Reno, 23 F.3d 525 (D.C. Cir. 1994); Linares v. City of White Plains, 773 F. Supp. 559 (S.D.N.Y. 1991); Walders v. Garrett, 765 F. Supp. 303 (E.D. Va. 1991).

74. *See, e.g.,* Mustafa v. Clark County School District, 876 F. Supp. 1177 (D. Nev. 1995) (explaining that classroom teaching is an essential function of a teacher's job), *affirmed in part, reversed in part and remanded* 157 F.3d 1169 (9th Cir. 1998).

75. Pandazides v. Virginia Board of Education, 804 F. Supp. 794 (E.D. Va. 1992), *reversed on other grounds* 13 F.3d 823 (4th Cir. 1994).

76. Falchenberg v. New York State Department of Education, 375 F. Supp. 2d 344, (S.D.N.Y. 2005), 457 F. Supp. 2d 490 (S.D.N.Y. 2006), 567 F. Supp. 2d 513 (S.D.N.Y. 2008), *affirmed* 338 F.3d 11 (2d Cir. 2009).

77. *See, e.g.,* Wilber v. Brady, 780 F. Supp. 837 (D.D.C. 1992) (upholding the dismissal of an employee who was convicted of driving under the influence).

78. Gonzalez v. California State Personnel Board, 39 Cal. Rptr. 2d 282 (Cal. Ct. App. 1995).

79. Gedney v. Board of Education of the Town of Groton, 703 A.2d 804 (Conn. Ct. App. 1997).

80. *See, e.g.,* Byrne v. Board of Education, School District of West Allis–West Milwaukee, 741 F. Supp. 167 (E.D. Wis. 1990) (finding that a school board had to show that accommodations would result in an unfair financial or administrative burden).

81. Johnson v. Cleveland City School, 2009 WL 2610833 (6th Cir. 2009).

82. Ramirez v. New York City Board of Education, 481 F. Supp. 2d 209 (E.D.N.Y. 2007).

83. Nichols v. Harford County Board of Education, 189 F. Supp. 2d 325 (D. Md. 2002).

84. Age Discrimination in Employment Act, 29 U.S.C. § 621 *et seq.*

85. Equal Employment Opportunity Commission v. Francis W. Parker School, 41 F.3d 1073 (7th Cir. 1994).

86. *See, e.g.,* Filar v. Board of Education of Chicago, 526 F.3d 1054 (7th Cir. 2008); Dragoness v. School Committee of Melrose, 833 N.E.2d 679 (Mass. Ct. App. 2005).

87. Equal Employment Opportunity Commission v. Atlantic Community School District, 879 F.2d 434 (8th Cir. 1989).

88. Richane v. Fairport Central School District, 179 F. Supp. 2d 81 (W.D.N.Y. 2001).

89. Stone v. Board of Education of Saranac Central School District, 153 F. App'x 44 (2d Cir. 2005).

90. *See, e.g.,* Brierly v. Deer Park Union Free School District, 359 F. Supp. 2d 275 (E.D.NY. 2005) (declaring that a teacher failed to rebut the school board's explanation for not appointing him to a supervisory position).

91. Auerbach v. Board of Education of the Harborfields Central School District, 136 F.3d 104 (2d Cir. 1998).

92. Jankovitz v. Des Moines Independent Community School District, 421 F.3d 649 (8th Cir. 2005).

93. Abrahamson v. Board of Education of Wappingers Falls Central School District, 374 F.3d 66 (2d Cir. 2004).

94. Solon v. Gary Community School Corporation, 180 F.3d 844 (7th Cir. 1999).

95. Overlie v. Owatonna Independent School District, 341 F. Supp. 2d 1081 (D. Minn. 2004); O'Brien v. Board of Education of Deer Park Union Free School District, 127 F. Supp. 2d 342 (E.D.N.Y. 2001); Equal Employment Opportunity Commission v. Hickman Mills Consolidated School District, 99 F. Supp. 2d 1070 (W.D. Mo. 2000).

96. Gabarczyk v. Board of Education of Poughkeepsie, 738 F. Supp. 118 (S.D.N.Y. 1990).

97. Cipriano v. Board of Education of North Yonawanda, 772 F. Supp. 1346 (W.D.N.Y. 1991).

98. Auerbach v. Board of Education of the Harborfields Central School District, 136 F.3d 104 (2d Cir. 1998).

99. Genetic Information Nondiscrimination Act of 2008, 122 Stat. 881, codified at 26 U.S.C.A. § 9834; 42 U.S.C.A. §§ 300gg-53, 1320d-9; 42 U.S.C.A. §§ 2000ff *et seq.*

100. Stewart v. Independent School District, 481 F.3d 1034 (8th Cir. 2007).

101. Taylor v. Brandywine School District, 202 F. App'x 570 (3d Cir. 2006).

102. Taxman v. Board of Education of the Township of Piscataway, 91 F.3d 1547 (3d Cir. 1996).

103. Wygant v. Jackson Board of Education, 476 U.S. 267 (1986).

104. Britton v. South Bend Community School Corporation, 819 F.2d 766 (7th Cir. 1987).

Teacher Discipline, Dismissal, and Due Process

7

KEY CONCEPTS IN THIS CHAPTER

❖ Probationary Employees

❖ Rights of Tenured Teachers

❖ Progressive Discipline

❖ Discharge for Cause

❖ Remedies for Wrongful Discharge

❖ Reduction in Force and Call Back

INTRODUCTION

Just as school boards have the authority to hire teachers, they have the power to terminate their employment when necessary. The causes for which teachers may be discharged are generally spelled out in state law along with the processes that school boards must follow in dismissing educators. Although boards must adhere to proper procedures, it is well established that they have not only the authority, but also the duty, to dismiss school personnel when necessary.[1] In addition to dismissing teachers for cause, in recent decades many school boards have had to release teachers without any personal fault on their part in reductions in force due to economic necessity or declining enrollments.

This chapter covers the legal aspects of teacher discipline and dismissal. It begins with an overview of the tenure rights of teachers and continues with a discussion of educator discipline and discharge for cause. The chapter emphasizes the legal grounds for teacher dismissals as well as the due process procedures that school boards must adhere to in the process of terminating the employment of teachers for cause. This section also provides information on the remedies available to teachers who have been wrongfully discharged. Finally, the chapter addresses reductions in force and call-back rights.

TENURE RIGHTS

Tenure is a continuing contract between teachers and their school boards that may not be terminated without cause.[2] Teachers attain tenure, referred to as a continuing contract in some states, after probationary periods as long as they have met established requirements that are set by a combination of state law and local board policy. Tenure has its roots in higher education, where it is granted to faculty members to ensure academic freedom and to protect those who may disagree with the prevailing opinions in their respective fields. By providing job security, tenure encourages dissent within fields of inquiry. At the elementary and secondary level, where teachers do not have as many rights to academic freedom, tenure protects educators from unjust or arbitrary discharge, particularly in politically charged environments. In this way, tenure protects teachers who may engage in union activity or openly disagree with school board policies that are matters of public concern (as opposed to internal operating rules). Further, tenure prevents school boards from taking arbitrary actions, such as discharging current teachers to open up positions for purposes of nepotism or patronage, or replacing experienced higher-paid teachers with inexperienced lower-paid teachers to save money.

> Tenure is a continuing contract between teachers and their school boards that may not be terminated without cause. Teachers attain tenure... after a probationary period as long as they have met established requirements that are set by a combination of state law and local board policy.

Probationary Periods

Probationary teachers are those who have not yet attained tenure[3] and thus lack the substantive due process protections of continuing employment.[4] Probationary periods vary from state to state, but most range from three to five consecutive school years in the same school system.[5]

During probationary periods boards usually employ teachers for specified periods of time, generally not exceeding one year. At the end of the contractual periods, the contracts may either be renewed for additional periods of time or not renewed at the discretion of school boards. As discussed below, when teacher contracts are allowed to expire, the courts generally refuse to treat these situations as adverse employment actions.

Once teachers complete their probationary periods, they may attain tenure automatically, simply by being retained in their positions. However, in most jurisdictions, tenure may be awarded only by affirmative votes of school boards[6] on the recommendations of educational administrators. Still, it is important to understand that service under so-called temporary or emergency contracts does not necessarily count toward the attainment of tenure.[7] For instance, many states permit the employment of uncertificated teachers on emergency or temporary bases when qualified candidates cannot be found to fill positions. Nevertheless, service under these terms normally does not accrue toward tenure. Courts have reached mixed results regarding the question of whether time spent as a part-time or substitute teacher counts toward tenure, with the results depending on the specific provisions of state laws.[8]

It is important to understand the difference between teacher dismissal and the nonrenewal of teachers' contracts. Dismissal refers to the actual termination of employment for cause, while nonrenewal refers to situations where school boards simply allow contracts to expire and do not offer teachers new contracts. Although dismissal is usually thought of in the context of tenured teachers, probationary teachers also may be dismissed for cause at any time during their contractual periods. To the extent that short-term contracts provide some procedural due process property rights, probationary teachers facing dismissal for cause before their contracts have expired may be entitled to due process protections that are similar to those afforded to tenured teachers.[9] Some states, for instance, require boards to provide notice to teachers who are not tenured before terminating their contracts.[10]

> It is important to understand the difference between teacher dismissal and the nonrenewal of teachers' contracts. Dismissal refers to the actual termination of employment for cause, while nonrenewal refers to situations where school boards simply allow contracts to expire and do not offer teachers new contracts.

For the most part, teachers facing the nonrenewal of their contracts are entitled to little in terms of procedural protections. School boards may decide to not offer new contracts to probationary teachers for any legitimate reason or even for no reason, as long as the grounds are not constitutionally impermissible.[11] This means that while boards may decide to not renew the contracts of teachers who exhibit excessive absenteeism,[12] they may not refuse to renew the contracts of those who need to take two days off per year for religious observances. Generally speaking, probationary teachers facing the nonrenewal of their contracts are not entitled to a statement of the reasons for the nonrenewals or to hearings challenging board actions. Yet, there are two important exceptions to this general rule. First, some states may require statements of reasons or even hearings when requested by teachers whose contracts are not renewed [13] as long as the teachers act within specified periods. Second, teachers who allege that their contracts were not renewed for impermissible or unconstitutional reasons such as race or gender typically have the opportunity to be heard, and school boards should investigate their complaints.

In most jurisdictions probationary teachers, either by statute or collective bargaining agreement, must be notified in writing by specified dates if boards elect not to renew their contracts, with the result that if boards fail to comply by the notification dates, typically April 15 or May 1, teachers may automatically have their contracts renewed.[14] In most states, teachers must actually receive the notification of nonrenewal by the specified date.[15] By way of illustration, mailing the notice by the statutory date is insufficient when boards do not provide ample time for it to travel through the postal system and reach recipients by designated dates. Further, state statutes may require that notifications be sent by certified or registered mail or even delivered in person. Courts may order teachers to be reinstated when boards fail to meet these requirements.[16] By the same token, teachers may not thwart receipt of the notice by such actions as failing to pick up their mail or refusing to sign for certified mail.

State laws and collective bargaining agreements often require school boards to ensure that probationary teachers are properly evaluated. These

> State laws and collective bargaining agreements often require school boards to ensure that probationary teachers are properly evaluated.

provisions may even require administrators to conduct a specified number of evaluations per school year[17] and give teachers the opportunity to correct their deficiencies. The failure of board officials to provide proper supervision for probationary teachers may result in courts overturning decisions not to renew their contracts. In such a case, the Supreme Court of Ohio held that a school board was bound by state statute and collective bargaining provisions specifying the procedures for evaluating teachers, and that the failure of administrators to follow these procedures and provide a teacher with specific recommendations for improvement resulted in an improper nonrenewal of her contract.[18] The court explained that such a failure permitted it to order the board to reemploy the teacher.

Guarantees of Job Security

Tenure is normally created by state statute and is awarded to teachers who have completed the requisite probationary period and have met any additional qualifications for attaining tenure. In some jurisdictions, state law may provide for probationary periods to be extended. On the other hand, unless they are specifically prohibited from doing so by state statute or collective bargaining agreements, school boards may award tenure before the full completion of probationary periods.[19]

Once teachers have attained tenure, they may be dismissed only for reasons specified by law. Most state statutes contain language stipulating that tenured teachers may be dismissed for grounds such as "inefficiency, incompetency, incapacity, conduct unbecoming a teacher, insubordination, or failure on the part of the teacher to satisfy teacher performance standards . . . or other just cause."[20] Even so, state statutes generally do not provide concise definitions of each of the enunciated grounds for dismissal, leaving it to the courts to decide on case-by-case bases whether school boards have sufficient cause to discharge teachers. This being said, as long as school board officials follow proper procedures and their actions do not violate state statutes or constitutional principles, courts are reluctant to substitute their judgments for those of boards regarding teacher dismissals.[21]

> Once teachers have attained tenure, they may be dismissed only for reasons specified by state law. . . . This being said, as long as school boards have followed proper procedures and their actions have not violated state statutes or constitutional principles, courts are reluctant to substitute their judgment for that of boards regarding teacher dismissals.

Tenured teachers may be dismissed, but only after they have received procedural due process that varies from one state to the next. Further, collective bargaining contracts may provide teachers with additional due process rights. Still, at the very least, teachers facing dismissal are normally entitled to notice of the grounds for their dismissals and hearings. At the hearings, school board officials present their arguments as to why teachers should be dismissed, while teachers are given opportunities to rebut these arguments. The next section of this chapter discusses in greater detail grounds for dismissal and the procedures that boards must follow to dismiss tenured teachers.

Tenure is generally associated with particular positions in school systems such that teachers who change jobs do not automatically have tenure in their new positions. In this regard, a tenured teacher who accepts a transfer to become a guidance counselor or administrator may need to serve a probationary period before earning tenure in the new role. When teachers change jobs within the same school system, such as moving from classroom teaching positions into administrative positions, they do not automatically give up tenure in their former positions.[22] On the other hand, tenure normally does not follow teachers who resign positions in their current school systems to accept similar jobs in other districts, although some state statutes allow school boards to award tenure earlier than mandated, particularly to teachers who had attained tenure status in their previous jobs.[23]

Tenure protects teachers from improper discharge but guarantees neither lifetime employment nor particular assignments. Instead, tenure "only" guarantees that teachers receive procedural due process before their employment is terminated. Moreover, local school boards usually have the authority to transfer or reassign teachers to positions for which the teachers are qualified. In other words, tenure provides a guarantee of continued employment as long as an individual performs satisfactorily but does not assure employment in any specific positions. Nonetheless, when educators are reassigned, their new positions must be substantially equal to their former jobs, or else the reassignments could be considered to be demotions, subject to state tenure laws. Thus, transferring individuals from one teaching position to another, with no loss in pay, would not run afoul of tenure statutes. On the other hand, reassigning tenured administrators to teaching positions with subsequent salary reductions would constitute demotions.

The issue can be complicated, as many positions with dissimilar titles may be considered equivalent. For instance, the positions of teacher and counselor would be equivalent if both were compensated according to the same salary scale. Conversely, the positions would not be equivalent if the counselor role came with an extra stipend or was considered to be a promotional or administrative position. Like many personnel issues, transfers and reassignments of employees also may be governed by collective bargaining agreements.

PROGRESSIVE DISCIPLINE AND DISMISSAL OF TEACHERS

Teachers should be given feedback on their performance, particularly with respect to any deficiencies they may have, and they should be given assistance in addressing their shortcomings.[24] It is inherently unfair to discipline or discharge teachers if they have not been given notice of their deficiencies and opportunities to improve. In fact, state statutes and contractual provisions typically require administrators to evaluate teachers, both probationary and tenured,

> State statutes and contractual provisions typically require administrators to evaluate teachers, both probationary and tenured, on a regular basis.

on a regular basis. Courts often examine the specific conduct leading to teacher dismissals to ascertain whether the conduct could have been remediated.[25] When courts determine that teacher actions can be remediated, it is not unusual for them to order school boards to provide educators with opportunities to improve their performance, if the boards have not already done so. By the same token, courts judge whether dismissals are proportionate to the reasons stated or whether lesser penalties would suffice. Even so, absent statutory or contractual mandates, school boards are under no obligation to warn teachers before initiating disciplinary actions or even to provide opportunities for correction.

This section of the chapter outlines common statutory grounds for teacher dismissal and the steps that school board officials must follow in taking such actions, emphasizing teachers' rights to procedural due process. Although much of what is written here applies predominantly to tenured teachers, it is relevant to probationary teachers who are dismissed before their contracts expire.

Progressive Discipline

Progressive discipline refers to a process of responding to teacher performance or behavior that fails to meet expected standards. School administrators use progressive discipline to inform teachers that performance or behavior issues need to be corrected while providing the teachers with the opportunity to improve. As the name implies, the process begins with less formal methods but may quickly move to more formal methods, particularly when improvement is not forthcoming. It is important to

> School administrators use progressive discipline to inform teachers that performance or behavior issues need to be corrected while providing the teachers with opportunities to improve.

understand that although the main purpose of progressive discipline is to help teachers improve, administrators document all steps in the process, including verbal warnings and reprimands. Documentation of this type can, and likely will, be used in dismissal proceedings.[26]

The initial step in progressive discipline is for supervisors to inform teachers verbally of their concerns and communicate their expectations for improved performance. If teachers do not take the corrective action requested, administrators typically issue verbal reprimands while reiterating their performance expectations. Administrators follow these initial steps by progressively taking more formal and serious actions, including written reprimands, formal evaluations, and written improvement plans.[27] Depending on the reasons for progressive discipline, the process may also involve suspensions. Throughout the process administrators should provide teachers with assistance in improving their performance and behavior.

School administrators commonly use a process known as clinical supervision to evaluate teachers.[28] This process, or another formal evaluation process, usually is incorporated as part of progressive discipline. The main purposes of clinical supervision are to provide teachers with objective feedback on their performances, help them improve their skills, and allow them to be active participants in their own professional development. Naturally, the results of the clinical supervision process are also used to make decisions regarding retention, tenure, and promotion. Although there are many variations, the clinical supervision process generally involves planning conferences, observations of teachers, analysis of their performance, a postobservation conference, and formal written evaluations.

Discharge for Cause

As indicated above, state statutes commonly provide for the discharge of teachers for cause. Although the grounds for dismissal vary from one jurisdiction to another, most states permit school boards to dismiss teachers for reasons such as insubordination, inefficiency, incompetence, neglect of duty, conduct unbecoming a teacher, and other good or just cause.

> Although the grounds for dismissal vary from one jurisdiction to another, most states permit school boards to dismiss teachers for reasons such as insubordination, inefficiency, incompetence, neglect of duty, conduct unbecoming a teacher, and other good or just cause.

Individual states may use other terminology but, by and large, all stipulated grounds for discharge would fall in one or another of these categories. For example, some states may list immorality as a specific reason for terminating teachers' contracts, but immorality could fall into the category of conduct unbecoming a teacher. Moreover, terms such as *inefficiency, incompetence,* and *neglect of duty* have considerable overlap and are most often treated as being synonymous.

The grounds listed in state statutes for teacher dismissals are broad and usually are not precisely defined. Thus, courts frequently are called upon to interpret the statutes and determine if school boards' proffered reasons for discharging teachers are legally permissible. In this respect, most courts interpret the enumerated grounds for dismissal broadly.[29] Further, inasmuch as the authority to set the grounds for teacher dismissal lies solely with the state legislatures, school boards may not establish additional bases for terminating teacher contracts. Even so, boards may need to let teachers go from time to time due to the changing needs of their systems. Reduction in force is discussed by itself in a later section of this chapter.

Insubordination

When teachers knowingly and intentionally fail to comply with the legitimate directives of their supervisors or with valid school board rules and regulations, they can be charged with insubordination. *Insubordination* has been defined as an unwillingness to submit to authority.[30] Courts are reluctant to uphold teacher dismissals when administrative directives were unreasonable or rules were not clearly spelled out. Although courts have supported dismissals for single acts of insubordination, they often look for persistent or continuing noncompliance before sanctioning teachers being discharged.

> Although courts have supported dismissals for single acts of insubordination, they often look for persistent or continuing noncompliance before sanctioning teachers being discharged.

The failure to obey a direct, lawful order, particularly after a warning has been issued, constitutes insubordination. The Supreme Court of Colorado affirmed the dismissal of a teacher who continued to use profanity in the presence of students even after having received a directive from the superintendent to discontinue his use of inappropriate language.[31] The court noted that insubordination encompassed a single incident of willful disobedience of a reasonable order as well as constant or persistent defiance. The same court also upheld the dismissal of a teacher who had shown an R-rated film without first obtaining an administrator's approval as required by school board policy.[32] The court found the policy to be reasonable and within the board's discretion.

Courts have upheld the dismissals of teachers who defied directives to cease proselytizing or conducting religious activities in their classrooms, consistently finding that the teachers' rights to free exercise of religion did not give them the right to carry out such activities.[33] Inasmuch as school boards have the authority to establish school curricula, as discussed in the next chapter, teachers may be dismissed for insubordination if they refuse or fail to implement the standard curriculum, utilize prescribed teaching methods, or adhere to established grading policies.[34]

The willful failure of teachers to fulfill assignments or professional responsibilities can be grounds for dismissal. The Supreme Court of Wyoming upheld the dismissal of a teacher who refused to teach an assigned class.[35] The court decided that the assignment was reasonable and had been given by proper authority, and the teacher willfully defied the order to teach the class. Similarly, an appellate court in Colorado found that a teacher's willful refusal to perform hall duty was grounds for his dismissal.[36] The Supreme Court of Appeals of West Virginia endorsed the dismissal of a teacher who, among other acts of insubordination, had

CASE SUMMARY 7.1: DISMISSAL FOR INSUBORDINATION AND NEGLECT OF DUTY

Bellairs v. Beaverton School District

136 P.3d 93 (Or. Ct. App. 2006)

Factual Summary: A middle school teacher was transferred to a high school following several complaints from students and colleagues. At the time of his transfer he was given a warning that his conduct created a severe situation. Additional incidents occurred after the transfer, including violations of school policy, outbursts at faculty meetings, making derisive comments about other employees, and unprofessional conduct. The teacher was subsequently suspended pending a meeting to discuss his situation. Student grades were due during the suspension period. The teacher failed to turn the grades in by the due date but, when contacted by administrators, agreed to bring them to the scheduled meeting. However, instead of bringing his grades to the meeting he submitted an ungraded pile of papers, stating that he did not grade them, because he was not allowed on school property during his suspension and could not retrieve his answer key. An assistant principal later testified that the ungraded papers contained essay questions as opposed to test items that required an answer key. Following this incident the teacher was dismissed for insubordination and neglect of duty. That decision was upheld by a fair dismissal appeals board, and the teacher appealed.

Issue: Does a teacher's failure to submit grades on time constitute insubordination sufficient to warrant dismissal?

Decision: Yes, the state appellate court affirmed the board's decision to dismiss the teacher.

Summary of Court's Rationale: As an initial matter the court accepted the fair dismissal appeals board's findings that the teacher failed to comply with the directive to turn in his grades. The court acknowledged that insubordination was an inexact legislative term, but nevertheless was convinced that it included an unwillingness to submit to authority. In the court's view, the teacher's failure to turn in his grades after ample time to do so had been allowed and after delivery arrangements had been made constituted an affirmative refusal that was readily attributable to a defiant intent. That, the court concluded, when combined with the teacher's long history of disrespectful behavior, was sufficient grounds for his dismissal. In its analysis the court also agreed with the fair dismissal appeals board's finding that the teacher's failure to communicate respectfully and professionally to students, parents, staff, and administrators amounted to neglect of duty.

willfully and knowingly refused to attend PTA and faculty meetings, meet or confer with parents in the principal's office as directed, issue a report card to a student as requested by supervisors, and return materials to the office as required by school board policy.[37] In finding that the teacher's discharge was reasonable, the court remarked that she had made her own rules and then followed them.

School boards have succeeded in discharging teachers who violated state laws or school board policies.[38] In particular, teachers frequently have been dismissed for using prohibited corporal punishment. In such a case, the Supreme Court of Colorado upheld the dismissal of a music teacher who struck a student on the head with a wooden pointer, since it was her fourth incident of inappropriate physical discipline, and she had been warned after the third occurrence that another violation could result in the termination of her employment.[39] Similarly, an appellate court in Tennessee affirmed the dismissal of a teacher who refused to refrain from striking students after being warned to not put her hands on children under any circumstances.[40] Other teachers have been dismissed for insubordination for failing to heed warnings not to touch students inappropriately.[41]

Teachers may not be dismissed for insubordination if they did not know and had no reason to know that their conduct violated school regulations or policy and could subject them to dismissal.[42] Put another way, teachers may not be disciplined for violating regulations that do not exist or of which they have not been made aware. Still, teachers may be disciplined for violating standards that should be obvious even if unstated.[43] Thus, courts uphold dismissals for conduct that is so unmistakably egregious that rules, regulations, or policies forbidding it are unnecessary.[44]

Courts have refused to uphold teacher dismissals in situations where the teachers failed to comply with unreasonable directives. In one such case the Supreme Court of Tennessee affirmed an order to reinstate a

CASE SUMMARY 7.2: DISMISSAL FOR INSUBORDINATION, INCOMPETENCY, AND INEFFICIENCY

Ketchersid v. Rhea County Board of Education

174 S.W.3d 163 (Tenn. Ct. App. 2005)

Factual Summary: A kindergarten teacher was transferred to teach a remedial class at another school due to her failure to meet the requirements of an improvement plan. Shortly after she began her new assignment, the principal of her new school reprimanded her for striking a student and warned her to not put her hands on students. The teacher was later suspended with pay after admitting that she had continued to hit students over the head with books, pinched their cheeks, and placed her hands on their faces. The school board subsequently dismissed her for insubordination, incompetence, and inefficiency. The teacher appealed, but a trial court found that she had received a fair hearing and that there was sufficient evidence to justify her dismissal. The teacher appealed.

Issue: Was the teacher's dismissal for insubordination, incompetence, and inefficiency justified?

Decision: Yes, the state appellate court affirmed that the teacher's dismissal was justified.

Summary of Court's Rationale: First, the court determined that the teacher's failure to follow her principal's instructions to refrain from putting her hands on students was an insubordinate act within the meaning of the state statutes. Second, the court found that the teacher's tactics of disciplining her students met the definition of incompetence, as they amounted to evidence of unfitness for service. Third, the court observed that the teacher's failure to maintain an orderly classroom and her need to resort to physical tactics constituted inefficiency.

teacher, pointing out that a superintendent's directing her to return to work was unreasonable inasmuch as she provided documentation that she was unable to return for medical reasons.[45] In a similar vein, an appellate court in Minnesota refused to allow a board to dismiss a teacher for insubordination for failing to submit to a psychological examination that was not required by statute under the circumstances.[46]

Incompetence, Neglect of Duty, and Inefficiency

Since the terms *incompetence, neglect of duty,* and *inefficiency,* when applied to teacher dismissal, are so closely related they are practically indistinguishable, they are treated together in this section. Moreover, since these grounds for dismissal are so similar, they often appear together in the same case.

Incompetence may be defined as an unfitness to teach or an inability to carry out the functions of the position. The inability may be due to physical, mental, emotional, or personal conditions that interfere with classroom performance or failure to perform up to expected standards caused by a lack of proper training and experience. School officials can prove that teachers are incompetent if they are unfit to teach, have deficiencies in knowledge of subject matter or pedagogy, or lack effectiveness in the classroom. Neglect of duty occurs when teachers fail to carry out the myriad obligations and responsibilities connected with classroom and other school sponsored activities. Teachers may be dismissed for neglect of duty for failing either to complete their assigned duties or to execute their duties effectively. Inefficiency has been defined as being below the standards of efficiency displayed by others for similar work and includes such offenses as being habitually tardy, inaccurate, or wanting in the effective performance of duties.[47] Inefficiency further encompasses shortcomings such as failing to establish appropriate rapport with students and parents and insufficient communication with parents.[48]

Inasmuch as teachers have many duties, both inside and outside of classrooms, incompetence, neglect of duty, and inefficiency encompass noninstructional as well as instructional obligations, such as maintaining proper classroom discipline, record keeping, and attending school functions.[49] To the extent that possession of teaching certificates implies competence, the burden of proof is on school boards to show that teachers they wish to discharge are incompetent. This burden becomes more difficult the longer teachers have served without documentation of their shortcomings, since school boards usually need to demonstrate that an inability to perform adequately existed over time. Although a single egregious incident, such as dating a student, can be grounds for dismissal, more often than not proceedings result from a pattern or combination of deficiencies exhibited over time.

> Inasmuch as teachers have many duties, both inside and outside of classrooms, incompetence, neglect of duty, and inefficiency encompass noninstructional as well as instructional obligations, such as maintaining proper classroom discipline, record keeping, and attending school functions.

One of the difficulties in establishing incompetence, neglect of duty, or inefficiency in teachers lies in defining the standards for professional proficiency. In one case, the Supreme Court of Nebraska commented that competence cannot be measured in a vacuum and does not require perfection, but rather should be judged according to the standard required of others performing the same function.[50] The court was not persuaded that the school board met this criterion, since it failed to show that the teacher's performance was below that of colleagues. In contrast, in a later case the same court affirmed a teacher's discharge, this time on the basis that her evaluations, which compared her performance with those of other similarly situated educators, did not measure up in light of such deficiencies as her inability to control her classes or her emotions when correcting students.[51]

It is important that criteria that school officials use to judge teachers' competence be as objective as possible. Not surprisingly, teachers often challenge evaluations conducted by administrators, given their inherent subjective nature. Since courts are reluctant to substitute their judgment for that of school officials, most are unwilling to void poor evaluations as long as the assessments have been conducted using professional criteria, are completed by competent supervisors, and are not arbitrary or capricious.[52] By way of illustration, an appellate court in New York refused to disturb an administrative decision upholding a number of unsatisfactory evaluations of a teacher conducted over a two-year period.[53] Similarly, on at least two occasions, appellate courts in Illinois upheld the dismissal of teachers who failed to improve their evaluation ratings following remediation periods during which they were given assistance.[54] As evidenced by a case from the Supreme Court of Minnesota, poor student progress can be the basis for a teacher's dismissal.[55] The court found that there was sufficient evidence to support a school board's action in discharging a tenured teacher due to his students' documented lack of progress.

Maintaining proper classroom discipline is an important function of all teachers. Teachers have been dismissed for incompetence for not establishing safe and orderly classrooms and, in general, failing to meet the needs of their students. The Supreme Court of Alaska determined that a school board was justified in discharging a tenured teacher who failed to deal effectively with student behavior management issues even after being given substantial support.[56] Similarly, an appellate court in Missouri refused to substitute its judgment for that of school administrators, upholding their dismissal of a teacher who failed to maintain classroom discipline, to provide sufficient individualized attention to students, and to offer administrators prompt and accurate information regarding student performances.[57] In another case, an appellate court in Tennessee affirmed the dismissal of a kindergarten teacher for inefficiency due to her inability to establish an orderly learning environment in her classroom.[58]

A major duty of classroom teachers is to supervise students properly. An appellate court in Mississippi agreed with a school board's termination of the contract of a teacher who left his classroom unattended on multiple occasions and failed to supervise students in other situations.[59] Similarly, the Supreme Court of Louisiana refused to second-guess the judgment of a school board that dismissed a tenured teacher who repeatedly sent unescorted students to the office in violation of her principal's directives.[60] In a particularly egregious case, the Supreme Court of Colorado affirmed the dismissal of a teacher who accompanied cheerleaders to a tournament and subsequently drank beer with them.[61] Interestingly, the court found that the teacher neglected her duty by not enforcing a board policy prohibiting the consumption of alcohol by students at school-sponsored activities.

Teachers may be dismissed for neglect of duty if they fail to implement approved curricula or use prescribed textbooks and materials. In such a case, an appellate court in Colorado upheld the dismissal of an educator who refused to teach the school board's adopted mathematics curriculum and distribute approved textbooks.[62] Since a hearing officer had previously determined that the teacher failed to fulfill her classroom duties and obligations, the court concluded that the board was not remiss in discharging her on this basis.

Teachers are expected to engage in noninstructional tasks such as evaluating or grading students' performances properly, providing students with feedback, giving students needed attention, maintaining student records, and completing required paperwork. An appellate court in Oregon upheld a school board's dismissal of a teacher who repeatedly failed to submit grades on time.[63] An appellate court in Missouri affirmed the termination of the contract of a special education teacher who failed to comply in a timely and accurate manner with the school system's paperwork requirements.[64] In upholding the teacher's dismissal, the court observed that case management and paperwork were integral parts of special education teachers' overall duties, and her deficiencies rose to the level of incompetency and inefficiency.

The Supreme Court of Nebraska ruled that a teacher who had taken days off due to the illness and death of her mother had not committed neglect of duty.[65] The court thought that since the teacher's absence did not violate the school system's leave policy, she had notified administrators that she needed to be absent, and she had provided lesson plans as required, her dismissal for unreasonable absenteeism was arbitrary and capricious. On the other hand, an appellate court in New York refused to overturn the dismissal of a school employee for excessive absenteeism and for failing to follow proper call-in procedures when he was absent.[66]

Similarly, in Florida, an appellate court upheld the dismissal of a teacher who failed to provide required lesson plans for her numerous absences.[67] By the same token, teachers who are consistently tardy or leave early without proper authorization may be dismissed.[68]

Teachers are expected to maintain and improve their skills by continuing to take courses or participating in other professional development activities. This requirement may be dictated by state regulations, school board rules, or contractual provisions. The Supreme Court, noting that school boards have an interest in providing students with competent, well-trained teachers, ruled that the dismissal of a teacher in Oklahoma who had failed to earn credits as required by a board rule did not deprive her of substantive due process or equal protection.[69]

Conduct Unbecoming a Teacher

Conduct unbecoming a teacher, sometimes referred to as *unprofessional conduct,* means that individuals displayed personal behavior inconsistent with professional standards, such as immoral acts, crimes, dishonesty, and/or failure to abide by professional ethics. It must be kept in mind that since teachers are role models, their conduct, even outside of school, must be exemplary.

> It must be kept in mind that since teachers are role models, their conduct, even outside of school, must be exemplary.

Teachers' use of unconventional disciplinary techniques often results in charges of unprofessional conduct. The Supreme Court of Nebraska, defining unprofessional conduct as that which breaches the rules or ethical code of a profession or is unbecoming to a member in good standing of a profession, upheld the dismissal of a teacher who, among other things, wrapped a student in an electrical cord, placed soap on a child's tongue, and shook a student while holding him by the jaw.[70]

Unprofessional behavior in the classroom can certainly be cause for dismissal, particularly when it clearly violates school board policy. For example, an appellate court in Missouri upheld the dismissal of a teacher who made racially discriminatory comments in class.[71] Similarly, the federal trial court in New Jersey refused to disturb the discharge of a teacher who was rude to students, belittled them in class, and used unconventional disciplinary techniques.[72] In yet another situation, an appellate court in Arizona affirmed that a school board was justified in dismissing a teacher who encouraged students to hit and kick each other as part of a game.[73] The court explained that the teacher's actions constituted physical abuse of children entrusted in his care. As in other areas, isolated incidents are generally insufficient to sustain the termination of teacher contracts, unless they are particularly egregious.[74]

Charges of immorality or moral turpitude often arise in teacher dismissal actions.[75] While teachers are entitled to privacy in their personal lives, their private actions can lead to discharges if these actions interfere with their abilities to be effective educators. To this end, as was discussed in Chapter 4, teachers do give up a degree of personal freedom when they accept employment as educators. Even so, due to changing standards, what was once considered to be immoral behavior may now be acceptable, even for educators. For example, an out of wedlock pregnancy today does not engender the disapproval it once did. In one such case, involving teachers' aides, the Fifth Circuit struck down a Mississippi school board's regulation prohibiting unwed parents from working in the system.[76] The court was not persuaded that the birth of a child out of wedlock, by itself, is evidence of immoral conduct or that unwed parents necessarily are unfit role models.[77] By the same token, it is just as unlikely that teachers who engage in adulterous affairs could be dismissed absent verification that the behavior had a negative impact on their work effectiveness.[78]

Courts consistently support the dismissal of teachers who engage in sexual relations with or sexually harass students.[79] Sexual contact with minors violates criminal codes, and a conviction for this crime can constitute grounds for termination.[80] Even absent criminal convictions, as would be expected, teachers may be fired for having sexual relations with students.[81] Courts sustain the removal of teachers who participate in consensual relationships with students even when the students are over the age of consent. In one case, an appellate court in Oklahoma upheld the termination of the contract of a female teacher who had a romantic relationship with a 17-year-old male student.[82]

At the same time, courts are disposed to support the dismissal of teachers who engage in relationships with former students, particularly those who only recently have graduated. For instance, the Sixth Circuit affirmed the denial of tenure to a teacher in Michigan who had a romantic relationship with a former student.[83] As another case from Michigan demonstrates, teachers may be removed for inappropriate sexual activity with students that occurred many years in the past.[84]

Teachers have been dismissed for off-campus conduct such as using illegal drugs.[85] To the extent that the arrests and convictions of teachers on drug charges may result in the revocation of their licenses, they are also grounds for dismissal. Still, teachers may be fired for using drugs even in the absence of criminal convictions.

As a rule, the standard of proof in dismissal hearings is less than is required for criminal convictions. Teachers may be dismissed if it can be shown that their misconduct leaves them ineffective. An appellate court in Connecticut upheld the dismissal of a tenured teacher who was charged

CASE SUMMARY 7.3: DISMISSAL FOR IMMORALITY

Zelno v. Lincoln Intermediate Unit No. 12 Board of Directors

786 A.2d 1022 (Pa. Commw. Ct. 2002)

Factual Summary: A tenured teacher assigned to an alternative education program operated by a drug and alcohol residential treatment facility for court-adjudicated youth pled guilty to a third offense of driving under the influence of alcohol and a second offense of driving after her license was suspended. The facility's board of directors voted to dismiss the teacher, contending that her conduct violated sections of the public school statutes regarding immorality. On appeal the state secretary of education affirmed the board's decision. The teacher appealed.

Issue: May a teacher be discharged for immorality as a result of multiple convictions for driving under the influence?

Decision: Yes, the state court upheld the decision of the secretary of education, thus ruling that teachers may be dismissed for immorality as a result of multiple convictions for driving under the influence.

Summary of Court's Rationale: The court noted that although a single incident of driving under the influence would have been a serious mistake, a third offense, which resulted in a criminal conviction, constituted immoral conduct as the term is used in the school code. The court also reasoned that the teacher's conduct made her a bad role model for students whose ideals she was supposed to foster. This, the court offered, affected her credibility and impacted her ability to teach. Further, the court noted that testimony at the teacher's hearing indicated that her behavior offended the morals of her community.

with possession of cocaine and drug paraphernalia but was never convicted of the crime, because he completed rehabilitation.[86] The court was convinced that the teacher's conduct undermined his ability to work with other faculty, set a poor example for students, and reflected personal values that were inconsistent with his role as a teacher. In another case, the Supreme Court of Appeals of West Virginia affirmed the dismissal of a teacher who was arrested but later acquitted of selling marijuana to an undercover police officer.[87] The teacher admitted to smoking marijuana during his trial, and the school board then received petitions opposing his continued employment. The court was satisfied that the notoriety surrounding the teacher was an adequate reason for his dismissal.[88]

Courts agree that actions compromising teachers' abilities to be role models are sufficient grounds for dismissal. In a sad situation, a teacher from Iowa was dismissed after she allowed her son and other students to drink alcohol illegally on her property. Unfortunately, four of the students were killed in an accident when they left the party to obtain more alcohol. The state's high court ascertained that the school board had just cause to terminate the teacher's contract, since she knew the students were drinking and did nothing to curtail the party, an action that constituted unprofessional conduct.[89] The court agreed that her actions damaged her reputation as a teacher and were detrimental to her ability to be an effective role model. Similarly, the Supreme Court of Iowa sustained the dismissal of a teacher who was arrested for shoplifting.[90] The court noted that the teacher's actions were not consistent with being a good role model for students and that being a role model is part of a teacher's effectiveness.

Analogously, courts have held that actions that are offensive to community values also provide adequate reasons for dismissals. In one such case, an appellate court in Pennsylvania was of the opinion that a teacher's federal conviction for trafficking in counterfeit goods or services was offensive to the community and warranted termination of his contract.[91] The court explained that the teacher's behavior presented a "bad example to the youth whose ideals a teacher is supposed to foster and elevate."[92] In another case, the same court refused to disturb the dismissal of a teacher who was convicted following multiple offenses of driving under the influence (of alcohol) and with a suspended license.[93] After hearing testimony that the teacher's behavior offended community values, the court acknowledged that her behavior made her a bad role model. In yet another example, an appellate court in Michigan upheld the discharge of a teacher who pled guilty to a charge of embezzling funds from a part-time employer.[94] The court was satisfied that due to the effect his actions had on students, parents, and his peers, the teacher could no longer serve as a role model. Using similar logic, an appellate court in New York supported the firing of a teacher who was convicted of grand larceny, finding that she was not an appropriate role model for young people.[95]

Other Good or Just Cause

The catchall terms *other good or just cause* or *other sufficient cause* are difficult to define but may encompass the other specific bases for discharge

Good or just cause refers to other conduct that interferes with the continued performance of duties. For the most part it is left to the courts to determine if reasons given for discharge constitute a good or just cause under applicable state statutes and regulations.

outlined within state statutes as well as other reasonable grounds that are not arbitrary or irrational.[96] Thus, in addition to other stipulated reasons for dismissal, good or just cause refers to other conduct that interferes with the continued performance of duties. For the most part, it is left to the courts to evaluate whether the reasons that school boards give for discharge constitute good or just cause under applicable state statutes and regulations.

As was explained in Chapter 4, teachers must be properly certificated to teach in public schools. Loss of teaching certificates, regardless of whether they are revoked by the state or lapse due to inaction on the part of teachers, certainly constitutes good and just cause for terminating teachers' contracts.[97] In one case, an appellate court in Colorado decided that the facts that a teacher let her license lapse, failed to inform school administrators that it had expired, continued to teach with it, and failed to take steps to renew her certification constituted good and just cause warranting her dismissal.[98] Similarly, the high court in that same state affirmed that the lapse in a teacher's certification that occurred while she was on a leave of absence warranted sufficient cause for her dismissal.[99] Similarly, school boards may dismiss teachers who fraudulently obtained their certifications[100] or submitted false information on their job applications.

In another case, an appellate court in Ohio agreed that a teacher's conduct in telling dirty jokes to students and referring to another teacher by a derogatory name in front of students constituted good and just cause to justify her termination.[101] In like manner, the Supreme Court of Iowa upheld a school board's dismissal of a teacher with a history of making sarcastic, offensive, and inappropriate comments to students despite being warned that his humor was objectionable.[102]

Conviction of a misdemeanor or felony, although normally falling under the category of conduct unbecoming a teacher, can be sufficient cause to terminate an individual's contract. An appellate court in Indiana affirmed that a school board was justified in discharging a teacher who pled guilty to charges of assault and battery and fleeing a police officer.[103] In refusing to disturb the termination of the teacher's contract, the court observed that an educator's behavior outside the classroom bears a reasonable relationship to his qualifications for employment.

CASE SUMMARY 7.4: DISMISSAL FOR OTHER GOOD OR JUST CAUSE

Hanes v. Board of Education of the City of Bridgeport

783 A.2d 1 (Conn. Ct. App. 2001)

Factual Summary: A tenured teacher who taught a language arts course designed to enhance student scores on a statutorily mandated statewide mastery test administered a subtest of the examination that measured students' vocabulary and spelling skills. An investigation into test disparities revealed that the teacher altered the answer sheets. Specifically, the investigation concluded that after collecting the answer sheets, the teacher filled in answers to questions that had been left blank by the students and changed answers that she believed were incorrect. After the school board terminated the teacher's employment contract, a trial court ruled in favor of the school board. This appeal followed.

Issue: Does a charge that a teacher altered student responses on student answer sheets on a standardized test justify dismissal for other good or just cause?

Decision: Yes, the state appellate court affirmed the decision of the trial court, thus ruling that the school board had adequate cause to dismiss a teacher who altered student answer sheets on a standardized test.

Summary of Court's Rationale: As an initial matter the court acknowledged that the evidence in the record supported the conclusion that the teacher tampered with the answer sheets. The court noted that in previous decisions, it defined good cause to include any grounds that are put forward by a school board in good faith and that are not arbitrary, irrational, unreasonable, or irrelevant to the board's task of maintaining an efficient school system. In the present case, the court agreed that the teacher's actions deprived students of appropriate placements, provided parents with inaccurate feedback, negatively impacted the school's eligibility for grant funds, and caused the school to submit false results to the statewide testing program. Thus, the court averred that since the teacher's conduct adversely affected the school's operations, the school board acted reasonably and rationally in terminating her employment.

Today, as a regular part of their duties, teachers are required to administer standardized examinations to students. Most of these examinations have strict rules regarding their administration that educators must follow to ensure the integrity of their results. In such a case, an appellate court in Connecticut acknowledged that a teacher's tampering with the administration of a statewide examination, by filling in answers that were left blank and changing incorrect answers, was sufficient cause for her dismissal.[104]

Procedures

Tenured teachers who have property interests in their jobs have an expectation of continued employment. Probationary teachers facing dismissal before the expiration of their contracts, depending on state law or collective bargaining agreements, may have comparable interests.[105] The Supreme Court, in *Cleveland Board of Education v. Loudermill*[106] ruled that public employees who can be discharged only for cause are entitled to oral or written notice of the charges brought against them, an explanation of the employer's evidence, and an opportunity to present their sides of the story. Although the Court did not establish an exact prescription for procedural due process for dismissals, it did indicate that, at a minimum, teachers facing discharge are entitled to notice and a hearing.[107] State statutes, school board policies, or collective bargaining agreements may provide additional procedural protections for teachers facing dismissal.

Notice

The purpose of providing notice is not only to inform teachers of school boards' intent to dismiss them, but also to specify the grounds on which the contemplated actions is based. In order to afford teachers facing dismissal fair opportunities to defend themselves against any charges, the notice must include a summary of the charges and the evidence against them. Notice must be specific enough to grant teachers the opportunity to refute the charges and to prepare defenses.[108] Notice must also provide a sufficient time in advance of scheduled hearings so that teachers have ample time to prepare.[109] In this respect, state statutes frequently specify the number of days before hearings that the notice must be rendered.

Teachers have often challenged the adequacy of the notice they received, claiming that it was too unclear to allow them to prepare properly for hearings. Notice should thus include particulars such as names, dates, facts, and

> In order to afford teachers facing dismissal a fair opportunity to defend themselves against the charges they face, notice must include a summary of the charges and the evidence against them.

other information that school board officials rely on in making dismissal decisions. For example, an appellate court in Louisiana held that a notice that failed to list the time and place of alleged offenses and the names of witnesses did not comply with state law requirements.[110] In contrast, the Fourth Circuit agreed that a notice outlining the charges against a teacher and providing him with the opportunity to present a defense was sufficient.[111]

As indicated in a previous section, school boards frequently allege patterns of continuing misconduct or deficiencies in their attempts to discharge teachers. In such cases, notice should include information regarding the alleged misconduct and the dates on which it occurred. By way of illustration, the Supreme Court of Arkansas reasoned that the teacher could not be discharged, because the notice he received did not state a reason indicative of a pattern of misconduct.[112]

Hearings

Hearings, which are less formal than judicial proceedings, are not subject to the same procedural requirements as trials, so the rules for admission of evidence and cross examination of witnesses[113] are greatly relaxed. Insofar as teacher dismissals are civil matters, courts are satisfied when decision makers apply the lesser standard of proof, that of a preponderance of the evidence, in order to substantiate cause for dismissal. Hearings may be conducted by independent hearing officers, arbitrators, or local school boards. Ultimately, regardless of who conducts hearings, boards have the authority to make dismissal decisions. In most jurisdictions, final hearing orders are subject to judicial review. Even so, when state statutes set down procedures for the conduct of hearings, they must be strictly followed.

Depending on state law, dismissal hearings may be either open to the public or conducted behind closed doors. Teachers facing dismissal are usually allowed to be represented by attorneys and may question witnesses. A federal trial court in Kentucky posited that at a minimum, employees facing discharge must be allowed to attend hearings, have the assistance of counsel, and be permitted to call witnesses, produce evidence on their own behalf, and challenge evidence against them.[114] Since decisions regarding dismissals must be based on credible documented evidence, courts generally do not disturb findings of fact unless they are clearly erroneous.

Teachers frequently mount challenges when school boards conduct dismissal hearings. It is well settled, however, that school boards may conduct such hearings.[115] The fact that school boards may have familiarity with the facts of situations does not disqualify them from acting as decision makers in dismissal

> Teachers frequently mount challenges when school boards conduct dismissal hearings. It is well settled, however, that school boards may conduct such hearings.

hearings. The impartiality of boards as decision makers is assumed, since they normally lack inherent bias toward teachers facing dismissal.[116] When teachers allege bias, then, the burden is ordinarily on them to show that board members are incapable of acting impartially.[117]

Remedies for Wrongful Dismissal

Teachers who are wrongfully discharged from their positions more often than not are entitled to reinstatement as well as some form of financial compensation. In addition to being reinstated to their former jobs, teachers are also entitled to restoration of their rightful positions on scales of salaries and benefits, including seniority.[118]

> Teachers who are wrongfully discharged from their positions more often than not are entitled to reinstatement as well as some form of financial compensation.

In order to receive compensation in the form of monetary damages, teachers must demonstrate that they suffered economic losses. In this regard, wrongfully discharged teachers are entitled to recover the amount of pay they would have earned had they not been discharged.[119] Damages awards normally consist of the lost salary, but they can be mitigated by the amount of money that teachers earned in alternative employment during periods when they were out of work with the systems that discharged them. In other words, if teachers secured other employment after being dismissed, damages awards are usually the difference between the salary they lost and what they actually earned in the other job. Naturally, no damages are awarded if teachers earned more in the alternative position. Further, in addition to recovering salaries, wrongfully discharged teachers may be entitled to recover retirement contributions and health care costs as well as the legal costs they incurred in successfully challenging school board dismissal actions.[120]

Teachers do have a duty to try to mitigate damages, meaning that they have an obligation to seek and accept alternative employment while contesting whether they were discharged improperly. Yet, there are limitations on the types of employment teachers may be expected to accept. For example, teachers are not expected to relocate to other geographic regions to mitigate damages or accept jobs that are not of the same general nature as the ones they formerly held. While the burden is on school boards to show that teachers failed to mitigate damages,[121] teachers may be required to show that they made reasonable efforts to obtain other employment.[122]

REDUCTION IN FORCE

In today's economic climate, school boards frequently must take action to cut budgets. Inasmuch as salaries make up the largest portion of school budgets, this necessarily requires reductions in staffing. Reductions in the teacher workforce also may occur when enrollments decline and school systems do not need as many teachers to serve their student populations. Most states now have statutes that specifically deal with the situations where teaching or other positions must be eliminated through no fault on the part of individual teachers, regardless of whether they are tenured. Thus, the overall grounds for reduction in force (RIF), the order in which teachers are dismissed, and call-back rights are generally outlined in state laws, with specific details enumerated in collective bargaining agreements or school board policies.[123]

Grounds for RIFs

The reasons school boards may dismiss teachers as part of RIFs are ordinarily established under state law but can be modified by the terms of their collective bargaining agreements. RIFs are most commonly permitted for declines in student enrollments;[124] financial exigencies;[125] discontinuation of programs;[126] and *other good or just cause* or *board discretion,*[127] terms that vary from one jurisdiction to the next.

Seniority Rights

In most situations involving RIFs, teachers are released in reverse order of seniority, meaning that the least senior faculty members are let go first. Since the order of release is usually dictated by state law or collective bargaining agreements, the sequence in which layoffs occur may vary from one jurisdiction to another. To further complicate matters, many teachers are certificated to teach more than one level or subject. Consequently, RIF statutes and policies typically establish "bumping" rights whereby teachers whose jobs have been eliminated may transfer into positions held by less senior colleagues as long as they have proper certification.[128] While school boards are usually required to consider whether laid off teachers are eligible for other positions, officials are not obligated to realign positions or rearrange schedules to create new positions for which dismissed teachers would be qualified.[129]

> In most situations involving RIFs, teachers are released in reverse order of seniority, meaning that the least senior faculty members are let go first.

Another issue is whether teachers who change positions during their careers accrue seniority according to the time spent in the position or the school system. While layoffs often occur according to individuals' seniority in the system, this can be modified by collective bargaining agreements or state statutes. In one such case, an appellate court in New York invalidated a provision in a collective bargaining agreement that allowed teaching time in other areas to be applied to seniority status in teachers' current areas.[130] The court ruled that under state statute, teachers with more seniority within their department were entitled to be retained over colleagues with less time in their departments but greater seniority in their school systems. Another corollary issue is whether teachers who changed positions retain seniority in their former positions. Again, this is often addressed by negotiated agreements, but it is not unusual for policies to stipulate that teachers lose bumping rights if they have not taught or taken courses in particular areas for a specified number of years. For instance, the Supreme Court of South Dakota observed that a teacher who had not taught within an area of certification for more than seven years could not bump into a position in that area.[131]

Whether seniority is a factor when probationary teachers are subject to RIFs varies. In some jurisdictions all probationary teachers may be treated alike, regardless of their seniority, since none of them have a property right to continued employment. In other locales probationary teachers may have the same seniority rights as all teachers.[132] Regardless, it goes without saying that a probationary teacher must be released before a tenured staff member when both are qualified for a given position.[133]

Additional Factors

Courts acknowledge seniority rights but recognize that other factors may be taken into considerations for both hiring and RIF purposes.[134] In such a case, the Supreme Court of Nebraska affirmed that a school board, pursuant to its own policy, could retain a less senior teacher who made a greater contribution to the school system's activities program.[135] The court noted that since state law neither authorized nor prohibited boards from considering teachers' contributions to activities programs as a criterion for a RIF, it was in their discretion to do so.

> Courts do acknowledge seniority rights but recognize that other factors may be taken into considerations for both hiring and RIF purposes.

Certification is an important criterion in any RIF decision. As a rule, certificated teachers may not be RIFed while noncertificated teachers are retained, regardless of seniority.[136] Teachers seeking to be transferred to new positions to avoid layoffs must be properly certificated for the new jobs. In such a case, an appellate court in New York determined that a school psychologist could not transfer to the position of elementary school counselor, because he was not properly certificated for that position.[137] A case from Illinois illustrates the importance of teachers notifying their school board when they have obtained additional certifications. The court held that a teacher had no right to bump a less senior teacher whose position he was qualified to fill where he had failed to demonstrate his qualifications before the school board sent out layoff notices.[138] In like fashion, the Supreme

Court of Indiana pointed out that when two teachers vie for the same position, and neither is fully certificated, a school board may retain the less senior teacher if that individual is closer to obtaining proper certification.[139]

School boards also may consider factors such as advanced degrees or the number of certifications teachers possess in selecting which teachers to retain. In eliminating teaching positions, boards, particularly in smaller school systems, may need to retain teachers who can provide instruction in more than one subject or discipline. In a case where this was at issue, the Supreme Court of Montana ruled that a school board's decision to retain teachers with multiple certifications over a more senior teacher with certification in only one subject was objective and fair.[140]

CASE SUMMARY 7.5: REDUCTION IN FORCE

Scobey School District v. Radakovich

135 P.3d 778 (Mont. 2006)

Factual Summary: In taking RIF action, a school board restructured teaching positions based on the certification status of existing staff. In doing so, the board eliminated a social studies teaching position in favor of creating jobs including multiple-subject teaching responsibilities. A tenured high school social studies teacher who was certificated only in social studies and had never taught any other subject was released, while two more junior teachers with multiple certificates were retained. The teacher challenged his dismissal, but it was upheld in arbitration and administrative appeals. After complicated judicial proceedings, a state trial court reversed these decisions, ruling in favor of the teacher.

Issue: May a school board consider multiple certifications when determining the priority of teachers to be retained in a RIF?

Decision: Yes, on further review, the Supreme Court of Montana, reversing in favor of the school board, agreed that the school board could consider multiple certifications when prioritizing which teachers could be retained as part of a RIF.

Summary of Court's Rationale: The court first observed that a school board has the duty to manage its district in a financially responsible manner and that tenured teachers did not have the right to teach in positions for which they were unqualified. After examining the evidence in the present situation, the court determined that the board's use of multiple certifications as a criterion in a RIF was objective and fairly applied. The court stated that the multiple certification criterion was objective and applied fairly, since all of the teachers who were retained had multiple certifications.

As was discussed in Chapter 6, many school boards have created diversity within their teaching corps via affirmative action plans. Unfortunately, many of those systems have been faced with the prospect of layoffs recreating an imbalance. For example, in many formerly racially segregated systems, the more senior members of a faculty may be nonminorities, while less senior members may be minorities. Consequently, many school boards have enacted RIF policies designed to preserve diversity. The Supreme Court, in *Wygant v. Jackson Board of Education,* [141] struck down an arrangement that resulted in the retention of minority teachers with less seniority than nonminority teachers. The Court was of the opinion that this practice violated the Equal Protection Clause, since it was based on racial or ethnic criteria, and there was no evidence that the retained minority teachers had been the victims of individual discrimination. A year later, a full panel of the Seventh Circuit decided that a collective bargaining agreement that stated that minority teachers would not be laid off in the event of a RIF violated the Equal Protection Clause. [142] The court was persuaded that the plan was not intended to remediate past discrimination, but rather, created a preference for one race. Similarly, in a case that was days away from oral arguments at the Supreme Court when the parties decided to enter into a settlement agreement, the Third Circuit struck down an affirmative action policy that resulted in the retention of a minority teacher over a white teacher with equal seniority. [143] The court explained that the policy was unconstitutional, because it was adopted to promote racial diversity rather than remedy discrimination.

Call-Back Rights

As districts gain enrollment or funding to be able to hire again after a RIF, teachers who have been dismissed due to RIFs typically have the right to be called back before school boards may fill available positions with new applicants. In other words, boards must offer open positions to qualified teachers who have been RIFed before offering them to individuals who have never worked in the school system. Subject to statutory provisions, school board policies, and collective bargaining agreements, teachers are usually called back according to their seniority.

> Subject to statutory provisions, school board policies, and collective bargaining agreements, teachers are usually called back according to their seniority.

The Supreme Court of Appeals in West Virginia, in a case on this point, ruled that individuals who were not former employees were ineligible to be hired for teaching positions until all qualified permanent employees and all qualified teachers on the recall list had been offered the opportunity for reemployment in positions for which they were qualified. [144]

State statutes and collective bargaining agreements may place some restrictions on call-back rights, particularly for probationary teachers. Still, teacher call-back rights are not indefinite. Many provisions stipulate that teachers may remain on a call-back list for a specified period of time such as two or three years, or until they are offered, and refuse, an open position.[145] Since probationary teachers lack property rights to employment in the first place, their call-back rights may be limited as well. For instance, an appellate court in California specified that, pursuant to state law, a school board was not required to rehire a probationary teacher who had been employed by the district less than two consecutive years prior to the teacher's dismissal in a RIF.[146]

Many of the same considerations exist for calling back teachers as for letting them go in the first place. In addition to seniority, certification is a prime consideration.[147] Even so, school boards have some discretion in assessing teachers' qualifications for open positions.[148] In other words, boards may consider other factors, such as experience, in addition to certification in recalling teachers.

SUMMARY AND RECOMMENDATIONS

State statutes provide teachers with protections from unfair or arbitrary termination of their contracts. These statutes confer what is generally referred to as tenure on teachers after they have satisfactorily served probationary periods and have met any other requirements for continued employment. Once teachers have attained tenure, they have continuing contracts and may be dismissed only for causes enumerated in state law. Conversely, prior to obtaining tenure, teachers are at-will employees who lack guarantees that their contracts will be extended.

Most state statutes provide that tenured teachers may be discharged for causes such as insubordination, incompetence, neglect of duty, inefficiency, conduct unbecoming a teacher, and other good or just cause. Since defining these terms has largely been left to the courts, there has been a considerable amount of litigation contesting adverse employment decisions. Even so, courts generally defer to school boards regarding teacher dismissals, reviewing their decisions only for procedural irregularities, arbitrariness, or abuse of discretion. Teachers facing dismissals are entitled to notice of the charges against them, an explanation of the evidence, and an opportunity to tell their side of the story. Wrongfully discharged teachers are usually entitled to reinstatement, an award of back pay, and restoration of benefits.

Teachers also may be dismissed without fault of their own when school boards must reduce the number of teaching positions due to declining enrollments, discontinuations of programs, or fiscal exigencies. School board RIF policies usually take factors such as seniority and certification into account but may be based on other considerations as well. In this respect, as long as boards adhere to all state laws and contractual provisions, and their decisions are not arbitrary, courts usually defer to their judgments regarding the needs of their school systems.

Even though tenure and fair dismissal statues vary considerably from state to state, a number of general principles have emerged from common law. The recommendations and points below are applicable in almost all jurisdictions.

- Since aspects of employment such as tenure, teacher discipline and dismissal, and reduction in force are governed predominantly by state statutes, teachers need to be aware of the laws of their own states.
- Probationary periods vary from one state to another, but most are between three and five years.
- Since probationary periods generally must be continuous, breaks in service may start calendars over again.
- Teachers should check their state laws to ascertain the required length of probationary periods and other conditions that may apply to attaining tenure.
- When teachers are dismissed for cause, courts generally do not disturb the actions of school boards, as long as the boards have followed proper procedures and reached judgments that are consistent with state law.
- Courts generally look for patterns of continuing or persistent insubordination before sustaining a teacher's discharge. Even so, single acts of insubordination may be cause for dismissal, especially for egregious behavior.
- Incompetence, neglect of duty, and inefficiency are the causes most often stated by school boards when attempting to terminate the contracts of teachers whose job performance does not measure up to expected standards.
- Teachers are expected to be positive role models for their students. Thus, any behavior, even off campus, that compromises teachers' role model status and impacts their effectiveness in the classroom can be justification for dismissal as conduct unbecoming a teacher.
- While it is difficult to define the term *other good or just cause*, school boards have successfully used the phrase to justify teacher discharge for reasons that may not be specifically enumerated in the statutes.

- Teachers who have been wrongfully discharged are entitled to back pay and restoration of their benefits. Restoration to positions on seniority lists may require the realignment of other educators on the lists.
- Teachers who are wrongfully discharged may have obligations to mitigate financial damages. In other words, teachers must diligently seek alternate employment in similar fields and geographic locations.
- While RIFs most often occur along lines of seniority, other factors may be taken into consideration. It is important for teachers to be aware of all of the terms of collective bargaining agreements in this regard.
- Seniority is usually the main factor in calling back teachers when new positions become available. Still, school boards may consider other qualifications such as certification and experience.

FREQUENTLY ASKED QUESTIONS

Q. Are school boards required to provide reasons and justifications for not renewing the contracts of probationary teachers?

A. As a rule, school boards do not need to provide probationary teachers with the reasons for nonrenewal of their contracts. Although it is fairly rare, some states do require boards to provide nonrenewed probationary teachers with the reasons for their nonrenewal. Also, when probationary teachers can satisfy courts that their contracts were not renewed for discriminatory reasons, the burden then shifts to school boards to show that they had legitimate reasons for not extending the teachers' contracts.

Q. Our teachers' association representatives generally advise that teachers should obey directives of administrators, even if they feel that the directives are unreasonable or in violation of the contract. Since courts generally do not sustain dismissals for insubordination when the directives were unreasonable, is this advice sound?

A. Yes. Although teachers may think that the directive is unreasonable, courts may not agree. It is always best to obey directives, if at all possible, and challenge them later through school systems' grievance procedures. This practice does not put teachers' jobs in jeopardy while the propriety of the directives is being questioned.

Q. I understand that teachers are expected to be good role models for their students, but how can my private out-of-school behavior be cause for dismissal?

A. If the private out-of-school behavior of teachers causes them to lose respect or in any way impairs the teacher's effectiveness in the classroom, it can be cause for dismissal. Courts have routinely accepted that teachers need to be positive role models, and when their private behavior essentially renders them incapable of fulfilling that function, they may be discharged.

Q. The phrase other good or just cause *as a reason for termination sounds vague. What constitutes good or just cause? Why aren't state legislatures more specific?*

A. As courts have recognized, it is nearly impossible for state legislatures to anticipate all possibilities when it comes to appropriate reasons to discharge teachers. For this reason, most state statutes contain a catchall phrase such as *other good or just cause*. As with other grounds for dismissal, this term has been left to the courts to define. Courts generally accept reasonable explanations from school boards as to why teachers should be discharged, as long as officials can demonstrate connections between the teachers' misconduct or deficiencies and the proper operation of schools.

Q. A former teacher in my school system was recently reinstated after having been wrongfully discharged. The teacher was unemployed for two years before being reinstated, and on his return those two years were added to his seniority, placing him ahead of me on the seniority list. I have actually worked in the system one more year than he has. Isn't this unfair?

A. The teacher was simply restored to the position on the seniority list he would have been in had he not been discharged. The fact that he did not work in the system for those two years was not his fault but that of the school board. Fairness dictates that wrongfully discharged personnel be restored to the positions they would have been in if the discharges had not occurred.

WHAT'S NEXT

The next chapter outlines the many legal issues that fall under the expansive topic of curriculum and instruction. It covers the state legislatures' and local school boards' authority to establish and control the curriculum and instructional methodologies, including controversial aspects of the instructional program. The chapter also examines the related subjects of grading policies and graduation requirements. It also discusses the current state of the law regarding testing and evaluating students, record keeping, copyright law, and technology in the classroom, along with the requirements to provide remedial programs.

ENDNOTES

1. Adler v. Board of Education, 342 U.S. 485 (1952).

2. Many states use terms other than *tenure* to describe continuing contracts, such as *professional teacher* or *permanent status*, or descriptors such as *fair dismissal policy*. This chapter uses the term *tenure* for the sake of simplicity to describe systems affording teachers protection from arbitrary or unjust dismissals.

3. The term *probationary teachers*, as used in this chapter, is synonymous with *nontenured teachers*.

4. *See, e.g.*, Roberts v. Lincoln County School District, 676 P.2d 577 (Wyo. 1984) (finding that an initial contract teacher had no claim, entitlement, or reasonable expectation of employment).

5. *See, e.g.*, 71 Massachusetts General Laws Annotated § 41, which states that teachers who have served for three previous consecutive school years are entitled to professional teacher status (tenure).

6. *See, e.g.*, Ray v. Board of Education of Oak Ridge Schools, 72 S.W.3d 657 (Tenn. Ct. App. 2001) (ruling that under state law the conferral of tenure status was dependent not only on completion of a probationary period but also on affirmative action by the school board).

7. *See, e.g.*, Smith v. Governing Board of Elk Grove Unified School District, 16 Cal. Rptr. 3d 1 (Cal. Ct. App. 2004) (finding a teacher ineligible for permanent status under a statute providing that time spent teaching under an emergency permit did not count toward permanent status); Scheer v. Independent School District N. I-26 of Ottawa County, 948 P.2d 275 (Okla. 1997) (ruling that teachers employed under temporary contracts were statutorily exempt from tenure laws).

8. *See, e.g.*, Reis v. Biggs Unified School District, 24 Cal. Rptr. 3d 393 (Cal. Ct. App. 2005); Emanuel v. Independent School District No. 273, 615 N.W.2d 415 (Minn. Ct. App. 2000); Bochner v. Providence School Committee, 490 A.2d 37 (R.I. 1985) (refusing to count short-term service as a substitute toward tenure); Harkins v. Ohio County Board of Education, 369 S.E.2d 224 (W.Va. 1988) (taking full-time substitute teaching into consideration in determining that a teacher was entitled to tenure); Dial v. Lathrop R-II School District, 871 S.W.2d 444 (Mo. 1994) (allowing part-time employment to accrue toward permanent status).

9. *See, e.g.*, Valter v. Orchard Farm School District, 511 S.W.2d 550 (Mo. 1976) (ruling that a probationary teacher dismissed during the contract period was entitled to due process); Jacob v. Board of Regents, 365 A.2d 430 (R.I. 1976) (pointing out that a probationary teacher dismissed during the school year was entitled to a hearing).

10. *See, e.g.*, Goodman v. Hasbrouck Heights School District, 275 F. App'x 105 (3d Cir. 2008) (noting that although a nontenured teacher lacked a property interest entitling him to due process, he may have had a state law claim, since New Jersey law required 60 days notice prior to dismissal).

11. *See, e.g.*, Back v. Hastings on Hudson Union Free School District, 365 F.3d 107 (2d Cir. 2004) (observing that the view that a female could not be a good

mother and work long hours, or that she would not demonstrate her prior level of commitment to teaching after having children, could constitute evidence of gender discrimination, supporting the employee's equal protection claims).

12. *See, e.g.,* McKinnon v. Board of Education of North Bellmore Union Free School District, 709 N.Y.S.2d 104 (N.Y. App. Div. 2000) (upholding the dismissal of an employee for excessive absenteeism).

13. *See, e.g.,* Palmer v. Louisiana State Board of Elementary and Secondary Education, 842 So. 2d 363 (La. 2003) (finding that a school board's failure to provide valid reasons for not renewing a probationary teacher's contract as required by state law amounted to an illegal discharge); Naylor v. Cardinal Local School District Board of Education, 630 N.E.2d 725 (Ohio 1994) (explaining that state law required the board to provide a clear and substantive basis for not renewing a probationary teacher's contract).

14. *See, e.g.,* Ottawa Education Association v. Unified School District No. 290, 666 P.2d 680 (Kan. 1983) (ruling that teachers who were not notified of the nonrenewal of their contracts by the statutorily mandated date would have a continuing contract for the following school year); Gillespie v. Board of Education of North Little Rock School District, 692 F.2d 529 (8th Cir. 1982) (affirming that state statute provided for the automatic renewal of teacher contracts absent affirmative action by the school board, such as timely written notice that the contracts would not be renewed).

15. *See, e.g.,* Kiel v. Green Local School District Board of Education, 630 N.E.2d 716 (Ohio 1994) (recognizing that mailing a nonrenewal notice to a high school address where it was received and signed for by an individual other than the intended recipient did not comply with state statute requiring written notice).

16. *See, e.g.,* Hoschler v. Sacramento City School District, 57 Cal. Rptr. 3d 115 (Cal. Ct. App. 2007) (affirming that a teacher who received his notice of nonrenewal in the mail, when the statutes required that it be delivered in person, was entitled to reinstatement).

17. *See, e.g.,* Snyder v. Mendon-Union District Board of Education, 661 N.E.2d 717 (Ohio 1996) (finding that state law prescribed that probationary teachers be evaluated twice per year based on two observations of at least 30 minutes).

18. Naylor v. Cardinal Local School District Board of Education, 630 N.E.2d 725 (Ohio 1994).

19. *For example,* Massachusetts permits superintendents to award tenure to teachers who have served for at least one year. 71 Massachusetts General Laws § 41.

20. 71 Massachusetts General Laws § 42.

21. Childs v. Roane County Board of Education, 929 S.W.2d 364 (Tenn. Ct. App. 1996).

22. *See, e.g.,* East Canton Education Association v. McIntosh, 709 N.E.2d 468 (Ohio 1999) (ruling that a teacher did not waive his continuing contract status by accepting an administrative position).

23. *See, e.g.,* 71 Massachusetts General Laws § 41, which authorizes superintendents to award tenure to teachers who attained tenure in another public school district in the state.

24. *See, e.g.,* Board of Education of Benton Harbor Area Schools v. Wolff, 361 N.W.2d 750 (Mich. Ct. App. 1984) (finding that a teacher may not be

discharged without first being notified of and given a reasonable opportunity to correct deficiencies).

25. *See, e.g.,* Hall v. Board of Trustees of Sumter County School District, 499 S.E.2d 216 (S.C. Ct. App. 1998) (remarking that a teacher who was discharged for insubordination and failure to supervise students should have been given a reasonable time for improvement); Board of Education of Chicago v. Harris, 578 N.E.2d 1244 (Ill. App. Ct. 1991) (maintaining that a teacher's refusal to accept a classroom assignment was irremediable). Criminal conduct is almost always considered to be irremediable. *See* City School District of City of New York v. Campbell, 798 N.Y.S.2d 54 (N.Y. App. Div. 2005); McBroom v. Board of Education, 494 N.E. 2d 1191 (Ill. App. Ct. 1986).

26. For an example of documentation that may be used in teacher dismissal proceedings, *see* Frels, K., & Horton, J. A. (2007). *A documentation system for teacher improvement or termination.* Dayton, OH: Education Law Association.

27. *See, e.g.,* Hope v. Charlotte-Mecklenburg Board of Education, 430 S.E.2d 472 (N.C. Ct. App. 1993) (upholding the dismissal of a teacher, in part, because she had failed to develop and implement a professional growth plan as directed by her principal).

28. Sullivan S. S., & Glanz, J. G. (2005). *Supervision that improves teaching: Strategies and techniques.* Thousand Oaks, CA: Corwin.

29. Russo, C. J. (2009). *Reutter's the law of public education* (7th ed.). New York: Foundation Press.

30. Bellairs v. Beaverton School District, 136 P.3d 93 (Or. Ct. App. 2006).

31. Ware v. Morgan County School District, 748 P.2d 1295 (Colo. 1988). *See also* Lackrow v. Department of Education of the City of New York, 859 N.Y.S.2d 52 (N.Y. App. Div. 2008) (upholding dismissal of a teacher who used inappropriate language in the classroom after having been warned about the inappropriateness of his behavior).

32. Board of Education of Jefferson County v. Wilder, 960 P.2d 695 (Colo. 1988).

33. Fink v. Board of Education of Warren County School District, 442 A.2d 837 (Pa. Commw. Ct. 1982); La Rocca v. Board of Education of Rye City School District, 406 N.Y.S.2d 348 (N.Y. App. Div. 1978).

34. *See, e.g.,* School District No. 1, City and County of Denver v. Cornish, 58 P.3d 1091 (Colo. Ct. App. 2002) (upholding the dismissal of a teacher who refused to teach the approved curriculum and refused to submit lesson plans to her principal); Hope v. Charlotte-Mecklenburg Board of Education, 430 S.E.2d 472 (N.C. Ct. App. 1993) (affirming the dismissal of a teacher, in part, because she had failed to discontinue a class project as directed by supervisors); In re Termination of James E. Johnson, 451 N.W.2d 343 (Minn. Ct. App. 1990) (upholding the dismissal of a teacher who failed to follow directives to change his instructional methods).

35. Board of Trustees of School District No. 4, Big Horn County v. Colwell, 611 P.2d 427 (Wyo. 1980).

36. Lockhart v. Arapahoe County School District No. 6, 735 P.2d 913 (Colo. Ct. App. 1987).

37. Meckley v. Kanawha County Board of Education, 383 S.E.2d 839 (W.Va. 1989).

38. *See, e.g.,* Choudhri v. New York City Department of Education, 852 N.Y.S.2d 133 (N.Y. App. Div. 2008) (confirming the dismissal of a teacher who,

among other charges, used the Internet excessively for nonschool reasons); Lacks v. Ferguson Reorganized School District R-2, 147 F.3d 718 (8th Cir. 1998) (affirming the termination of a teacher who had violated school board policy by allowing students to use profanity in plays and poetry).

39. Board of Education of West Yuma School District v. Flaming, 938 P.2d 151 (Colo. 1997).

40. Ketchersid v. Rhea County Board of Education, 174 S.W.3d 163 (Tenn. Ct. App. 2005).

41. *See, e.g.,* Forte v. Mills, 672 N.Y.S.2d 497 (N.Y. App. Div. 1998) (upholding charges of insubordination against a teacher who continued to touch students after he had been given verbal and written warnings against engaging in any physical contact).

42. *For example,* in two separate decisions, the First Circuit ruled that teachers could not be dismissed for using methods that, while questionable, had not specifically been prohibited: Mailloux v. Kiley, 448 F.2d 1242 (1st Cir. 1971) and Keefe v. Geanakos, 418 F.2d 359 (1st Cir. 1969). These cases are discussed in greater detail in Chapter 8. *See also* Lindros v. Governing Board of Torrance Unified School District, 510 P.2d 361 (Cal. 1973) (determining that a teacher could not be dismissed for using a teaching technique that was not barred by any school regulation).

43. *See, e.g.,* Lackrow v. Department of Education of the City of New York, 859 N.Y.S.2d 52 (N.Y. App. Div. 2008) (upholding dismissal of a teacher, noting that even if he had not been warned to cease the use of inappropriate language, his conduct was clearly unacceptable).

44. *See, e.g.,* Spurlock v. East Feliciana Parish School Board, 885 So. 2d 1225 (La. Ct. App. 2004) (affirming the dismissal of a teacher who allowed second grade students to simulate sex acts in her classroom); Fowler v. Board of Education of Lincoln County, 819 F.2d 657 (6th Cir. 1987) (affirming that a teacher could be dismissed for showing a violent and sexually explicit film to high school students); Altsheler v. Board of Education of Great Neck Union Free School District, 476 N.Y.S.2d 281 (N.Y. 1984) (upholding the discharge of a teacher who had revealed items from a standardized achievement test to her students); Gatewood v. Little Rock Public Schools, 616 S.W.2d 784 (Ark. Ct. App. 1981) (concluding that a teacher could be dismissed for offering to give students higher grades if they bought raffle tickets from her).

45. McGhee v. Miller. 753 S.W.2d 354 (Tenn. 1988).

46. In re Mary Silvestri's Teaching Contract, 480 N.W.3d 117 (Minn. Ct. App. 1992).

47. Tennessee Code Annotated § 49-5-501(6).

48. In re Termination of James E. Johnson, 451 N.W.2d 343 (Minn. Ct. App. 1990).

49. *See, e.g.,* Meckley v. Kanawha County Board of Education, 383 S.E.2d 839 (W.Va. 1989) (upholding the dismissal of a teacher who, among other transgressions, refused to attend PTA and faculty meetings).

50. Sanders v. Board of Education of South Sioux City Community School District, 263 N.W.2d 461 (Neb. 1978).

51. Eshom v. Board of Education of School District No. 54, 364 N.W.2d 7 (Neb. 1985).

52. Russo, C. J. (2009). *Reutter's the law of public education* (7th ed.). New York: Foundation Press. *See also* Wise v. Bossier Parish School Board, 851 So. 2d 1090 (La. 2003) (ruling that a school board's dismissal of a tenured teacher could not be reversed absent a clear showing of abuse of discretion).

53. Batyreva v. New York City Department of Education, 854 N.Y.S.2d 390 (N.Y. App. Div. 2008).

54. Raitzik v. Board of Education of Chicago, 826 N.E.2d 568 (Ill. App. Ct. 2005); Davis v. Board of Education of the City of Chicago, 659 N.E.2d 86 (Ill. App. Ct. 1995).

55. Whaley v. Anora-Hennepin Independent School District, 325 N.W.2d 128 (Minn. 1982).

56. Linstad v. Sitka School District, 963 P.2d 246 (Ala. 1998).

57. Johnson v. Francis Howell R-3 Board of Education, 868 S.W.2d 191 (Mo. Ct. App. 1994). *See also* Childs v. Roane County Board of Education, 929 S.W.2d 364 (Tenn. Ct. App. 1996) (affirming the dismissal of a teacher who was unable to control her classroom, used questionable methods for grading students, and required extraordinary assistance to maintain discipline).

58. Ketchersid v. Rhea County Board of Education, 174 S.W.3d 163 (Tenn. Ct. App. 2005).

59. Gordon v. Lafayette County School District, 923 So. 2d 260 (Miss. Ct. App. 2006).

60. Wise v. Bossier Parish School Board, 851 So. 2d 1090 (La. 2003).

61. Blaine v. Moffat County School District, 748 P.2d 1280 (Colo. 1998).

62. School District No. 1, City and County of Denver v. Cornish, 58 P.3d 1091 (Colo. Ct. App. 2002).

63. Bellairs v. Beaverton School District, 136 P.3d 93 (Or. Ct. App. 2006).

64. Hellmann v. Union School District, 170 S.W.3d 52 (Mo. Ct. App. 2005).

65. Drain v. Board of Education of Frontier County School District No. 46, 508 N.W.2d 255 (Neb. 1993).

66. McKinnon v. Board of Education of North Bellmore Union Free School District, 709 N.Y.S.2d 104 (N.Y. App. Div. 2000).

67. Dolega v. School Board of Miami-Dade County, 840 So. 2d 445 (Fla. Ct. App. 2003).

68. *See, e.g.,* Choudhri v. New York City Department of Education, 852 N.Y.S.2d 133 (N.Y. App. Div. 2008) (upholding the dismissal of a teacher for, among other charges, disruptive absences, late arrivals, and early departures).

69. Harrah Independent School District v. Martin, 440 U.S. 194 (1979).

70. Johanson v. Board of Education of Lincoln County School District, 589 N.W.2d 815 (Neb. 1999). *See also* Walker v. Highlands County School Board, 752 So. 2d 127 (Fla. Ct. App. 2000) (sustaining the dismissal of a teacher who violated school board policy resulting in a loss of classroom control); Daily v. Board of Education of Morrill County School District, 588 N.W.2d 813 (Neb. 1999) (upholding a school board's suspension without pay of a teacher who struck a student on the back of his head).

71. Loeffelman v. Board of Education, 134 S.W.2d 637 (Mo. Ct. App. 2004).

72. Emri v. Evesham Township Board of Education, 327 F. Supp. 2d 463 (D.N.J. 2004).

73. Roberts v. Santa Cruz Valley Unified School District, 778 P.2d 1294 (Ariz. Ct. App. 1989).

74. *See, e.g.,* Trustees of Lincoln County School District v. Holden, 754 P.2d 506 (Mont. 1988) (rejecting isolated disrespectful remarks as a sufficient cause for dismissal).

75. *See, e.g.,* Chaplin v. New York City Department of Education, 850 N.Y.S.2d 425 (N.Y. App. Div. 2008) (finding that a teacher could be dismissed for moral turpitude in that it compromised her ability to function in her job).

76. Andrews v. Drew Municipal Separate School District, 507 F.2d 611 (5th Cir. 1975). Mississippi is now part of the Eleventh Circuit after the Fifth Circuit was split in 1981 to form a new circuit.

77. *See also* New Mexico State Board of Education v. Stoudt, 571 P.2d 1188 (N.M. 1977) (commenting that a teacher's discharge for being unmarried and pregnant was arbitrary and unreasonable given that other unwed mothers were retained in the school system).

78. *See, e.g.,* Bertolini v. Whitehall City School District Board of Education, 744 N.E.2d 1245 (Ohio Ct. App. 2000) (ruling that an assistant superintendent's adulterous affair was not grounds for termination); Erb v. Iowa State Board of Public Instruction, 216 N.W.2d 339 (Iowa 1974) (rejecting adultery as grounds for revocation of a teaching certificate absent evidence that it had an adverse effect on a male teacher's fitness to perform his duties).

79. *See, e.g.,* Rivers v. Board of Trustees, Forrest County Agricultural High School, 876 So. 2d 1043 (Miss. Ct. App. 2004) (sustaining the discharge of a teacher for improperly touching students); Hierlmeir v. North Judson–San Pierre Board of School Trustees, 730 N.E.2d 821 (Ind. Ct. App. 2000) (recognizing sexual harassment of students as good and just cause for dismissal); Conrad v. Cambridge School Committee, 171 F.3d 12 (1st Cir. 1999) (ruling that a teacher's discharge for giving a lewd document to a student was not a pretense for racial discrimination); Governing Board of the ABC Unified School District v. Haar, 33 Cal. Rptr. 2d 744 (Cal. Ct. App. 1994) (affirming the firing of a teacher who had engaged in immoral conduct by sexually harassing students); Board of Education of Sparta Community Unit School District No. 140 v. State Board of Education, 577 N.E.2d 900 (Ill. App. Ct. 1991) (allowing the dismissal of a teacher who gave female students unsolicited kisses and hugs, gifts, and affectionate letters); Miller v. Grand Haven Board of Education, 390 N.W.2d 255 (Mich. Ct. App. 1986) (permitting the suspension of a teacher who exposed himself to students).

80. *See, e.g.,* Baltrip v. Norris, 23 S.W.3d 336 (Tenn. Ct. App. 2000) (upholding the dismissal of a teacher who had been charged with sexual battery but pled guilty to assault, a misdemeanor).

81. *See, e.g.,* In re Binghampton City School District, 848 N.Y.S.2d 382 (N.Y. App. Div. 2007) (finding that dismissal was the appropriate penalty for a teacher who had engaged in an inappropriate relationship with a student); Board of Education of City School District of the City of New York v. Mills, 680 N.Y.S.2d 683 (N.Y. App. Div. 1998) (affirming the suspension of a teacher who had a romantic relationship with a student); Johnson v. Beaverhead County High School District, 771 P.2d 137 (Mont. 1989) (affirming the discharge of a teacher who had sexual contact with students).

82. Andrews v. Independent School District, 12 P.3d 491 (Okla. Civ. App. 2000). *See also* Dixon v. Clem, 492 F.3d 665 (6th Cir. 2007) (refusing to disturb

the firing of a teacher who took topless photographs of a female student, presumably with her consent); Welch v. Board of Education of Chandler Unified School District No. 80, 667 P.2d 746 (Ariz. Ct. App. 1983) (supporting the dismissal of a teacher who failed to cooperate with an investigation into his relationship with a student that culminated in marriage).

83. Flaskamp v. Dearborn Public Schools, 385 F.3d 935 (6th Cir. 2004).

84. Parker v. Board of Education of the Byron Center Public Schools, 582 N.W.2d 859 (Mich. Ct. App. 1998). *See also* Toney v. Fairbanks North Star Borough School District Board of Education, 881 P.2d 1112 (Alaska 1994) (explaining that evidence that a teacher engaged in a sexual relationship with a minor while employed in another state was an adequate basis for dismissal for immorality).

85. *See, e.g.,* Board of Education of Hopkins County v. Wood, 717 S.W.2d 837 (Ky. 1986) (affirming that teachers who smoked marijuana with two students off campus during the summer could be dismissed on charges of conduct unbecoming a teacher; specifically rejecting their argument that they could not be fired for acts committed during off-duty hours, during the summer, and in the privacy of their own apartment).

86. Gedney v. Board of Education of the Town of Groton, 703 A.2d 804 (Conn. Ct. App. 1997). *See also* Dubuclet v. Home Insurance Co., 660 So. 2d 67 (La. Ct. App. 1995) (holding that a school board had the authority to dismiss a teacher for immorality based on his possession of drugs, even though criminal proceedings were dropped after he completed probation).

87. Woo v. Putnam County Board of Education, 504 S.E.2d 644 (W.Va. 1998).

88. *See also* Bergerson v. Salem-Keizer School District, 144 P.2d 918 (Or. 2006) (upholding the dismissal of a teacher who pled no contest to criminal mischief charges and parents objected to her returning to teaching).

89. Walthart v. Board of Directors of Edgewood-Colesburg Community School District, 694 N.W.2d 740 (Iowa 2005). *See also* Blaine v. Moffat County School District, 748 P.2d 1280 (Colo. 1998) (affirming the dismissal of a teacher who drank beer with students on a school-sponsored trip).

90. Board of Directors of the Lawton-Bronson Community School District v. Davies, 489 N.W.2d 19 (Iowa 1992).

91. Kinniry v. Abington School District, 673 A.2d 429 (Pa. Commw. Ct. 1996).

92. *Id.* at 432 citing Appeal of Flannery, 178 A.2d 751 at 754 (Pa. 1962).

93. Zelno v. Lincoln Intermediate Unit, 786 A.2d 1022 (Pa. Commw. Ct. 2001).

94. Satterfield v. Board of Education of the Grand Rapids Public Schools, 556 N.W.2d 888 (Mich. Ct. App. 1996).

95. Green v. New York City Department of Education, 793 N.Y.S.2d 405 (N.Y. App. Div. 2005).

96. The Second Circuit acknowledged that such catchall phrases are necessary due to the many situations that may arise in the school context that the state legislature could not reasonably be expected to specifically include within the statutes as proscribed conduct. diLeo v. Greenfield, 541 F.2d 949 (2d Cir. 1976).

97. *See* Chapter 4 for a discussion of the revocation of certificates. *See also* Rettie v. Unified School District, 167 P.3d 810 (Kan. Ct. App. 2007) (finding that

a teacher was entitled to a dismissal hearing even though she allowed her certificate to lapse, thus failing to meet an essential requirement of continued employment).

98. School District No. 1, City and County of Denver v. Cornish, 58 P.3d 1091 (Colo. Ct. App. 2002).

99. Snyder v. Jefferson County School District R-1, 842 P.2d 624 (Colo. 1992).

100. *See, e.g.*, Mitchell v. School Board of Miami–Dade County, 972 So. 2d 900 (Fla. Ct. App. 2007) (affirming the dismissal of a teacher whose certification was obtained using college credits for courses in which he did no work).

101. Oleske v. Hilliard City School District Board of Education, 764 N.E.2d 1110 (Ohio Ct. App. 2001).

102. Sheldon Community School District Board of Directors v. Lundblad, 528 N.W.2d 593 (Iowa 1995). *See also* diLeo v. Greenfield, 541 F.2d 949 (2d Cir. 1976) (ruling that improper and harassing conduct toward students on several occasions constituted sufficient cause for dismissal).

103. Gary Teachers Union v. School City of Gary, 332 N.E.2d 256 (Ind. Ct. App. 1975).

104. Hanes v. Board of Education of the City of Bridgeport, 783 A.2d 1 (Conn. Ct. App. 2001). *See also* Rodriguez v. Ysleta Independent School District, 217 F. App'x 294 (5th Cir. 2007) (affirming the dismissal of a teacher who inappropriately helped her students on a state mandated test, finding that she had been given sufficient due process).

105. As indicated earlier, probationary teachers facing nonrenewal do not have an expectation or a property right in continued employment, and are thus not entitled to due process. *See, e.g.*, Gibson v. Caruthersville School District, 336 F.3d 768 (8th Cir. 2003) (ruling that probationary teachers have a property interest in employment only until the end of the school year).

106. 470 U.S. 532 (1985). Although this case did not involve teachers, it applies to tenured teachers, as they are public employees who can be discharged only for cause.

107. *See, e.g.*, Martin v. School District No. 394, 393 F. Supp. 2d 1028 (D. Idaho 2005) (noting that a teacher who received a letter describing the evidence to support the charges against him and an opportunity to tell his side of the story was given adequate procedural protections).

108. *See, e.g.*, Simmons v. New Public School District No. Eight, 574 N.W.2d 561 (N.D. 1988) (observing that a notice that listed ability and competence as reasons for discharge did not meet statutory requirements, as it gave no specific reasons or factual assertions to which the employee could respond).

109. *See, e.g.*, Clark County School District v. Riley, 14 P.3d 22 (Nev. 2000) (ruling that four days' notice was not sufficient).

110. Richard v. Lafayette Parish School Board, 984 So. 2d 218 (La. Ct. App. 2008).

111. Curtis v. Montgomery County Public Schools, 242 F. App'x 109 (4th Cir. 2007).

112. Allen v. Texarkana Public Schools, 794 S.W.2d 138 (Ark. 1990).

113. Head v. Chicago School Reform Board of Trustees, 225 F.3d 794 (7th Cir. 2000).

114. Lafferty v. Board of Education of Floyd County, 133 F. Supp. 2d 941 (E.D. Ky. 2001). *See also* Coleman v. Reed, 147 F.3d 751 (8th Cir. 1998) (affirming that a dismissed principal had been given adequate due process in that she was given notice of the charges, was represented by an attorney, and had an opportunity to rebut the charges).

115. Hortonville Joint School District No. 1 v. Hortonville Education Association, 426 U.S. 482 (1976) (pointing out that a school board could validly conduct termination hearings for striking teachers in the absence of bias or malice).

116. *See, e.g.,* Felder v. Charleston County School District, 489 S.E.2d 191 (S.C. 1997) (presuming that school board members are honest and have integrity in carrying out their duties and decision-making responsibilities); Riter v. Woonsocket School District, 504 N.W.2d 572 (S.D. 1993) (acknowledging that a school board and its members are afforded a strong presumption of good faith).

117. *See, e.g.,* Riter v. Woonsocket School District, 504 N.W.2d 572 (S.D. 1993) (finding that a teacher showed bias on the part of the school board where, prior to the teacher's dismissal hearing, a board member offered the teacher's position to another person and informed the teacher that he should resign, because he probably would not get his job back). *But see* Wilder v. Board of Trustees of Hazelhurst City School District, 969 So. 2d 83 (Miss. Ct. App. 2007) (finding that a school board member who supported another candidate for the position of superintendent could still be unbiased); Vukadinovich v. Board of School Trustees of North Newton School Corp., 278 F.3d 693 (7th Cir. 2002) (affirming that a terminated teacher failed to show that school board members who participated in his hearing, and whom he had previously criticized publicly, acted with actual or potential bias).

118. *See, e.g.,* Harms v. Independent School District No. 300, 450 N.W.2d 571 (Minn. 1990) (ruling that a reinstated teacher's seniority rights should be restored even if that meant realigning the seniority of other teachers).

119. *See, e.g.,* Hosford v. School Committee of Sandwich, 659 N.E.2d 1178 (Mass. 1996) (concluding that a teacher who was not reemployed, for actions that were later determined to be within her free speech rights, was entitled to reinstatement and monetary damages).

120. McDaniel v. Princeton City School District Board of Education, 45 F. App'x 354 (6th Cir. 2002).

121. Assad v. Berlin-Bolyston Regional School Committee, 550 N.E.2d 357 (Mass. 1990).

122. *See, e.g.,* Martin v. Santa Clara Unified School District, 125 Cal. Rptr. 2d 337 (Cal. Ct. App. 2002) (ruling that a school board could deduct from an award of back pay the amount a teacher might have earned had she sought employment); California Teachers Association v. Governing Board of the Golden Valley Unified School District, 119 Cal. Rptr. 2d 642 (Cal. App. Ct. 2002) (directing a trial court to consider whether a teacher failed to mitigate damages by diligently seeking other employment).

123. Hartmeister, F., & Russo, C. J. (1999). "Taxing" the system when selecting teachers for reduction-in-force. *Education Law Reporter, 130,* 989–1008.

124. Nickel v. Saline County School District No. 163, 559 N.W.2d 480 (Neb. 1997).

125. Impey v. Board of Educ. of Borough of Shrewsbury, 662 A.2d 960 (N.J. 1995).

126. Howard v. West Baton Rouge Parish School Board, 865 So. 2d 708 (La. 2004).

127. Ballato v. Board of Educ. of Town of Stonington, 633 A.2d 323 (Conn. Ct. App. 1993).

128. *See, e.g.,* Duncan v. Rochester Area School Board, 571 A.2d 365 (Pa. 1990) (deciding that the public school code required the school board to provide the opportunity for a teacher to avoid dismissal by taking the position of a less senior teacher in another area for which the first teacher was certificated); Dallap v. Sharon City School District, 571 A.2d 368 (Pa. 1990) (ruling that a school board had no choice but to replace less senior teachers with more senior ones who held proper certification). *See also* Hancon v. Board of Education of Barrington Community Unit School District, 474 N.E.2d 407 (Ill. App. Ct. 1985) (finding that a teacher who was eligible for certification but was not yet certificated could not bump a less senior certificated teacher).

129. *See, e.g.,* Moe v. Independent School District No. 696, 623 N.W.2d 899 (Minn. Ct. App. 2001) (indicating that a teacher was entitled to bump less senior teachers as long as it did not require scheduling adverse to students); Butler v. Board of Education, Unified School District No. 440, 769 P.2d 651 (Kan. 1989) (ruling that a teacher was not entitled to be retained if his retention required a rearrangement of class schedules, and that the school board was not required to give him additional time to obtain certification in another area); Peters v. Board of Education of Rantoul Township High School District No. 193, 454 N.E.2d 310 (Ill. 1983) (finding that a school board was not required to combine classes from other positions to create a position for which a RIFed teacher would be qualified).

130. Szumigala v. Hicksville Union Free School District Board of Education, 539 N.Y.S.2d 83 (N.Y. App. Div. 1989). *See also* Davis v. School District of City of Niagara Falls, 772 N.Y.S.2d 180 (N.Y. App. Div. 2004) (observing that a drafting teacher was not entitled to transfer into positions in areas that were not similar and required different certification).

131. Hanson v. Vermillion School District, 727 N.W.2d 459 (S.D. 2007).

132. *See, e.g.,* Lezette v. Board of Education of Hudson City School District, 360 N.Y.S.2d 869 (N.Y. 1974) (interpreting tenure statutes broadly to include seniority rights for probationary teachers).

133. *See, e.g.,* Babb v. Independent School District No. I-5, 829 P.2d 973 (Okla. 1992) (pointing out that state law gave a tenured teacher priority for renewal over a probationary teacher where the tenured teacher was certificated to teach all of the courses for which the probationary teacher was retained).

134. *See, e.g.,* Board of Education of the County of Wood v. Enoch, 414 S.E.2d 630 (W.Va. 1992) (remarking that hiring for a summer school program should be based on qualifications first with seniority being a factor only when all qualifications were equal).

135. Dykeman v. Board of Education of the School District of Coleridge, 316 N.W.2d 69 (Neb. 1982).

136. Nickel v. Saline County School District No. 163, 559 N.W.2d 480 (Neb. 1997).

137. Donato v. Board of Education of the Plainview–Old Bethpage Central School District, 729 N.Y.S.2d 187 (N.Y. App. Div. 2001). *See also* Dees v. Marion-Florence Unified School District No. 408, 149 P.2d 1 (Kan. Ct. App. 2006) (affirming that an elementary school counselor could not bump into a high school position, since she did not have the proper qualifications).

138. Hancon v. Board of Education of Barrington Community Unit School District, 474 N.E.2d 407 (Ill. App. Ct. 1985).

139. Stewart v. Fort Wayne Community Schools, 564 N.E.2d 274 (Ind. 1990).

140. Scobey School District v. Radakovich, 135 P.3d 778 (Mont. 2006).

141. 476 U.S. 267 (1986).

142. Britton v. South Bend Community School Corporation, 819 F.2d 766 (7th Cir. 1987).

143. Taxman v. Board of Education of Township of Piscataway, 91 F.3d 1547 (3d Cir. 1996), *cert. granted,* 521 U.S. 1117 (1997), *cert. dismissed,* 522 U.S. 1010 (1997).

144. Board of Education of the County of Mercer v. Owensby, 526 S.E.2d 831 (W. Va. 1999).

145. *See, e.g.,* Lee v. Franklin Special School District Board of Education, 237 S.W.2d 322 (Tenn. Ct. App. 2007) (ruling that a teacher had the right to remain on a preferred list for reemployment until she refused a bona fide offer of employment or, if an offer had not been made, a minimum of two years).

146. California Teachers Association v. Mendocino Unified School District, 111 Cal. Rptr. 2d 879 (Cal. Ct. App. 2001).

147. Greater Johnstown School District v. Greater Johnstown Education Association, 647 A.2d 611 (Pa. Commw. Ct. 1994).

148. *See, e.g.,* Chester v. Harper Woods School District, 273 N.W.2d 916 (Mich. Ct. App. 1978) (declaring that a school board's determination of qualifications is entitled to some deference unless it is arbitrary, unreasonable, or promulgated in bad faith).

Curricular and Instructional Issues   **8**

INTRODUCTION

The days when schools were responsible for teaching only the "three Rs" are long gone. Teachers in 21st century schools are required to teach ever-expanding curricula designed to prepare students for a world that will likely be very different on the day they graduate. Along with offering standard subjects such as English, mathematics, social studies, science, and technology, many schools provide programs designed to keep students safe as a regular part of their instructional framework. Consequently, it is now common for schools to offer drug and alcohol awareness, child assault prevention, and antibullying programs as standard components of their overall instructional programs.[1]

This chapter examines the many legal issues falling under the broad category of curriculum and instruction. It begins with a discussion of the authority of state legislatures and local school boards to establish and control curricula and instructional methodologies, including controversial aspects of the instructional program. The chapter also addresses the corollary issues of grading policies and graduation requirements before presenting information on current requirements regarding testing and evaluating students, record keeping, copyright law, and technology in the classroom, along with the need to provide remedial programs.

CONTROL OF THE CURRICULUM AND ACADEMIC FREEDOM

It is well settled that states have the authority to establish curricula in their public schools. Consistent with this authority, state legislatures may establish the conditions and parameters under which curricula are to be taught. Put another way, pursuant to the Tenth Amendment, states may dictate what is to be taught in the public schools and how it will be taught. The authority of states in this regard may go so far as to approve the textbooks that may be used for given courses.[2] Even so, states frequently delegate decisions regarding specific course offerings to local school boards. By way of example, while states may mandate that high school students must have three years of science to graduate, local school boards are generally given the discretion to determine what specific courses to offer under the rubric of science instruction in order to satisfy the state requirement.

Courts generally defer to the judgment of state and local school authorities regarding curricula, as long as they abide by constitutional principles. In this respect, the courts ordinarily reject parental challenges to curricular content or the use of specific textbooks.[3] As in other areas of education, since judges do not consider themselves to be curricular experts, they prefer to leave decisions regarding course content to education officials who have a greater expertise in this arena.

Academic freedom does not exist at the elementary and secondary level to the same extent that it does in higher education.[4] Insofar as students between specified ages are required to attend school, the state's interest in creating an educated citizenry, combined with the impressionable nature of immature minds, means that public officials can justify the

curricular requirements and restrictions that
are placed on public schools. Even so, courts
have recognized that teachers do not lose all of
their constitutional rights to freedom of speech
and expression once inside school buildings.[5]
As the following sections illustrate, it is impor-
tant to strike a balance between the rights of teachers to free expression
and the states' obligation to educate their young citizens.[6]

> Academic freedom does not exist at the elementary and secondary level to the same extent that it does in higher education.

Authority to Establish Curriculum

Courts have long acknowledged that the state legislatures have the
authority to establish curricula for their public schools within constitutional parameters. In this respect most states establish minimum standards regarding the subjects to be taught and the content of those
subjects. This means that local school boards are generally free to set
higher standards or offer additional courses of study.[7] The authority to
establish curricula extends to the ability to select and approve instructional materials and methods. Many states leave almost exclusive control
over selection of materials to local school boards, while others distribute
lists of approved materials, and others go so far as to dictate the contents
of the texts that are used for specified courses.[8]

The authority to establish the curriculum lies predominantly with the
states and local school boards. Even so, as indicated in previous chapters, the
federal government in recent years has assumed
an ever-increasing role in the operation of the
schools, particularly in the areas of curriculum
and instruction. The federal government is able
to influence curricula by offering federal funds to
states and local school boards if they meet specified requirements. The most notable example in
this regard is the No Child Left Behind Act
(NCLB),[9] which provides funds to states for redistribution to school boards as
long as they meet the act's mandates. The purpose of the NCLB is to create a
framework for the improvement of elementary and secondary education by
establishing standards for annual student progress and making school systems accountable for that progress.[10] Under the NCLB, in order to receive
funds, school systems must utilize teaching methods and materials that are
research based and have been proven to be effective.

> The authority to establish curricula lies predominantly with the states and local school boards. Even so, . . . the federal government in recent years has assumed an ever-increasing role in the operation of the schools.

The NCLB's Reading First program provides an excellent illustration
of how the federal government has influenced curricular choices. States
were given substantial grant funds to distribute to local school boards for

the implementation of new literacy programs in kindergarten through Grade 3. As noted, in order to qualify for funds, school systems had to meet strict federal guidelines regarding the instructional program implemented and the reading materials purchased with the federal monies. By providing these funds, then, the federal government is able to exert control over curricula through the power of the purse.

Required Subjects

As indicated above, states have full authority to determine what should be taught in public schools. Within constitutional limits, states may require, or forbid, that certain subjects be taught. Yet, since most state requirements are general, local school boards are normally given the discretion to develop specific course content and teaching methodologies. In other words, while state laws dictate that reading and English classes are to be taught in elementary and secondary schools, beyond the minimum number of contact hours, they leave it to local school boards to determine how many hours per week subjects are taught at each grade level and what materials are to be used for instruction.

> Within constitutional limits, states may require, or forbid, that certain subjects be taught. Yet, since most state requirements are general, local school boards are normally given the discretion to develop specific course content and teaching methodologies.

States also commonly dictate that schools should offer courses in mathematics and science. Although the wording varies from state to state, instruction in specific topics within the realm of social studies, such as U.S. history and citizenship, is generally mandated by state law.[11] Further, most states require at least a minimum amount of instruction in physical education. In today's world where special efforts must be taken to protect children and keep them safe, it is not unusual for states or school boards to mandate instruction in such areas as health and nutrition, driver education, sex education, drug and alcohol awareness, and assault prevention. Even though instruction in these areas may be mandated, older cases indicated that school personnel must make special provisions allowing parents to exclude their children from classes in controversial topics such as sex education,[12] a trend that is now largely ignored.[13]

Many states have recently adopted comprehensive testing programs, in part in response to the accountability sections of the NCLB. While student testing and evaluation is discussed below, it is worth noting that states influence curricular content through their choices of what subject matter content is tested, particularly since school boards may face considerable penalties and stigma for poor performance on these tests.

In addition to subjects required by state law, school boards have the authority to offer elective courses. By and large courts have recognized that school boards need to have flexibility in regard to course offerings to meet the changing needs of the educational system. Once electives have been created, boards are free to drop them from curricula or replace them with newer course offerings.[14] Unless state law provides otherwise, school boards cannot be compelled to offer specific electives.[15] Moreover, school boards generally have the authority to mandate prerequisites or other criteria for admission into specified courses.

Controversial or Prohibited Subjects

As indicated earlier, curricular control is left to the state legislatures, which, in turn, delegate decisions regarding the specifics of implementation to local school boards. This means that state and local education officials have significant discretion in determining what is to be taught and how it is to be taught. However, there are limitations on the authority of the states and local school boards. State and local school officials may not make decisions that would contravene federal law or constitutional principles.

> There are limitations on the authority of the states and local school boards. State and local school officials may not make decisions that contravene federal law or constitutional principles.

An early example of a limitation on state authority occurred at the height of World War I, when many states enacted legislation, under the guise of supporting the war effort, emanating from anti-German sentiment. In the most notable example, Nebraska passed a law prohibiting the teaching of any modern foreign language or of any subject in a foreign language to students who had not yet completed the eighth grade. When a teacher appealed a conviction for violating this statute, the Supreme Court, in *Meyer v. Nebraska*,[16] seeing no danger stemming from young children learning a foreign language, struck down the law as violating the Fourteenth Amendment, because it was unreasonable and arbitrary.

One of the more controversial curricular issues subject to litigation during the past century involves the teaching of evolution and, more recently, creationism. Most readers are probably familiar with the Scopes monkey trial[17] due to its fictionalization in the movie *Inherit the Wind*.[18] In this early case, a science teacher was convicted and fined $100 for violating a state statute prohibiting the teaching of evolution. Although the Supreme Court of Tennessee reversed the fine, the law was never struck down. However, four decades later, in *Epperson v. Arkansas*,[19] the Supreme Court overturned a statute that was an adaptation of the Tennessee law; it forbade the teaching of evolution in public schools and universities. The Court held that the statute was contrary to the freedom of religion mandate of the First Amendment and further violated the Fourteenth Amendment. Specifically, the Court, in finding that the purpose of the law was to prevent teachers from discussing evolution because it was contrary to the belief of many in the divine creation of humans, decreed that the First Amendment did not permit a state to require teaching tailored to the principles or prohibitions of any particular religious sect or dogma.

Perhaps to counteract the effects of the Supreme Court's decision striking down the Arkansas antievolution statute, state legislatures enacted legislation directing school systems to provide instruction on the biblical version of the creation along with evolution. In 1987 the Supreme Court invalidated one such statute as violating the First Amendment in *Edwards v. Aguillard.*[20] Louisiana passed a law, known as the Creationism Act, that forbade the teaching of evolution in public schools unless it was accompanied by instruction in creation science. Schools were not required to teach either theory, but if either one were taught, the other theory also had to be taught. In striking down the statute, the Court wrote that the act served no identified secular purpose, but rather, its purpose was to promote a particular religious belief. The Court concluded that the legislation was unconstitutional, because it endorsed religion in violation of the First Amendment.

Many school boards in the United States have instituted requirements for students to complete a set number of hours of community service during their high school years. In some schools students who do not complete this requirement do not graduate. The issue has become controversial, with opponents of mandatory community service programs questioning the constitutionality of such requirements. Even so, courts have generally upheld mandatory community service programs. In what was apparently the first litigated case on this point, the Third Circuit upheld a Pennsylvania school board's requirement that students complete 60 hours of community service to graduate.[21] The court dismissed arguments that the requirement compelled students to engage in expression contrary to their personal beliefs in violation of the First Amendment, and that mandatory community service constituted involuntary servitude in violation of the Thirteenth Amendment. Similarly, the Second Circuit affirmed that a New York school board's community service requirement did not violate the Constitution.[22] The court explained that the requirement was reasonably related to the state's function of educating its students and did not violate their rights to personal liberty or privacy. Courts in other jurisdictions have reached similar outcomes.[23]

The issue of removing or excluding materials from curricula or school libraries has been controversial, particularly since many parents raise objections to specific texts on religious grounds. School boards certainly have the right to prohibit material that is generally considered to be obscene or inappropriate for young children. On the other hand, legitimate instructional materials may not be removed from school shelves simply because board members or the general public may not agree with their message. In the leading case on the topic, the Supreme Court overturned a New York school board's decision to remove books from the junior and senior high schools' libraries in *Board of Education, Island Trees Union Free School District v. Pico (Pico)*.[24] In a press release, the board described the books in question as being "anti-American, anti-Christian, anti-Semitic, and just plain filthy."[25] In a plurality, meaning that it is not binding precedent, the Court decided that there was sufficient evidence of improper motive in the board's action to warrant a trial on the merits of the issue. The Court noted that although school boards may remove vulgar and educationally unsuitable materials from school shelves, they may not exercise this discretion in a partisan or political way as a guise for protecting orthodoxy. Relying on guidance from *Pico*, lower courts have struck down restrictions on student access to controversial books. In one such case, a federal trial court in Arkansas ruled that a school board violated the rights of children to receive information when it tried to require students to have prior written approval from their parents before borrowing copies of the popular *Harry Potter* book series from their school library.[26]

School officials have been fairly successful in removing material that they consider to be obscene, vulgar, or sexually explicit.[27] In these situations, the ages of the students can be an important factor in determining whether challenged material is inappropriate. By and large the courts defer to the judgment of school officials regarding what is appropriate for children of a given age and whether challenged material has pedagogical value, especially where educators can tie their concerns to curricular values.

It is not uncommon for parents to object to having their children exposed to material in a classroom that is inconsistent with their religious beliefs. In such instances, many school systems give students the option of completing alternate assignments. Even so, parents have had limited success in having texts entirely removed from curricula or in having their children excused from studying specified aspects of the curriculum simply because the material may not correspond with their own religious beliefs. In one such challenge, parents objected on religious grounds to themes that were included in the reading series that the school board adopted. When the board voted to eliminate alternate reading programs, thus requiring all students to be instructed using the officially adopted texts, the Sixth Circuit, in a long-running dispute, affirmed an order in the board's favor, pointing out that the requirement did not create an unconstitutional burden under the Free Exercise Clause of the First Amendment.[28] Similarly, in other challenges to curricular materials, the Seventh[29] and Ninth[30] Circuits agreed that schools may expose students to stories about witchcraft without violating their

> Parents have had limited success in having texts entirely removed from curricula or in having their children excused from studying specified aspects of curricula simply because the materials may not correspond with their own religious beliefs.

constitutional rights. In like fashion, the Eleventh Circuit rejected a parental challenge asserting that materials approved for use in history, social studies, and home economics amounted to teaching secular humanism.[31]

CASE SUMMARY 8.1: PARENTAL CHALLENGE TO CURRICULAR CONTENT

Mozert v. Hawkins County Board of Education

827 F.3d 1058 (6th Cir. 1987)

Factual Summary: A school board adopted a program for teaching reading in the first through eighth grades. The school system's teachers also used an integrated approach, whereby the ideas presented in the reading series were carried over into other subjects. When a parent who described herself as a "born again Christian" objected on religious grounds to the themes presented in many of the texts, the principal of her daughter's school agreed to allow students whose parents objected to the material to be taught using an alternative series. However, the school board later voted to eliminate all use of alternative reading programs. The parents of several children then filed suit, asserting that they had sincere religious beliefs that were contrary to the values being taught in the approved reading series, and that forcing the students to read the selected texts violated their rights to free exercise of religion. After protracted litigation a federal trial court held in favor of the parents, finding that requiring the students to read the challenged books burdened their free exercise of religion. The school board appealed.

Issue: Does the use of the challenged curricular material burden the students' free exercise of religion rights?

Decision: No, reversing in favor of the school board, the Sixth Circuit reasoned that the board had the authority to select the reading program of its choice.

Summary of Court's Rationale: The court held that requiring students to study a specific reading series approved by the school board did not create an unconstitutional burden under the Free Exercise Clause. Moreover, the court pointed out that students were not required to affirm or deny a belief, to engage or refrain from engaging in a practice prohibited or required by their religion, or to engage in any conduct that was forbidden by their religion. In the court's view the fact that students might draw conclusions that were contrary to the teachings of their religion was not sufficient to establish an unconstitutional burden.

Many parents have objected to the content of sex education courses, particularly when those classes deal with topics such as homosexuality. In one such situation the Sixth Circuit refused to sustain a parental challenge to portions of a diversity course relating to sexual orientation.[32] Parents objected to the course because of their belief that homosexuality was sinful. Similarly, the Second Circuit held that a school board did not violate a parent's free exercise of religion rights by refusing to excuse his child from a required health education course that included instruction on family life, physical growth and development, and AIDS.[33] In another action the First Circuit affirmed that school officials did not violate parental rights to due process or free exercise of religion by allowing teachers to use materials that depicted same sex marriages and diverse families, including those with parents of the same gender.[34]

Instructional Methodologies

Just as states have the authority to establish curricula and select instructional materials, they also may dictate instructional methods. Even so, absent state laws, decisions regarding instructional methods are generally left to school boards, school administrators, and teachers.[35] For the most part, courts have been reluctant to interfere with the judgment of local school boards regarding pedagogical concerns.[36] In this respect, lawsuits brought by parents to exert control over teaching methodologies largely have been unsuccessful.[37]

Much of the litigation in this area involves challenges to instructional techniques chosen by teachers and so involves issues of academic freedom. In most such challenges, whether brought by parents or resulting from administrative discipline, courts consider whether the teaching profession in general supports disputed methodologies or whether regulations existed proscribing the instructional techniques at issue.[38] In this respect, when teachers are given substantial discretion to choose appropriate instructional strategies, they generally may not be disciplined for their choices, unless they exhibit flagrant abuses of that discretion.

> When teachers are given substantial discretion to choose appropriate instructional strategies, they generally may not be disciplined for their choices, unless they exhibit flagrant abuses of that discretion.

In one high-profile early case, an English teacher was dismissed for conduct unbecoming a teacher after he had written a four-letter word on the chalkboard during a discussion of taboo language. The teacher did not orally state the word but did ask students to define it. In ordering the teacher's reinstatement, the First Circuit noted that there was no regulation prohibiting the teacher's choice of methodology.[39] Similarly, two

CASE SUMMARY 8.2: TEACHER'S CHOICE OF INSTRUCTIONAL METHODOLOGY

Mailloux v. Kiley

448 F.2d 1242 (1st Cir. 1971)

Factual Summary: An 11th grade English teacher assigned chapters in the novel *The Thread That Runs So True* by Jesse Stuart for outside reading. During a class discussion of the book, the teacher introduced the subject of society and its ways as illustrated by taboo words. As part of the discussion the teacher wrote what is considered to be a taboo word on the board and asked students to define it. After getting a synonymous phrase the teacher, without using the taboo word, commented on how one was acceptable and the other was not. Following a complaint by a parent, the teacher was subsequently dismissed. After the teacher filed suit, a federal trial court reinstated him, ruling that he could not be discharged for using the chosen methodology inasmuch as he had not been given notice by regulation or otherwise that he should not use such a method. The court reasoned that even though it was not shown that the challenged methodology had universal support from the teaching profession, it was relevant to the subject and students, served a serious educational purpose, and was used by the teacher in good faith. School authorities appealed.

Issue: Can the teacher be discharged for using the method he chose?

Decision: No, reversing in his favor, the First Circuit acknowledged that the teacher could not be dismissed for teaching about a word that is considered to be taboo.

Summary of Court's Rationale: The appeals court posited that the grounds relied on by the trial court were dispositive insofar as they were sound and sufficient. The court found that a statement in the Code of Ethics of the Education Profession presented by school officials—indicating that a teacher recognizes the supreme importance of the pursuit of the truth, devotion to excellence, and nurture of democratic citizenship—was impermissibly vague; it was not sufficient to have provided the teacher with notice that the use of his chosen methodology was grounds for discharge. Thus, the court treated the sanctions under the circumstances as a denial of due process.

years earlier the same court had overturned the suspension of a high school teacher who had asked students to read a magazine article containing a vulgar term.[40] The teacher discussed the word and its use in the article in class, and offered an alternative assignment to students who found the assignment distasteful. Conceding that the article was scholarly and that a proper study of the piece could not avoid consideration of the word, the court commented that the sensibilities of parents who may have been offended were not determinative. At the same time, the court was of the opinion that the teacher would prevail if an argument were put forward that the teacher had not received notice from administrators that a class discussion of the article was forbidden, particularly since the school's library contained at least five books that used the same word. Conversely, rejecting her First Amendment and academic freedom claims, the Sixth Circuit upheld the dismissal of a teacher based on insubordination after she played a violent and sexually suggestive movie for her class without having previewed its contents, because the film was unrelated to an educational purpose.[41]

As was true in the three preceding cases, it must be kept in mind that the age of the students is an important consideration in evaluating whether controversial or questionable methodology is within professional bounds. The courts might have reached different results in the first two cases if the challenged instructional techniques had been used with elementary school students[42] or if the teacher in the third dispute had sought prior approval before playing the video.

In a broader context, school boards have the power to establish school schedules, set the number of hours in school days, and create the overall grade and school structure as long as they meet minimum state standards This means that school boards may have the freedom to group grade levels into schools or houses within schools as they see fit while working with carefully designed criteria,[43] such as offering classes for students who have expressed an interest to enter higher education once they graduate from high school.[44] In this regard, an appellate court in Michigan was convinced that a board had the authority to create a nongraded elementary school.[45] Since the practice was not prohibited by state law or regulations, the court decided that local officials could set the school up as they best saw fit.

Graduation Requirements

Consistent with the powers of states to establish curricula while exerting control over materials and methodologies, states have the authority to set graduation requirements. If states do not explicitly establish graduation requirements, the authority of local school boards to do so is implied. Unless state law dictates otherwise, school boards may set more stringent requirements than those established by the state. Although requirements for earning a high school diploma vary from state to state, almost all entail a minimum total number of credits and further specify that a set number of credits must be earned in particular subjects, such as English.

In recent years, many states have added the requirement that students must pass comprehensive tests to earn high school diplomas. For the most part, courts do not interfere with judgments of school officials regarding graduation requirements as long as those requirements are reasonable and are not applied unfairly or arbitrarily. In this respect school boards may deny diplomas to students who have not met all graduation requirements.[46]

School boards may, and under many circumstances do, waive established graduation requirements or allow for alternative means of meeting them. Waivers or alternative requirements often are issued, for example, when students are unable to satisfy usual standards for religious reasons or because of their disabilities. For example, it would be a clear violation of Section 504 of the Rehabilitation Act[47] to deny diplomas to students with physical challenges for not meeting physical education requirements. Allowing students to meet the requirements by participating in adaptive physical education classes would be a reasonable accommodation. In a case that arose at the height of the Vietnam conflict, the Sixth Circuit held that strict adherence to a Tennessee school board's requirement that all male students take a Reserved Officers Training Corps course to earn diplomas violated the free exercise of religion rights of a student who was a conscientious objector for religious reasons.[48]

Whether students may be required to pass comprehensive curricular or competency tests, also referred to as minimum competency tests, to earn high school diplomas has been controversial. As an initial matter, fairness dictates that students must be exposed to the material on the test and must be given proper notice that passing the test is necessary to earn diplomas.[49] For the most part, as long as school officials have met these requirements, courts will not interfere with the discretion of educational authorities to set diploma requirements.[50]

As illustrated by an early case from Iowa, it is important to separate the right to earn a diploma from the privilege of attending graduation exercises. The state's high court declared that a school board could not deny a diploma to a student who refused to wear a cap and gown at graduation exercises but could refuse to allow him to participate in the graduation exercises.[51]

> It is important to separate the right to earn diplomas from the privilege of attending graduation exercises.

By the same token, students who have met all graduation requirements generally may not be denied diplomas for disciplinary reasons but may be excluded from graduation ceremonies or denied other privileges associated with graduation.[52]

It must be kept in mind that while an earned high school diploma is a property right,[53] there is no constitutional right to participate in graduation ceremonies.[54] To this end, courts have agreed that diplomas may not be withheld from students who have met all requirements, even when they have engaged in serious misconduct.[55] On the other hand, the Second Circuit wrote that since attendance at a graduation ceremony was not a prerequisite for receiving a diploma, a school board did not infringe a student's free exercise of religion rights by scheduling the program on a day that he could not attend for religious reasons.[56]

Grading Policies

As in other matters of educational policy, courts are reluctant to interfere with school board grading policies, preferring that judgments regarding grades and the granting of course credit be left to educators. Since most states do not dictate grading policies, the authority of local school boards to create and enforce grading policies is implied. Much of the controversy over grading policies stems not from the policies themselves, but rather, from their application. Accordingly, it is important for grading policies, particularly those involving grade reductions, to be clearly spelled out in student handbooks or course syllabi.[57]

> As in other matters of educational policy, courts are reluctant to interfere with school board grading policies, preferring that judgments regarding grades and the granting of course credit be left to educators.

It is not uncommon for school officials to reduce students' grades for poor attendance under the theory that attendance and participation in class can be a component of an individual student's overall rating.[58] An appellate court in Michigan determined that establishing an attendance policy was within a school board's discretion.[59] The court added that the policy in question, which permitted letter grade reductions for students who were absent a specified number of days and failed to attend mandatory afterschool study sessions, did not violate a student's rights to substantive or procedural due process. Earlier, the Supreme Court of Connecticut did not find any error in the application of a school board policy of imposing academic sanctions, including grade reductions, for nonattendance.[60] The court decided that creating such a policy was within the board's authority and did not jeopardize any fundamental student rights under the state's constitution.

Courts largely have agreed that grades may not be reduced for disciplinary infractions.[61] In one such case, an appellate court in Pennsylvania affirmed that a policy that called for a reduction in class grades of two points for every day of suspension for an infraction not related to the offending student's academic performance amounted to a clear misrepresentation of his scholastic achievement and was therefore an illegal application of the school board's discretion.[62]

Whether suspension days may be counted as unexcused absences for purposes of grade reductions or whether it is permissible for teachers to assign no credit for suspension days depends on the circumstances. The answer may well turn on whether educators give students opportunities to make up missed assignments. Suspension days are usually classified as unexcused absences and can be treated as such. For example, the Supreme Court of Mississippi held that the school board's policy of not granting credit for suspension days was enforceable when students failed to attend an offered alternative program on those days, but that its refusal to allow students to attend the alternative program when suspended for infractions involving alcohol was arbitrary and capricious.[63] By the same token, even though grades generally may not be reduced for suspension days by themselves, suspension days generally may be counted along with all other unexcused absences when policies provide for a grade reduction after so many days of unexcused absences in a term.

Testing and Evaluation of Students

In response to the NCLB's call for greater accountability, states have instituted comprehensive testing programs, whereby students are required to be evaluated on their curricular mastery at selected grade levels. Specifically, the NCLB directs states to conduct annual testing of students in grades 3 through 8 in reading and mathematics and at specified grade intervals in science. Further, the NCLB requires states to administer tests in core subjects at least once to students in grades 10 to 12.[64] While these tests are most commonly used to decide which curricular objectives individual students have achieved and whether states and school systems have met the NCLB's goal of establishing high standards, they may be used to make decisions relative to graduation, student promotion,[65] or whether given students should be referred for remedial services. At the same time, the Individuals with Disabilities Education Act (IDEA)[66] requires states to include students with disabilities

> In response to the NCLB's call for greater accountability, states have instituted comprehensive testing programs, whereby students are required to be evaluated on their curricular mastery at selected grade levels.

in general state or school district assessment programs.[67] Also, the NCLB requires English language learners to take state assessments in English after as little as 12 months attending school in the United States.[68] Yet, at least one court has held that it is not practical for states to provide testing in students' native languages, particularly in light of the many languages that can be spoken by students in the public schools coupled with the fact that native language testing is not mandated by NCLB.[69]

There are two essential criteria for all tests: validity and reliability. Validity refers to the degree to which tests measure what they are intended to measure. Reliability, on the other hand, refers to the ability of tests to produce consistent results. Basic principles of fairness dictate that high-stakes, or minimum competency, tests are both valid and reliable. In this regard it is well settled that when tests are used for such important milestones as graduation or promotion to the next grade, students must be given both notice that the tests are to be used for such purposes and sufficient exposure to the objectives or materials being tested.[70] Inasmuch as the NCLB has been law since 2002, at this point all students have, or should have, received notice, and instructional systems should be aligned with the objectives being tested. Moreover, these tests may not be racially, linguistically, or ethnically discriminatory.[71] These principles apply regardless of whether the tests have been developed by the state or are commercially available standardized measures.

As indicated above, it is well settled that states have the authority to establish graduation requirements and may expect students to pass competency tests before being able to receive standard high school diplomas. Courts have upheld the requirement that students, including children with disabilities, must pass tests to receive standard high school diplomas.[72] Further, courts agree that the individualized education programs (IEPs) of students with disabilities should include instruction in the areas to be tested.

Students with disabilities may require some modifications to testing procedures. This means that test administrators may be required to modify how tests are administered but may not be obligated to alter the actual content of examinations. By way of illustration, students who are visually impaired may need Braille versions of tests, while students with physical challenges may require assistance writing or filling in the circles on machine-scored answer sheets. On the other hand, school personnel are not required to develop and administer tests with fewer items or easier items for students with intellectual or cognitive impairments.[73] Stated another way, school officials must make accommodations that allow students to take tests but are not obligated to modify the content of items.

State tests may be used as part of the evaluation process to determine whether children have disabilities. Even so, one court remarked that the

NCLB does not require school boards to use a student's results on a state test as a basis for decisions as to whether a student with disabilities has received a free appropriate public education (FAPE).[74] The court emphasized that the NCLB does not oblige educators to develop IEPs specifically to enhance a student's scores on state tests. Still, the court acknowledged that the NCLB's assessments could be used as one factor in the overall evaluation of whether students received a meaningful education. In sum, while it appears that the failure of students to pass state mandated tests does not mean that school boards did not provide them with a FAPE, passing test scores may be one indicator that school boards have complied with the law.

STUDENT RECORDS

The Family Educational Rights and Privacy Act (FERPA),[75] sometimes referred to as the Buckley Amendment after its primary sponsor, then New York Senator James Buckley, created privacy rights for qualified students, meaning those over the age of 18 as discussed below, and their parents with regard to educational records. FERPA accomplished the dual goals of granting parents and eligible students access to their educational records while limiting the access of outsiders to these records. Although students' records are generally maintained by personnel in school offices, it is important for teachers to know and understand the specific provisions in FERPA, since teachers frequently need to access student records in order to obtain needed information, especially for children with disabilities.

Records Covered

FERPA applies to all records maintained by educational agencies, or by persons acting on their behalf, containing personally identifiable information about students.[76] While teachers often think of student records in the context of each child's cumulative folder, it is important to understand that all records, including temporary records, come under FERPA's umbrella.

> FERPA applies to all records maintained by educational agencies, or by persons acting on their behalf, containing personally identifiable information about students.

Two cases involving children with disabilities underscore the importance of safeguarding student records. In the first case, the federal trial court in Connecticut ruled that school officials violated the privacy rights of parents by releasing their names and that of their son to a local newspaper following a due process hearing.[77] In the second case, the Eighth Circuit, noting that public policy favors protection of the privacy of minors where sensitive matters are concerned, affirmed that judicial proceedings under the IDEA may be closed to the public.[78] The court acknowledged that the IDEA, mirroring FERPA, restricts the release of information about students with disabilities without parental permission. In order to ensure that critical information was safeguarded and to prevent the stigmatization of the student, the court decided that access to the courtroom could be restricted and the files sealed.

Schools also maintain so-called directory information. FERPA defines directory information as a child's

> name, address, telephone listing, date and place of birth, major field of study, participation in officially recognized activities and sports, weight and height of members of athletic teams, degrees and awards received, and the most recent previous educational agency or institution attended by the student.[79]

Before any such information may be released, school officials must provide parents and qualified students with notice of the categories of records that are designated as directory information while affording them a reasonable time to request that such information not be released without their consent.[80] To the extent that the disclosure provisions relating to directory information do not apply to former students, school officials may release such data without obtaining any prior approvals.[81]

FERPA requires school officials to notify parents and qualified students annually of their rights to inspect and review, request amendment of, and consent to disclosure of educational records as well as to file complaints with the federal Department of Education alleging failures to comply with the statute's provisions.[82] Typically, parents and students are notified of these rights by means that are reasonably likely to reach them, such as school newsletters, student handbooks, notes home, local access TV, e-mail, or other methods or combination of means designed to ensure that they receive notice.

FERPA does include four major exceptions regarding documents that are not classified as educational records subject to the act's mandatory disclosure provisions.[83] First, records created by educational personnel that are in the sole possession of their makers and are not accessible by or revealed to any other persons except temporary substitutes are not subject to release.[84] The material covered under this exception includes notes about students that teachers may keep to serve as their own memory jogs or information about students that would be necessary for substitutes to properly carry out their duties. Second, records kept separately by law enforcement units of educational agencies that are used only for their own purposes may not be accessed by third parties.[85] Third, records that are made in the ordinary course of events relating to individuals who work at, but who do not attend, educational institutions, and that refer exclusively to their capacity as employees and are not available for any other purpose are not covered by FERPA.[86] Fourth, records relating to students who are 18 years of age or older, or who attend postsecondary educational institutions, that are made by physicians, psychiatrists, psychologists, or other professionals or paraprofessionals for use in their treatment and are not available to others, except at the request of the students, may not be released.[87]

Access Rights

Parents and qualified students have the right to inspect and review records containing personally identifiable information relating to the education of their children or themselves.[88] When educational records include information about more than one student, parents reviewing the records of their children may access only that portion of group data that is specific to their own children.[89] With respect to student records, absent court orders or applicable state law, FERPA grants noncustodial parents the same right of access to their children's records as custodial parents.[90] Along with access rights, FERPA requires school officials to provide parents with reasonable interpretations and explanations of information contained in the records of their children.[91]

> Parents ... have the right to inspect and review records containing personally identifiable information relating to the education of their children.

Provisions regarding parental permission or consent are transferred to eligible students who reach their 18th birthdays or who attend postsecondary institutions, unless they are legally incapable, due to their intellectual or emotional disabilities, of managing their own affairs.[92] Further, postsecondary institutions do not have to permit students to inspect financial records in their files that include information about the resources of their parents[93] or letters of recommendation if they waived their rights of access.[94] School officials also are not required to grant access to records pertaining to individuals who are not or never were students at their institutions.[95]

Third parties normally may access school records, other than directory information, only when parents or qualified students provide written consent.[96] FERPA contains nine major exceptions where permission is not required before officials may review educational records. These exceptions, outlined below, were included to assist in the smooth operation of schools, especially as officials in different systems interact with one another and school personnel work with officials from other agencies. The nine exceptions are as follows:

1. School employees who have legitimate educational interests may access student records.[97] By way of example, at the end of a school year, or over a summer, teachers may review the records of students who will be in their classes in the fall to prepare for the upcoming school year. On the other hand, teachers usually do not have a legitimate need to see the files of students they will not be instructing or interacting with in any official capacity, including their own former students.

2. Officials representing schools to which students apply for admission may access the students' records as long as parents receive proper notice that the information will be sent to the receiving institutions.[98]

3. Authorized representatives of the U.S. comptroller general, the secretary of the Department of Education, and state and local education officials with authorization to do so by state law may view student records for law enforcement purposes.[99]

4. Officials who are charged with evaluating the eligibility of students for financial aid may review appropriate educational records.[100]

5. Members of organizations conducting studies on behalf of educational agencies or institutions developing predictive tests or administering aid programs and improving instruction may view records as long as doing so does not lead to the release of personal information about students.[101]

6. Personnel acting in the course of their duties for accrediting organizations may review student records.[102]

7. Parents of dependent children may access student records pertaining to their own children.[103]

8. In emergency situations, persons who protect the health and safety of students or other persons may view records.[104]

9. School officials must release records when they are subpoenaed or otherwise sought via judicial orders. Be that as it may, the parents must be notified in advance of compliance by school boards.[105] Nonetheless, prior to ordering the release of information, courts usually weigh the need for access against the privacy interests of students. FERPA also adds that its provisions do not prohibit educational officials from disclosing information concerning registered sex offenders who are required to register by federal law.

Third parties seeking disclosure of student records must have written consent from parents or eligible students specifying the specific records to be released, the reasons for the proposed release, and to whom the information is being given.[106] FERPA specifies that parents and qualified students have the right to receive copies of the materials to be released.[107] At the same time, school officials must keep logs of all individuals or groups, except exempted parties, who request or obtain access to student records.[108] These records must not only explain the legitimate interests of those who were granted access to the educational files but also must be maintained with the records of the student in question.[109]

Educational agencies that retain student records must fulfill requests for review without unnecessary delay. In this respect, unless parents agree otherwise, officials must grant access no later than 45 days after receiving requests.[110] It should go without saying that nothing prohibits school officials from granting requests for access to student records sooner. Agencies responding to requests for access to records may not charge fees to search for or retrieve student records.[111] However, once records are located, school officials may charge for copies as long as a payment does not effectively prevent parents or qualified students from exercising their rights to inspect and review the desired educational records.[112]

Amending Records

If parents or qualified students disagree with anything contained in the educational records that they seek to review, they may ask school officials to remove or amend the disputed information.[113] If officials decline to amend the disputed records or fail to take action within a reasonable time, parents or students are entitled to hearings at which hearing officers evaluate whether the challenged material is accurate and appropriately contained within the educational records of the students.[114] Hearing officers also must conduct the hearings and render decisions within a reasonable time.[115] If hearing officers are convinced that contested materials are inaccurate, misleading, or otherwise violate the rights of students to privacy, school officials must amend the materials accordingly and inform students' parents in writing that this been done.[116] If, however, hearing officers are satisfied that the materials in

> If parents or qualified students disagree with anything contained within the educational records that they seek to review, they may ask school officials to remove or amend the disputed information.

educational records are not inaccurate or misleading, or do not other-wise violate the privacy rights of students, the records need not be removed or amended.[117] Parents or students who are concerned over the content of the educational records, even after hearing officers decide that they are acceptable, may add statements explaining their objections to the records. These statements must be kept with the contested records for as long as they are kept on file.[118]

Enforcement

When parents or eligible children are denied the opportunity to review the records they seek, or if protected information is released impermissibly, the educational offi-cials responsible can be charged with violating FERPA, thereby triggering its enforcement pro-visions. In order to activate FERPA's enforce-ment provisions, aggrieved parties must file written complaints detailing the specifics of alleged violations with the federal Department of Education's Family Policy Compliance Office (FPCO).[119]

> In order to activate FERPA's enforcement provisions, aggrieved parties must file written complaints detailing the specifics of alleged violations with the federal Department of Education's Family Policy Compliance Office (FPCO).

Student record violation complaints must be filed within 180 days of either the alleged violations or the dates when claimants knew or reason-ably should have known about the violations.[120] When the FPCO receives complaints, its staff must notify officials at the responsible educational institutions in writing, detailing the substance of the alleged violations and asking them to respond before considering whether to proceed with any investigations.[121] If, after investigations are completed, the FPCO offi-cials agree that violations occurred, the Department of Education can withhold future payments under its programs, issue orders to compel compliance, or ultimately terminate an institution's eligibility to receive federal funding if school personnel refuse to comply within a reasonable time.[122]

In the only Supreme Court case involving FERPA at the elementary and secondary level, *Owasso Independent School District v. Falvo*,[123] the Justices held that the practice of "peer grading," whereby teachers allow students to grade the papers of classmates, does not violate the statute. The Court indicated that since the practice does not turn the papers into educational records covered by FERPA, a school board in Oklahoma did not violate the law by permitting teachers to use peer grading over the objection of a mother whose children attended schools in the district.[124]

CASE SUMMARY 8.3: PEER GRADING

Owasso Independent School District v. Falvo

534 U.S. 426 (2002)

Factual Summary: Teachers in the Owasso school system, like their colleagues in other systems across the country, used peer grading, whereby they asked students to score each other's tests, papers, and assignments as the teacher explains the correct answers to the entire class. A parent complained, alleging that the practice embarrassed her children. When school officials declined to ban the practice, the parent brought suit, contending that the peer grading practice violated FERPA. A federal trial court ruled in favor of the school board, finding that grades put on papers by other students were not records as defined by the statute. The Tenth Circuit reversed, holding that peer grading violated FERPA, because grades marked by students on each other's work were educational records such that the act of grading was an impermissible release of the information to the student grader. The school board appealed.

Issue: Does the practice of peer grading violate FERPA?

Decision: No, reversing in favor of the school board, the Supreme Court ruled that peer grading does not violate FERPA.

Summary of Court's Rationale: At the outset the Court noted that education records are defined in FERPA as "records, files, documents, and other materials" containing information directly related to students, which are "maintained by an educational agency," but the law contains an exception for records that are in the sole possession of their maker. In the Court's view students' papers were not maintained by the school within the meaning of FERPA when they were in the possession of other students. In this regard, the Court observed that construing the term *education records* to encompass student homework or class assignments would impose a substantial burden on teachers. Thus, the Court concluded that student grades are not protected by FERPA until teachers collected and recorded them in their mark books.

The Court explained that student papers do not become educational records within the meaning of FERPA until their scores are entered into the grade books of teachers.

COPYRIGHT LAW

Teachers use a variety of sources to obtain materials for their classrooms. Many teachers reproduce or copy materials without any thought as to whether they have the right to do so. The Copyright Act of 1976[125] codifies the rights of copyright holders, affording protection to "original works of authorship fixed in any tangible medium of expression, now known or later developed, from which they can be perceived, reproduced, or otherwise communicated, either directly or with the aid of a machine or device."[126] Works of authorship include literary; musical; dramatic; pantomime and choreographic; pictorial, graphic, and sculptural; and architectural creations. The act also includes motion picture, audiovisual, and sound recordings. Under the statute, copyright owners have exclusive rights to reproduce their work; create derivative works; sell, lease or rent copies of the work to the public; perform the work publicly; and display the work.[127]

Even so, educators do have some rights to use copyrighted works in their classrooms under the fair use doctrine. Fair use includes, but is not limited to, use of copyrighted works for criticism, news reporting, teaching, scholarship, and research.[128] In evaluating whether uses of copyrighted works fall within the parameters of fair use, courts consider the purpose and character of the use, the nature of the work, the amount and portion of the original work used, and the effect the use has on the market or potential market for the work. In essence, fair use allows individuals other than the copyright owner to use the material in a reasonable manner without the owner's consent.

> Educators do have some rights to use copyrighted works in their classrooms under the fair use doctrine. Fair use does not, though, give educators unrestricted permission to use copyrighted materials in their classrooms.

Fair use does not, though, give educators unrestricted permission to use copyrighted materials in their classrooms. Teachers may make single copies of copyrighted works for instructional purposes but are not as free to make multiple copies. One of the restrictions on making multiple copies lies with the length of materials. For example, poems of more than 250 words may not be copied. As to longer works, teachers may copy only 1,000 words or 10% of the work, whichever is less. Teachers have more flexibility to copy material when it is not reasonable to make timely requests for permission to do so. By the same token, copies may be made for one-time use only. Future use of the same material would require permission. Finally, it should go without saying that teachers may not copy materials to avoid purchasing the works. In other words, it is a violation of the statute to copy workbooks for class use as a substitute for buying them.[129]

USING TECHNOLOGY IN THE CLASSROOM

Technology provides teachers with unprecedented opportunities, not only in terms of what is taught, but how it is taught. It also provides a new set of pedagogical as well as legal challenges. Traditional instructional tools are being replaced by computers, multimedia projectors, and smartboards.[130] There is no question that technology provides teachers with greater access to information while simultaneously giving them a new means of conveying that information to their students. Technology also has given students new ways to research and present reports and projects.

As an initial matter, as Chapter 4 emphasized, it is important for teachers to be familiar with the Internet-use policies of their school systems. Most school boards require teachers and students to read and sign their acceptable use policies.[131] Although these policies vary from one system to another, most address the types of sites or content that may be accessed, instructional use of the Internet, personal use of district-provided computers, and copyright issues.

This section of the chapter explores emerging legal issues relating to the use of technology in classrooms, focusing on the challenge of applying copyright law to technological applications. Chapter 4 discussed issues surrounding teachers' use of email and privacy issues connected with both teacher and student use of social networking sites. While that discussion is not repeated here, readers may wish to refer to it in reviewing this material.

The rapidly increasing use of technology as an instructional tool in classrooms not only presents a unique set of opportunities for educators but also raises a unique set of legal implications. In this rapidly expanding area, the legal issues are just beginning to emerge. In fact, the law is having difficulty keeping pace with technological developments.

Teachers' ability to easily copy a wide array of materials for use in the classroom provides them with an almost endless supply of instructional

> Teachers' ability to easily copy a wide array of materials for use in the classroom provides them with an almost endless supply of instructional materials. Even so, teachers need to exercise caution in this regard so as not to violate the Copyright Act.

materials. Even so, teachers need to exercise caution in this regard so as not to violate the Copyright Act,[132] as discussed in the previous section. For example, teachers are able to easily record television shows for later showing in the classroom, but due to the possible infringement of the copyright owners' rights to market the materials, restrictions apply.[133] In 1981 Congress issued guidelines for using off-air recordings for educational purposes.[134] The guidelines are included in their entirety in Figure 8.1. In sum, the guidelines state that recordings may be made only at the request of the teacher and may be used in the

Figure 8.1   Federal Guidelines for Off-Air Recording of Broadcast Programming for Educational Purposes

Congressional Record, October 14, 1981, pp. E4750–E4752

1. The guidelines were developed to apply only to off-air recording by nonprofit educational institutions.

2. A broadcast program may be recorded off-air simultaneously with broadcast transmission—(including simultaneous cable re-transmission) and retained by a nonprofit educational institution for a period not to exceed the first forty-five (45) consecutive calendar days after date of recording. Upon conclusion of such retention period, all off-air recordings must be ceased or destroyed immediately. "Broadcast programs" are television programs transmitted by television stations for reception by the general public without charge.

3. Off-air recordings may be used by individual teachers in the course of relevant teaching activities, and repeated once only when instructional reinforcement is necessary, in classrooms and similar places devoted to instruction within a single buildings, cluster, or campus, as well as in the homes of students receiving formalized home instruction, during the first ten (10) consecutive school days in the forty-five (45) day calendar day retention period. "School days" are school session days—not counting weekends, holidays, vacations, examination periods, or other scheduled interruptions—within the forty-five (45) calendar day retention period.

4. Off-air recordings may be made only at the request of and used by individual teachers, and may not be regularly recorded in anticipation of requests. No broadcast program may be recorded off-air more than once at the request of the same teacher, regardless of the number of times the program may be broadcast.

5. A limited number of copies may be reproduced from each off-air recording to meet the legitimate needs of teachers under these guidelines. Each such additional copy shall be subject to all provisions governing the original recording.

6. After the first ten (10) consecutive school days, off-air recordings may be used up to the end of the forty-five (45) calendar day retention period only for teacher evaluation purposes, i.e., to determine whether or not to include the broadcast program in the teaching curriculum, and may not be used in the recording institution for student exhibition or any other non-evaluation purpose without authorization.

7. Off-air recordings need not be used in their entirety, but the recorded programs may not be altered from their original content. Off-air recordings may not be physically or electronically combined or merged to constitute teaching anthologies or compilations.

8. All copies of off-air recordings must include the copyright notice on the broadcast programs as recorded.

9. Educational institutions are expected to establish the appropriate control procedures to maintain the integrity of these guidelines.

classroom only once within 10 days of recording. A second showing within the 10-day period is allowed for reinforcement purposes. Although the guidelines allow for the recording to be maintained for 45 days, after the initial 10 days it may be used only for evaluative purposes.

Computer software is protected under an amendment to the Copyright Act that applies to intellectual property.[135] Software vendors typically issue licenses allowing software to be installed on a limited number of computers at one time. For instance, many software programs designed for personal use allow the software to be installed on only three computers. School systems can purchase lab, building, or site licenses that will allow for the economical installation of software on multiple computers or on a server that can be accessed by many computers. Even so, it is important to adhere to license restrictions. In this regard, a lab license might allow for installation of a program on up to 25 computers or simultaneous access by 25 students when the software is loaded onto a server; additional usages would be violations of license agreements. Generally, schools are allowed to make one back-up copy of software programs, but any additional copying would constitute copyright violations.

Current widespread use of the Internet has created new copyright issues. While general copyright principles apply to Internet material, the unique nature of digital media caused Congress to amend the Copyright Act in 1998 to address the emerging issues.[136] Inasmuch as technology is constantly evolving, even this law does not answer all of the questions that can arise regarding the use of Internet sources. Although the amendment did extend the fair use doctrine to digital media, it is safe to say that material found on the Internet can be fully protected by the copyright law, and it should be used only in accordance with the basic principles of the law.

SPECIAL EDUCATION AND PROGRAMS FOR ENGLISH LANGUAGE LEARNERS

A major challenge facing teachers is meeting the needs of diverse groups of learners in their classrooms. Current laws require the inclusion of students with disabilities and those whose primary language is not English. Further, many students classified as regular education students require additional remedial services. Teachers are further challenged by the fact that all of these students must take the state mandated tests discussed earlier.

Requirements for Educating Students With Disabilities

The delivery of special education services, whether in regular classrooms or separate locations, is governed by the IDEA and state law.

Inasmuch as each of the 50 states has its own sets of laws, few of which do little more than reiterate the basic federal standards, this section focuses on the federal statute. The IDEA requires states, and by delegation, local school boards, to provide a free appropriate public education (FAPE) in the least restrictive environment to all qualifying students with disabilities between the ages of 3 and 21 based on the contents of their IEPs.[137] Students with disabilities covered by the statute are those who have identified disabilities[138] and who need special education and related services because of their conditions.[139]

The IDEA requires school boards to give students with disabilities a FAPE consisting of any needed special education and related services,[140] but it does not establish substantive standards by which the adequacy of those services can be assessed. The IDEA states only that students are to be given specially designed instruction[141] in conformance with their IEPs.[142] In *Board of Education of Hendrick Hudson Central School District v. Rowley* (*Rowley*),[143] its first case on special education, the Supreme Court provided some guidance by explaining that students with disabilities are entitled to personalized instruction with support services sufficient to permit them to benefit from the education they receive. All the same, hearing officers and judges are often asked to decide what level of services is required to meet the IDEA's minimum standards.

> The IDEA requires school boards to give students with disabilities a FAPE consisting of any needed special education and related services. . . . The Supreme Court provided some guidance by explaining that students with disabilities are entitled to personalized instruction with support services sufficient to permit them to benefit from the education they receive.

The IDEA includes a detailed system of due process safeguards designed to ensure that students with disabilities are properly identified, evaluated, and placed according to the law's mandates.[144] The act requires school boards to give the parents or guardians of children with disabilities the opportunity to participate in the development of the IEPs for and placement of their children.[145] The IDEA also directs school boards to provide written notice and obtain parental consent prior to evaluating any children[146] or making any initial placements.[147] After students have been placed in special education programs, boards must provide parents with proper notice before initiating any changes in placement.[148] Nevertheless, while administrative or judicial actions are pending, boards may not change students' placements without parental consent,[149] hearing officers' orders,[150] or court decrees.[151] One of the many distinctive aspects of the IDEA is that it contains an elaborate system to resolve disputes between parents and school boards, including resolution meetings between parents and school officials, mediation, administrative due process hearings, and, as a final resort, appeals to the courts.

CASE SUMMARY 8.4: APPROPRIATE EDUCATION DEFINED

Board of Education of the Hendrick Hudson Central School District v. Rowley

458 U.S. 176 (1982)

Factual Summary: Parents sued a school board on behalf of their daughter who was hearing-impaired and whose IEP provided for regular class placement, an FM hearing aid, one hour of instruction per day from a tutor for the deaf, and three hours of speech therapy per week, but it did not include the services of a sign language interpreter that her parents requested. After considering the request, school officials determined that the interpreter was not needed. A due process hearing officer upheld that decision, finding that the student was achieving educationally, academically, and socially without the interpreter. A federal trial court, finding that the student performed better than average but understood considerably less of what went on in class than she would understand if she were not deaf, ruled that the student was not receiving a FAPE. The court postulated that an appropriate education was one that provided a child with disabilities an opportunity to achieve her full potential commensurate with the opportunity provided to nondisabled peers. The Second Circuit affirmed and the school board appealed.

Issue: Does the provision of a FAPE require a school board to provide an opportunity for students with disabilities to achieve their full potential commensurate with the opportunity given to students who do not have disabilities?

Decision: No, reversing in favor of the school board, the Supreme Court explained that an appropriate education merely provides a floor of opportunities for students with disabilities.

Summary of Court's Rationale: The Supreme Court asserted that the lower courts erred in interpreting federal special education law (now the IDEA) as requiring school personnel to maximize the potential of students with disabilities commensurate with opportunities provided to their peers who are not disabled. To the extent that school boards are required to provide a FAPE, the Court stated that they satisfy this requirement by providing personalized instruction with sufficient services to permit children to benefit educationally from that instruction. According to the Court such instruction and services must be provided at public expense, must meet the state's educational standards, must approximate the grade levels used in the state's regular education program, and must comport with the child's IEP. Further, the Court declared that the IEP, and therefore the personalized instruction, should be formulated in accordance with the requirements of the statute and, if the child is being educated in the regular classrooms of the public education system, should be reasonably calculated to enable the child to achieve passing marks and advance from grade to grade. Inasmuch as the student in this case performed better than the average students in her class, was advancing easily from grade to grade, and was receiving personalized instruction that was reasonably calculated to meet her educational needs, the Court determined that the student was not entitled to the services of a sign language interpreter.

In implementing the IDEA's mandates, school personnel must conduct initial evaluations before placing students in special education programs.[152] These evaluations must be completed within 60 days of the date when school officials received parental consent to conduct testing.[153] All evaluations are to be multidisciplinary, meaning that they should consist of a variety of assessment tools and strategies to obtain relevant information in the suspected areas of disability.[154] As another safeguard, students with disabilities are entitled to independent evaluations at public expense if their parents disagree with board evaluations.[155] Still, school boards may challenge requests for independent evaluations via administrative hearings, and parents are not entitled to obtain independent evaluations at public expense if the school boards' evaluations are deemed to be appropriate.[156] Although IEP teams must consider the results of independent evaluations, whether paid for by the school board or the parents, they are not required to adopt any of the recommendations that come out of those assessments.[157]

The IDEA specifically requires IEPs to include statements of students' current educational performance, annual goals and short-term objectives, specific educational services to be provided, the extent to which each child can participate in general education, the dates of initiation and duration of services, and evaluation criteria to determine if the objectives are being met.[158] IEPs also must include statements about how students' disabilities affect their abilities to be involved in and progress in general educational curricula along with comments about modifications that may be needed to allow children to participate in their school's general education program. IEP teams must review all IEPs at least annually,[159] and students who have IEPs need to be reevaluated at least every three years.[160]

School boards must offer a "continuum of alternative placements" to meet the needs of students with disabilities for special education and related services.[161] That continuum may range from placements in general education to private residential facilities as well as homebound services. The placements chosen for all students must be in the least restrictive environment, meaning that students may be removed from general education only to the extent necessary to provide special education and related services.[162] All placements must be made at public expense and must meet state educational standards.[163] In *Rowley* the Supreme Court explained that an appropriate education is one that is developed in compliance with the IDEA's procedures and is reasonably calculated to enable children to receive educational benefits.[164] Although states are required to adopt policies and procedures that are consistent with the IDEA, they may provide greater benefits than those mandated by the federal law. If states do establish higher standards, courts consider those standards in assessing the appropriateness of IEPs.[165] Since the implementation of the IDEA, the courts have examined literally thousands of cases where parents have challenged proposed IEPs.[166] While courts generally leave decisions regarding proper methodology to educators, they do pass judgment on whether or not the IDEA's basic requirements have been met.[167]

Along with special education, school boards need to provide related, or supportive, services to students with disabilities, if such services are needed to assist the students in benefiting from their special education programs.[168] The IDEA specifically lists transportation and such developmental, supportive, and corrective services as speech pathology, audiology, psychological services, physical therapy, occupational therapy, recreation (including therapeutic recreation), social work services, counseling services (including rehabilitation counseling), orientation and mobility services, medical services (for diagnostic or evaluative purposes only), and early identification and assessment as related services, but that list is not exclusive.[169] In *Irving Independent School District v. Tatro*,[170] the Supreme Court emphasized that related services must be provided only to students receiving special education. The Court added that only those services that are necessary for students to benefit from special education must be incorporated into their IEPs. The only limits placed on what school boards must provide under the related services clause is that medical services (unless they are specifically for diagnostic or evaluative purposes), medical devices that are surgically implanted, and the replacement of such devices are exempted.[171]

The IDEA requires school boards to provide assistive technology devices and services. Assistive technology devices are items, pieces of equipment, or product systems that are used to increase, maintain, or improve the functional capabilities of individuals with disabilities. These devices may include commercially available, modified, or customized equipment.[172] Assistive technology services are designed to assist individuals in the selection, acquisition, or use of assistive technology devices, including evaluations of children's needs, provision of assistive technology devices, training in their use, coordination of other services with assistive technology, and maintenance and repair of devices.[173] Under this provision school boards often are required to provide students with computer technology.

School personnel must develop transition services to help students with disabilities move from school to postschool activities such as employment, vocational training, or independent living. Transition services encompass related services, instruction, community experiences, and the acquisition of daily living skills.[174] Beginning when students turn 16 years of age, IEP teams must include statements of transition services in their IEPs.[175]

In one of the many controversial amendments to the IDEA, Congress added specific provisions outlining disciplinary requirements for students with disabilities.[176] These provisions were included, in part, in response to many cases involving disciplinary sanctions as applied to special education students. In its only decision on point, *Honig v. Doe (Honig)*,[177] the Supreme Court held that special education students could not be expelled for disciplinary reasons where their infractions were manifestations of, or caused by, their disabilities.

The Supreme Court's decision in *Honig* and the current language of the IDEA have not left school disciplinarians without recourse when students with disabilities misbehave. School administrators may transfer students to interim alternative settings for up to 45 days for possession of weapons or drugs or infliction of serious bodily injury, as long as their peers who are not disabled are subject to similar punishments.[178] The act makes it clear that educational services for students with disabilities must continue during expulsion periods.[179] Another important section of the IDEA requires school boards to conduct functional behavioral assessments (FBAs) and develop behavior intervention plans (BIPs) under specified circumstances[180] in order to help them better respond to the educational needs of students of disabilities who misbehave.

Students with disabilities may be suspended temporarily, and are subject to other normal disciplinary sanctions that do not result in changes in placement. If necessary, when educators cannot reach agreements with the parents of dangerous students concerning proper placement, school boards may seek interventions from hearing officers or courts pending completion of administrative due process hearings to remove these students from the classroom.[181] Prior to taking disciplinary actions, school personnel must first determine whether students' misconduct was a manifestation of, or caused by, their disabilities.[182] The purpose of this requirement is to ensure that students with disabilities are not disciplined for behavior over which they have no control or that results from the failure of school boards to provide a FAPE.

Unfortunately, from time to time school boards fail to provide appropriate placements for students with disabilities. In those circumstances the courts are empowered to grant such relief as they determine to be appropriate.[183] The relief often involves reimbursement of costs borne by parents in unilaterally obtaining appropriate services for their children. In one high-profile case, *Burlington School Committee v. Department of Education, Commonwealth of Massachusetts*,[184] the Supreme Court ruled that school boards may be required to reimburse parents for costs incurred in providing their children with special education and related services if they prevail in having their chosen placements deemed appropriate. The IDEA now includes language limiting reimbursement awards when parents do not provide school boards with prior notice of their dissatisfaction with their children's placements and their intent to enroll them in private schools.[185] In light of the Supreme Court's opinion in *Florence County School District Four v. Carter*,[186] reimbursement is an available remedy even when the parents' chosen facilities are not state approved, as long as the unapproved facilities offer otherwise appropriate programs. The Supreme Court's decision in *Forest Grove School District v. T.A.*[187] makes it evident that this is so even if the student in the private facility has not previously received services from the public schools. Courts often grant awards of compensatory educational services when parents lack the financial means to obtain private services while litigation is pending. Further, parents are entitled to recover their legal expenses in most situations where they prevail in administrative or judicial actions against school boards.[188]

Requirements for Educating English Language Learners

English language learners are students whose second language is English and who need support services and/or remedial instruction to succeed in school. School boards are required to provide educational programs for students with limited English proficiency. For many years bilingual education classes, whereby students were taught in both their primary languages and English, predominated. The practice has come under controversy and in many jurisdictions has been replaced with programs such as structured English immersion classes where students are taught in English for the majority of the school day.

In 1974 the Supreme Court recognized the right of non-English-speaking students to equal educational opportunities. In *Lau v. Nichols*[189] the Court reasoned that school boards receiving federal funds must provide non-English-speaking learners with specialized instruction when their language barriers hindered their educations. The Court interpreted Title VI of the Civil Rights Act of 1964[190] as requiring school boards to provide remedial instruction to non-English-speaking students as a condition for receiving federal assistance. The Court was not swayed by the school board's contention that it lacked the funds to provide such instruction, stating that in accepting federal funds, the board agreed to abide by Title VI's requirements. However, the Court did not specifically mandate the provision of bilingual programs, leaving the decision on methodology to educators and the lower courts.

> As early as 1974 the U.S. Supreme Court recognized the right of non-English-speaking students to equal educational opportunities. . . . The Court asserted that school boards receiving federal funds must provide non-English-speaking learners with specialized instruction when their language barriers hindered their educations.

Lower courts have been frequently called on to settle methodology issues. As the discussion below illustrates, the situation is complicated in that it is often intertwined with other issues such as desegregation. The Tenth Circuit, recognizing that many students did not speak English at home, ordered a school board to implement a bilingual education program for its Spanish-speaking students.[191] On the other hand, the same court struck down a segregated bilingual plan. On remand from the Supreme Court in *Keyes v. School District No. 1, Denver, Colorado*,[192] a federal trial court approved a desegregation plan[193] calling for the implementation of a bilingual-bicultural education program for minority students.[194] The Tenth Circuit reversed the trial court's earlier approval of this plan, maintaining that bilingual education was not a substitute for desegregation, since the Spanish-speaking students in the school system had a constitutional entitlement to a nonsegregated education that provided them with the chance to attain proficiency in English.

As an order of the Ninth Circuit shows, students do not have a right to bilingual education, although such programs are not necessarily barred.[195] The court was convinced that a school board met its obligations under Title VI by adopting measures to cure the non-English-speaking students' existing language deficiencies. In another case, the Fifth Circuit, reversing an earlier order involving desegregation issues, established criteria by which a program designed to overcome language barriers could be evaluated.[196] The court advised that any such programs should

CASE SUMMARY 8.5: ENGLISH LANGUAGE INSTRUCTION

Lau v. Nichols

414 U.S. 563 (1974)

Factual Summary: Parents filed a class action lawsuit against the San Francisco public schools on behalf of their Chinese-speaking children, alleging unequal educational opportunities insofar as the children were not provided with instruction in the English language. The suit claimed that the school board violated the Equal Protection Clause of the Fourteenth Amendment and Title VI of the Civil Rights Act of 1964 by not meeting the lingual needs of approximately 1,800 members of the class. The school board responded that it was unable to do so due to a lack of funds. A federal trial court denied relief, and the Ninth Circuit affirmed.

Issue: Did the school board's failure to provide English language instruction to large numbers of the class deny them a meaningful opportunity to participate in public education?

Decision: Yes, reversing in favor of the parents, the Supreme Court decided that the school board violated the Fourteenth Amendment and Civil Rights Act by not providing children who spoke Chinese with instruction in English.

Summary of Court's Rationale: The Supreme Court ruled that the school board's failure to provide English language instruction to approximately 1,800 students of Chinese ancestry who did not speak English, or to provide them with other adequate instructional procedures, denied them a meaningful opportunity to participate in the public educational program and thus violated the Civil Rights Act of 1964, which bans discrimination based on race, color, or national origin in any program or activity receiving federal funding. The Court noted that the Chinese-speaking minority received fewer benefits than the English-speaking majority from the school system, which denied them a meaningful opportunity to participate in the educational program. The Court commented that federal regulations require that where inability to speak and understand the English language excludes national-origin–minority children from effective participation in the educational program offered by a school board, officials must take affirmative steps to rectify the language deficiencies in order to open their instructional programs to these students.

be based on sound educational theory, reasonably calculated to implement the theory, and involve good faith efforts consistent with local circumstances and resources.

More recently, in *Horne v. Flores*,[197] the Supreme Court reversed and remanded a judgment of the Ninth Circuit, because the high Court did not think that officials in the state of Arizona had made sufficient progress in providing educational programming for English language learners to warrant relief from trial court orders. The dispute began when the parents of English language learners filed a class action suit, claiming that the state's funding system violated a provision of the Equal Educational Opportunities Act[198] that requires states to take appropriate action to overcome language barriers in schools.[199] Following protracted litigation, in which a federal trial court found the state to be in civil contempt for failing to fund English language learner programs adequately, the Ninth Circuit concluded that sufficient progress in funding and programming for English language learners had not occurred to warrant relief from the trial court's previous orders.[200] In remanding, the Supreme Court instructed lower courts to consider whether four factors warranted relief: a transition from bilingual classes to structured English immersion, compliance with the NCLB, structural and management improvements, and an increase in overall education funding. The Court observed that research indicates that there is documented support for the proposition that structured English immersion is more effective than bilingual education.[201]

SUMMARY AND RECOMMENDATIONS

The federal government is currently more involved in education than ever. Still, state legislatures and local school boards exert great control over curricular matters such as determining what is to be taught and how it will be taught, establishing grading policies, setting graduation requirements, and overseeing the evaluation of students. State legislatures have the authority to establish curricula and set guidelines as to how they are to be implemented. However, in doing so, officials may not violate the constitutional rights of students and faculty. Even so, since all states accept federal funds, the terms of statutes such as the NCLB and IDEA must be implemented as a condition of receiving those much-needed dollars.

Teachers need to be aware of other federal requirements in addition to the laws that directly affect curricula. For example, FERPA protects the privacy of students by limiting access to the contents of their school records. Although much of the management of FERPA falls on administrators and office personnel, teachers need to be attentive in their own use of student records to ensure that they do not inadvertently violate the law. Teachers certainly may access the records of their current students but do not have full access to the records of children not in their charge unless they have legitimate needs for such access.

Teachers need to be aware of copyright laws, especially in the age of technology where the development of new media has created challenges to the interpretation of old legal principles. The fair use doctrine allows teachers to use copyrighted material for instructional purposes, but there are many limitations on its use. Teachers need to be cognizant of these restrictions in order to avoid liability for copyright infringement.

In today's educational settings teachers are required to instruct a diverse group of students. While this presents methodological and curricular challenges, teachers need to be conscious of the legal ramifications of their actions. Students with disabilities and English language learners in particular have rights to equal educational opportunities that teachers must respect. Since the laws governing the education of students with disabilities are complex, teachers should communicate frequently with special educators and administrators regarding the needs and legal rights of the students in their classes.

In light of the myriad laws that impact the delivery of instruction, teachers should be responsive to and follow these principles and guidelines:

- Although states and, by delegation, school boards have plenary power over curricula, the federal government has been increasing its role in the establishment of curricular objectives and standards of achievement. Inasmuch as the federal government is able to exert control over curricula by making receipt of federal funds contingent on full implementation of federal laws, it is imperative for all educators to keep abreast of all federal developments in education.
- As with many aspects of education, constitutional principles must be respected in terms of what may be taught in the public schools.
- Most state legislation regarding curricula is general, leaving it up to local school boards to select specific subject matter content and means of instruction. Teachers should be familiar with all school board policies regarding the curriculum and instructional methodologies.
- Inasmuch as students have reasonable expectations of receiving diplomas upon completing all requirements, diplomas are property rights that may not be denied without due process of law.
- Grading policies, particularly those involving grade reductions for absences or other factors, should be clearly detailed in student handbooks and course syllabi, and should be reiterated orally in class.
- Since state laws regarding the permissibility of grade reductions for excess absenteeism or disciplinary purposes vary, it is important to

be familiar with state statutes and regulations as well as local school board policies.

- Even though school board policies may call for grade reductions after specified numbers of unexcused absences, such policies may not permit the reduction of grades for disciplinary purposes unrelated to academics. However, suspension days may be treated as unexcused absences, particularly if students do not make up the work they missed.

- Teachers may access student records when they have a legitimate need to do so but may not share protected student information with others. An exception exists for sharing only necessary information with substitutes.

- When court orders or state laws prohibit disclosure of educational records to noncustodial parents, school officials should consider keeping files in two separate locations. In order to avoid the risk of accidentally granting record access to noncustodial parents or their representatives, educators should place essentially blank files in the main set of student records directing individuals who need to see them to a second, more secure location.

- Parents and qualified students may request that statements or material in their records be amended or even removed. School officials are not required to amend or remove the challenged material if, after examining the issues, they believe that the material is appropriate. Regardless of the outcome, parents and qualified students have the right to have statements explaining their objections to the material included with the student records.

- Teachers need to exercise caution when copying or reproducing materials so as not to violate the Copyright Act. Although rare, suits for copyright infringement can be expensive.

- Technology provides teachers with many new curricular opportunities but many legal pitfalls as well. Teachers need to be familiar with guidelines for off-air recordings of digital media, software licensing restrictions, and other copyright limitations regarding technology.

- Students with disabilities have a right to a FAPE in the least restrictive environment. As such, it is more common for special education students to be taught alongside their peers in typical, inclusive, educational settings rather than in more restrictive segregated environments. Teachers need to be aware of the provisions in these students' IEPs so that they can employ appropriate educational strategies in all classroom situations.

- English language learners also have rights to equal educational opportunities. The law requires that barriers, particularly artificial barriers, to the achievement of this goal be removed.

FREQUENTLY ASKED QUESTIONS

Q. If education is a state function and the authority to establish the curriculum lies with state legislatures, how can the federal government enforce the mandates included in the NCLB for states to set higher curriculum standards?

A. The federal government provides significant educational funding to all states. In granting these funds, the government can and does attach conditions. One of these conditions is that states must implement the provisions of federal laws such as the NCLB. States are free to either accept or reject the federal funding. Practically speaking, if states want the money, they must accept the conditions. While states that do not want to implement the federal statutes are free to decline federal dollars, since the funds are significant, states would be hard pressed to operate their educational systems without these monies.

Q. May students be denied credit for days they do not attend school because they have been suspended?

A. Yes, students may be denied credit for not attending school during suspensions as long as they were given the opportunity to make up class work and failed to do so. Students do not usually earn credit for assignments they failed to complete. Students may be denied credit for failing to complete assignments they missed on days they were absent when they do not make up the work. Suspension days should be treated the same way as other unexcused absences. If students are normally given the option of making up assignments missed on days of unexcused absences, they should be given the same opportunity for days missed due to suspensions.

Q. May a teacher look at the records of former students to see how they are doing?

A. No. Under FERPA only those who have a legitimate educational reason to access the records may do so. Former teachers, although they may be well intentioned, no longer have a need or right to know what is contained in the records of their former charges. Curiosity about how students have fared is not a sufficient reason to access the records. As with many things, there are exceptions to when teachers may access the records of former students, but these exceptions exist only when educators have legitimate reasons for looking at the records. For example, when teachers are asked to write letters of recommendation for former students, they may consult the students' records for information needed to compose the letters.

Q. How careful do I need to be when adding information to a student's file? I've been told that I should never put anything negative in a student's file.

A. In addition to transcript records, student files often include comments by teachers. The information placed in student files should be objective and accurate. This does not mean that negative statements cannot be included in the files, especially when that information is needed to provide a complete and accurate picture of the student. By way of illustration, a notation that a student is not very motivated is problematic, as it is subjective and open to interpretation. On the other hand, a statement that a student has failed to complete 6 class and 14 homework assignments is objective, as it can be easily documented and supported.

Q. May a teacher copy a few pages from a workbook to include in an instructional packet? May recordings be made of television shows for viewing in the classroom?

A. The practice of copying workbook pages may be common, but in most cases is a violation of the Copyright Act of 1976. First, the fair use doctrine would allow only one-time use of the copied material without permission from the copyright owner. Second, reproducing multiple pages could run afoul of the quantity restrictions placed on fair use of copyrighted material. Similar principles apply to recording television shows for classroom use. A one-time showing of the video, particularly when time does not allow teachers to seek permission for its use, namely within 10 days of making recordings, is acceptable, but multiple showings over time is not. Copying material, whether it is in print or in other media, simply to avoid paying for it is unacceptable and a clear violation of the copyright law.

WHAT'S NEXT

The final chapter deals with the important issue of tort liability. The chapter opens with definitions and descriptions of various forms of torts. The bulk of the chapter covers the topic of negligence and the situations teachers need to guard against to avoid legal liability for student injuries. In addition, the chapter addresses related issues such as educational malpractice and liability for civil rights violations.

ENDNOTES

1. As an example of the ever-increasing responsibilities placed on schools to provide instruction in social areas, Massachusetts recently became the 42nd state to enact an antibullying law. This legislation, among other provisions, requires instruction on bullying at all grade levels as part of the curriculum. Chapter 92 of the Acts of 2010, *An Act Relative to Bullying,* codified at 71 Massachusetts General Laws § 370.

2. Leeper v. State of Tennessee, 53 S.W. 962 (Tenn. 1899).

3. Todd v. Rochester Community Schools, 200 N.W.2d 90 (Mich. Ct. App. 1972).

4. As the Third Circuit observed, no court has granted teachers the right to choose their own curricula or classroom management techniques in contravention of school policy or dictates. Bradley v. Pittsburgh Board of Education, 910 F.2d 1172 (3d Cir. 1990).

5. *See* Tinker v. Des Moines Independent Community School District, 393 U.S. 503, 506 (1969). ("It can hardly be argued that either students or teachers shed their constitutional rights to freedom of speech or expression at the schoolhouse gate.")

6. *See, e.g.,* Kirkland v. Northside Independent School District, 890 F.2d 794 (5th Cir. 1989) (permitting officials to place restrictions on speech in public schools as long as the restrictions are reasonably related to legitimate pedagogical concerns).

7. State Tax Commission v. Board of Education of Holton, 73 P.2d 49 (Kan. 1937); State *ex rel.* Andrews v. Webber, 8 N.E. 708 (Ind. 1886).

8. Dixon, S. (Ed.). (2010, March 7). Texas textbook changes stir controversy. *My Fox Atlanta.* Retrieved from http://www.myfoxatlanta.com/dpp/news/texas-textbook-changes-stir-controversy-030607.

9. No Child Left Behind Act, 20 U.S.C. §§ 6301 *et seq.* (2006).

10. Raisch, C. D., & Russo, C .J. (2006). The No Child Left Behind Act: Federal over-reaching or necessary educational reform? *Education Law Journal, 7,* 255–265.

11. *See, e.g.,* 71 Massachusetts General Laws § 2 (requiring that courses in American history and civics must be offered that include instruction in "the constitution of the United States, the declaration of independence and the bill of rights, and in all public high schools the constitution of the commonwealth and local history and government").

12. *See, e.g.,* Valent v. New Jersey State Board of Education, 274 A.2d 832 (N.J. 1971); Medeiros v. Kijosaki, 478 P.2d 314 (Haw. 1970).

13. Brown v. Hot, Sexy and Safer Productions, 68 F.3d 525 (1st Cir. 1995), *cert. denied,* 516 U.S. 1159 (1996); Fields v. Palmdale School District, 427 F.3d 1197 (9th Cir. 2005), *opinion amended on denial of rehearing,* 447 F.3d 1187 (9th Cir. 2006), *cert. denied,* 549 U.S. 1089 (2006); Parker v. Hurley, 514 F.3d 87 (1st Cir. 2008), *cert. denied,* 129 S. Ct. 56 (2008). For a commentary on this issue, *see* Russo, C. J., & Thro, W. E. (2007). Curricular control and parental rights: Balancing the rights of educators and parents in American public schools. *Australia & New Zealand Journal of Law and Education, 12*(2), 91–102.

14. Jones v. Holes, 6 A.2d 102 (Pa. 1939).

15. Zykan v. Warsaw Community School Corp., 631 F.2d 1300 (7th Cir. 1980); Board of Education of Okay Independent School District v. Carroll, 513 P.2d 872 (Okla. 1973). *But see* 70 Massachusetts General Laws. § 13:
"In every public school having not less than one hundred and fifty pupils, any course not included in the regular curriculum shall be taught if the parents or guardians of not less than thirty pupils or of a number of pupils equivalent to five per cent of the pupil enrollment in the high school, whichever is less, request in writing the teaching thereof; provided that said request is made and said enrollment is completed before the preceding August first; provided, further, a qualified

teacher is available to teach the course; and provided, further, that the approval and implementation of said course is voted by two-thirds or more of the full membership of the school committee. The teaching of any course as provided by this section may be discontinued if the enrollment of pupils falls below fifteen. Such courses as may be taught under this section shall be given the same academic credit necessary for a high school diploma as is given to similar courses taught in said public high school, provided that the school committee shall make a determination as to the credit equivalency of such course prior to its being offered."

16. 262 U.S. 390 (1923). *See also* the companion case of Bartels v. Iowa, 262 U.S. 404 (1923), (striking down similar laws from Iowa and Ohio).

17. Scopes v. State of Tennessee, 278 S.W. 57 (Tenn. Cir. Ct. 1925), *reversed* 289 S.W. 363 (Tenn. 1927).

18. Kramer, S. (Director) (1960). *Inherit the Wind.* United Artists.

19. 393 U.S. 97 (1968). For commentary on this issue, *see* Russo, C. J. (2002), Evolution v. creation science in the US: Can the courts divine a solution? *Education Law Journal, 3*(3), 152–158.

20. 482 U.S. 578 (1987).

21. Steirer v. Bethlehem Area School District, 987 F.2d 989 (3d Cir. 1993).

22. Immediato v. Rye Neck School District, 73 F.3d 454 (2d Cir. 1996).

23. *See, e.g.,* Herndon v. Chapel Hill–Carrboro City Board of Education, 89 F.3d 174 (4th Cir. 1996).

24. 457 U.S. 853 (1982).

25. *Id.* at 857

26. Counts v. Cedarville School District, 295 F. Supp. 2d 996 (W.D. Ark. 2003).

27. *See* Virgil v. School Board of Columbia County, 862 F.2d 1517 (11th Cir. 1989) (finding that a school board's actions in removing a previously approved book from an elective high school class due to objections to its vulgarity and sexual explicitness were reasonably related to legitimate pedagogical concerns).

28. Mozert v. Hawkins County Board of Education, 579 F. Supp. 1051 (E.D. Tenn. 1984), *reversed,* 765 F.2d 75 (6th Cir. 1985), *on remand,* 647 F. Supp. 1194 (E.D. Tenn. 1986), *reversed,* 827 F.2d 1058 (6th Cir. 1987), *cert. denied,* 484 U.S. 1066 (1988).

29. Fleischfresser v. Directors of School District, 200, 15 F.3d 680 (7th Cir. 1994) (finding that exposing students to stories about witchcraft did not endorse or enhance a religion).

30. Brown v. Woodland Joint Unified School District, 27 F.3d 1373 (9th Cir. 1994) (ruling that using curricular materials on witchcraft did not promote the religion of Wicca in violation of the Establishment Clause of the First Amendment).

31. *See, e.g.,* Smith v. Board of School Commissioners of Mobile County, 827 F.2d 684 (11th Cir. 1984).

32. Morrison v. Board of Education of Boyd County, 507 F.3d 494 (6th Cir. 2007), 521 F.3d 602 (6th Cir. 2008).

33. Leebaert v. Harrington, 332 F.3d 134 (2d Cir. 2003).

34. Parker v. Hurley, 514 F.3d 87 (1st Cir. 2008). For a commentary on this case, *see* Russo, C. J. (2008). The child is not the mere creature of the state: Controversy over teaching about same-sex marriage in public schools. *Education Law Reporter, 232,* 1–17.

35. Wulff v. Inhabitants of Wakefield, 109 N.E. 358 (Mass. 1915).

36. *See, e.g.,* Lacks v. Ferguson Reorganized School District R-2, 147 F.3d 718 (8th Cir. 1998); Boring v. Buncombe County Board of Education, 136 F.3d 364 (4th Cir. 1998).

37. *See, e.g.,* Leebaert v. Harrington, 332 F.3d 134 (2d Cir. 2003).

38. *See, e.g.,* Simineo v. School District No. 16, 594 F.2d 1353 (10th Cir. 1979).

39. Mailloux v. Kiley, 448 F.2d 1242 (1st Cir. 1971).

40. Keefe v. Geanakos, 418 F.2d 359 (1st Cir. 1969).

41. Fowler v. Board of Education of Lincoln County, Ky., 819 F.2d 657 (6th Cir. 1987), *cert. denied,* 484 U.S. 986 (1987).

42. In *Mailloux v. Kiley* the court declared, "We also recognized, however, that free speech does not grant teachers a license to say or write in class whatever they may feel like, and that the propriety of regulations or sanctions must depend on such circumstances as the age and sophistication of the students, the closeness of the relation between the specific technique used and some concededly valid educational objective, and the context and manner of presentation." 448 F.2d at 1243.

43. For the seminal case rejecting the use of tracking, *see* Hobson v. Hansen, 269 F. Supp. 401 (D.D.C. 1967), *affirmed sub nom.* Smuck v. Hobson, 408 F.2d 175 (D.C. Cir. 1969).

44. Andrews v. City of Monroe, 730 F.2d 1050 (5th Cir. 1984).

45. Schwan v. Board of Education of Lansing School District, 183 N.W.2d 594 (Mich. Ct. App. 1970).

46. *See, e.g.,* Swany v. San Ramon Valley Unified School District, 720 F. Supp. 764 (N.D. Cal. 1989) (finding that it was not unreasonable for a school board to withhold a diploma from a student who had not passed in all assignments).

47. Rehabilitation Act, Section 504, 29 U.S.C. § 794 (2006). For a more complete discussion of accommodations that need to be made for students with disabilities, *see* Russo, C. J., & Osborne, A. G. (2009). *Section 504 and the ADA.* Thousand Oaks, CA: Corwin.

48. Spence v. Bailey, 465 F.2d 797 (6th Cir. 1972).

49. Debra P. v. Turlington, 644 F.2d 397 (5th Cir. 1981), 730 F.2d 1405 (11th Cir. 1984). [Authors' note: The Fifth Circuit was divided on October 1, 1981, creating the Eleventh Circuit, which is why these two decisions involving the same case are cited to different federal appeals courts.] *See also* Crump v. Gilmer Independent School District, 797 F. Supp. 552 (E.D. Tex. 1992).

50. *See, e.g.,* Hancock v. Commissioner of Education, 822 N.E.2d 1134 (Mass. 2005); Student No. 9 v. Board of Education, 802 N.E.2d 105 (Mass. 2004); Edgewood Independent School District v. Paiz, 856 S.W.2d 269 (Tex. Ct. App. 1993); Williams v. Austin Independent School District, 796 F. Supp. 251 (W.D. Tex. 1992).

51. Valentine v. Independent School District, 183 N.W. 434 (Iowa 1921).

52. *See, e.g.,* Kahn v. Fort Bend Independent School District, 561 F. Supp. 2d 760 (S.D. Tex. 2008) (rejecting a student's request for a preliminary injunction to prohibit implementation of a school board's decision denying him the opportunity to make the valedictory address due to his poor conduct).

53. The Supreme Court has defined a property interest as a benefit in which an individual has a legitimate claim to entitlement. Board of Regents v. Roth, 408 U.S. 564 (1972).

54. Dolinger v. Driver, 498 S.E.2d 252 (Ga. 1998); Swany v. San Ramon Valley Unified School District, 720 F. Supp. 764 (N.D. Cal. 1989).

55. *See, e.g.,* Ream v. Centennial School District, 765 A.2d 1195 (Pa. Commw. Ct. 2001); Shuman v. Cumberland Valley School District Board of Directors, 536 A.2d 490 (Pa. Commw. Ct. 1988).

56. Smith *ex rel.* Smith v. Board of Education of North Babylon Union Free School District, 844 F.2d 90 (2d Cir. 1988).

57. R.J.J. *ex rel.* Johnson v. Shineman, 638 S.W.2d 910 (Mo. Ct. App. 1983).

58. Knight v. Board of Education, 348 N.E.2d 299 (Ill. 1976) (commenting that a policy of grade reduction for nonattendance discouraged truancy and that good grades are dependent on effort, including school attendance).

59. Slocum v. Holton Board of Education, 429 N.W. 2d 607 (Mich. Ct. App. 1988).

60. Campbell v. Board of Education of Town of New Milford, 475 A.2d 289 (Conn. 1984).

61. *See, e.g.,* Hamer v. Board of Education of Township High School District No. 13, 363 N.E.2d 231 (Ill. App. Ct. 1978) (ruling that a school board did not have the authority to employ academic sanctions for student misconduct). *But see* South Gibson School Board v. Sollman, 768 N.E.2d 467 (Ind. 2002) (overturning earlier orders taking away credits previously earned as arbitrary and capricious).

62. Katzman *ex rel.* Katzman v. Cumberland Valley School District, 479 A.2d 671 (Pa. Commw. Ct. 1984). *See also* Dorsey v. Bale, 521 S.W.2d 76 (Ky. Ct. App. 1975) (finding that a school board lacked authority to implement a reduction in grades policy as a punitive measure); Smith v. School City of Hobart, 811 F. Supp. 391 (N.D. Ind. 1993) (pointing out that a reduction in grades for each day of suspension violated a student's substantive due process rights).

63. In re T.H., 681 So. 2d 110 (Miss. 1996).

64. NCLB, 20 U.S.C. § 6311.

65. Bester v. Tuscaloosa City Board of Education, 722 F.2d 1514 (11th Cir. 1984).

66. Individuals with Disabilities Education Act, 20 U.S.C. §§ 1400–1482 (2006).

67. IDEA, 20 U.S.C. § 1412(a)(16).

68. NCLB Regulations, 34 C.F.R. § 200.6(b).

69. Reading School District v. Department of Education, 855 A.2d 166 (Pa. Commw. Ct. 2004).

70. Debra P. v. Turlington, 730 F.2d 1405 (11th Cir. 1984).

71. *Id.*

72. *See, e.g.,* Brookhart v. Illinois State Board of Education, 697 F.2d 179 (7th Cir. 1983); Board of Education of Northport–East Northport Union Free School District v. Ambach, 469 N.Y.S.2d 699 (N.Y. 1983); Anderson v. Banks, 520 F. Supp. 472 (S.D. Ga. 1981), *modified,* 540 F. Supp. 761 (S.D. Ga. 1982).

73. Rene v. Reed, 751 N.E.2d 736 (Ind. App. Ct. 2001); Brookhart v. Illinois State Board of Education, 697 F.2d 179 (7th Cir. 1983).

74. Leighty v. Laurel School District, 457 F. Supp. 2d 546 (W.D. Pa. 2006).

75. Family Educational Rights and Privacy Act, 20 U.S.C. § 1232g (2006).

76. *Id.* § 1232g(a)(4)(A).

77. Sean R. v. Board of Education of the Town of Woodbridge, 794 F. Supp. 467 (D. Conn. 1992).

78. Webster Groves School District v. Pulitzer Publishing Co., 898 F.2d 1371 (8th Cir. 1990).

79. FERPA, 20 U.S.C. § 1232g(a)(5)(A).

80. *Id.* § 1232g(a)(5)(B).

81. FERPA Regulations, 34 C.F.R. § 99.37(b).

82. *Id.* §§ 99.7, 300.612.

83. *Id.* § 99.3(b).

84. FERPA, 20 U.S.C. § 1232g(a)(4)(B)(1).

85. *Id.* § 1232g(a)(4)(B)(2).

86. *Id.* § 1232g(a)(4)(B)(3).

87. *Id.* § 1232g(a)(4)(B)(4).

88. *Id.* § 1232g(a)(1)(A).

89. *Id.* § 1232g(a)(1)(A).

90. FERPA Regulations, 34 C.F.R. § 99.4.

91. *Id.* § 99.10(c).

92. FERPA, 20 U.S.C. § 1232g(d).

93. *Id.* § 1232g(a)(1)(B).

94. *Id.* § 1232g(a)(1)(C).

95. *Id.* § 1232g(a)(6).

96. *Id.* §§ 1232g(b)(1).

97. *Id.* § 1232g(b)(1)(A).

98. *Id.* § 1232g(b)(1)(B).

99. *Id.* § 1232g(b)(1)(C)(E).

100. *Id.* § 1232g(b)(1)(D).

101. *Id.* § 1232g(b)(1)(F).

102. *Id.* § 1232g(b)(1)(G).

103. *Id.* § 1232g(b)(1)(H).

104. *Id.* § 1232g(b)(1)(I).

105. *Id.* §§ 1232g(b)(1)(J).

106. FERPA Regulations, 34 C.F.R. § 99.30.

107. FERPA, 20 U.S.C. § 1232g(b)(2)(A).

108. *Id.* § 1232g(b)(4)(A).

109. *Id.* § 1232g(b)(4)(A).

110. *Id.* § 1232g(a)(1)(A).

111. FERPA Regulations, 34 C.F.R. §§ 99.11(b).

112. *Id.* 34 §§ 99.11(a).

113. *Id.* § 99.20(a).

114. *Id.* §§ 99.21.

115. *Id.* § 99.22.

116. *Id.* §§ 99.21(b)(1).

117. *Id.* §§ 99.21(b)(2).

118. *Id.* §§ 99.21(c).

119. *Id.* § 99.63. *See also* Gonzaga University v. Doe, 536 U.S. 273 (2002) (reasoning that FERPA does not grant aggrieved parties private rights of action).

120. 34 C.F.R. § 99.64.

121. *Id.* § 99.65.

122. *Id.* §§ 99.66, 99.67.

123. 534 U.S. 426 (2002).

124. For commentary on this case, *see* Russo, C. J., & Mawdsley, R. D. (2002). Owasso Independent School District v. Falvo: The Supreme Court upholds peer-grading. *School Business Affairs, 68*(5), 34–36.

125. Copyright Act of 1976, 17 U.S.C. § 101 *et seq.* (2006).

126. *Id.* § 102.

127. *Id.* § 106.

128. *Id.* § 107.

129. *See, e.g.,* Marcus v. Rowley, 695 F.2d 1171 (9th Cir. 1983) (finding that a teacher violated the Copyright Act for reproducing a booklet to incorporate into a learning packet).

130. A smartboard is an interactive board that connects to a computer so that the two devices communicate with each other. A user can write on the smartboard and transfer what is written to the computer, where the text can be converted to standard fonts.

131. *See* Russo, C. J. (2011). Acceptable use policies for school computers. *School Business Affairs, 77*(1), 32–34.

132. Copyright Act of 1976, 17 U.S.C. § 101 *et seq.* (2006).

133. *See, e.g.,* Encyclopedia Britannica Educational Corp. v. Crooks, 542 F. Supp. 1156 (W.D.N.Y. 1982), 558 F. Supp. 1247 (W.D.N.Y. 1983).

134. *Guidelines for Off-the-Air Recording of Broadcast Programming for Educational Purposes.* Congressional Record, E4750–E4752 (Oct. 14, 1981).

135. Copyright Act, 17 U.S.C. § 117.

136. Digital Millennium Copyright Act, 17 U.S.C. §§ 1201 *et seq.* (2006).

137. For a more thorough treatment of special education law, *see* Russo, C. J. & Osborne A. G. (2008). *Essential concepts & school-based cases in special education law.* Thousand Oaks, CA: Corwin. Osborne, A. G., & Russo, C. J. (2006). *Special education and the law: A guide for practitioners.* Thousand Oaks, CA: Corwin.

138. According to 20 U.S.C. § 1401(3)(A)(i), The term "child with a disability" means a child "(i) with mental retardation, hearing impairments (including deafness), speech or language impairments, visual impairments (including blindness), serious emotional disturbance (referred to in this chapter as 'emotional disturbance'), orthopedic impairments, autism, traumatic brain injury, other health impairments, or specific learning disabilities. . . ."

139. IDEA, 20 U.S.C. § 1401(3).

140. *Id.* §§ 1401(9), 1412(a)(1)A).

141. *Id.* § 1401(29).

142. *Id.* §§ 1401(14), 1414(d).

143. 458 U.S. 176 (1982).

144. 20 U.S.C. § 1415. *See also* Board of Education of Hendrick Hudson Central School District v. Rowley, 458 U.S. 176 (1982).

145. 20 U.S.C. §§ 1414(d)(1)(B)(i), 1414(f).

146. *Id.* § 1414(a)(1)(D).

147. *Id.* § 1415(b)(3).

148. *Id.* § 1415(b)(3)(A).

149. *Id.* § 1415(j).

150. *Id.* § 1415(k)(3)(B)(ii).

151. Honig v. Doe, 484 U.S. 305 (1988).

152. IDEA, 20 U.S.C. § 1414(a)(1)(A).

153. *Id.* § 1414(a)(1)(C)(i)(I).

154. *Id.* § 1414(b)(2), (3).

155. *Id.* § 1415(b)(1).

156. IDEA Regulations, 34 C.F.R. § 300.502(b).

157. *See, e.g.,* James and Lee Anne D. *ex rel.* Sarah D. v. Board of Education of Aptakisic-Tripp Community Consolidated School District No. 102, 642 F. Supp. 2d 804 (N.D. Ill. 2009) (finding that the IDEA does not require school personnel to implement recommendations from independent evaluations or even engage in a substantive discussion of their findings).

158. IDEA, 20 U.S.C. § 1414(d)(1)(A).

159. *Id.* § 1414(d)(4)(A).

160. *Id.* § 1414(a)(2)(A).

161. IDEA Regulations, 34 C.F.R. § 300.115.

162. IDEA Regulations, 34 C.F.R. § 300.115; *see also* 20 U.S.C. § 1412(a)(5).

163. IDEA Regulations, 34 C.F.R. § 300.115; *see also* 20 U.S.C. § 1401(9).

164. Board of Education of Hendrick Hudson Central School District v. Rowley, 458 U.S. 176 (1982).

165. *See, e.g.,* David D. v. Dartmouth School Committee, 775 F.2d 411 (1st Cir. 1985); Geis v. Board of Education of Parsippany–Troy Hills, 774 F.2d 575 (3d Cir. 1985).

166. For an annual review of these cases *see* the "Students with Disabilities" chapter in the *Yearbook of Education Law* (edited by C. F. Russo) published each year by the Education Law Association.

167. *See, e.g.,* Adrianne and Joshua D. v. Lakeland Central School District, 686 F. Supp. 2d 361 (S.D.N.Y. 2010) (finding that a student received a FAPE inasmuch as he had made progress); Souderton Area School District v. J.H. *ex rel.* J.H. and S.H., 351 F. App'x 755 (3d Cir. 2009) (allowing the proposed use of a rubric-based writing program for a student with a disability, since the program was approved for use with all student populations in the public schools in the state).

168. IDEA, 20 U.S.C. § 1401(26).

169. *Id.*

170. 468 U.S. 883 (1984). It is important to keep in mind that supportive services are frequently provided under Section 504 of the Rehabilitation Act, 29 U.S.C. § 794 (2006), to students who are not receiving special education.

171. IDEA, 20 U.S.C. § 1401(26).

172. *Id.* § 1401(1).

173. *Id.* § 1401(2).

174. *Id.* § 1401(34).

175. *Id.* § 1414(d)(1)(A)(i)(VIII).

176. *Id.* § 1415(k).

177. 484 U.S. 305 (1988).

178. IDEA, 20 U.S.C. § 1415(k)(1)(G).

179. *Id.* § 1415(k)(1)(D).

180. *Id.* § 1415(k)(1)(D), (E).

181. For a more thorough treatment of the IDEA's disciplinary provisions, *see* Osborne, A. G., & Russo, C. J. (2009). *Discipline in special education.* Thousand Oaks, CA: Corwin.

182. IDEA, 20 U.S.C. § 1415(k)(1)(E).

183. *Id.* § 1415(i)(2)(C)(iii). Even so, the Supreme Court has cautioned lower courts to not substitute their judgment regarding proper educational methodologies and techniques for those of educators. *See* Board of Education of Hendrick Hudson Central School District v. Rowley, 458 U.S. 176 (1982).

184. 471 U.S. 359 (1985).

185. IDEA, 20 U.S.C. § 1412(a)(10)(C)(iii).

186. 510 U.S. 7 (1993).

187. 129 S. Ct. 2484 (2009).

188. IDEA, 20 U.S.C. §§ 1415(i)(3)(B) *et seq.*

189. 414 U.S. 563 (1974).

190. Civil Rights Act of 1964, Title VI, 42 U.S.C. §§ 2000d *et seq.* (2006). Title VI bars discrimination in federally funded programs on the basis of race, color, or national origin.

191. Serna v. Portales Municipal Schools, 499 F.2d 1147 (10th Cir. 1974).

192. 413 U.S. 189 (1973).

193. 380 F. Supp. 673 (D. Colo. 1974).

194. 521 F.2d 465 (10th Cir. 1975).

195. Guadalupe Organization v. Tempe Elementary School District, 587 F.2d 1022 (9th Cir. 1978).

196. United States v. State of Texas, 680 F.2d 356 (5th Cir. 1982).

197. 129 S. Ct. 2579 (2009).

198. Equal Educational Opportunities Act of 1974, 20 U.S.C. §§ 1701 *et seq.* (2006).

199. The Equal Educational Opportunities Commission requires states to take "appropriate action to overcome language barriers that impede equal participation by its students in its instructional programs" (20 U.S.C. § 1703f).

200. Flores v. Arizona, 172 F. Supp. 2d 1225 (D. Ariz. 2000), 2001 WL 1028369 (D. Ariz. 2001), 405 F. Supp. 2d 1112 (D. Ariz. 2005), *remanded* 204 F. App'x 580 (9th Cir. 2006), *on remand,* 480 F. Supp. 2d 1157 (D. Ariz. 2007), *affirmed* 516 F.3d 1140 (9th Cir. 2008).

201. Horne v. Flores, 129 S. Ct. at 2601.

Tort Liability   9

KEY CONCEPTS IN THIS CHAPTER

❖ Types of Torts

❖ Intentional Torts

❖ Negligence

❖ Standard of Care

❖ Defenses to Charges of Negligence

❖ Educational Malpractice

❖ Civil Rights Violations

INTRODUCTION

Teachers everywhere, understandably, are concerned about their liability in the event that children in their care are injured through their either intentional or negligent actions. Tort liability, which is largely rooted in common law or judge-made law, is premised on the legal theory that parties who are injured through the intentional or negligent actions of others are entitled to compensation, most often in the form of monetary damages, to right the wrongs. It is a fact of life in schools that children get hurt. Many factors determine whether school personnel may be rendered liable for student injuries. Negligent behavior on the part of those charged with supervising children is alleged in a majority of tort claims arising in educational settings. Moreover, in recent years several lawsuits alleged that school officials committed educational malpractice and/or civil rights violations when students failed to learn.

This chapter reviews the different types of torts and the standard of care that teachers must exercise to avoid liability. The chapter begins with the definition of a tort and descriptions of the various types of torts before examining the intentional torts of assault, battery, false imprisonment, and defamation. The chapter proceeds with discussions of negligence, the standard of care expected of educators, the elements of negligence charges, how to avoid negligence, and the various defenses to charges of negligence. The chapter rounds out with information on educational malpractice and civil rights torts. As with previous chapters in this book, it ends with a summary of major points and a list of frequently asked questions.

DEFINITIONS AND TYPES OF TORTS

Torts are civil, as opposed to criminal, wrongs or injuries, other than breaches of contracts, for which courts provide remedies, generally in the form of monetary damages. The word *tort* is derived from the Latin and Old French words for *twisted.* There are essentially four types of torts: intentional torts, negligence, products liability, and constitutional torts.

> Torts are civil, as opposed to criminal, wrongs or injuries, other than breaches of contracts, for which courts provide remedies, generally in the form of monetary damages.

Intentional torts, as the term implies, occur when individuals purposefully violate the rights of others and cause them harm. Negligence, on the other hand, involves unintentional behavior, such as when students are injured because those responsible for their care failed to properly fulfill their duties. Educational malpractice takes place when teachers fail to provide proper instruction. Products liability, which is beyond the scope of this book because it has little impact on the professional activities of teachers, deals with injuries that buyers, users, or bystanders suffer as a result of defective products. Finally, constitutional torts arise when those responsible acted to intentionally discriminate, with deliberate indifference, or with gross misjudgment with regards to the civil rights of others.

Intentional Torts

Insofar as intentional torts stem from the deliberate acts of others, remedies in the form of compensation for damages are often higher than for other torts and may include punitive damages. Even so, it is often difficult to prove intentional torts, because plaintiffs must establish specific intent or state of mind by those causing alleged injuries. In order to prevail, plaintiffs must prove that defendants acted deliberately and purposefully with the intention of knowingly causing harm. By way of illustration, if a teacher injures a student while breaking up a fight in which the child was involved, it is unlikely that the teacher would be liable for an intentional tort, as long as the educator's actions were reasonable under the circumstances. On the other hand, if the teacher became angry and punched the student several times, the teacher may

> Insofar as intentional torts stem from the deliberate acts of others, remedies in the form of compensation for damages are often higher than for other torts and may include punitive damages.

be liable for the intentional torts of assault and battery, not to mention the possibility of criminal charges, a topic that is beyond the scope of this chapter and book. In the first scenario, as long as the teacher was following standard procedures, the student would have a difficult time proving that the teacher intended to cause the injury. In the latter case, the student would probably have little difficulty establishing that the teacher intended to cause harm.

It is important to note that teachers who commit intentional torts can be rendered personally liable for their actions. Put another way, school boards do not indemnify teachers who are assessed monetary damages for their intentional torts, because the teachers' misdeeds constitute conduct that is outside the scope of their normal duties. However, judgments against teachers for intentional torts are relatively uncommon.

Assault and Battery

As an initial matter, it is worth keeping in mind that assault and battery often go together like salt and pepper. In other words, as explained in the coming paragraphs, assault is a verbal threat of an unwanted touch, while battery is the actual unwanted touch. It is important to recognize that the intentional torts of assault and battery may be related to but are different from their criminal counterparts, the elements of which vary from one jurisdiction to the next.

> Assaults are threats to commit immediate unwanted touches of others, as opposed to actual acts of physical force. . . . Battery, on the other hand, refers to unwanted and unlawful touching or striking of individuals.

Assaults are threats to commit immediate unwanted touches of others, as opposed to actual acts of physical force. Assaults occur when individuals' overt actions put others in fear or apprehension of an immediate harm or unconsented-to touch. An assault occurs, for instance, to the extent that a student feels endangered when a teacher brandishes a ruler and verbally threatens to use it on the student. Yet, words alone do not normally constitute assaults, since the words must be combined with immediate threatening actions. Accordingly, if a teacher threatens to strike a student the next day if the child misbehaves again, this is not assault, because there is no threat of immediacy.

Battery, on the other hand, refers to unwanted and unlawful intentional touching or striking of individuals. A battery is committed, using the above example, if the teacher follows through on the threat and strikes the student with the ruler. A battery does not always need to be violent, as many forms of unwanted touching, such as sexual harassment, constitute batteries. Not surprisingly, most suits charging school officials with assault and battery arise in the context of student discipline and sexual harassment.

Before turning to specific cases, it is worth noting that a teacher can assault one child while battering another. For example, if a teacher threatens a child that he will strike him with the piece of chalk that he is holding and throws it at the student but misses and hits a second child, he may well have assaulted the first child by placing him in the situation of fearing an unwanted touch while battering the second child due to the unconsented-to touch. As should be clear from this hypothetical scenario, while students must be aware that they are being assaulted, they can be battered without advanced warning, such as where a teacher might discipline a child with a slap to the back of the head as the teacher walks down a row of desks in a classroom. Accordingly, in one sequence of events, it is possible for a teacher to assault one student while battering another.

When students and their parents file suit over the related infliction of corporal punishment, they often seek damages under tort law. In states that do not permit corporal punishment, its use can predictably result in allegations of assault and battery. Even in states where corporal punishment is authorized, students frequently allege that the penalty was not administered in accordance with requirements, was unreasonable, or was executed with excessive force. Overall, courts are reluctant to interfere with school authorities' disciplinary measures but do take notice when the actions are particularly egregious. In the most significant case on point, the Supreme Court ruled in *Ingraham v. Wright*,[1] a dispute from Florida, that subject to state law, school officials have the right to impose corporal punishment. Two years earlier, in a summary approval of a trial court order from North Carolina, *Baker v. Owen*,[2] the Court had affirmed that school officials had the right to administer corporal punishment as they saw fit, regardless of whether parents agreed.

On the other hand, corporal punishment that is so grossly excessive that it is shocking to the conscience can rise to the level of constitutional violations of students' substantive due process rights. In the school context, substantive due process prohibits school authorities from infringing on students' fundamental constitutional liberties. For example, a paddling that leaves a student with deep bruises, bleeding, and a permanent scar[3] or that sends a student to the emergency room[4] infringes on the student's right to be free from excessive force. In one particularly flagrant situation, the Eleventh Circuit ruled that a coach's hitting a student with a metal weight lock, which resulted in the loss of the use of one eye, violated the student's right to be free from excessive corporal punishment, supporting his claim of a substantive due process violation.[5]

The Eighth Circuit established a test for lower courts to use in evaluating substantive due process claims in the context of corporal punishment.[6] The panel instructed lower courts to determine the need for corporal punishment, the relationship between the need and the amount of punishment administered, the extent of any injuries inflicted, and whether the punishment was administered in a good faith effort to maintain discipline as opposed to maliciously and sadistically intending to cause harm. In the case before it, the court was convinced that the corporal punishment, which consisted of two strikes with a wooden paddle, was not excessive and did not exceed that which is permissible under common law.

Students and their parents have filed a fair number of lawsuits alleging that school officials used excessive force in either disciplining or restraining them. In an early case a student in Louisiana successfully claimed that it was unnecessary, either for discipline or his own protection, when a teacher shook him, lifted him, and then let him fall.[7] In another case from Louisiana, an appellate court agreed that a teacher's actions greatly exceeded the boundaries of reasonable corporal punishment when he punched the child several times.[8]

As noted, students have the right to be free from the use of excessive force by school personnel.[9] Still, teachers and administrators are free to use reasonable force in controlling students who pose a danger to themselves or others. Educators are typically not deemed liable when students resist and are injured in the process as long as restrainers used no more force than was necessary. In such a case, the Seventh Circuit decided that a teacher in Illinois did not violate a disruptive student's rights when he grabbed her by her wrist and elbow as he escorted her from his classroom.[10] Similarly, the Eighth Circuit held that a coach who dragged a student along a cafeteria floor did not use excessive force, because the student had disobeyed the coach's orders and fought back.[11] Subsequently, the Eighth Circuit was convinced that a principal's action in forcefully restraining a student, who violently kicked a vending machine while resisting the efforts of a teacher to calm him down, was appropriate and did not rise to the level of a substantive due process violation.[12] Even though the principal's

CASE SUMMARY 9.1: USE OF FORCE IN RESTRAINING STUDENTS

Golden ex rel. Balch v. Anders

324 F.3d 650 (8th Cir. 2003)

Factual Summary: A fairly large sixth grade student in an elementary school who was violently kicking a vending machine resisted the efforts of a teacher who attempted to settle him down. In the process the student held one of the teacher's arms to keep his balance. A high school principal arrived on the scene, and seeing the student with his hands on the teacher, grabbed the student and escorted him out of the area. The principal then allegedly threw the student onto a bench and forcefully kept him there. The school's resource officer, under instructions from the principal, subsequently handcuffed the student who was later diagnosed as having a pulled nerve and a strained neck. His mother sued the principal seeking compensatory damages. The federal trial court dismissed the suit, and the mother appealed.

Issue: Did the principal violate the student's substantive due process rights?

Decision: No, the Eight Circuit affirmed the decision of the trial court, agreeing that the principal had the authority to act as he did.

Summary of Court's Rationale: The court observed that the principal was in a position where he had to make an instant judgment regarding how to quell the immediate danger posed by the student. Acknowledging that school administrators are given substantial deference in matters such as school discipline and maintaining order and that the principal needed to act quickly and decisively to respond to an incident of serious student misconduct, the court rejected the notion that the principal's actions were conscience-shocking. The court concluded that his use of force in subduing the student was not excessive but was appropriate under the circumstances, since the student ignored a teacher's order and resisted the principal's efforts to restrain his violent actions.

restraint caused an injury to the student, the court did not find that it was shocking to the conscience. Rather, the court concluded that the principal's behavior was reasonable under the circumstances, since the student resisted the principal's efforts to subdue him.

Teachers also may file assault and battery charges when they are attacked and injured by students. Although it is uncommon, such suits are not unheard of. In one case, a teacher from Wisconsin sued a student, who had a reputation for aggressive behavior, for battery after the student punched him in the face and pushed his head into a corner. An appellate court affirmed a substantial monetary award of punitive damages against the student, pointing out that he had a malicious intent in attacking the teacher and was old enough to know that his actions were wrong.[13] The court expressed the hope that the damages award would provide the student with a lesson he would not soon forget while serving as a warning to other students.

False Imprisonment

False imprisonment takes place when individuals intentionally and unlawfully detain others against their wills. A case from Florida shows that unintentional confinement does not amount to false imprisonment. Where a bus driver became lost and, consequently, a student remained on board the bus for hours, the court refused to render the driver liable for false imprisonment, since he had no intent to detain the student unlawfully.[14] At the same time, false imprisonment does not necessarily require individuals to be locked in rooms but may occur when they are restrained or otherwise prevented from freely moving about.

> False imprisonment takes place when individuals intentionally and unlawfully detain others against their wills.

Traditional disciplinary measures used in schools, such as detentions, do not amount to false imprisonment. It has long been a common practice for educators to detain students after school as a form of discipline. In fact, as early as 1887, courts recognized that school personnel had the authority to keep students after school and that the practice did not amount to false imprisonment.[15] By the same token, placing students in time-out areas or in-house suspensions is fairly universal. In keeping with their overall reluctance to interfere with educators' necessity to discipline students, courts, by and large, have not impeded this practice. In one case a federal trial court in Arkansas held that removing a disruptive student and requiring her to sit in an isolated area did not constitute false imprisonment.[16] If possible, teachers should notify parents that their children will be in detention. In fact, educators should consider not imposing detention on the same day that an infraction occurs so that parents can ensure needed after-school transportation or supervision for their children.

Educators may use detentions, time-outs, and in-house suspensions as disciplinary tools with students with disabilities as long as the use of these methods is not inconsistent with the students' individualized education programs.[17] Although detentions and time-outs are considered to be minor disciplinary sanctions, an excessive amount of time spent in such situations is not permissible. Of course, students must be properly supervised while detained.

School officials may use physical restraints when necessary to protect themselves and/or others from danger but must act with extreme care. In Virginia a federal trial court dismissed charges that parents filed against a teacher and aide who restrained a special education student, since the child's individualized education program specifically provided for restraints to be used if he became a danger to himself or others, and the force used was not disproportionate to the need presented.[18] Similarly, a federal trial court in Texas dismissed a claim against school personnel who wrapped an out-of-control student in a blanket for safety reasons.[19] The court decided that the student's substantive due process rights did not include the right to be free from restraints used to control her outbursts for the purpose of preventing harm to herself and school staff. In yet another case, the federal trial court in Connecticut agreed that school authorities who used restraints in response to a student's misbehavior exercised professional judgment in accordance with professionally accepted standards.[20] Educators must be careful when they use physical restraints, and those who do so should be properly trained in restraint techniques.

Unfortunately, when educators fail to exercise wise judgment in their disciplinary measures, courts intervene in egregious situations. For example, courts agree that students presented viable claims in situations where they were locked in rooms or chained to trees.[21] A federal trial court in New York allowed a suit to proceed in light of evidence that a teacher used disproportionate force to restrain a child under the circumstances.[22]

Defamation

Defamation refers to the intentional communication of a false statement that injures the reputation of the person against whom it is directed. In essence, defamation is a false accusation that damages the good name of another. There are two types of defamation: slander and libel. Slander involves oral communications, and libel occurs with written communications. Those who need to pass information on to others are given some protection from allegations of defamation. Defamation is thus an important topic for teachers, since they are often in positions where they must share information about their students.

> Defamation refers to the intentional communication of a false statement that injures the reputation of the person against whom it is directed. In essence, defamation is a false accusation that damages the good name of another.

Educators enjoy a qualified or conditional immunity from liability when they must transmit information in students' best interests. Even so, teacher statements must be made in good faith and not in malice. Teachers are protected, for instance, when they make good faith comments, even negative or critical observations, on student report cards or college recommendation letters. All statements must be made in good faith, since gossip is not privileged, meaning that its use does not enjoy immunity from liability, as the use of good-faith statements does. In addition to privilege, truth is a defense against charges of defamation, as true statements can never be defamatory. Of course, an individual may not violate another's privacy right in making such oral or written statements. Opinion statements may have some protections, especially when it is very clear that they are opinions rather than statements of fact.

Parents may claim privilege as a defense to charges of defamation brought by educators, particularly when the allegations stem from criticisms or complaints they level against school personnel. Parents are particularly privileged when their concerns are raised through proper channels. In one case, teachers from Louisiana filed suit after parents relayed their concerns to school authorities that the teachers inappropriately touched students. The court emphasized that such communications, even if false, were privileged as long as they were made in good faith and without malice.[23] In another case, a teacher unsuccessfully sued a student and her parents for monetary damages after they made oral and written statements suggesting that the teacher was incompetent. An appellate court in New York affirmed the trial court's dismissal on the basis that the statements were protected as expressions of pure personal opinion.[24] Similarly, an appellate court in Michigan agreed that statements were privileged that a father made in a letter to the principal of his son's school complaining that a teacher's actions were unprofessional and not in keeping with good teaching practices.[25] Even so, not all statements made by parents are protected. Teachers can succeed in defamation actions against parents when they can demonstrate that the statements were clearly false and made with malice.

CASE SUMMARY 9.2: DAMAGES FOR DEFAMATION OF TEACHER

Ansorian v. Zimmerman

627 N.Y.S.2d 706 (N.Y. App. Div. 1995)

Factual Summary: A high school French teacher filed suit seeking damages for defamation against a student and her parents after they charged that she was incompetent and requested that she be replaced as the child's teacher. The trial court dismissed the complaint, and the teacher appealed.

Issue: Are the student and her parents liable for damages for defamation?

Decision: No, the appellate court affirmed that the parents and student were not liable for defamation, since their comments were privileged.

Summary of Court's Rationale: The court found that the challenged statements were protected by the state constitution. The court added that an examination of the statements indicated that they were not reasonably susceptible to a defamatory meaning, since they constituted personal opinion and rhetorical hyperbole. Also, the court observed that the expressions of opinion in the challenged statements were sufficiently supported by a recitation of the underlying facts.

In a case where a newspaper columnist wrote that a coach lied during a hearing, the Supreme Court found that the statement was not an opinion inasmuch as its veracity could be shown to be either true or false.[26] The Court declared that a public figure or official may sue for damages only when so-called opinion statements imply false and defamatory facts, are made with the knowledge that they are false, or are made with a reckless disregard for the truth. Accordingly, courts view public officials and public figures, those who voluntarily place themselves in the public consciousness—such as coaches or superintendents, but usually not teachers—in a different light than private persons when it comes to defamation. Public officials and public figures must prove that alleged defamatory statements were made with malice. As noted, it is fairly well settled that school board members and superintendents are public figures, but courts are divided as to whether teachers and coaches are public figures.[27]

School administrators may claim privilege when it comes to statements they make about teachers in their professional capacities. As such, comments that principals make in teachers' evaluations are protected. Moreover, statements made in letters of recommendation or communications to other administrators are privileged.[28] Again, though, administrators are not protected from defamation claims when they make statements that they know are false or with malicious intentions.

Infliction of Emotional Distress

The tort of infliction of emotional or mental distress—a tort of relatively recent origin, stems from conduct resulting in extreme emotional distress. The term refers to emotional suffering or anguish manifested by feelings such as fright, anxiety, nervousness, and even physical pain. Suits alleging the intentional or unreasonable infliction of emotional distress, whether filed by teachers or students, are largely unsuccessful. Emotional distress is difficult to prove, since claimants must provide evidence that the "defendants acted intentionally or recklessly; that the conduct was extreme and outrageous; that the defendants' actions caused the plaintiffs severe emotional distress; that the conduct exceeded all possible bounds of decency; and that it was utterly intolerable in a civilized community."[29]

> Lawsuits alleging the intentional or unreasonable infliction of emotional distress, whether filed by teachers or students, are largely unsuccessful.

In a rare successful application of this doctrine, an appellate court in Florida noted that a teacher, who alleged that two students inflicted emotional distress on her, raised a viable claim, since the students' behavior was so outrageous and extreme that it went beyond all limits of decency.[30] The students had produced and distributed a publication in which they referred to the teacher in derogatory and vulgar ways, threatened to rape and kill her and rape her children and their cousins.

Teachers have generally been unsuccessful when they have raised allegations of emotional distress in the face of adverse employment actions. In one instance, a kindergarten teacher in Virginia, who was suspended and required to undergo a medical and psychiatric examination after threatening other employees, failed to establish that the school board's actions violated her rights or amounted to outrageous and intolerable conduct.[31] In another case, a teacher who was not hired for a coaching position failed to prove that the board's actions amounted to extreme and outrageous behavior that would be utterly intolerable in a civilized community.[32] The teacher claimed that the board's failure to appoint him to the position caused him humiliation, serious emotional distress, and loss of self-esteem.

CASE SUMMARY 9.3: INFLICTION OF EMOTIONAL DISTRESS

*Katterhenrich v. Federal Hocking Local School
District Board of Education*

700 N.E.2d 626 (Ohio Ct. App. 1997)

Factual Summary: A teacher who applied for the position of assistant boys' basketball coach filed suit after he was not appointed to the position. After determining that the teacher was not qualified for the position, the school board eventually appointed a noncertificated individual to fill the vacancy. In his suit, the teacher alleged, among other things, intentional infliction of emotional distress and negligent infliction of emotional distress. In his complaint, the teacher claimed to have suffered humiliation, serious emotional distress, and a loss of self-esteem. A state trial court entered a judgment in favor of the school board, and the teacher appealed.

Issue: Is the school board liable for intentional infliction of emotional distress for failing to appoint the applicant to the vacant coaching position?

Decision: No, the court of appeals affirmed that the school board did not intentionally inflict emotional harm on the teacher when it chose not to hire him for a coaching position.

Summary of Court's Rationale: After examining the record of the trial court, the appellate court determined that the evidence showed that the teacher did not suffer emotional distress of the magnitude necessary to sustain a viable claim for infliction of emotional distress. The court noted that the teacher's own testimony clearly indicated that he did not suffer from a severe and debilitating emotional injury. The court reasoned that the school board's conduct could not be characterized as going beyond all possible bounds of decency, a criterion needed for a finding of infliction of emotional distress. The court concluded that the board's action, as a matter of law, did not constitute extreme and outrageous conduct.

Litigation charging teachers with inflicting emotional distress are relatively rare. In one action where the parents of a kindergarten student were successful, an appellate court in Louisiana sustained a substantial award of damages against a school board after the student suffered emotional trauma following an incident involving a teacher employed by the board.[33] The teacher had led the child to believe that he had hanged two of the child's friends with a jump rope. Two psychologists testified that the student's behavior changed after the incident and diagnosed him as having a multitude of emotional problems, including post-traumatic stress disorder.

Negligence

Negligence is a common law tort wherein one's unintentional behavior breaches a duty of care and injures another person or persons. In educational settings, school boards, administrators, teachers, and employees have a duty to protect students from reasonably foreseeable risks of harm. That is not to say that school personnel may be liable every time students are injured. Educators are not ensurers of student safety insofar as most injuries in schools derive from unavoidable accidents. No legal fault lies in these situations, since school employees cannot reasonably be expected to supervise and control students continuously.

> Negligence is a common law tort wherein one's unintentional behavior breaches a duty of care and injures another person or persons.

It has always been a major challenge for teachers to maintain safe, risk-free learning environments for students. Children will be children, and whether they are in class, playing in school yards, or participating in extracurricular activities, school personnel run the risk of liability for injuries that children suffer when supervisors breach their duty to protect their charges from unreasonable risks of harm. It is impossible, then, to be able to prevent all schoolhouse injuries. Of course, awareness of the principles constituting the legal duty to supervise students properly and the defenses to the tort of negligence can go a long way toward protecting school boards and their teachers.

Elements of Negligence

In order to maintain viable negligence claims, litigants must show that the alleged injuries were avoidable via the exercise of reasonable care. In other words, parties alleging negligence must establish the presence of the following elements: duty and the related concept of foreseeability, breach, injury, and causation. Each element is discussed below.

> In order to maintain viable negligence claims, litigants must show that the alleged injuries were avoidable via the exercise of reasonable care.

Figure 9.1   Criteria for Determining Liability for Negligence

---

1. The defendant had a legal duty to the plaintiff.

2. The defendant breached that duty.

3. The plaintiff suffered a compensable injury.

4. The defendant's breach of duty was the proximate cause of the plaintiff's injury.

Duty. According to the common law of negligence, a person has no duty to act absent a legal relationship. In this respect, it is significant to note that school personnel who act within the scope of their duties must assist all students in a group, even if they do not know the children personally. This duty arises from educators' legal relationship with their school boards and is not limited to students (or others) from the buildings in which they work. Given the importance of duty, many negligence cases can be seen in the context of adequacy of supervision. To the extent that adequate supervision should prevent students from being injured by reasonably foreseeable dangers, all school activities must be supervised. The degree of supervision needed depends on such factors as the nature of the activities and the ages and mental capacities of the children involved.

Once the existence of a legal relationship is established, administrators and teachers have the duty to anticipate reasonably foreseeable injuries or risks to students and take logical steps to protect them from harm. Foreseeability is a highly flexible concept based on students' ages and physical-emotional conditions along with the extent of danger inherent in activities. To this end, the law does not expect teachers to anticipate all harm that might befall the students in their care. To the contrary, teachers, and their school boards, are responsible for only those accidents of which they are reasonably aware or that can reasonably be anticipated.

Whether injuries can be foreseen cannot be based on speculation. Teachers are not likely to be liable when intervening acts that could not have been foreseen occur, as long as they take realistic precautions. By way of example, when a supervising classroom aide could not have anticipated that a student would pull a chair out from under a classmate who was attempting to sit down, the court refused to impose liability.[34] Similarly, another court refused to impose liability where a student slipped and was injured during a classroom skit, since the fall could not have been anticipated.[35]

Unfortunately, even when properly supervised, students sometimes get into fights. Although school officials cannot always anticipate spontaneous altercations, they are required to intervene when one occurs. An appellate court in New York dismissed a negligence suit brought by the parents of a high school student who was injured in an exchange with peers.[36] The court found that school authorities had not breached their duty to supervise the students properly, commenting that they could not "be expected to guard against all of the sudden, spontaneous acts that take place among students on a daily basis."[37] On the other hand, teachers have an obligation to intervene when they observe children engaging in aggressive behavior, inasmuch as a failure to intervene would be tantamount to inadequate supervision.[38]

The required level of supervision may be lessened before the start of a school day and after students are dismissed, as compared to the supervision required during the school day itself. Even so, once personnel know, or should know, that students are present on school property, they must take precautions to ensure the children's safety. Accordingly, an appellate court in Louisiana decided that a board was responsible for the injuries a child sustained when he was playing in the school yard prior to the start of classes.[39] The court indicated that although the board operated a breakfast program, and officials knew that many students would therefore be in attendance, a supervising teacher was not present on the playground when the child was injured. Conversely, the Supreme Court of Kansas refused to impose liability on a school board or teacher in an unfortunate situation where a student was struck by a car after being chased off of school grounds by a peer before class.[40] The court thought that the student could not recover for negligence without proving that officials took on a duty to protect or supervise him before classes began, since he was not in their custody or control.

Breach. Two essential considerations must be taken into account when examining whether school authorities have breached their duty of care. The first relates to how educators performed, or failed to perform, their duties. The second involves the standard of care that is expected of school personnel.

Regarding the performance of duties, teachers can breach their duty by failing to act when there is a responsibility to act; this is known as *nonfeasance.* Further, school staff can breach their duty by failing to act properly when there is a duty to act; this is known as *misfeasance.* On the other hand, where educators act improperly, or with evil intent, they commit *malfeasance,* which is an intentional tort, a topic discussed earlier in this chapter. Even though malfeasance is an intentional tort, it is mentioned and distinguished here because the three terms sound similar. If administrators are aware that employees are failing to meet their duties, then they, and their boards, may share in tort liability of those individuals.

The second major consideration under breach is the standard of care that teachers must follow. In assessing whether defendants met the appropriate level of care, courts adopted a common law standard of reasonableness. Judges typically instruct juries to consider defendants' behavior in light of the legal principle known as the *reasonable person,* or the *reasonably prudent person,* discussed in greater detail below. Courts have stopped short of creating a clear hierarchy of expectation but, when evaluating what is reasonable, consider such factors as individuals' ages, educational levels, experience, maturity, and other relevant characteristics. Even so, courts are likely to expect a reasonable teacher to provide a higher standard of care than a reasonable person but less than a reasonable parent. In applying this rationale, courts have sought to create an objective standard that requires teachers to provide the same level of care as a reasonably prudent professional of similar education and experience.

A case from athletics highlights the implications of applying the proper standard in negligence cases. After a high school football player, who was under consideration for a college athletic scholarship, broke his neck while correctly executing a block, New York's highest court ruled that the coach should not be judged under the same standard of care as a reasonably prudent parent.[41] Instead, the court applied the lower standard of ordinary reasonable care for a coach. The court was convinced that the coach satisfied the less demanding standard, since the student voluntarily participated in the game, implicating the defense of assumption of risk, and was under no inherent obligation to play (thereby also involving the defense of assumption of risk, discussed below), and he was properly equipped and well trained.

Injury. In order for an aggrieved party to prevail in a negligence claim, an injury must be one for which compensation can be awarded. This means that if a student running in the school cafeteria slips on food that was spilled during a previous lunch period, courts examine four factors. The first inquiry is whether school officials have a duty to keep the floor safe and clean. Obviously, such a duty exists so that foreseeability comes into play, particularly where food is often spilled in school lunch rooms. To the extent that school personnel can see and even predict that such an accident will occur, they should have the spillage cleaned up reasonably quickly. Next, the question of educators' duty and possible breach, in terms of supervising the area, must be addressed. Put another way, courts address whether teachers met their duty to keep students away from any mess on the floor. The final concern is the nature of the child's injuries. If the child's only injuries are soiled clothing and mild discomfort, a negligence claim is unlikely to succeed. On the other hand, if a child breaks a bone on falling, there is a greater chance that this may be judged an injury for which compensation can be awarded. The fourth factor, causation, focusing on liability of a supervising teacher, administrator, or staff member, is examined in the next paragraph.

Causation. The final element for establishing liability in negligence litigation is that school officials must be the legal, or proximate, cause of injuries brought about by their breaches. Stated another way, as situations evolve, the last person in a series of events who could have taken steps to prevent an injury from occurring is typically considered as at least contributing to the legal cause.

CASE SUMMARY 9.4: NEGLIGENCE FOR STUDENT INJURY

Janukajtis v. Fallon

726 N.Y.S.2d 451 (N.Y. App. Div. 2001)

Factual Summary: A 14-year-old middle school student was injured when he was struck in the eye by a stick thrown by a fellow student during recess. The incident had been preceded by horseplay between the two students. At the time of the incident there were approximately 75 students on the playground, supervised by one monitor. The student's parents sued, seeking damages for personal injury. A state trial court denied the school board's motion for summary judgment, finding that there was an issue of fact regarding whether proper supervision had been provided. The board appealed.

Issue: Is the school board liable for the student's injuries?

Decision: No, reversing in favor of the board, the court decided that the board was not liable, because the incident could not have reasonably been foreseen.

Summary of Court's Rationale: As an initial matter the court noted that school officials have a duty to provide proper supervision and can be liable for foreseeable injuries proximately related to inadequate supervision. Even so, the court pointed out that educators cannot reasonably be expected to provide continuous supervision and control all student movements. The court maintained that the school board sustained its burden of showing that it had no actual or constructive notice of prior similar conduct. Further, the court did not find evidence to establish that negligence on the part of school officials was the proximate cause of the student's injuries since he voluntarily chose to engage in an activity in violation of school rules and so assumed the risk of the injuries that he sustained. The court declared that where an accident occurs in such a short period of time, as it did here, even the most intense supervision would not have prevented it, and therefore lack of supervision is not the proximate cause of the injury. Finally, the court determined that the student had been a willing and active participant in the incident so that any alleged failure of the school board to provide proper supervision was not a proximate cause of his injuries.

A case from New York highlights judicial reasoning in this regard, where a middle school student threw a stick and injured the eye of another while the two adolescents were engaged in horseplay during recess. In response to the parents' negligence claim, an appellate court observed that where there was insufficient actual notice of dangerous conduct that such an injury would have occurred, school officials did not breach their duty of adequate supervision.[42] The court added that any negligence on the part of those charged with supervising the students was not the proximate cause of the child's injury, because the time span between the horseplay and the stick-throwing incident was so short that even the most intense supervision could not have prevented the injury. Not surprisingly, when students knowingly violate school rules and are injured in the process, courts usually agree that those who violate school rules, rather than school officials, are the proximate causes of their own injuries.[43]

Defenses to Negligence

In order to be held liable, school officials must be unable to assert a defense such as immunity, assumption of risk, and or contributory/ comparative negligence. Even if an injured party has established that the elements of negligence are present, boards and their employees may use any one of these three primary defenses to limit or eliminate liability. These defenses recognize that even though boards and officials have the duty to supervise students, they may not be accountable for all conceivable harms that occur during school hours.

> In order to be held liable, school officials must be unable to assert a defense such as immunity, assumption of risk, and or contributory/ comparative negligence.

Immunity. Immunity, sometimes referred to as sovereign or statutory immunity, is the defense most often used by boards and their employees. Immunity is based on the common law theory, supplemented by statutes on such aspects as recreational and discretionary function immunity laws, that the government, or the sovereign, may not be liable for the torts committed by its members or employees. In many states, to encourage the use of public facilities, laws have been passed to absolve school boards of any immunity for injuries incurred in the recreational use of their property. (Of course, liability can ensue if the property is not properly maintained.) Hence, in many situations where parents file suit against both school boards and school personnel, the boards are able to successfully claim immunity. Further, school boards may, in some instances, be able to claim sovereign immunity if this form of immunity is specifically granted by statute.

Contributory and Comparative Negligence. Contributory and comparative negligence are premised on individuals' having played a part in causing their injuries. The difference between these similar-sounding defenses, each of which applies in an almost equal number of states, is significant. Contributory negligence wholly bars individuals from recovering for their injuries if they contributed in any way to the harm that they suffered.[44]

Courts and legislatures have recognized that the contributory negligence defense often led to unfair results, so increasing numbers of states have established comparative negligence as a defense. Comparative negligence allows juries to apportion liability based on a percentage of relative fault between the parties. Most states that rely on comparative negligence allow plaintiffs to recover for the harm that they suffered if they were not more than 50% liable.[45] Some states may apply pure comparative negligence, which permits plaintiffs to recover even if they contributed more than 50% to their injuries.

Assumption of Risk. Assumption of risk, which is also based on comparative fault, can reduce injured parties' recovery in proportion to the degree to which their responsible conduct contributed to an accident where the individuals voluntarily exposed themselves to known and appreciated risks of harm. Assumption of risk is an important defense in many educational contexts, particularly athletics. For example, an appellate court in New York affirmed that a cheerleader who was injured during practice could not recover damages from her school board, since she assumed the risks of her sport and was practicing voluntarily under the supervision of her coach.[46] Another appellate court in New York agreed that a board was not liable for injuries that an experienced high school varsity softball player sustained when she collided with a chain link fence while chasing a fly ball.[47] The court was convinced that since the player fully assumed and appreciated the risks inherent in playing softball, and the existence of the fence was open and obvious, there was no issue as to whether the fence unreasonably increased her risk of injury. Other courts have reached similar results regarding injuries in other sports, including baseball,[48] basketball,[49] gymnastics,[50] ice hockey,[51] swimming,[52] and wrestling.[53]

Standard of Care: The Reasonable Person

As indicated above, teachers and other school personnel are expected to provide a standard of care for their students consistent with what would be expected of a reasonable person in the same situation. The degree of care or supervision required under any given circumstances is variable. In this respect, elementary school students require more supervision than those in high schools, simply because of their lack of maturity and judgment. Moreover, preschool children may even be entitled to a standard of care equal to that of a reasonable parent.[54] Greater supervision may be necessary in situations carrying heightened risks of inherent danger, such as in shop classes where students are operating machinery. Also, situations where problems can reasonably be expected require a higher level of supervision. For example, two children who have reputations for animosity toward each other should not be left alone in a room unsupervised, particularly if they have had physical altercations in the past.

It should thus be obvious that the reasonable person standard must be applied on a case-by-case basis. Courts and juries assessing whether teachers acted properly in given situations essentially ask the question, "What would a reasonable person have done under the circumstances?" The answer to the question revolves not only around the characteristics of the students but also around those of the teacher. By way of illustration, consider the situation of two fairly large athletes getting into a fight during a supervised study hall. A teacher of small physical stature would not be obligated under these circumstances to step between the students and physically break up the fight but would be expected to verbally order them to stop their fighting and seek assistance. On the other hand, a physically fit coach might be expected to do more.

The reasonable person is strictly a hypothetical concept, but the conceptual person resembles the defendant in many ways. When a teacher is the defendant, the reasonable person would have physical characteristics similar to those of the teacher, meaning the same gender, age, size, and strength. In this respect courts typically take any disabilities that teachers may have into consideration when determining liability. However, when it comes to mental capacities, the standard becomes one of typicality. In other words, the courts view the reasonable person as having normal intelligence, with average abilities in terms of factors such as memory, perception, and problem-solving skills. Consequently, courts do not take into consideration that a defendant may have less than average intelligence. Even so, when it comes to teachers, courts consider their levels of education and levels of training such that the standard of reasonableness is higher for teachers than it is for laypersons.

General Supervision

One of the most common claims in negligence actions is that school personnel failed to supervise students properly. As indicated above, the amount of supervision required varies from situation to situation. To this end, prudent school officials should always make sure that more, not less, supervision is provided. In examining whether provided supervision was adequate, courts often assess whether increased supervision might have prevented the accident. Teachers provide supervision in a number of situations besides their own classrooms. Teachers in most jurisdictions are regularly assigned to supervise students on playgrounds, in lunchrooms, and in corridors. At the same time, teachers may be assigned to watch over students in extracurricular activities or at other school functions such as athletic or social events.

Proper classroom supervision involves more than just watching out for students. Teachers also must provide appropriate instruction in the use of equipment in the classroom and make sure that students understand any safety precautions that need to be followed. In this way, chemistry teachers need to ensure that students wear proper protective clothing, such as goggles, when working with caustic chemicals. The degree of supervision and instruction in safety procedures required varies with the age of the students. Younger, less-mature, and less-skilled students require greater supervision, just as potentially dangerous situations require much more oversight than normal activities. Teachers need to be constantly alert to conditions within their classrooms that might lead to potential injury. In this respect, maintaining proper discipline is important, as the risk of injury is exponentially increased when students are rowdy.

It is not uncommon for teachers to step out of their classrooms for a few minutes. It only takes a few seconds for an accident to happen, so leaving students unsupervised, even for a few moments, can lead to liability on the part of the teacher in the event of an injury. While teachers' presence in their classrooms does not guarantee perfect student behavior, since the probability of misconduct increases when the teacher is absent, educators would be wise not to leave students unattended.

Special Circumstances

Four situations in schools today require a heightened awareness of their inherent liability: physical education and sports, playground equipment, field trips, and students with disabilities.

Physical Education Classes and Sports Activities. Participation in physical education classes and sports activities can increase students' chances of injury simply due to the nature of the activities. Proper instruction and supervision are critical when students engage in activities involving physical contact or use of equipment. For the most part, courts recognize that students engaging in athletic activities assume the risks inherent in those activities. Consequently, plaintiffs must demonstrate a direct connection between teachers' failure to provide adequate instruction or supervision in order to substantiate negligence charges. In one such case from Louisiana, a student who was injured while attempting a long jump was successful in his negligence claim when he proved that he had not been properly instructed in landing techniques.[55] It is common for school officials to require parents to sign release forms prior to students' participating in activities that can cause injuries. By and large courts do not impose liability when forms are carefully written but do not put much credence in forms that are overly broad or vague.[56]

Playground Equipment. Courts have reached mixed results in cases over the liability of school boards and personnel for accidents that occur on playground equipment. Plaintiffs generally are unsuccessful unless they can prove educators provided insufficient supervision or that the equipment was known to be defective. In one instance, in which a student was injured after falling off parallel bars, an appellate court in New York refused to impose liability where a board demonstrated that it provided adequate supervision.[57] On the other hand, another appellate court in New York recognized that questions of fact existed as to whether a lack of adequate supervision contributed to a student's injuries when he fell off monkey bars.[58] Yet another case from New York shows that school officials cannot be liable for defective equipment if they are not aware of the problem. A student was injured when a swing collapsed, but the board satisfactorily demonstrated that it had conducted daily inspections of the equipment and had not found any defects.[59] Similarly, another board in New York was successful in response to a negligence claim filed by the parents of a student who fell from playground apparatus, in part, because it was able to show that personnel had properly maintained the playground equipment.[60] Even so, school personnel should instruct students on the safe use of playground equipment and warn them of any potential dangers.[61]

Field Trips. When students are on field trips, educational officials must provide greater supervision than they do in schools, in large part because students are in unfamiliar places. Again, as in other areas, the amount of required supervision varies depending on the ages and maturity of the students. It is appropriate at this juncture to repeat the advice given earlier that prudent school personnel should always provide more, rather than less, supervision, particularly in situations that are inherently risky.

In one unfortunate situation, New York's highest court upheld a jury's award of damages to a student who was sexually assaulted by acquaintances after she left a field trip with her teacher's permission.[62] The court agreed that the award was supported by the evidence, since the child's teacher neither provided proper supervision nor informed authorities that she was missing. On the other hand, when a kindergarten student fell from her seat to the floor of a wagon on a hayride during a field trip to a farm, another court in New York was satisfied that the school board had not breached its duty to provide adequate supervision.[63] The court pointed out that there were 12 adults for approximately 40 students present, and a chaperone had been sitting next to the child when she fell. The court relied on testimony that the board had no knowledge of any hazard inherent in the hay ride insofar as there had been no analogous incidents in prior field trips to the farm.

Another interesting suit involved injuries that were inflicted on others by students who allegedly were improperly supervised during a field trip. An injured student filed suit, alleging that he was injured when he was assaulted by improperly supervised students from a school for at-risk youths. The federal trial court in the District of Columbia refused to dismiss the suit, holding that officials from the school the attackers attended had a duty to supervise them to prevent foreseeable harm from occurring to the general public.[64]

Students With Disabilities. Students with disabilities also require a higher standard of care, since their disabilities may increase the likelihood of injury.[65] Even so, an appellate court in Louisiana indicated that school boards are unlikely to be liable for injuries received by students who were mainstreamed as long as such placements are reasonable.[66] Rather, the court explained that the heightened standard of care applies more to the supervision that must be provided with students who have severe disabilities.

In another case, the parents of a student, who required close supervision when he ate, filed suit after the child choked on food and consequently went into a coma. A paraprofessional supervising the student had momentarily stepped back a few feet to retrieve a paper towel to clean up milk the child had spilled. An appellate court in Illinois was satisfied that school personnel provided sufficient supervision for the student and that there was no evidence that school staff showed an utter disregard for his safety.[67] In another case, the parents of a student who was visually impaired who fell and was injured while descending stairs were unsuccessful in their negligence suit. The court was of the view that the board

CASE SUMMARY 9.5: FAILURE TO ADEQUATELY SUPERVISE STUDENTS

Bell v. Board of Education of the City of New York

665 N.Y.S.2d 42 (N.Y. 1997)

Factual Summary: When several fifth and sixth grade classes attended a drug awareness fair held at a local park that was sponsored by the school board and the police department, they were allowed to walk through the park on their own to participate in the activities. Prior to the fair, teachers made arrangements with their students regarding the time and place to meet to return to the school. During the course of the day, one teacher gave a student permission to leave the park to have lunch with friends. When it was time to return to the school, the teacher noticed that the student was missing but failed to inform any of the other teachers or police officers. On the way back to the school, the teacher did stop at the student's house and informed the student's mother of her disappearance. He failed, however, to inform school officials that the child was missing. When the student returned to the park, she could not find her class and started to walk home alone. On the way she met three male students who took her to the home of one of the students, where they raped her. After the student's mother filed suit and a jury awarded the mother and daughter damages of $2,250,000, an appellate court reversed in favor of the board on the ground that the incident was an unforeseeable event. The student and her parent sought further review from the state's high court.

Issue: Was the school board liable for damages?

Decision: Yes, reversing in favor of the plaintiffs, the court held that since the negligence of the defendants led to the student's being raped, the board was liable for her injuries.

Summary of Court's Rationale: The court observed that third party criminal interventions may be a reasonably foreseeable consequence of circumstances created by a defendant, and it could not determine that the act of rape was unforeseeable as a matter of law. The court concluded that a reasonable jury could have found that the foreseeable result of the danger created by the school board's alleged lack of supervision could be an injury such as occurred in this case.

was not liable, since the child failed to wait for the teacher who normally escorted her.[68]

Most courts agree that damages awards for students with disabilities must come from state tort law and not the Individuals with Disabilities Education Act (IDEA),[69] the federal special education law.[70] For example, in a case filed by the parents of a student who died after his tracheotomy tube had become dislodged, the Eleventh Circuit proclaimed that the IDEA does not provide tort-like relief.[71] In like manner, a federal trial court in Wisconsin commented that it is unlikely that Congress intended for the IDEA to be converted into a tort law for playground accidents.[72] Similarly, a federal trial court in Arkansas dismissed a damages claim under the IDEA filed by the parents of a special education student who had been raped in a locker room.[73] Earlier, the Sixth Circuit had concluded that a student could not receive a damages award for the emotional injury he allegedly suffered when he was wrongfully barred from participating in sports.[74]

EDUCATIONAL MALPRACTICE

Malpractice generally refers to professional wrongdoing resulting in harm or injury to a client. Moreover, many malpractice claims allege improper, negligent, or unethical treatment of clients by professional practitioners in medicine or law. To date, malpractice claims in education have been unsuccessful. Yet, it is hard to know whether future courts will be open to allegations of educational malpractice, particularly in an era of increased accountability for educators.

In perhaps the earliest case alleging educational malpractice, an appellate court in California dismissed the claims of a student who graduated but was able to read at only an eighth grade level.[75] The court rejected the claim because the allegations did not show a workable rule of care against which the conduct of educators could be measured, lacked an injury within the meaning of negligence, and failed to establish a connection between the student's injury and the educators' conduct. More recent challenges have failed, in part, because of judicial concerns over the public policy implications of making educational malpractice actionable.

Special education may be particularly vulnerable to allegations of educational malpractice because of the statutory nature of student rights. Even so, cases in special education are generally unsuccessful, because the IDEA provides remedies when school officials fail to provide the free appropriate public education (FAPE) called for in the statute.[76] These remedies include reimbursing parents for their expenses in obtaining appropriate services privately or giving students compensatory educational services to make up for the loss. To this end courts have unanimously agreed that compensatory damages as well as punitive awards (a topic beyond the scope of this discussion) are unavailable under the IDEA.[77] In California, an appellate court denied tort damages under the IDEA for a claim that a student was denied a FAPE.[78] The court decided that the appropriate remedy for a denial of services was an award of compensatory educational services, which was allowed under the IDEA. Similarly, a court in Michigan observed that damages for negligence were not recoverable under the IDEA for a board's failure to properly evaluate a student.[79] The court refused to interpret the IDEA as being intended to serve as a vehicle for a private cause of action for damages. Subsequently, the Sixth Circuit affirmed that the IDEA does not create any right to recover damages for loss of earning power attributed to the failure of a school board to provide a student with a FAPE.[80] In this case the student sued to recover lost wages allegedly resulting from the insufficient education that he received.

CIVIL RIGHTS VIOLATIONS

When educators allegedly violate the civil rights of students or others, injured parties may seek redress, either in the form of equitable relief or monetary damages, under Section 1983 of the Civil Rights Act of 1871.[81] According to Section 1983,

> every person who, under color of any statute, ordinance, regulation, custom, or usage, of any State or Territory or the District of Columbia, subjects, or causes to be subjected, any citizen of the United States or other person within the jurisdiction thereof to the deprivation of any rights, privileges, or immunities secured by the Constitution and laws, shall be liable to the party injured in an action at law, suit in equity, or other proper proceeding for redress, except that in any action brought against a judicial officer for an act or omission taken in such officer's judicial capacity, injunctive relief shall not be granted unless a declaratory decree was violated or declaratory relief was unavailable.

Section 1983 is a potent legal tool to the extent that it allows aggrieved parties to sue individuals for violating their constitutional and statutory rights "under the color of state law," meaning that offending individuals committed the offenses in the performance of their official duties. In this way, school officials can be liable for their actions if courts determine that their behavior had the effect of depriving individuals of their civil rights.[82]

Section 1983 does not create any new civil rights. Instead, Section 1983 provides a means of redress for civil rights torts, by creating a vehicle for individuals to sue public officials for constitutional and statutory violations. In this respect, Section 1983 affords a powerful remedy against discrimination based on race, national origin, sex, sexual orientation, disability, and religion as well as violations of the Fourth Amendment's prohibition on unreasonable search and seizure. As its wording indicates, Section 1983 imposes liability on persons, in this case meaning either individuals or corporate bodies such as school boards. Accordingly, parties can file damages claims against school personnel in their official capacities. In order to succeed, plaintiffs must demonstrate that the educators knowingly acted "under the color of state law," or in their official capacity, for the suits to be successful. The Supreme Court has clearly affirmed that school board members can be sued under Section 1983.[83] Although the Court recognized that board members must be able to exercise judgment, it emphasized that those who act with disregard of the law can be liable if they do so with an impermissible motivation or in bad faith.

Section 1983 provides litigants with a powerful tool to enforce their rights under constitutional and statutory law. Teachers and other school personnel can be personally liable under Section 1983, particularly if their actions have the effect of discriminating against individuals in protected classes such as those defined by age, race, and disability. The adage that ignorance of the law is no excuse is particularly germane in regard to Section 1983 actions, since teachers can be held liable not only for knowingly violating the law but also for actions clearly violating established rights, even when no ill intent was present.

As exemplified by a case from West Virginia, teachers can be personally liable for violating the civil rights of students. A jury awarded $15,000 in compensatory and punitive damages against a teacher who had failed to comply with the terms of an individualized education program (IEP) for a student with learning disabilities.[84] The child's IEP called for tests to be administered orally by a special education teacher. Yet, one of the student's teachers refused to comply with the oral testing accommodation and continued to administer written tests in spite of having received several notices and directives regarding the oral testing. To make matters worse, the parents alleged that the teacher insulted and belittled the student in class in front of other students. As a consequence, the student failed the course and was rendered ineligible for extracurricular activities, opening the door to the teacher's liability.

SUMMARY AND RECOMMENDATIONS

As Americans become increasingly litigious, teachers are justified in being concerned that they can be subjected to litigation and being rendered liable for tort damages, even if their actions were not intentional. Teachers can be liable for their negligent conduct or for failing to meet the appropriate standard of care.

Claims for monetary damages are predominantly based on state tort laws. Tort laws vary from state to state but are more similar than dissimilar. Given the increasing number of suits filed each year with plaintiffs seeking damages, teachers need to be aware of the following principles:

- Teachers can be liable for deliberate acts that cause injuries to students. As a result, teachers need to exercise caution when disciplining or restraining students.
- Unfortunately, teachers need to restrain students from time to time. In doing so, teachers should apply the minimum amount of force necessary to control students.
- Teachers should never discipline or restrain children in anger, since it increases the chance of using excessive force.
- Educators who are in positions where they frequently may be required to restrain students should consider formal training in restraint techniques. Properly administering physical restraints can minimize student injuries and, consequently, reduce liability. At the same time, teachers should attend annual sessions to make sure that they can maintain their skill levels.
- Keeping students after school is a common disciplinary tool that does not amount to false imprisonment. Even so, teachers should detain students only for a reasonable amount of time and must properly supervise them during the detention. For added safety, teachers should notify parents that their children will be in detention and should consider not imposing such a penalty until the parents have been informed of the detentions. Adopting this approach should afford parents the opportunity to ensure needed afterschool transportation or supervision for their children to avoid any claims of negligent supervision or lack of supervision if children are hurt while heading home unattended.
- Teachers are often required to make evaluative comments about students. Negative comments made in this regard do not amount to defamation unless they are made maliciously or with disregard for the truth, or if they have the effect of invading another person's privacy.

- Allegations of intentional infliction of emotional distress are difficult to prove. Still, this is a topic to watch, because claims of infliction of emotional distress are often included along with other tort allegations.
- Teachers have been unsuccessful in suits alleging infliction of emotional distress based on adverse employment decisions. In order to make a viable claim of emotional distress, teachers need to show more than the fact that they were distraught, suffered hurt feelings, or sustained damage to their professional reputations.
- Most tort claims in education arise from alleged negligent supervision or care of students.
- Accidents will happen, and teachers are not liable every time students in their care are injured. Liability ensues when teachers fail to provide the standard of care expected of someone in their position.
- Since playgrounds are attractive places for children, it is natural that they will use school property for recreational purposes during nonschool hours. Even so, school officials must make it clear to parents that supervision is not provided at all times.
- School officials must properly maintain playground equipment. School boards can be liable for injuries caused by knowingly defective equipment.
- Educators must pay particular attention to providing proper instruction and supervision in inherently risky activities such as sports and field trips.
- Educational malpractice suits have been unsuccessful. Still, with the increasing accountability that is being expected of educators, this is an area of the law that needs to be monitored.
- Failure to adhere to the terms of students' IEPs is a civil rights violation that can subject teachers to personal liability for substantial damages awards.

FREQUENTLY ASKED QUESTIONS

Q. When does the infliction of corporal punishment amount to assault and battery?

A. In states that have banned corporal punishment, intentional striking of children for the purpose of causing pain or injury may constitute assault and/or battery. In states allowing corporal punishment, the use of excessive force resulting in serious or permanent injuries to the child can lead to assault and/or battery charges. Most states that sanction corporal punishment have set up guidelines on how it is to be administered. In order to avoid liability, educators should strictly adhere to these guidelines when administering corporal punishment.

Q. Can teachers be sued for defamation for writing negative comments, such as noting that students are not motivated, on their report cards?

A. Teachers should exercise care when making subjective comments about students. As part of their duties teachers are required to make many qualitative assessments about students. Teachers should not be reluctant to make negative comments about students when such comments are warranted. That being said, writing statements that are knowingly false, made with a blatant disregard for the truth, and/or made with malicious intent can amount to defamation. Thus, teachers must be prepared to document statements they make regarding students.

Q. Can teachers be liable for injuries that occur to students when they have left classrooms unsupervised for even a few moments?

A. While the answer depends on many factors, teachers generally can be liable when students are injured, in part, because they were not properly supervised. Among the factors courts consider in such cases are the age of the students left unsupervised, the proximity of teachers to unsupervised classrooms, the length of teachers' absences, and whether the injuries still would have occurred with proper supervision. Even so, insofar as it is reasonable to assume that unsupervised students can get into mischief, teachers should never leave their classes completely unattended. When teachers must leave their classrooms, they should make sure that other responsible adults are looking in on the students.

Q. How can school personnel protect themselves from liability when students typically congregate on school playgrounds well before school personnel provide supervision?

A. First, school officials should make it clear to parents what time supervision is provided, that students should not be on playgrounds before or after that time, and that school personnel cannot take responsibility for the children during the times supervision is not provided. This should be done frequently via specific notices to parents and reminders in parent newsletters. Second, when students do congregate on the playground during times that supervision is not provided, their parents should be individually informed that staff cannot be responsible for them at that time. In egregious situations, such as when parents ignore notices not to bring their very young children to school before the time supervision begins, if all else fails, officials should notify the proper authorities, such as a state's protection and advocacy group. While all of this takes time and diligence, it is necessary to protect schools from liability.

ENDNOTES

1. 430 U.S. 651 (1977).

2. 395 F. Supp. 294 (M.D.N.C. 1975), *affirmed*, 423 U.S. 907 (1975).

3. *See, e.g.*, Garcia v. Miera, 817 F.2d 650 (10th Cir. 1987).

4. *See, e.g.*, Hall v. Tawney, 621 F.2d 607 (4th Cir. 1980).

5. Neal v. Fulton County Board of Education, 229 F.3d 1069 (11th Cir. 2000).

6. Wise v. Pea Ridge School District, 855 F.2d 560 (8th Cir. 1988).

7. Frank v. Orleans Parish School Board, 195 So. 2d 451 (La. Ct. App. 1967).

8. Thomas v. Bedford, 389 So. 2d 405 (La. Ct. App. 1980).

9. *See, e.g.*, Johnson v. Newburgh Enlarged School District, 239 F.3d 246 (2d Cir. 2001) (affirming that a student who claimed to have been assaulted by a teacher had an actionable claim for a violation of his substantive due process right to be free of excessive force).

10. Wallace by Wallace v. Batavia School District 101, 68 F.3d 1010 (7th Cir. 1995).

11. Louden v. Directors of the DeWitt Public Schools, 194 F.3d 873 (8th Cir. 1999).

12. Golden *ex rel.* Balch v. Anders, 324 F.3d 650 (8th Cir. 2003).

13. Anello v. Savignac, 342 N.W.2d 440 (Wis. Ct. App. 1983).

14. School Board of Miami–Dade County v. Trujillo, 906 So. 2d 1109 (Fla. Ct. App. 2005).

15. Fertich v. Michener, 11 N.E. 605 (Ind. 1887).

16. Wallace v. Bryant School District, 46 F. Supp. 2d 863 (E.D. Ark. 1999).

17. Osborne, A. G., & Russo, C. J. (2009). *Discipline in special education.* Thousand Oaks, CA: Corwin.

18. Brown v. Ramsey, 121 F. Supp. 2d 911 (E.D. Va. 2000).

19. Doe v. S & S Consolidated Independent School District, 149 F. Supp. 2d 274 (E.D. Tex. 2001).

20. M.H. by Mr. and Mrs. H. v. Bristol Board of Education, 2002 WL 33802431 (D. Conn. 2002).

21. *See, e.g.*, Banks v. Fritsch, 39 S.W.3d 474 (Ky. Ct. App. 2001); Newman v. Obersteller, 915 S.W.2d 198 (Tex. Ct. App. 1996); Gerks v. Deathe, 832 F. Supp. 1450 (W.D. Okla. 1993).

22. Dockery v. Barnett, 167 F. Supp. 2d 597 (S.D.N.Y. 2001).

23. Desselle v. Guillory, 407 So. 2d 79 (La. Ct. App. 1981).

24. Ansorian v. Zimmerman, 627 N.Y.S.2d 706 (N.Y. App. Div. 1995).

25. Swenson-Davis v. Martel, 354 N.W.2d 288 (Mich. Ct. App. 1984).

26. Milkovich v. Lorain Journal Company, 497 U.S. 1 (1990).

27. Russo, C. J. (2009). *Reutter's the law of public education* (7th ed.). New York: Foundation Press.

28. *See, e.g.*, McGowen v. Prentice, 341 So. 2d 55 (La. Ct. App. 1976) (finding that a principal did not defame a teacher by recommending that she not be hired).

29. Russo, C. J. (2009). *Reutter's the law of public education* (7th ed.). New York: Foundation Press, p. 440.

30. Nims v. Harrison, 768 So. 2d 1198 (Fla. Ct. App. 2000).

31. Early v. Marion, 540 F. Supp. 2d 680 (W.D. Va. 2008).

32. Katterhenrich v. Federal Hocking Local School District Board of Education, 700 N.E.2d 626 (Ohio Ct. App. 1997).

33. Spears v. Jefferson Parish School Board, 646 So. 2d 1104 (La. Ct. App. 1994).

34. Tomlinson v. Board of Education of Elmira, 583 N.Y.S.2d 664 (N.Y. App. Div. 1992).

35. Jones v. Jackson Public Schools, 760 So. 2d 730 (Miss. 2000).

36. Johnsen v. Carmel Central School District, 716 N.Y.S.2d 403 (N.Y. App. Div. 2000).

37. *Id.* at 404.

38. *See, e.g.,* Shoemaker v. Whitney Point Central School District, 750 N.Y.S.2d 355 (N.Y. App. Div. 2002) (finding that school personnel have an affirmative duty to supervise students adequately and may be held liable for foreseeable injuries proximately related to the lack of adequate supervision).

39. Laneheart v. Orleans Parish School Board, 524 So. 2d 138 (La. Ct. App. 1988).

40. Glaser *ex rel.* Glaser v. Emporia Unified School District No. 253, 21 P.3d 573 (Kan. 2001).

41. Benitez v. New York City Board of Education, 543 N.Y.S.2d 29 (N.Y. 1989).

42. Janukajtis v. Fallon, 726 N.Y.S.2d 451 (N.Y. App. Div. 2001).

43. *See, e.g.,* Mastropolo v. Goshen Central School District, 837 N.Y.S.2d 236 (N.Y. App. Div. 2000) (finding that the sole proximate causes of a student's injuries were activities he engaged in knowing they were violations of school rules).

44. *See, e.g.,* Daniel v. City of Morganton, 479 S.E.2d 263 (N.C. Ct. App. 1997) (finding that an athlete's own negligence barred recovery of damages).

45. *See, e.g.,* Johnson *ex rel.* Johnson v. Dumas, 811 So. 2d 1085 (La. Ct. App. 2002); Millus v. Milford, 735 N.Y.S.2d 202 (N.Y. App. Div. 2002).

46. Fisher v. Syosset Central School District, 694 N.Y.S.2d 691 (N.Y. App. Div. 1999).

47. Schoppman v. Plainedge Union Free School District, 746 N.Y.S.2d 325 (N.Y. App. Div. 2002).

48. Yanero v. Davis, 65 S.W.3d 510 (Ky. 2001).

49. Milea v. Our Lady of Miracles, 736 N.Y.S.2d 84 (N.Y. App. Div. 2002).

50. Weber v. William Floyd School District, 707 N.Y.S.2d 231 (N.Y. App. Div. 2000).

51. Greenberg by Greenberg v. North Shore Central School District No. 1, 619 N.Y.S.2d 151 (N.Y. App. Div. 1994).

52. Kahn v. East Side Union High School District, 117 Cal. Rptr. 2d 356 (Cal. Ct. App. 2002).

53. Lilley v. Elk Grove Unified School District, 80 Cal. Rptr. 2d 638 (Cal. Ct. App. 1998).

54. Russo, C. J., & Russo, D. L. (2008). Risk management, pre-schools, and young children. *School Business Affairs, 74*(6), 18–20.

55. Scott v. Rapides Parish School Board, 732 So. 2d 749 (La. Ct. App. 1999).

56. Russo, C. J. (2009). *Reutter's the law of public education* (7th ed.). New York: Foundation Press.

57. Navarra v. Lynbrook Public Schools, 733 N.Y.S.2d 730 (N.Y. App. Div. 2001).

58. Vonungern v. Morris Central School District, 658 N.Y.S.2d 760 (N.Y. App. Div. 1997).

59. Sinto v. City of Long Beach, 736 N.Y.S.2d 700 (N.Y. App. Div. 2002).

60. Lopez v. Freeport Union Free School District, 734 N.Y.S.2d 97 (N.Y. App. Div. 2001).

61. *See, e.g.,* Merson v. Syosset Central School District, 730 N.Y.S.2d 132 (N.Y. App. Div. 2001) (noting that genuine issues of material fact existed as to whether school officials had properly instructed students on the use of playground equipment).

62. Bell v. Board of Education of the City of New York, 665 N.Y.S.2d 42 (N.Y. 1997).

63. David v. City of New York, 835 N.Y.S.2d 377 (N.Y. App. Div. 2007).

64. Thomas v. City Lights School, 124 F. Supp. 2d 707 (D.D.C. 2000).

65. Mawdsley, R. D. (2010). Standard of care for students with disabilities: The intersection of liability under the IDEA and tort theories. *Education Law Reporter, 252,* 527–550.

66. Brooks v. St. Tammany Parish School Board, 510 So. 2d 51 (La. Ct. App. 1987).

67. Mitchell *ex rel.* Lambert v. Special Education Joint Agreement School District, 897 N.E.2d 352 (Ill. Ct. App. 2008).

68. Mercado v. Board of Education of New York, 563 N.Y.S.2d 450 (N.Y. App. Div. 1990).

69. Individuals with Disabilities Education Act, 20 U.S.C. § 1400 *et seq.* (2006).

70. Russo, C. J., & Osborne, A. G. (2008). *Essential concepts & school-based cases in special education law.* Thousand Oaks, CA: Corwin.

71. Ortega v. Bibb County School District, 397 F.3d 1321 (11th Cir. 2005).

72. Edwards v. School District of Baraboo, 570 F. Supp. 2d 1077 (W.D. Wis. 2008).

73. Finch v. Texarkana School District No. 7, 557 F. Supp. 2d 976 (W.D. Ark. 2008).

74. Crocker v. Tennessee Secondary School Athletic Association, 980 F.2d 382 (6th Cir. 1992).

75. Peter W. v. San Francisco Unified School District, 131 Cal. Rptr. 854 (Cal. Ct. App. 1976).

76. *See, e.g.,* Brantley v. District of Columbia, 640 A.2d 181 (D.C. 1994); Suriano v. Hyde Park Central School District, 611 N.Y.S.2d 20 (N.Y. App. Div. 1994).

77. Osborne, A. G., & Russo, C. J. (2007). *Special education and the law: A guide for practitioners.* Thousand Oaks, CA: Corwin.

78. White v. State of California, 240 Cal. Rptr. 732 (Cal. Ct. App. 1987).

79. Johnson v. Clark, 418 N.W.2d 466 (Mich. Ct. App. 1987).

80. Hall v. Knott County Board of Education, 941 F.2d 402 (6th Cir. 1991).

81. Civil Rights Act of 1871, Section 1983, 42 U.S.C. § 1983 (2006).

82. *Id.*

83. Wood v. Strickland, 420 U.S. 308 (1975).

84. Doe v. Withers, Civil Action No. 92-C-92 (W. Va. Cir. Ct. 1993).

Resource A:
Court Systems and
the Authority of Courts

FUNCTIONS AND DUTIES OF THE COURTS

The basic purpose of courts is to interpret the law a process generally involving interpreting statutes and regulations. Even so, when there is no codified law, or if statutes or regulations are unclear, courts apply common law. Common law is also referred to as judge-made law, meaning that courts may interpret the law to adapt to new or changing circumstances. The collective decisions of the courts make up the body of *case law* or *common law*. When legal disputes involve the interpretation of legislation, the job of the courts is to determine, as best they can, the intent of the legislative bodies that enacted the statutes. To the extent that judicial pronouncements establish precedent, they have considerable weight in terms of providing guidance on how statutes and regulations are to be applied to everyday situations.

ORGANIZATION OF THE FEDERAL COURT SYSTEM

The federal court system has three levels: trial courts, intermediate appellate courts, and the Supreme Court. On the lowest level are the trial courts, officially known as the district courts. District courts are the basic triers of fact in legal disputes. The trial courts review evidence and render decisions based on the evidence presented by the parties to disputes. Depending on the factual situation, trial courts may review the records of any prior administrative proceedings, may hear additional evidence, and/ or may hear the testimony of witnesses. Each state has at least one federal district court, while larger states, such as California and New York, have as many as four.

Parties unhappy with the decisions of trial courts may appeal to the court of appeals in the federal circuit in which their states are located. For example, a decision issued by a federal trial court in New York would be appealed to the Second Circuit, which, in addition to New York, includes of the states of Connecticut and Vermont. There are 13 federal judicial circuits in the United States. The circuits were created for judicial and administrative convenience so that parties seeking to appeal judgments with which they disagreed would not have to travel too far from home to do so. The table below shows the organization of the federal circuits:

Federal Circuit	Jurisdictions Within the Circuit
First	Maine, Massachusetts, New Hampshire, Puerto Rico, Rhode Island
Second	Connecticut, New York, Vermont
Third	Delaware, New Jersey, Pennsylvania, Virgin Islands
Fourth	Maryland, North Carolina, Virginia, West Virginia
Fifth	Louisiana, Mississippi, Texas
Sixth	Kentucky, Michigan, Ohio, Tennessee
Seventh	Illinois, Indiana, Wisconsin
Eighth	Arkansas, Iowa, Minnesota, Missouri, Nebraska, North Dakota, South Dakota
Ninth	Alaska, Arizona, California, Guam, Hawaii, Idaho, Montana, Nevada, Northern Mariana Islands, Oregon, Washington
Tenth	Colorado, Kansas, New Mexico, Oklahoma, Utah, Wyoming
Eleventh	Alabama, Florida, Georgia, South Carolina
District of Columbia	District of Columbia
Federal	Special cases such as those involving patent laws and appeals from the Court of International Trade and the Court of Federal Claims

Litigants who are still dissatisfied with the judgments of the circuit courts may appeal to the ultimate court of last resort, the U.S. Supreme Court. Due to the sheer volume of cases appealed, the Supreme Court accepts less than 1% of the approximately 8,000 cases annually in which parties seek further review. Cases typically reach the Court in requests for a writ of *certiorari,* which literally means "to be informed of." When the Supreme Court agrees to hear an appeal, it issues a writ of certiorari. At least four of the nine Justices must vote to grant certiorari for a case to be heard. Denying a writ of certiorari has the effect of leaving a lower court's decision unchanged but is of no precedential value, meaning that the lower court's decision remains binding only within that circuit.

STATE COURTS

The court systems in each of the 50 states and various territories are arranged in an organizational fashion that is similar to the federal format except that the names of the courts may differ. In most states, there are also three levels of courts: trial courts, intermediate appellate courts, and courts of last resort. Readers are cautioned to pay particular attention to the names of state courts, as they are not consistent from state to state. For example, people generally think of a supreme court as being the highest court. Nevertheless, in New York, the trial court is known as the Supreme Court, the intermediate level is named the Supreme Court Appellate Division, while the state's high court is called the Court of Appeals, typically the name for intermediate appellate courts in most jurisdictions.

COURT JURISDICTIONS

When courts deliver their decisions, their opinions are binding only within their jurisdictions. In other words, a verdict of the federal trial court for Ohio is binding only in Ohio. The federal trial court in Kentucky, which is in the same federal circuit, may find a decision of the Ohio court persuasive, but it is not bound by the Ohio court's order. Even so, a ruling of the Sixth Circuit Court of Appeals is binding on all states within its jurisdiction, and lower courts in Kentucky, Ohio, Michigan, and Tennessee must rule consistently. A decision by the Supreme Court of the United States is, of course, enforceable in all 50 states and in American territories.

Readers should keep in mind that a court's jurisdiction can refer to either the types of cases that it can hear or the geographic area over which it has authority. The preceding paragraph referred to jurisdiction by geographic area. At the same time, courts are typically limited by the type of jurisdiction, or ability to hear cases, with which they are empowered. As discussed in a bit more detail in the next paragraph, trial courts typically have jurisdiction over cases that have yet to be tried, while the judicial authority of appellate courts is usually restricted to cases that have already proceeded through at least one level of judicial review.

To summarize, the complex American court systems operate at both the federal and state levels. The most common arrangement of these systems is a three-tiered organization with trial courts, intermediate appellate courts, and courts of last resort. Trial courts, which have general jurisdiction so that there are few limits on the types of cases that they may hear, typically hear the facts behind disputes and apply the law to the circumstances. Trial courts are generally presided over by a single judge or justice.

Intermediate courts, generally known as appellate courts or courts of appeal, hear cases when parties are dissatisfied with the decisions of lower courts. Appellate courts are not triers of fact, but rather, review lower courts' application of the law. In rare cases an appellate court may reject a lower court's interpretation of the facts of a case, if it is convinced that the lower court's interpretation was clearly erroneous. However, appellate court decisions are usually resolved only on points of law. Appellate courts typically consist of a panel of judges. For example, at the federal level, and in many state systems, appeals are heard by a panel of three judges. Finally, legal disputes may be appealed to a court of last resort. At the federal level this is the Supreme Court. The Supreme Court has discretion to review rulings of lower federal courts and state high courts that involve federal constitutional, statutory, or regulatory issues.

Insofar as education is a state function and federal courts exist for federal matters, most disputes involving education are resolved by state courts. Unless there is a substantial federal question, such as a disagreement over a provision in the U.S. Constitution, a federal statute, or a federal regulation, cases must be tried in state courts. If a substantial federal question is involved with a state question, a dispute may be litigated either in a state or federal court. When federal courts examine cases involving both state and federal law, they must follow interpretations of state law made by the state courts within which they sit. Special education disputes provide a good example of cases that frequently have mixed questions of federal and state law. To the extent that special education is governed by state laws as well as federal laws, claims are often brought on the basis of both sets of statutes. Even though final due process hearing decisions in special education disagreements may be appealed to either the federal or state courts, the vast majority of published opinions come from the federal courts.

Resource B:
Legal Resources
and References

LAWS AND REGULATIONS

Federal statues appear in the United States Code (U.S.C.), the official version, or the United State Code Annotated (U.S.C.A.), an unofficial version published by West Publishing Company. Most education statutes are found in Title 20, and most civil rights statutes are located in Title 42. Agency regulations are published in the Code of Federal Regulations (C.F.R.). Copies of education statutes and regulations can be downloaded via links on the U.S. Department of Education's website. Legal materials also are available online from a variety of sources, most notably WestLaw and LexisNexis. State laws and regulations are commonly available online from the websites of their states. Resource C provides a list of websites on which legal materials can be found.

COURT DECISIONS

The written opinions of most courts generally are available in a variety of officially published formats as well as from several unofficial sources. The official versions of U.S. Supreme Court opinions are found in the United States Reports, abbreviated U.S. The same opinions, with additional research aids, are published in the Supreme Court Reporter (S. Ct.) and the Lawyer's Edition, now in its second series (L. Ed. 2d). Opinions issued by the federal circuit courts of appeal are located in the Federal Reporter, currently in its third series (F. 3d) while federal district court decisions are published in the Federal Supplement, presently in its second series (F. Supp. 2d). State court cases are published in a variety of publications, most notably West's National Reporter system, which divides the country up into seven regions: Atlantic (A.), North Eastern (N.E.), North Western (N.W.), Pacific (P.), South Eastern (S.E.), South Western (S.W.), and Southern (S). Most education-related cases also are republished in West's *Education Law Reporter.*

Before being published in hardbound volumes, nearly all decisions are released in what are known as *slip opinions*; these are published through a variety of loose-leaf services and electronic sources. There also are many commercial services available that each publish decisions in a specialized area.

UNDERSTANDING LEGAL CITATIONS

As complicated as they may seem to readers who are unfamiliar with them, legal citations are fairly easy to read once one understands the format. The following brief description of how to interpret legal citations should help put the minds of readers at ease. For the most part citations begin with a number followed by an abbreviation and another number. The first number in a citation indicates the volume in which the case, statute, or regulation is located; it is followed by the abbreviation (sometimes including an ordinal number such as *2d* or *3d*) of the book or series in which the material may be found. The second number designates the page on which a case begins or the section number of a statute or regulation. For references to judicial opinions, the last part of a citation provides the name of the court, for lower court cases, and the year in which the dispute was resolved. For example, the citation for *Saunders v. City of New York,* 594 F. Supp. 2d 346 (S.D.N.Y. 2008) can be located in volume 594 of the Federal Supplement Second Series beginning on page 346. The case was decided by the District Court for the Southern District of New York in 2008.

In similar fashion, the citation for the No Child Left Behind Act, 20 U.S.C. §§ 6301–7941 (2006) can be found in Title 20 of the United States Code beginning with section 6301 and continuing through section 7941. Official versions of the United States Code have been published every six years since 1925 by the Office of the Law Revision Counsel of the U.S. House of Representatives. Statutes are always cited to the most recent updates to the code, not the year the particular statute was enacted.

The format for legal citations is dictated by *The Bluebook: A Uniform System of Citation* published jointly by the Columbia Law Review Association, the Harvard Law Review Association, the University of Pennsylvania Law Review, and the Yale Law Journal. The *User's Guide to The Bluebook* (2006) by Alan L. Dworsky, published by William S. Hein & Co., is an excellent quick resource for legal citations.

Resource C:
Basic Legal Research

Maintaining Currency in an
Evolving Legal Environment

KEEPING ABREAST OF LEGAL DEVELOPMENTS

The best way to deal with legal challenges is to prevent them from occurring. The best way to prevent legal challenges in the school environment is for all to be aware of their legal responsibilities. However, as readers of this book should be well aware, maintaining one's knowledge in an era of rapidly evolving legal principles, where thousands of new court decisions are handed down each year, can be daunting. Reading this book and others like it should provide school personnel with a basic knowledge of the issues and the results of previous litigation. Even so, new cases that can alter the status of the law are decided daily. Teachers and all school employees need to take affirmative steps to stay abreast of new legal developments.

Today numerous sources of information exist about issues and developments in education law. The Education Law Association (ELA), headquartered at the University of Dayton, in Dayton, Ohio, publishes *The Yearbook of Education Law*, which is called simply "the Yearbook" and includes chapters on all areas of education law, such as employee rights, collective bargaining, school governance, student rights, special education, tort liability, and sports. It also contains a chapter on new legislation. ELA also publishes a monthly newsletter, *ELA Notes*, and a reporter, *School Law Reporter*, as well as monographs that provide up-to-date information on school law. In the interests of full disclosure, we as authors of this book would like to point out that we are both past presidents of ELA. In addition, we have both worked on *The Yearbook of Education Law*: Allan G. Osborne has written the chapter on students with disabilities in the *Yearbook* since 1990, and Charles J. Russo has been editor of the *Yearbook* since 1995.

Many association newsletters and professional journals in education frequently contain articles on legal issues, particularly those of interest to the members of the organization publishing the journal or newsletter. Most professional organizations also include sessions at their annual conventions that address legal issues. The websites of these organizations also may contain updated legal information. In addition, the colleges or schools of education in many colleges and universities offer courses on school law that can serve as excellent resources for educators. Workshops on education law may (and should) be part of every school system's professional development program. In providing such ongoing professional development for staff, school officials should consider having the school board's attorneys join in the presentations so that they can provide up-to-date legal perspectives.

Reading the professional literature, attending conference sessions, and participating in local professional development workshops should be sufficient to keep most professionals updated on legal developments in education. It is our hope, however, that reading this book will spur an interest in some to conduct more extensive research on legal issues in education. Those who are interested in more comprehensive information on legal research may wish to consult *Research Methods for Studying Legal Issues in Education,* edited by Steve Permuth and Ralph Mawdsley and published by the Education Law Association. The websites listed below also are excellent resources for legal materials.

USEFUL EDUCATION LAW WEBSITES

Legal Search Engines

http://washlaw.edu
This website lists and links to law-related sources on the Internet.

http://www.findlaw.com
FindLaw is an Internet resource that helps to find any website that is law related.

http://www.alllaw.com
AllLaw is another resource for locating law-related websites.

http://www.law.cornell.edu/
This is a website sponsored by Cornell Law School; it provides access to federal and state cases and regulations.

U.S. Supreme Court, Federal Courts, and Federal Government Websites

http://www.supremecourtus.gov
This is the official website of the Supreme Court of the United States.

http://supct.law.cornell.edu/supct/index.html
This website contains decisions of the Supreme Court. It also has free e-mail publication to distribute the syllabi of the Court's rulings within hours after they are handed down.

http://thomas.loc.gov/
This website is maintained by the U.S. Library of Congress and has links to the federal court system.

http://www.uscourts.gov
This is the U.S. federal judiciary website.

http://www.gpoaccess.gov/uscode/
This website provides searchable access to the United States Code.

http://www.gpoaccess.gov/cfr/index.html
This website provides searchable access to the Code of Federal Regulations.

http://www.gpoaccess.gov/fr/index.html
This website contains the *Federal Register.*

http://www.ed.gov/about/offices/list/ocr/index.html?src=mr
This is the website of the Office for Civil Rights.

http://www.house.gov/
This is the U.S. House of Representatives website.

http://www.senate.gov
This is the U.S. Senate website.

http://www.whitehouse.gov
This is the website of the White House.

http://www.ed.gov
This is the U.S. Department of Education website.

http://www.ed.gov/nclb/landing.jhtml?src=pb
This website contains the No Child Left Behind Act.

Glossary of Terms, Acronyms, and Abbreviations

A.2d: Abbreviation for the Atlantic Reporter, now in its second series, one of the regional reporters published by the West Group. It contains state court decisions from Connecticut; Delaware; Washington, D.C.; Maine; Maryland; New Hampshire; New Jersey; Pennsylvania; Rhode Island; and Vermont.

ADA: Acronym for the Americans with Disabilities Act, a civil rights statute prohibiting discrimination against individuals with disabilities in employment and programs.

ADEA: Acronym for the Age Discrimination in Employment Act, a federal law that makes it illegal for employers to discriminate against individuals 40 years of age and older.

Affirm: To uphold the decision of a lower court in an appeal.

Appeal: A resort to a higher court seeking review of a judicial action.

Cal. Rptr. 3d: Abbreviation for the California Reporter, now in its third series, a compilation of state court decisions from California.

Cert. Abbreviation for *certiorari,* a writ issued by an appeals court indicating its willingness to review a lower court's decision.

C.F.R.: Abbreviation for the Code of Federal Regulations; the set of regulations promulgated by various federal agencies to implement laws passed by Congress.

Civil rights: Personal rights guaranteed by the U.S. Constitution or a state constitution or by a federal or state statute.

Common law: The body of law that has developed as a result of court decisions, customs, and precedents. Common law is also known as case law or judge-made law.

Defendant: The party against whom a lawsuit is brought.

ED: Official acronym for the U.S. Department of Education. The Department of Education is often abbreviated as DOE; however, ED is the official acronym for the department to avoid confusion with the Department of Energy, which uses the official acronym of DOE.

EEOA: Acronym for the Equal Educational Opportunities Act of 1974, a federal statute prohibiting discrimination and requiring schools to take action to overcome barriers to students' equal participation.

ESEA: Acronym for the Elementary and Secondary Education Act of 1965, a federal statute providing funding for elementary and secondary schools for professional development, instructional materials, educational programs such as Title I, and parental involvement. NCLB is the current reauthorization of the ESEA.

F.3d: Abbreviation for the Federal Reporter, now in its third series. The Federal Reporter contains decisions of the federal circuit courts of appeal. The second series was abbreviated as F.2d and the first as F.

F. App'x: Abbreviation for the Federal Appendix, a West Group unofficial publication that includes decisions of federal circuit courts of appeal that were not released for official publication.

FERPA: Acronym for the Family Educational Rights and Privacy Act, a federal law protecting the privacy of school records.

F. Supp. 2d: The abbreviation for the Federal Supplement, now in its second series. The Federal Supplement contains published decisions of federal trial, or district, courts. The first series was abbreviated as F. Supp.

GINA: Acronym for the Genetic Information Nondiscrimination Act, a federal law that prohibits discrimination in health coverage and employment based on genetic information.

IDEA: Acronym for the Individuals with Disabilities Education Act, the federal special education law.

Indemnify: To compensate a party for damage, loss, or injury.

Injunction: An equitable remedy, or court order, forbidding a party from taking a contemplated action, restraining a party from continuing an action, or requiring a party to take some action.

In re (literally, "in the matter of"): Indicates that there are no adversarial parties in a judicial proceeding, this refers to the fact that a court is considering only a *res* ("thing"), not a person.

LEA: Acronym for *local education agency*. The term is roughly synonymous with *school district*.

Litigant: A party to a lawsuit, either the plaintiff or the defendant.

NCLB: Acronym for the No Child Left Behind Act, the current reauthorization of the ESEA, the NCLB is aimed at improving the performance of public schools by establishing high standards and accountability.

NDEA: Acronym for the National Defense Education Act of 1958; a federal law providing aid to education at all levels, both public and private.

N.E.2d: Abbreviation for the North Eastern Reporter, now in its second series, one of the regional reporters published by the West Group. It contains state court decisions from Illinois, Indiana, Massachusetts, New York, and, Ohio.

N.Y.S.2d: Abbreviation for the New York Supplement, now in its second series, a compilation of decisions of state courts from New York.

N.W.2d: Abbreviation for the North Western Reporter, now in its second series, one of the regional reporters published by the West Group. It contains state court decisions from Iowa, Michigan, Minnesota, Nebraska, North Dakota, South Dakota, and Wisconsin.

OCR: Acronym for the Office for Civil Rights, a federal agency within the Department of Education that deals with issues of discrimination.

Opinion: A court's written explanation of its judgment.

P.3d: Abbreviation for the Pacific Reporter, now in its third series, one of the regional reporters published by the West Group. It contains state court decisions from Alaska, Arizona, California, Colorado, Hawaii, Idaho, Kansas, Montana, Nevada, New Mexico, Oklahoma, Oregon, Utah, Washington, and Wyoming. The second series was abbreviated as P.2d.

PDA: Acronym for the Pregnancy Discrimination Act, a federal statute prohibiting discrimination on the basis of pregnancy, childbirth, or a medical condition caused by pregnancy or childbirth.

P.L.: Abbreviation for Public Law. When bills are passed by Congress, they are each assigned a number indicating the session of Congress and the order in which the bill was enacted. For example, P.L. 94-142 was the 142nd piece of legislation passed by the 94th session of Congress.

Plaintiff: The party filing a lawsuit.

Remand: To return a case to a lower court for further consideration, often with specific instructions.

Reverse: To revoke a lower court's decision in an appeal.

School board: The governing body of a local education agency or school district. School boards also are known by various other names, such as *school committee, board of education,* or *board of trustees.*

S. Ct.: Abbreviation for the Supreme Court Reporter, an unofficial source of Supreme Court opinions published by the West Group.

S.E.2d: Abbreviation for the South Eastern Reporter, now in its second series, one of the regional reporters published by the West Group. It contains state court decisions from Georgia, North Carolina, South Carolina, Virginia, and West Virginia.

SEA: Acronym for *state education agency.* It is often used in citations to designate state administrative hearing decisions.

Section 504: A section of the federal Rehabilitation Act prohibiting a recipient of federal financial assistance from discriminating against an individual on the basis of a disability.

So. 2d: Abbreviation for the Southern Reporter, now in its second series, one of the regional reporters published by the West Group. It contains state court decisions from Alabama, Florida, Louisiana, and Mississippi.

Sovereign immunity: The maxim that litigants may not sue the government without its consent. The theory of governmental immunity originated in common law under the doctrine that "the king can do no wrong." Courts have interpreted the Eleventh Amendment to provide immunity to federal and state governments and their agencies, unless that immunity has specifically been abrogated by statute.

S.W.3d: Abbreviation for the South Western Reporter, now in its third series, one of the regional reporters published by the West Group. It contains state court decisions from Arkansas, Kentucky, Missouri, Tennessee, and Texas. The second series was abbreviated as S.W.2d.

Title VI of the Civil Rights Act of 1964: A statute forbidding discrimination based on race, color, or national origin, in programs receiving federal financial assistance.

Title VII of the Civil Rights Act of 1964: A statue prohibiting employment discrimination based on race, color, religion, sex, or national origin.

Tort: A civil wrong or injury for which a court will provide a remedy, generally in the form of monetary damages.

U.S.: As used in case citations, the abbreviation for the United States Reports, the official reporter of Supreme Court decisions.

U.S.C.: Abbreviation for the United States Code; the official compilation of statutes enacted by Congress. An unofficial version published by the West Group, known as the United States Code Annotated, is abbreviated as U.S.C.A.

Vacate: To set aside a lower court's decision in an appeal.

WL: Abbreviation for WestLaw, an online legal reporting system.

Index

Abood v. Detroit Board of Education (1977), 122, 123

Absenteeism. *See* Excessive absenteeism

Academic freedom, 218–232, 256 (n4)

Adultery, 83, 110 (n48)

Affirmative action, 162–164

Age discrimination:
  antidiscrimination legislation, 13–14, 158, 160–161
  case summary, 159
  early retirement incentives, 160–161
  economic factors, 158
  employment, 13–14, 158–161
  federal circuit review, 158, 159, 160, 161
  qualifications assessment, 158–160, 171 (n90)
  state court review, 158–159, 160–161

Age Discrimination in Employment Act (ADEA) (1967):
  employment discrimination, 158, 160–161
  provisions, 13–14, 158

Agency/representation fee, 119, 121–124
  See also Fair share fees

Agency shops, 121–124

Alabama:
  leave of absence, 98
  resignation, 103

Alaska, 186

American Federation of Labor (AFL), 116

American Federation of Teachers (AFT), 116

Americans with Disabilities Act (ADA) (1990):
  employees with disabilities, 153–157
  provisions, 13
  school governance, 24
  Title I, 153
  Title II, 153

Americans with Disabilities Act Amendments Act of 2008, 153

A Nation at Risk, 4

Ansonia Board of Education v. Philbrook (1986), 99

Ansorian v. Zimmerman (1995), 274

Arbitration, 124–126

Arizona:
  bilingual education, 251
  certification/licensure, 79
  dismissal, 188

Arkansas:
  curriculum and instruction, 221–222, 223
  dismissal, 195
  tort liability, 271, 289

Arrocha v. Board of Education of the City of New York (1999), 76

Assault and battery, 266–271

Assignments, 94–95, 112 (n103), 113 (n105)

Assistive technology, 246–247

Association rights:
  case summary, 51
  collective bargaining, 49, 50–51, 67 (n32)
  constitutional rights, 7, 49–52, 82, 118
  federal circuit review, 49–51
  political activity, 49–50, 66 (n26)
  Supreme Court review, 49, 50

Assumption of risk, 280, 283

Attendance policy, 229, 259 (n58)

Baker v. Owen (1975), 268

Bellairs v. Beaverton School District (2006), 182–183

Bell v. Board of Education of the City of New York (1997), 288

Bilingual education, 248, 249, 251

Bill of Rights, 6, 8–9, 42

Binding precedent, 5

Bluebook, The, 304
Board of Education, Island Trees Union Free School District v. Pico (1982), 223
Board of Education of the Hendrick Hudson Central School District v. Rowley (1982), 243, 244–245, 246
Bona fide occupational qualification, 13, 144
Brannen v. Kings Local School District Board of Education (2001), 57
Branti v. Finkel (1980), 50
Breach of duty, 277, 279–280
Broadcast recordings, 240, 241 (figure), 242
Brown v. Board of Education (1954), 3–4, 12
Buckley, J., 232
Buckley Amendment. *See* Family Educational Rights and Privacy Act (FERPA)
Bumping rights, 197–199, 214 (n129)
Burlington School Committee v. Department of Education, Commonwealth of Massachusetts (1985), 248

California:
  dismissal, 201
  employment discrimination, 156
  tort liability, 289, 290
Call-back rights, 200–201
Carter, J., 24
Case law. *See* Common law
Causation, negligence, 277, 280–282
Certification/licensure:
  basic standards, 74–75
  case summary, 76
  citizenship, 75
  criminal activity, 76, 78
  dismissal, 192, 211 (n97), 212 (n100)
  employees with disabilities, 77, 155–156
  employment discrimination, 143
  employment terms, 72–80
  examinations, 77
  highly qualified teachers, 72, 77
  loyalty oath, 75
  moral character, 75–77, 80
  reduction in force, 198–199
  requirements, 72–77, 80
  revised standards, 80
  state court review, 77, 78, 79, 80
  state education agency (SEA), 27, 72–80

Certification/licensure revocation:
  criminal activity, 78
  moral character, 78
  procedural issues, 80
  sexual misconduct, 78
  state education agency (SEA), 77–80
  unprofessional conduct, 79–80
Character misalignment, 59–60, 68 (n61), 69 (n62)
Chicago Teachers Union v. Hudson (1986), 122
Child-rearing:
  gender discrimination, 148–149
  leave of absence, 98
Citizenship, 75
Civil rights:
  curriculum and instruction, 4, 249, 250, 251
  employment discrimination, 12–13, 138, 139, 140, 144, 146–147, 148, 149–152, 153, 163, 164
  religious rights, 98–100
  student discrimination, 12, 13
Civil Rights Act (1871), 290–291
Civil Rights Act (1964), 12–13
  See also specific statute
Civil rights statutes, 12–14
Civil rights violations, 12, 140, 290–291
Classroom observations, 101
Cleveland Board of Education v. Loudermill (1985), 61, 194, 212 (n106)
Clinical supervision, 180
Closed union shops, 121
Code of Federal Regulations (C.F.R.), 303
Collective bargaining:
  agency/representation fee, 119, 121–124
  agency shops, 121–124
  arbitration, 124–126
  association rights, 49, 50–51, 67 (n32)
  bargaining topics, 119–121
  bargaining units, 118–121
  case summary, 51, 117, 123
  closed shops, 121
  communities of interest, 119
  constitutional rights, 118, 121–122, 123
  dispute resolution, 124–127
  fact-finding resolution, 124, 127
  fair share fees, 121–122, 124
  fair share shops, 121–124
  federal circuit review, 51
  frequently asked questions, 132

historical background, 116–118
leave of absence, 97, 98
mandatory bargaining topics, 119–120
mediation, 124, 127
nonmember fees, 121–124
open shops, 121
permissive bargaining topics, 120
probationary teachers, 176
prohibited bargaining topics,
    120–121
reduction in force, 197–198, 200–201
representatives, 118–119
right-to-work states, 118
state court review, 117, 119, 127
strikes, 126–127
Supreme Court review, 118,
    122–124
teacher recommendations, 128–131
union rights, 121–124
work stoppages, 126–127
zipper clauses, 120
Colorado:
bilingual education, 249
dismissal, 181, 183, 187, 192, 207
    (n31)
leave of absence, 99–100
Color-based discrimination, 140–143
See also Race discrimination
Columbia Law Review Association, 304
Common law:
binding precedent, 5
persuasive precedent, 5
Communities of interest, 119
Community service, 222
Comparative negligence, 283
Competitive grants, 33, 34
Computer software, 242
Conduct unbecoming a teacher. See
    Unprofessional conduct
Connecticut:
certification/licensure, 78, 80
collective bargaining, 117, 127
curriculum and instruction, 229
dismissal, 189–190, 193, 194,
    211 (n86)
employment discrimination, 156
First Amendment rights, 48
historical law, 3
privacy rights, 84, 85, 92
salary, 94–95
student records, 232
tort liability, 272
Connick v. Myers (1983), 46

Constitutional rights:
association rights, 7, 49–52, 118
collective bargaining, 118,
    121–122, 123
curriculum and instruction, 218,
    221–225, 227, 250
dismissal, 200
due process, 8, 9–10, 59–62
employment discrimination, 137–138,
    140, 143, 163, 164
free speech rights, 7, 42–48, 90, 151
frequently asked questions, 63–65
privacy rights, 7–8, 54–59, 81,
    82, 86, 90
religious rights, 7, 11, 52–54, 149,
    221–223
school governance, 6, 8–9, 11
search and seizure, 54, 55–57, 86
teacher recommendations, 62–63
See also specific amendment
Constitutional torts, 266
Constitutions:
federal constitution, 6–10
state constitutions, 10–11
See also U.S. Constitution
Contract nonrenewal, 175–176
Contracts Clause, 6–7
Contributory negligence, 283
Copyright Act (1976), 239, 240, 242
Copyright law, 239, 261 (n129)
Corporal punishment, 183, 268–270, 272
Corporate funds, 34
Court system:
court jurisdictions, 301–302
federal level, 299–301
functions and duties, 299
geographical jurisdictions, 300, 301
state level, 301
See also U.S. Supreme Court; specific
    federal court circuit
Creationism, 221, 222
Creationism Act (Louisiana), 222
Criminal activity:
certification/licensure, 76, 78
dismissal, 189–191, 192
drug abuse, 76, 84, 156, 189–191
privacy rights, 84
Curriculum and instruction:
academic freedom, 218–232, 256 (n4)
attendance policy, 229, 259 (n58)
authoritative control, 218–232
broadcast recordings, 240, 241
    (figure), 242

case summary, 224, 226, 238, 244–245, 249–250
civil rights, 4, 249, 250, 251
community service, 222
constitutional rights, 218, 221–225, 227, 250
controversial subjects, 221–225
copyright law, 239, 261 (n129)
creationism, 221, 222
curriculum establishment, 219–220
dismissal, 181, 187, 207 (n34)
elective courses, 220–221, 256 (n15)
English language instruction, 4, 231, 248–251
evaluation and testing, 228, 230–232
evolution, 152, 169 (n54), 221–222
federal circuit review, 222, 223–224, 225–227, 228, 229, 232–233, 249, 251
free speech rights, 219, 256 (n6)
frequently asked questions, 254–255
grading policy, 229–230
graduation requirements, 227–229, 258 (n46)
instructional methodology, 225–227
instructional technology, 240–242, 246–247
patriotism, 152, 169 (n55)
prohibited subjects, 221–225
religious rights, 54, 67 (n42), 151, 152, 221–225, 228, 229
required subjects, 220–221, 256 (n11)
safety programs, 217–218, 255 (n1)
sex education, 225
state court review, 221, 222, 223, 227, 229, 230, 232
student records, 232–238
Supreme Court review, 221–222, 249, 250, 251
suspensions, 230, 247–248, 259 (n62)
teacher recommendations, 251–253
textbook restrictions, 222–223, 224–225, 226
See also Special education
Cyberbullying, 91–92

Davenport v. Washington Education Association (2007), 122
Defamation, 272–275, 295 (n28)
case summary, 274
Delaware, 127

Department of Education Organization Act, 24–25
Detentions, 271–272
Disabilities. See Employees with disabilities; Special education; specific legislation; Students with disabilities
Disciplinary actions:
corporal punishment, 183, 268–270, 272
detentions, 271–272
in-house suspensions, 271–272
progressive discipline, 178–196
special education, 247–248
student suspensions, 230, 247–248, 259 (n62)
time-out, 271–272
Discretionary duties, 29, 38
Dismissal:
case summary, 182–183, 184, 190, 193, 199
certification/licensure, 192, 211 (n97), 212 (n100)
constitutional rights, 200
contract nonrenewal, 175–176
criminal activity, 189–191, 192
curriculum and instruction, 181, 187, 207 (n34)
drug abuse, 189–191
due process, 59, 60–62, 174, 175–176, 177, 194
excessive absenteeism, 187–188, 209 (n68)
federal circuit review, 189, 195
frequently asked questions, 203–204
grounds for dismissal, 180–194
hearings, 194, 195–196, 213 (n115)
incompetency, 180, 184, 185–188
inefficiency, 180, 184, 185–188
insubordination, 181–184
moral character, 189–191
neglect of duty, 180, 182–183, 185–188
notice for, 194–195, 212 (n108)
other good or just cause, 191–194, 211 (n96)
probationary teachers, 60–61, 174–176, 177, 194, 205 (n3)
procedural due process, 175–176, 177, 194, 205 (n9)
procedures for, 194–196
professional ethics, 188, 193, 194

progressive discipline, 178–196
religious rights, 175–176, 181
state court review, 176, 181–184,
    186–194, 195, 197–199, 201
substantive due process, 174, 205 (n4)
Supreme Court review, 188, 194, 200
teacher recommendations, 202–203
tenured teachers, 174, 177–178,
    205 (n2)
unprofessional conduct, 188–191
wrongful dismissal, 196
See also Reduction in force
Disparate impact, 138–139
Disparate treatment, 138–139
District of Columbia:
    employment discrimination, 154–155
    geographical jurisdiction, 300
    privacy rights, 86
    tort liability, 287
Drug abuse:
    criminal activity, 76, 84, 156,
        189–191
    dismissal, 189–191
    employees with disabilities, 156
    privacy rights, 58, 84
Drug/alcohol testing, 56–57, 86–88
Due process:
    case summary, 61
    character misalignment, 59–60, 68
        (n61), 69 (n62)
    constitutional rights, 8, 9–10, 45,
        59–62
    dismissal, 59, 60–62, 174, 175–176,
        177, 194
    hearings, 27–28, 60–62
    probationary teachers, 174, 175
    tenured teachers, 59, 60–62, 177
    See also Procedural due process;
        Substantive due process
Due Process Clause, 8, 9–10, 61–62
Duty, negligence, 277, 278–279, 282
Dworsky, A. L., 304

Early retirement incentives:
    age discrimination, 160–161
    resignation, 103
Educational foundations:
    common law, 15–16
    constitutions, 5–11
    educational statistics, 1
    frequently asked questions, 17–18
    historical context, 2–5
    legal fundamentals, 5–16

statutes and regulations, 11–15
teacher recommendations, 17
Educational malpractice:
    defined, 266
    tort liability, 289–290
Education for All Handicapped Children
    Act (1975), 4, 14
Education Law Association (ELA), 305
Education Law Reporter (West Publishing
    Company), 303–304
Edwards v. Aguillard (1987), 222
Eighth Circuit:
    employment discrimination, 145–146,
        148, 160, 162
    geographical jurisdiction, 300
    privacy rights, 82, 83
    student records, 232–233
    tort liability, 269–270
ELA Notes (Education Law
    Association), 305
Elective courses, 220–221, 256 (n15)
Elementary and Secondary Education Act
    (ESEA) (1965), 3, 14
Eleventh Amendment, 9
Eleventh Circuit:
    curriculum and instruction, 224
    employment discrimination, 146
    geographical jurisdiction, 300
    leave of absence, 98
    privacy rights, 83, 87
    tort liability, 269, 289
Elrod v. Burns (1976), 50
E-mail, 88–93
Employees with disabilities:
    antidiscrimination legislation, 13,
        152–157
    case summary, 157
    certification/licensure, 77, 155–156
    discrimination claims, 154–155
    employment discrimination, 152–157
    excessive absenteeism, 155, 157,
        170 (n72)
    federal circuit review, 154–156
    medical examinations, 153
    otherwise qualified, 153–154,
        155–156
    reasonable accommodations, 153–154,
        156–157, 171 (n80)
    state court review, 154, 155,
        156, 157
Employment discrimination:
    affirmative action, 162–164
    age discrimination, 13–14, 158–161

antidiscrimination legislation, 13, 138, 139, 140, 144, 147, 148, 149–150, 152–158, 160–162, 163
bona fide occupational qualification, 13, 144
case summary, 142, 145
civil rights, 12–13, 138, 139, 140, 144, 146–147, 148, 149–152, 153, 163, 164
color-based discrimination, 140–143
constitutional rights, 137–138, 140, 143, 163, 164
disability discrimination, 152–157
disparate impact, 138–139
disparate treatment, 138–139
employer retaliation, 139, 162
employment tests, 143
ethnic discrimination, 140–143
frequently asked questions, 166–167
gender discrimination, 144–149
genetic information, 161–162
national origin discrimination, 140, 142–143
race discrimination, 140–143
religious discrimination, 149–152
sexual orientation, 148
Supreme Court review, 138, 140, 147, 149, 150, 155, 163
teacher recommendations, 165–166
Employment terms:
certification/licensure, 72–80
evaluation system, 100–101
frequently asked questions, 106–107
leave of absence, 96–100
privacy rights, 81–93
resignation, 102–103
salary, 93–95
Supreme Court review, 75
teacher recommendations, 104–106
Employment tests, 143
English language instruction, 4, 231, 248–251
bilingual education, 248, 249, 251
case summary, 250
civil rights, 4, 249, 250, 251
immersion classes, 248, 251
Entitlement grants, 33
Epperson v. Arkansas (1968), 221–222
Equal Educational Opportunities Act, 251, 263 (n199)
Equal Employment Opportunity Commission (EEOC), 139

Equal Pay Act (EPA) (1963), 94, 144
Equal Protection Clause, 9–10, 137–138, 140, 143, 163, 164, 200, 250
Establishment Clause, 11, 53, 151
Ethnic discrimination, 140–143
Evaluation system:
classroom observations, 101
clinical supervision, 180
curriculum and instruction, 228, 230–232
employment terms, 100–101
formative evaluations, 100
progressive discipline, 179–180, 207 (n27)
students with disabilities, 230–232
summative evaluations, 100
Evolution, 152, 169 (n54), 221–222
Examinations. *See* Tests
Excessive absenteeism:
dismissal, 187–188, 209 (n68)
employees with disabilities, 155, 157, 170 (n72)
leave of absence, 97, 113 (n113)
probationary teachers, 175–176, 206 (n12)
Executive Order 49, 118
Executive Order 10998, 118
Executive Order 11491, 118
Express powers, 29

Facebook, 91–92
Fact-finding resolution, 124, 127
Fair share fees, 121–122, 124
Fair share shops, 121–124
Fair use doctrine, 239
False imprisonment, 271–272
Family and Medical Leave Act (FMLA) (1993), 96–97
Family Educational Rights and Privacy Act (FERPA), 232–238
Family medical leave, 96–98
Family Policy Compliance Office (FPCO), 237
Federal constitution. *See* U.S. Constitution
Federal court system:
court jurisdictions, 301–302
federal circuits, 300
functions and duties, 300
geographical jurisdictions, 300, 301
organization of, 299–301
See also U.S. Supreme Court; *specific circuit court*
Federal funds, 25, 33

Federal Reporter (F.3d), 303
Federal Supplement (F.Supp.2d), 303
Field trips, 286–287, 288
Fifth Amendment:
　due process, 8, 59
　provisions, 8
Fifth Circuit:
　bilingual education, 249, 251
　dismissal, 189
　employment discrimination,
　　140–141, 143
　First Amendment rights, 50
　geographical jurisdiction, 300
　privacy rights, 83, 87–88
First Amendment:
　association rights, 7, 49–52, 82, 118
　case summary, 44
　collective bargaining, 118,
　　121–122, 123
　constitutional rights, 7, 42–54
　curriculum and instruction,
　　221–223, 227
　Establishment Clause, 11, 53, 151
　Free Exercise Clause, 53, 223
　free speech rights, 7, 42–48, 90, 151
　provisions, 7, 42
　religious rights, 7, 11, 52–54, 149,
　　221–223
　Supreme Court review, 43, 44, 45–47,
　　49, 50, 66 (n10), 67 (n31), 118,
　　221–222
First Circuit:
　curriculum and instruction, 225–227
　First Amendment rights, 47–48
　geographical jurisdiction, 300
　resignation, 103
*Florence County School District Four v.
　Carter* (1993), 248
Florida:
　certification/licensure, 79
　dismissal, 188
　employment discrimination, 147
　privacy rights, 91–92
　tort liability, 268, 271, 275
Foreseeability, negligence, 277
Forest Grove School District v. T.A.
　(2009), 248
Formative evaluations, 100
Fourteenth Amendment:
　curriculum and instruction, 221, 250
　dismissal, 200
　Due Process Clause, 8, 9–10, 61–62
　due process rights, 8, 9–10, 45, 59–62

employment discrimination, 137–138,
　140, 143, 163, 164
　Equal Protection Clause, 9–10,
　　137–138, 140, 143, 163, 164,
　　200, 250
　privacy rights, 54, 57, 82
　provisions, 9–10
Fourth Amendment:
　privacy rights, 7–8, 54, 55–59
　provisions, 7–8
　search and seizure, 54, 55–57, 86
Fourth Circuit:
　dismissal, 195
　employment discrimination, 139, 148
　First Amendment rights, 48
　geographical jurisdiction, 300
Free, appropriate public education (FAPE):
　educational malpractice, 289–290
　legislative mandate, 4, 14
　special education programs, 243,
　　244–245, 246, 248
　testing and evaluation, 232
Freedom of association. *See* Association
　rights
Freedom of religion. *See* Religious rights
Free Exercise Clause, 53, 223
Free speech rights:
　case summary, 44
　classroom restrictions, 47–48
　constitutional rights, 7, 42–48,
　　90, 151
　curriculum and instruction, 219, 256
　　(n6)
　federal circuit review, 45, 47–48
　matters of public concern, 42,
　　43–47, 65 (n2)
　Supreme Court review, 43–47, 65 (n1)

Garcetti v. Ceballos (2006), 46–47
Gender discrimination:
　affirmative action, 162–164
　antidiscrimination legislation, 144,
　　146–147, 148, 149
　bona fide occupational
　　qualification, 144
　case summary, 145
　child-rearing, 148–149
　discrimination claims, 144–146
　employment, 144–149
　federal circuit review, 145–146,
　　148–149
　hostile work environment, 146–147,
　　148, 169 (n38)

pregnancy, 148–149
salary, 94, 144
sexual harassment, 144, 146–147, 168 (n25)
sexual orientation, 148
state court review, 146, 147, 148
students, 13
transgendered status, 148
General Welfare and Spending Clause, 6, 9, 11
Genetic information, 161–162
Genetic Information Nondiscrimination Act (GINA) (2008):
  Title I, 161
  Title II, 161–162
Georgia:
  certification/licensure, 79–80
  privacy rights, 88
Golden ex rel. Balch v. Anders (2003), 270
Grading policy, 229–230
Graduate Record Exam (GRE), 143
Graduation requirements, 227–229, 258 (n46)
Grievance arbitration, 124–125
Grossman v. South Shore Public School District (2007), 53

Hanes v. Board of Education of the City of Bridgeport (2001), 193
Harvard Law Review Association, 304
Hawaii, 28
Hazelwood School District v. United States (1977), 140
Head Start, 3
Healy v. James (1972), 49
Hearings:
  dismissal, 194, 195–196, 213 (n115)
  due process hearings, 27–28, 60–62
  special education, 27–28
  student records, 236–237
Hickman v. Valley Local School District Board of Education (1980), 51
Highly qualified teachers, 72, 77
Homosexuality. See Sexual orientation
Honig v. Doe (1988), 247
Horne v. Flores (2009), 251
Hostile work environment, 146–147, 148, 169 (n38)

Illinois:
  certification/licensure, 79
  dismissal, 198
  salary, 94
  tort liability, 269, 287

Immersion classes, 248, 251
Immunity defense, negligence, 282–283
Implied powers, 29
Incompetency, 180, 184, 185–188
Indiana, 192, 198–199
Individualized education program (IEP):
  civil rights violations, 291
  legislative mandate, 4, 14
  special education programs, 243, 244, 245, 246, 247
  testing and evaluation, 231–232
Individuals with Disabilities Education Act (IDEA) (1975):
  due process, 60
  due process hearings, 27–28
  free, appropriate public education (FAPE), 4, 14, 243
  individualized education program (IEP), 4, 14, 243
  least restrictive environment (LRE), 4, 14, 243
  mandates, 4, 14
  negligence, 289
  provisions, 4, 14
  school governance, 24
  special education programs, 242–248
  testing and evaluation, 230–231
Inefficiency, 180, 184, 185–188
Infliction of emotional distress, 275–277
  case summary, 276
Informational picketing, 127
Ingraham v. Wright (1977), 268
Inherit the Wind, 221
In-house suspensions, 271–272
Injury, negligence, 277, 278–279, 280, 281, 282, 296 (n43)
Instructional methodology, 225–227
Instructional technology, 240–242, 246–247
Insubordination, 181–184
Intentional torts, 266–277
  assault and battery, 266–271
  case summary, 270, 274, 276
  defamation, 272–275, 295 (n28)
  defined, 266
  false imprisonment, 271–272
  infliction of emotional distress, 275–277
Interest arbitration, 124
Internet:
  instructional methodology, 240, 242
  legal resources, 303, 306–307
  privacy rights, 88–93

Iowa:
    curriculum and instruction, 228
    dismissal, 191, 192, 211 (n89), 212
        (n102)
Irving Independent School District v. Tatro
    (1984), 246, 262 (n170)

Janukajtis v. Fallon (2001), 281
Johnson, L. B., 138
J.S. v. Bethlehem Area School District
    (2002), 90

Kansas, 279
*Katterhenrich v. Federal Hocking Local
    School District Board of Education*
    (1997), 276
Kennedy, J. F., 118, 138
Kentucky:
    dismissal, 195, 213 (n114)
    employment discrimination, 152
    privacy rights, 87
*Ketchersid v. Rhea County Board of
    Education* (2005), 184
*Keyes v. School District No. 1, Denver,
    Colorado* (1973), 249

Labor strikes, 126–127
Labor unions. *See* Collective bargaining
Landrum-Griffin Act (1950), 116
Lau v. Nichols (1974), 4, 249, 250
Lawyer's Edition (L.Ed.2d.), 303
Least restrictive environment (LRE):
    legislative mandate, 4, 14
    special education programs, 243
Leave of absence:
    case summary, 97, 99
    child-rearing, 98
    collective bargaining, 97, 98
    employment terms, 96–100
    excessive absenteeism, 97, 113
        (n113)
    family medical leave, 96–98
    federal circuit review, 98, 99–100
    maternity leave, 98, 113 (n114)
    military service, 100
    personal medical leave, 96–98, 113
        (n115)
    religious obligations, 98–100
    state court review, 97
    Supreme Court review, 98
Legal resources:
    court decisions, 303–304
    current law, 305–306
    Internet websites, 303, 306–307

laws and regulations, 303
    legal citations, 304
Lehnert v. Ferris Faculty Association
    (1991), 122
LexisNexis, 303
Libel, 272
Louisiana:
    curriculum and instruction, 222
    dismissal, 187, 195
    tort liability, 269, 273, 276–277, 279,
        286, 287
Loyalty oath, 75

Mailloux v. Kiley (1971), 226
Maine:
    employment discrimination, 154
    resignation, 103
Malfeasance, 279
Mandatory functions, 29, 38
Marbury v. Madison (1803), 15
Marriage, 82, 83, 84
Maryland, 157
Massachusetts:
    collective bargaining, 127
    employment discrimination, 146
    historical law, 2, 3
    salary, 95
    school governance, 29
Maternity leave, 98, 113 (n114)
Mawdsley, R., 306
Mediation, 124, 127
Medical examinations, 153
Meyer v. Nebraska (1923), 221,
    257 (n16)
Michigan:
    collective bargaining, 122, 123
    curriculum and instruction, 227, 229
    dismissal, 189, 191, 211 (n84)
    privacy rights, 83, 85
    tort liability, 273, 290
Military service:
    leave of absence, 100
    salary compensation, 94, 112 (n97)
Ministerial duties, 29, 38
Minnesota:
    collective bargaining, 119
    dismissal, 184, 186
    privacy rights, 85
Misfeasance, 279
Mississippi:
    curriculum and instruction, 230
    dismissal, 187, 189, 210 (n76)
    employment discrimination, 143, 152
    privacy rights, 83

Missouri:
  certification/licensure, 79
  dismissal, 186, 187, 188, 209 (n57)
  employment discrimination, 146
  privacy rights, 87, 91
Montana, 199
Moral character:
  case summary, 76
  certification/licensure, 75–77, 80
  dismissal, 189–191
  privacy rights, 82–83
*Mozert v. Hawkins County Board of
  Education* (1987), 224
*Mt. Healthy City Board of Education v.
  Doyle* (1977), 45
MySpace, 91, 92

National Defense Education Act (NDEA)
  (1958), 3
National Education Association
  (NEA), 116
National Labor Relations Act (NLRA)
  (1935), 116
National origin discrimination, 140,
  142–143
National Reporter (West Publishing
  Company), 303–304
National Teachers Examination,
  143, 155
*National Treasury Employees Union v. Von
  Raab* (1989), 55
NEAFT Partnership, 116
Nebraska:
  curriculum and instruction, 221
  dismissal, 186, 187, 188, 198, 209
    (n70)
Neglect of duty, 180, 182–183, 185–188
Negligence:
  assumption of risk, 280, 283
  breach of duty, 277, 279–280
  case summary, 281, 288
  causation, 277, 280–282
  comparative negligence, 283
  contributory negligence, 283
  defenses to, 282–283
  defined, 266
  duty, 277, 278–279, 282
  field trips, 286–287, 288
  foreseeability, 277
  immunity defense, 282–283
  injury, 277, 278–279, 280, 281, 282,
    296 (n43)
  litigation criteria, 277–282

malfeasance, 279
misfeasance, 279
nonfeasance, 279
physical education class, 285–286
playground equipment, 286
reasonable person criteria, 279–280,
  283–284
sports activities, 285–286
standard of care, 283–284
students with disabilities, 287, 289
supervision, 282, 284–289
tort liability, 277–289
Nepotism:
  association rights, 52, 67 (n36)
  dismissal, 174
  employment discrimination, 139
  privacy rights, 81, 84
New Hampshire, 78
New Jersey:
  dismissal, 188
  employment discrimination, 146
New Jersey v. T.L.O. (1985), 55, 68 (n47)
New York:
  certification/licensure, 75, 76, 77, 78
  collective bargaining, 118, 119, 127
  curriculum and instruction, 222–223
  dismissal, 186, 187, 191, 197–198,
    214 (n130), 215 (n137)
  employment discrimination, 142–143,
    149, 152, 154, 155–156, 157,
    158–159, 160–161
  historical law, 3
  privacy rights, 86, 88
  tort liability, 272, 273, 274, 278–279,
    280, 281, 282, 283, 286, 287,
    288, 296 (n38), 297 (n61)
New York State Labor Relations
  Board, 127
Ninth Amendment:
  privacy rights, 54
  provisions, 8
Ninth Circuit:
  bilingual education, 249, 251
  curriculum and instruction, 223–224,
    257 (n30)
  First Amendment rights, 48, 54
  geographical jurisdiction, 300
Nixon, R., 118
No Child Left Behind Act (NCLB) (2002):
  certification/licensure, 72–73, 77, 80
  curriculum and instruction, 219–220,
    230, 231–232
  enactment, 4–5, 14

federal funds, 33
provisions, 5, 14
Reading First program, 33, 219–220
reauthorization, 3, 14
school governance, 24
teacher evaluation, 101
Title I, 33
Nonfeasance, 279
Nonmarital living arrangements, 82–83
North Carolina:
certification/licensure, 80
collective bargaining, 118
tort liability, 268
North Dakota, 152
Norwalk Teachers' Association v. Board of Education of the City of Norwalk (1951), 117
Notice for dismissal, 194–195, 212 (n108)

O'Connor v. Ortega (1987), 55
Ohio:
certification/licensure, 78
dismissal, 176, 192
due process, 61
employment discrimination, 142, 148
privacy rights, 57, 84, 85–86
resignation, 103
state constitution, 10–11
tort liability, 276
Oklahoma:
dismissal, 188, 189, 210 (n82)
privacy rights, 83
student records, 237–238
Open union shops, 121
Oregon:
certification/licensure, 78
dismissal, 187
employment discrimination, 152
Owasso Independent School District v. Falvo (2002), 237–238

Parental gifts, 95
Patriotism, 152, 169 (n55)
Peer grading, 237–238
Pennsylvania:
certification/licensure, 78, 80
collective bargaining, 120
curriculum and instruction, 222, 230
dismissal, 190, 191
employment discrimination, 143, 152
leave of absence, 97
privacy rights, 82–83, 85, 91, 92

Pensions, 102–103
Permuth, S., 306
Perry v. Sinderman (1972), 43, 45
Personal information, 84–86
Personal medical leave, 96–98, 113 (n115)
Personal privacy, 58–59, 81–84
Personnel records, 56, 84–86
Persuasive precedent, 5
Physical education, 285–286
Pickering v. Board of Education of Township High School District 205 (1968), 43, 44, 46
Pittman v. Cuyahoga Valley Career Center (2006), 142
Playground equipment, 286
Political activity, 49–50, 66 (n26)
Pregnancy, 148–149
Pregnancy Discrimination Act (PDA), 144, 148
Privacy rights:
case summary, 57
constitutional rights, 7–8, 54–59, 81, 82, 86, 90
drug abuse, 58, 84
drug/alcohol testing, 56–57, 58–59, 86–88
e-mail, 88–93
employment terms, 81–93
federal circuit review, 82, 83, 84, 86–88, 91, 92
moral character, 82–83
personal information, 84–86
personal privacy, 58–59, 81–84
personnel records, 56, 84–86
role models, 81, 82–83, 109 (n45)
search and seizure, 86–88
sexual misconduct, 58, 82–83, 110 (n50)
sexual orientation, 82, 83, 110 (n46)
social networking sites, 88–93
state court review, 58, 82–83, 84, 85–86, 87, 88
student records, 232–238
Supreme Court review, 55
video surveillance, 57
workplace privacy, 55–57
Probationary teachers, 60–61
dismissal, 60–61, 174–176, 177, 194, 205 (n3)
reduction in force, 198, 214 (n132)
Procedural due process:
defined, 10, 60
dismissal, 175–176, 177, 194, 205 (n9)

free speech rights, 45
probationary teachers, 175–176,
205 (n9)
provisions, 60–62
Products liability, 266
Profanity, 181, 225, 227
Professional certification/licensure. *See*
Certification/licensure
Professional ethics:
certification/licensure revocation,
79–80
dismissal, 188, 193, 194
Progressive discipline, 178–196

Race discrimination:
affirmative action, 162–164
case summary, 142
discrimination claims, 141–143
employment, 140–143
racially balanced workforce, 140–141,
163–164, 200
*Ramirez v. New York City Board of
Education* (2007), 157
Reading First program, 33, 219–220
Reasonable accommodations:
employees with disabilities, 153–154,
156–157, 171 (n80)
religious discrimination, 150–152
Reasonable person criteria, 279–280,
283–284
Reassignments, 177–178
Records:
personnel records, 56, 84–86
student records, 232–238
Reduction in force:
bumping rights, 197–199, 214 (n129)
call-back rights, 200–201
case summary, 199
certification/licensure, 198–199
collective bargaining, 197–198,
200–201
dismissal, 196–201
grounds for, 197
probationary teachers, 198,
214 (n132)
racially balanced workforce,
163–164, 200
seniority rights, 197–200, 214 (n128)
state court review, 197–199, 200, 201
Regulations, 5, 11
Religious discrimination:
antidiscrimination legislation, 149–150
case summary, 151

constitutional rights, 149
curriculum and instruction, 151, 152
employment, 149–152
garments, 150, 152
reasonable accommodations, 150–152
state court review, 152
Religious rights:
case summary, 53, 151
civil rights, 98–100
constitutional rights, 7, 11, 52–54,
149, 221–223
curriculum and instruction, 54, 67
(n42), 151, 152, 221–225,
228, 229
dismissal, 175–176, 181
federal circuit review, 52–54
garments, 54, 67 (n43), 150, 152
leave of absence, 98–100
observances, 54, 67 (n45), 149–150
*Research Methods for Studying Legal Issues
in Education* (Permuth and
Mawdsley), 306
Reserved Officer Training Corps
(ROTC), 228
Resignation:
early retirement incentives, 103
employment terms, 102–103
federal circuit review, 103
pensions, 102–103
retirement systems, 102–103
Retaliation, employment discrimination,
139, 162
Retirement, 102–103
age discrimination, 160–161
early retirement incentives, 103,
160–161
Rights arbitration, 124
Right-to-work states, 118
*Riverview School District v. Riverview
Education Association* (1994), 97
Robert's Rules of Order, 31
Role models:
certification/licensure, 76
dismissal, 190–191
privacy rights, 81, 82–83, 109 (n45)

Safety programs, 217–218, 255 (n1)
Salary:
additional compensation, 95
assignments, 94–95, 112 (n103),
113 (n105)
employment terms, 93–95
federal circuit review, 94–95

gender discrimination, 94, 144
merit pay, 94
military service, 94, 112 (n97)
parental gifts, 95
salary schedules, 93–94
school finance, 34
tutoring, 95
School accreditation, 28
School boards:
  authority, 28–29
  closed meeting, 31
  discretionary duties, 29, 38
  dismissal hearings, 195–196, 213
    (n117)
  express powers, 29
  implied powers, 29
  mandatory functions, 29, 38
  meeting minutes, 32
  meetings and procedures, 30–32
  membership criteria, 29–30
  ministerial duties, 29, 38
  open meeting, 30–31
  organizational structure, 28
  school finance management, 32,
    33–36
  school governance, 28–32
School desegregation, 3–4, 12
School fees, 35–36
School finance:
  competitive grants, 33, 34
  corporate funds, 34
  entitlement grants, 33
  federal funds, 25, 33
  financial responsibilities, 33–34
  governance of, 32–36
  local funding, 33
  salaries, 34
  school board management, 32,
    33–36
  school fees, 35–36
  state funds, 33
School governance:
  constitutional rights, 6, 8–9, 11
  federal government role, 24–25
  frequently asked questions, 37–38
  school boards, 28–32
  school finance, 32–36
  school property, 32, 35
  state education agency (SEA), 25–28
  teacher recommendations, 36–37
School Law Reporter (Education Law
  Association), 305
School property, 32, 35

Scobey School District v. Radakovich
  (2006), 199
Search and seizure:
  civil rights violations, 291
  constitutional rights, 54, 55–57, 86
  privacy rights, 86–88
Second Circuit:
  collective bargaining, 127
  curriculum and instruction, 222,
    225, 229
  employment discrimination, 148–149,
    155–156, 159, 160, 161
  geographical jurisdiction, 300
  leave of absence, 99
  privacy rights, 86, 91, 112 (n87)
Section 504, Rehabilitation Act (1973):
  certification/licensure, 77
  employees with disabilities, 152–156
  graduation requirements, 228
  provisions, 13
Seniority rights, 197–200, 214 (n128)
Seventh Circuit:
  curriculum and instruction, 223–224,
    257 (n29)
  dismissal, 200
  employment discrimination, 154, 158,
    160, 163
  First Amendment rights, 48, 50, 52,
    53, 54
  geographical jurisdiction, 300
  tort liability, 269
Sex education, 225
Sexual harassment, 144, 146–147,
  168 (n25)
Sexual misconduct:
  certification/licensure revocation, 78
  dismissal, 189, 210 (n79)
  privacy rights, 58, 82–83, 110 (n50)
Sexual orientation:
  curriculum and instruction, 225
  employment discrimination, 148
  privacy rights, 82, 83, 110 (n46)
Sixth Circuit:
  curriculum and instruction, 223, 224,
    225, 227, 228
  dismissal, 189
  due process, 61
  employment discrimination, 156
  First Amendment rights, 45, 49,
    50–51, 66 (n28), 67 (n34)
  geographical jurisdiction, 300
  privacy rights, 83, 84, 87
  tort liability, 289, 290

*Skinner v. Railway Labor Executives'
    Association* (1989), 55
Slander, 272
Slip opinions, 304
Smartboards, 240, 261 (n130)
Social networking sites, 88–93
    case summary, 90
    cyberbullying, 91–92
    student postings, 89–92
    teacher postings, 92–93
South Carolina, 143
South Dakota:
    dismissal, 198
    privacy rights, 82
Special education:
    alternative placements, 246
    assistive technology, 246–247
    case summary, 244–245, 250
    disciplinary actions, 247–248
    due process, 60
    due process hearings, 27–28
    educational malpractice, 289–290
    English language instruction, 4, 231,
        248–251
    free, appropriate public education
        (FAPE), 4, 14, 232, 243,
        244–245, 246, 248, 289–290
    graduation requirements, 228, 231
    individualized education program (IEP),
        4, 14, 231–232, 243, 244, 245,
        246, 247
    least restrictive environment (LRE),
        4, 14, 243
    legislative requirements, 242–251
    school governance, 24
    supportive services, 246
    Supreme Court review, 243, 244–245,
        246, 247, 248
    transition services, 247
    See also specific legislation
Sports activities, 285–286
Standard of care, 283–284
State constitutions:
    educational foundations, 10–11
    loyalty oath, 75
State court system:
    court jurisdictions, 301–302
    functions and duties, 299
    organization of, 301
    See also specific state
State education agency (SEA):
    administrative due process hearings,
        27–28
    authority, 26–27

certification/licensure, 27, 72–80
certification/licensure revocation,
    77–80
judicial review, 27
organizational structure, 25–26
responsibilities, 26
rule-making, 27
school accreditation, 28
school governance, 25–28
State funds, 33
State statutes, 15
Statutes:
    civil rights, 12–14
    defined, 5, 11
    state statutes, 15
*Stone v. Board of Education of Saranac
    Central School District* (2005), 159
Stuart, J., 226
Student discrimination:
    civil rights, 12, 13
    gender discrimination, 13
    school desegregation, 3–4, 12
Student records:
    access enforcement, 237
    access rights, 234–236, 237
    amending records, 236–237
    case summary, 238
    educational classification exceptions,
        233–234
    hearings, 236–237
    peer grading, 237–238
    privacy complaints, 237
    privacy rights, 232–238
    Supreme Court review, 237–238
Students with disabilities:
    antidiscrimination legislation, 13, 14
    graduation requirements, 228, 231
    negligence, 287, 289
    student records, 232–233
    testing and evaluation, 230–232
    See also Special education
Substantive due process:
    corporal punishment, 268–270,
        272, 295 (n9)
    defined, 10, 59
    dismissal, 174, 205 (n4)
    probationary teachers, 174, 205 (n4)
    provisions, 59–60
Summative evaluations, 100
Sunshine laws, 30–31
Supervision, negligence, 282, 284–289
Supremacy Clause, 10
Supreme Court Reporter (S.Ct.), 303
Suspensions, 230, 247–248, 259 (n62)

Taft-Hartley Act (1947), 116
Technology:
  assistive technology, 246–247
  broadcast recordings, 240, 241
    (figure), 242
  computer software, 242
  smartboards, 240, 261 (n130)
  See also Internet
Tennessee:
  curriculum and instruction,
    221, 228
  dismissal, 183–184, 186
  privacy rights, 87
Tenth Amendment:
  curriculum and instruction, 218
  provisions, 8–9
  school governance, 6, 8–9, 11
Tenth Circuit:
  bilingual education, 249
  First Amendment rights, 47
  geographical jurisdiction, 300
  student records, 238
Tenured teachers:
  dismissal, 174, 177–178, 205 (n2)
  dismissal rights, 174, 177–178
  due process, 59, 60–62, 177
Tests:
  certification/licensure, 77
  drug/alcohol testing, 56–57, 58–59
  employment tests, 143
  Graduate Record Exam (GRE), 143
  National Teachers Examination,
    143, 155
  student evaluation, 228, 230–232
Texas:
  certification/licensure, 80
  collective bargaining, 118
  privacy rights, 58
  tort liability, 272
Textbook restrictions, 222–223,
    224–225, 226
Third Circuit:
  curriculum and instruction, 222
  dismissal, 200
  employment discrimination, 143,
    162, 163
  geographical jurisdiction, 300
  privacy rights, 91, 92
Thirteenth Amendment, 222
Thread That Runs So True (Stuart), 226
Time-out, 271–272
*Tinker v. Des Moines Independent
    Community School District* (1969), 17
Title IV, Civil Rights Act (1964), 12

Title IX, Education Amendments (1972):
  employment discrimination,
    144, 149
  provisions, 13
Title VI, Civil Rights Act (1964):
  curriculum and instruction, 4, 249,
    250, 251
  employment discrimination,
    140, 153
  provisions, 12
Title VII, Civil Rights Act (1964):
  employment discrimination, 138, 139,
    140, 144, 146–147, 148,
    149–152, 153, 163, 164
  provisions, 12–13
  religious rights, 98–100
Tort liability:
  case summary, 270, 274, 276,
    281, 288
  civil rights violations, 290–291
  constitutional torts, 266
  educational malpractice, 289–290
  federal circuit review, 268–270
  frequently asked questions, 293–294
  intentional torts, 266–277
  negligence, 277–289
  products liability, 266
  state court review, 268, 269,
    272, 273, 274, 275–277,
    278–279, 280, 281, 282, 283,
    286, 287, 288–289, 290
  Supreme Court review, 268,
    274, 291
  teacher recommendations, 292–293
Transgendered status, 148
Tutoring, 95

Uniformed Services Employment and
    Reemployment Rights Act
    (1994), 100
Unions. *See* Collective bargaining
United Federation of Teachers, 118
United States Code Annotated
    (U.S.C.A.), 303
United States Code (U.S.C.), 303, 304
United States Reports (U.S.), 303
University of Pennsylvania
    Law Review, 304
Unprofessional conduct:
  certification/licensure revocation,
    79–80
  dismissal, 188–191
Unreasonable searches. *See* Search and
    seizure

U.S. Constitution:
Bill of Rights, 6, 8–9, 42
Contracts Clause, 6–7
educational foundations, 6–10
General Welfare and Spending Clause, 6, 9, 11
loyalty oath, 75
Supremacy Clause, 10
See also Constitutional rights; *specific amendment*
U.S. Customs Service, 55
U.S. Department of Education (ED):
Family Policy Compliance Office (FPCO), 237
legal resources, 303
legislative requirements, 25
regulations, 12
school governance, 24–25
subdivisions, 24–25
U.S. Department of Health, Education, and Welfare (HEW), 4, 24
U.S. Department of Justice (DOJ), 12, 140
U.S. Department of Labor, 96
U.S. Supreme Court:
association rights, 49, 50
collective bargaining, 118, 122–124
common law, 15–16
curriculum and instruction, 221–222, 249, 250, 251
dismissal, 188, 194, 200
due process, 59
educational foundations, 3–4, 6, 13
employment discrimination, 138, 140, 147, 149, 150, 155, 163
employment terms, 75
English language instruction, 249–250, 251
First Amendment rights, 43, 44, 45–47, 49, 50, 66 (n10), 67 (n31), 118, 221–222
free speech rights, 43–47, 65 (n1)
leave of absence, 98
privacy rights, 55
special education programs, 243, 244–245, 246, 247, 248
student records, 237–238

tort liability, 268, 274, 291
See also specific court case
User's Guide to The Bluebook (Dworsky), 304

Video surveillance, 57
Virginia:
collective bargaining, 118
employment discrimination, 139, 155
tort liability, 272, 275

Wagner, R. F., 118
Wagner Act. *See* National Labor Relations Act (NLRA) (1935)
Warrants, 55–56
WestLaw, 303
West Publishing Company, 303
West Virginia:
dismissal, 181, 183, 190–191, 200, 211 (n88)
employment discrimination, 146
privacy rights, 84, 110 (n54)
tort liability, 291
Williams v. Vidmar (2005), 151
Willis v. Watson Chapel School District (1990), 145
Wisconsin:
collective bargaining, 118
tort liability, 271, 289
Witchcraft, 223–224
Work stoppages, 126–127
World War I, 221
Wrongful dismissal, 196
Wygant v. Jackson Board of Education (1986), 200
Wyoming, 181

Yale Law Journal, 304
Yearbook of Education Law, The (Education Law Association), 305–306
Ysursa v. Pocatello Education Association (2009), 122, 124

Zelno v. Lincoln Intermediate Unit No. 12 Board of Directors (2002), 190
Zipper clauses, 120

CORWIN
A SAGE Company

The Corwin logo—a raven striding across an open book—represents the union of courage and learning. Corwin is committed to improving education for all learners by publishing books and other professional development resources for those serving the field of PreK–12 education. By providing practical, hands-on materials, Corwin continues to carry out the promise of its motto: **"Helping Educators Do Their Work Better."**